PATTERNS IN CRIMINAL HOMICIDE

PATTERSON SMITH SERIES IN
CRIMINOLOGY, LAW ENFORCEMENT, AND SOCIAL PROBLEMS

A listing of publications in the SERIES *will be found at rear of volume*

PUBLICATION NO. 211: PATTERSON SMITH SERIES IN
CRIMINOLOGY, LAW ENFORCEMENT, AND SOCIAL PROBLEMS

PATTERNS IN
CRIMINAL HOMICIDE

by

MARVIN E. WOLFGANG

PATTERSON SMITH
Montclair, N. J.
1975

67097

Library of Congress Cataloging in Publication Data

Wolfgang, Marvin E   (1924-   )
    Patterns in criminal homicide.

    (Patterson Smith series in criminology, law enforcement, and social problems. Publication no. 211)
    Reprint of the 1958 ed.
    An analysis of all criminal homicides listed by police in Philadelphia between Jan. 1, 1948, and Dec. 31, 1952.
    1. Homicide—Case studies. 2. Homicide—Philadelphia. I. Title

[HV6534.P5W6   1975]   364.1'52   74-34157
                        ISBN 0-87585-211-4

CONTENTS

Acknowledgments   *page* ix
Foreword   xiii

I. INTRODUCTION
  1. The Nature of This Research   3
  2. A General Perspective of Criminal Homicide   20

II. THE VICTIM AND THE OFFENDER IN THE HOMICIDE DRAMA
  3. Race and Sex Differences   31
  4. Age Differences   65
  5. Methods and Weapons of Inflicting Death   79
  6. Temporal Patterns   96
  7. Spatial Patterns   120
  8. Alcohol and Violence   134
  9. Previous Record   168
  10. Motives   185

III. THE VICTIM-OFFENDER RELATIONSHIP
  11. The Interpersonal Relationship between Victim
      and Offender   203
  12. Race and Sex Relationships   222
  13. Homicide During Commission of Another Felony   238
  14. Victim-Precipitated Criminal Homicide   245

IV. THE OFFENDER AFTER THE CRIME
  15. Homicide-Suicide   269
  16. Unsolved Homicides   284
  17. Adjudication   295
  18. Summary   318
  19. Implications and Suggestions for Research   328

BIBLIOGRAPHY   341

APPENDIX I
  TABLE 1. Criminal Homicide, Victims and Offenders, by Race,
    Sex, and Age, Philadelphia, 1948–1952.   361
  TABLE 2. Distribution of Philadelphia Population, 1950; by
    Race, Sex, and Age.   362

v

67097

TABLE 3. Method and Weapon of Criminal Homicide, by Race and Sex of Victim and Offender, Philadelphia, 1948–1952. 363

TABLE 4. Weapon Employed by Offender in Criminal Homicide, by Age, Philadelphia, 1948–1952. 364

TABLE 5. Month, Day, and Hours at Place of Occurrence of Criminal Homicide, by Race and Sex of Victim, Philadelphia, 1948–1952. 364

TABLE 6. Distribution of Total Victims who Died Within Various Periods of Time Between Assault and Death, According to Method by which Victim Met Death, Philadelphia, 1948–1952. 366

TABLE 7. Place of Occurrence and Method of Criminal Homicide, by Race and Sex of Victim, Philadelphia, 1948–1952. 366

TABLE 8. Place of Occurrence of Criminal Homicide, by Race and Sex of Offender, Philadelphia, 1948–1952. 368

TABLE 9. Criminal Homicide and the Presence of Alcohol, by Race and Sex of Victim, Philadelphia, 1948–1952. 368

TABLE 10. Presence of Alcohol During Criminal Homicide by Method, by Place, and by Race and Sex of Victim, Philadelphia, 1948–1952. 369

TABLE 11. Total Presence of Alcohol During Criminal Homicide, by Method, by Place, and by Race and Sex of Victim, Philadelphia, 1948–1952. 370

TABLE 12. Violence in Criminal Homicide, by Race and Sex of Offender, by Degree of Violence and by Presence of Alcohol in the Offender, Philadelphia, 1948–1952. 371

TABLE 13. Violence in Criminal Homicide, by Race and Sex of Victim and by Degree of Violence, by Method, by Place, and by Presence of Alcohol in the Victim, Philadelphia, 1948–1952. 372

TABLE 14. Presence of Alcohol in the Victim in Violent and Non-Violent Criminal Homicide, by Race and Sex of Victim, Philadelphia, 1948–1952. 373

TABLE 15. Type of Previous Arrest Record, by Race and Sex of Victim and Offender in Criminal Homicide, Philadelphia, 1948–1952. 374

TABLE 16. Numbers of Offenses for which Offender had been Arrested Prior to Instant Offense of Criminal Homicide, by Race, and Sex, Philadelphia, 1948–1952. 375

TABLE 17. Motive in Criminal Homicide, by Race and Sex of Victim and of Offender, Philadelphia, 1948–1952. 376

TABLE 18. Motive in Criminal Homicide by Age of Offender, Philadelphia, 1948–1952. 377

TABLE 19. Motive in Criminal Homicide by Age of Offender, Philadelphia, 1948–1952 (in per cent.) 377

TABLE 20. Type of Interpersonal Relationship Between Victim and Principal Offender, by Race and Sex of Victim, by Place, and Violence, Criminal Homicide, Philadelphia, 1948–1952. 378

TABLE 21. Age Relationship between Victim and Offender, by Differential Number of Years. 379

vi

TABLE 22. Race and Sex of Victim by Race and Sex of Offender, Criminal Homicide, Philadelphia, 1948–1952.   379

TABLE 23. Time Interval between Death of Victim and Subsequent Legal Processes, by Race and Sex of Offender, Criminal Homicide, Philadelphia, 1948–1952.   380

TABLE 24. Time Interval between Arrest and Preliminary Hearing, by Race and Sex of Offender, Criminal Homicide, Philadelphia, 1948–1952.   381

TABLE 25. Disposition of Offender in Criminal Homicide, by Race and Sex, Philadelphia, 1948–1952.   381

TABLE 26. Disposition, by Motive of Offender in Criminal Homicide, Philadelphia, 1948–1952.   382

TABLE 27. Degree of Criminal Homicide Designated by a Court of Record, by Race and Sex of Three Classifications of Offenders, Philadelphia, 1948–1952.   382

TABLE 28. Degree of Criminal Homicide Designated by a Court of Record, by Age of Offender Available for Prosecution, Philadelphia, 1948–1952.   383

TABLE 29. Degree of Criminal Homicide Designated by a Court of Record, by Age of Offender Available for Prosecution, Philadelphia, 1948–1952 (in per cent.).   383

APPENDIX II

Number of Criminal Homicides by Police District, Philadelphia, 1948–1952   385

Maps:

    Philadelphia Police Department District Boundaries   386

    Criminal Homicides, Philadelphia, 1948–1952, by Census Tracts   387

Philadelphia Police Recording Forms:

    Résumé of Homicide Case   388

    Witness Sheet   389

    Report of Investigating Officer   390

    Request for Firearm Examination   391

INDEX   393

ACKNOWLEDGMENTS

FOR suggesting this undertaking, providing insight and encouragement at propitious moments, the writer is deeply indebted to Thorsten Sellin. Dr. Sellin placed at the disposal of the writer his excellent library of criminology and penology, without which this study would have been much less comprehensive.

J. P. Shalloo and Otto Pollak assisted the author's work from its beginning, and are equally responsible for the incisive counsel, experienced guidance, and organizational perspective so necessary to the myopic eyes of the compiler of data. It was Dr. Shalloo who provided the means by which essential contacts were first made with the Philadelphia Police Department. In addition to his generosity in time, Dr. Pollak contributed also to the author's collection of homicide literature.

For their patient scrutiny of the methodology employed in this research, for their aid in proper use of the statistical technique, their guidance in construction of tables, and for their editorial counsel, the writer is indebted to Dorothy S. Thomas and Everett Lee. Frequent discussions regarding chi-square theory and usage with Rolf Strohm, as well as his valuable assistance in code construction on the McBee punch card, and the many computations required throughout the study, greatly aided the author.

Office proximity and close friendship subjected Richard Lambert and Marvin Bressler to much of the author's preoccupation with homicide during the past few years. For many valuable suggestions and encouragement the writer is grateful.

The present work could not have been compiled without

the co-operation of Police Commissioner Thomas J. Gibbons and the Homicide Squad of the Philadelphia Police Department. The list of names is too large to include, but every man on the Homicide Squad, including some who have left police service, has rendered invaluable aid in collecting data and providing suggestive insights for analysis. For their patience in guiding the author through the voluminous police files, for permitting him to observe and participate in the apprehension and interrogation of several suspects of criminal homicide, for educating him to the skilled manner in which they conduct their investigations, the writer is deeply grateful.

Special acknowledgment is due Margaret Dietshe both for her many hours spent in recording data from the files of the Homicide Squad and for her very capable editorial and secretarial assistance.

For consultation on medical questions and editorial advice, the author is pleased to acknowledge the assistance of Murray G. Smyth, Jr., of the Hospital of the University of Pennsylvania. Similar advice and suggestions were given by the late William S. Wadsworth, Chief Medical Examiner of Philadelphia.

For aid in checking criminal records and for assistance with legal questions, special gratitude is expressed to the Central Records Division of the Police Department and to the District Attorney's Office respectively.

More than gratitude must be expressed to Lenora Wolfgang for painstaking tabulations and for her tireless nights critically reading over the manuscript and proofs for publication.

The author owes a special debt to all the members of the Department of Sociology at the University of Pennsylvania and to his students who have been subjected ceaselessly to a concern with the subject of criminal homicide. Several informal suggestions made in the corridors of Dietrich Hall or in the classroom have found their way into the core of this study.

For several important quotations appreciation is extended to the following: *Journal of Criminal Law, Criminology, and Police Science*; G. E. C. Gads Forlag; The Free Press; William F. Hoffman; The University of North Carolina Press.

M.E.W.

University of Pennsylvania

June 1957

FOREWORD

OF the many actions made punishable by criminal law, the taking of the life of a human being is generally regarded as the most abominable, especially when it is done deliberately and with that degree of foresight which places it in the category of murder in the first degree. No other offense—not even treason—is so often threatened with the death penalty by the criminal codes of American states. This fact alone would furnish a potent reason for the intensive study of all the conditions and circumstances that produce criminal homicides and of the persons who commit the various kinds of offenses grouped under that general title, in order to discover how to prevent such crimes and how to deal effectively with those who commit them.

The scientific literature on homicide is extensive. It contains innumerable case studies of offenders and an array of statistical investigations. Yet it is unlikely that it contains a counterpart to the research which the author of this monograph has undertaken. Using the detailed case files of the homicide squad of the police department of the city of Philadelphia, a community with a population of about two million, Dr. Wolfgang has produced a most interesting and valuable study of the 588 cases of criminal homicide, involving a total of 621 offenders, which occurred during the five-year period of 1948–1952. He has been concerned with exactly where and when these crimes were committed, the weapons used, the characteristics of the offenders and the victims, the relationship of the antagonists to one another, the circumstances of the crimes, the motives involved, and what happened later to the offenders. As a result of the statistical analysis of his data, he has uncovered a number of significant facts; many of his findings confirm the results of earlier researches, but others enlarge the scope of our knowledge about various aspects of the subject. Throughout the monograph, the results of prior studies pertinent to a particular question have been reported and compared with the author's own results.

Although the entire monograph is worth serious study, there are parts which deserve special attention. The author has, for instance, analyzed the offenses in terms of the relationship between the offender and his victim more fully than in any previously reported research. His discussion of what he calls victim-precipitated homicides is especially important in that connection, one out of four of his cases falling into this class. From an examination of previous arrest records, he has found that two out of three offenders and almost half of the victims had such a record and that in such instances about half of the offenders and over a third of the victims had previous arrests for aggravated assault. The study also reveals the great significance which alcohol played in the homicide situation, the relatively small number of cases where the crime was the by-product of the commission of some other felony, the relative rarity of the offender's suicide or his legal insanity as compared with British data, for instance, and the modest proportion (about 20 per cent) of the convictions for murder in the first degree among the total convictions following upon the crimes. The race differentials in homicide shown by the author are noteworthy.

It is a special pleasure to introduce this book to criminologists and police administrators, for whom it is likely to have a particular appeal. Having followed closely the author's career as student and teacher, the undersigned is certain that the research that he now offers us is but the first of many that will enhance his reputation as a careful, imaginative and productive scholar.

THORSTEN SELLIN

I
INTRODUCTION

I

THE NATURE OF THIS RESEARCH

Purpose

SINCE the nineteenth century, criminology has made steady but unspectacular progress toward a fuller understanding of many aspects of criminal behavior. The lack of any adequate theory of crime has been frequently remarked by sociologists. Although attempts have been made to provide some all-encompassing theories, they have been largely of modest value in the control or prediction of crime. Furthermore, relationship between the causal theory and the behavior examined has been so vague and amorphous that "disconnectedness"[1] has characterized most of these attempts. If the criminologist is to acquire general principles that are essential to effective control, prevention, and treatment, he must seek patterns, similarities, and repetitions that can become the basis for classifications and generalizations. But these patterns should not be so broad that the resulting generalizations become superficial. "Perhaps it is time," Albert Morris suggests, "that we faced the fact that the generally used concept of 'crime' is altogether too broad to be of much use to the serious investigator of criminal behavior."[2] The same author calls for examination of specific and particular types of criminal behavior: "To put it in semantically unrefined and unsophisticated terms, I am suggesting that if we are to get on with the business of learning to deal more effectively with crime we had better stop

---

[1] This is the term used by Daniel Glaser in "Criminality Theories and Behavioral Images," *The American Journal of Sociology* (March, 1956), 61: 433–444. The author contends that great gaps exist between sociological theory and the behavior it purports to explain, and says that disconnectedness refers to the failure to specify intervening variables between a dependent and an independent variable.

[2] Albert Morris, *Homicide: An Approach to the Problem of Crime*, Boston: Boston University Press, 1955, p. 4.

talking about crime and begin to identify and study with as much care and thoroughness as is possible the nature and workings of the significant factors essential to each type of criminal behavior."[1]

Analysis of a particular type of crime, the individuals who commit it, and those who are victims of it, is relatively rare. Such analysis, provided it is as detailed and specific as the best available data permit, may produce insights into etiology, prediction, and control as yet unknown and unexplored.

It is the purpose of the present study to examine and to analyze in detail the specific offense of criminal homicide. Despite interest in the illegal killing of another person manifested in our culture and indicated by the number of novels, plays, cinema and television performances that use this theme; and despite the numerous psychological case studies that have examined murder—usually of a bizarre nature—there has been very little research which analyzes criminal slayings from a sociological perspective.

Descriptive data revealing significant relationships of meaningful social attributes and variables is the first requirement of this perspective. Such an approach applied to homicide affords an objective body of facts regarding many social variables related to homicide, and thereby provides data on which a practical program of control and prevention might be based. The present study is just a beginning, and though not detailed enough to provide a basis for a program of social control of homicide, it indicates fields that might be further explored with this end in view. Only brief and passing allusions are made to biological, psychological, psychiatric, and even to different sociological emphases. In no sense are these other emphases considered less important. As personality and social environment are inseparable, so must the bio-psychological and sociological approaches to homicide and other problems also be interdependent. None alone can provide a complete account of homicide.

Thus, the process of learning about criminal homicide begins with some *a priori* knowledge and interrogative hypo-

[1] *Ibid.*, p. 6.

4

theses which lead to the accumulation of empirical data in order to answer meaningful questions. From these data new hypotheses may be formed and tested for significant associations. Finally, cautious, plausible, and suggested interpretations of the collected and analyzed data may then provide clues to the ways in which general theories of behavior might be applied or tested.

The purpose of this research is to analyze criminal homicide by using Philadelphia, Pennsylvania, as a community case study. Analysis has been made of all criminal homicides listed by the police in this city between January 1, 1948, and December 31, 1952. A critical review of scientifically important homicide literature in this country is provided, and whenever feasible, comparison is made of criminal homicides in Philadelphia with research elsewhere. Whether the general or specific conclusions regarding criminal homicide in Philadelphia may be projected beyond the present study so that more formalized and universal statements might be made about this particular crime, remains the task of future research to confirm or deny.

The present study is not an historical survey of homicide, provides no cross-cultural analysis, and does not directly examine causality.[1] Historically different interpretations of the more constant statutes; population changes; variations in police efficiency; technological developments of detecting, reporting, recording, and investigating procedures; and general socio-economic changes are major impediments to an adequate historical treatment of homicide. State and

[1] For discussion of some of the problems involved in such analyses, see: E. Roy Calvert, *Capital Punishment in the Twentieth Century*, London: G. P. Putnam's Sons, 1927, pp. 45–47; F. L. Hoffman, "The Increase in Murder," *The Annals of the American Academy of Political and Social Science* (1926), 125: 20–29; T. Sellin, "Is Murder Increasing in Europe?" *The Annals of the American Academy of Political and Social Science* (1926), 125: 29–34; A. H. Hobbs, "Criminality in Philadelphia: 1790–1810 Compared with 1937," *American Sociological Review* (1943), 8: 198–202; Viscount Templewood, *The Shadow of the Gallows*, London: Victor Gollancz, Ltd., 1951, p. 83; V. Verkko, "Survey of Current Practices in Criminal Statistics," Part I (December 5, 1950) and Part III (December 6, 1950), International Group of Experts on the Prevention of Crime and the Treatment of Offenders, Social Commission, Economic and Social Council, United Nations; Raymond T. Bye, *Capital Punishment in the United States*, Philadelphia: The Committee on Philanthropic Labor of Philadelphia, 1918, especially pp. 41–42.

5

national differences in definitions of criminal homicide make cultural comparisons unreliable. Causality is just one kind of order sought by the scientist, and it is assumed that a thorough psychological examination of the victim and offender combined with a sociological analysis would be necessary to unravel the skein of conscious and unconscious causal relationships that exist in this type of phenomenon. However, broad social statistics and interpersonal relationships analyzed in this study inferentially point to new and more precise areas of causation that have been heretofore overlooked and that require further research.

This research *does* seek to determine whether criminal homicide exhibits definite objective order, regularities, patterns, and if so, what this concatenation of phenomena is. Although criminal homicide is largely an unplanned act of violence, it is assumed, nonetheless, that there are in the act discernible and empirical uniformities of specific social characteristics. On the basis of this assumption, of previous research, and of examination of the raw data available in police files, answers to meaningful and important questions about criminal homicide are sought through the present analysis.

Because at least two persons are involved in every homicide —the victim and the offender—it is of interest to know what the differences are, if any, between them. Are there important race, sex, and age differences between victims and offenders? Is one race, sex, or age group likely to predominate in this crime? Do these same predominate attributes exist among offenders as well as among victims?

If there are significant race, sex, and age differences with respect to the rate or frequency of criminal homicide, are they also manifested with respect to methods or weapons used to inflict death, motives, types of interpersonal relationships between victims and offenders, etc.? Do there appear to be any cultural preferences for particular types of weapons? Are men and women, Negroes and whites, likely to use certain weapons with such high frequency that we may speak of definite race and sex patterns? Do persons who kill usually slay those with whom they have close social relationships or more distant ones? How often do family relationships appear among those who slay and are slain?

Much human behavior has some periodicity and occurs more frequently during certain seasons, months, days, or hours. Man is primarily a diurnal animal, but under the protective cloak of darkness often engages in socially un-approved nocturnal behavior. What can be said about criminal homicide? Is it primarily a nighttime occurrence? With an economic culture pattern of the five-day working week and a week-end of leisure, is criminal homicide largely a week-end phenomenon? Are there significant seasonal changes? Some persons are shot or stabbed and die imme-diately, thus allowing no opportunity for police questioning regarding the nature of the assault, the person who did it, and other important facts. It may be, therefore, of importance to the police to know something about the amount of time that elapses between the moment of assault and death. We may ask, for example, how many victims of what types of assault die within the first hour, the first day, or the first week after the assault. In general, is criminal homicide characterized by important temporal patterns?

Every crime occurs somewhere—at some particular place in space. Are there spatial patterns observable in criminal homicide? Does the crime occur most often in a home? If so, whose home and where?—the bedroom? kitchen? living room? If there are significant spatial patterns by race and sex, what meaning do they have? How often does homicide occur outside the home? Where outside the home?

Some previous criminological research refers to the rela-tionship between alcohol and offenses against the person. Usually reference is made to a study of victims who had been drinking and who suffered a violent death *or* of assailants who had been drinking. The present research seeks to dis-cover whether an association exists between criminal homi-cide and the presence of alcohol in either the victim, the offender, or both. Nowhere throughout this research are victims alone examined as if they were in a kind of social vacuum. Nor are only offenders analyzed. Relative to all aspects covered in the present study, victims *and* offenders are analyzed to determine important differences. Especially is this true for analysis of the presence of alcohol. It is meaningful to ask how many homicides occurred during which any of the persons—either victim, offender, or both—had alcohol present in his organism. Are offenders more likely to have alcohol present than victims? Are there, again, race and sex differences that may be called significant with respect to the presence of alcohol and the commission of homicide?

All victims of criminal homicide are by definition killed— i.e., do not die a natural death. But some persons are killed with one act of violence, while others are repeatedly and brutally assaulted. An attempt is made in the present study to distinguish between criminal homicides that are violent and those committed without violence, and to measure and analyze differences between them.

Because criminal homicide is a crime against the person it is a meaningful question to ask whether the offender of such a crime has been arrested previously, and particularly if he has been arrested for other and lesser offenses against the person. If offenders in criminal homicide often began their criminality by committing minor offenses which led up to the major crime of homicide, perhaps some clue to homicide prevention and control may be attained. What proportion of victims, we might also ask, have a previous police record? For both victims and offenders, are there significant race, sex, and age associations with a past record of arrest?

Analysis and comparison of victims, on the one hand, and of offenders, on the other, are believed to be important contributions of this study. However, when each of the victims is specifically compared to his own slayer with respect to race, sex, age, and other attributes, a new dimension of analysis is provided. We might then ask to what extent is criminal homicide a racially intra-group phenomenon. Does homicide occur most frequently within primary group relationships? With what frequency and under what kinds of interpersonal relationships are victims and their respective

8

slayers of the opposite sex? When a woman kills a man, is the recorded motive, method, weapon, and other factors different from a case in which a man kills a woman? Do more Negroes kill whites than vice versa?

In most states, homicide which occurs during commission of certain types of felonies is designated as first degree murder. In Pennsylvania, a killing occurring during commission of burglary, rape, arson, robbery, or kidnapping is a felony murder or first degree murder. It is important to know, therefore, how many such felony-murders occur. Is race or sex related to this type of homicide? Is the felony-murder offender more likely to have a previous arrest record than the offender who does not commit felony-murder?

Theories of social interaction maintain that criminal behavior is more indicative of a subject-object relation than of the perpetrator alone, and that the agent and his victim work upon each other profoundly and continually, even before the moment of disaster. One of the purposes of this research is an attempt to test empirically this hypothesis. To know one person involved in a homicide situation, we must be acquainted with the other. Does an analysis of criminal homicide show that there are uniformities of interpersonal relationships in the commission of the act, and are these patterns classifiable according to significant attributes? Such an analysis enters a relatively unexplored field and asks important questions about the victim's contribution to his own victimization. Are males or females, Negroes or whites more likely to precipitate their own death by extreme provocation of their slayers? After defining and identifying those cases of criminal homicide in which the victim precipitated the offense, are there significant differences to be noted when compared to those killings in which the victim did not precipitate the offense? Is the victim who contributes to his own death by provoking the slayer likely to have been involved previously in similar, though less drastic episodes?

After the crime of homicide has been committed, the offender may be voluntarily or reluctantly taken into custody by the police. He may escape arrest, however, by fleeing, or by committing suicide. Proportionately how many homicide-suicides are there? How do they differ from those cases in which the offender does not kill himself? Which race and sex groups are more likely to commit homicide-suicide?

In the absence of a standardized and formal definition of an unsolved criminal homicide, it has become part of the purpose of this study to establish an operational definition of unsolved homicide. If one can be made, we are faced with such obvious questions as: What proportion of homicides known to the police are unsolved? From data available on unsolved cases, are there significant differences between the solved and the unsolved criminal homicides with respect to the nature of the offense and the *dramatis personae* involved?

Part of the ethos of our culture is the emphasis placed on efficiency and speed. It is reasonable, therefore, to ask how quickly after arrest a person charged with criminal homicide passes through the major legal processes of a preliminary hearing, coroner's inquest, grand jury, and court trial. Emphasis on individual rights and protection is also part of our culture pattern, and until convicted, a defendant is presumed innocent. An unreasonable amount of time spent in detention awaiting final court adjudication is interpreted as unjust. The tempo of legal procedure thus becomes an important consideration in the analysis of any crime.

Court disposition of persons charged with the offense of criminal homicide is obviously of concern to an analysis of this crime. What proportion of persons so charged are acquitted, found guilty, or otherwise disposed? Are there race and sex differences of any significance according to court disposition? Are Negroes and males—as is suspected—more likely to be convicted than whites and females? It is one of the functions of the court to determine the degree of homicide committed and to pronounce sentence—in classical Beccarian terms—according to the seriousness of the offense. Data collected for the present study make it possible to answer such questions as: What proportion of all criminal homicides so listed by the police are first degree murders?

10

second degree murders? voluntary or involuntary man-slaughters? Are race, sex, and other attributes associated with any of the degrees of criminal homicide? How severe are the punishments for offenders in each of these degrees? Are murderers likely to be first offenders, as is often suggested in homicide literature? Or, is the incidence of a previous police record as high among murderers as among persons who commit homicide of lesser degree?

Insanity is a legal, not a psychiatric, term. To be a valid defense, insanity must actually exist in the defendant at the time of the act. The burden of proof is on the defendant, and, in Pennsylvania, it is for the jury to decide whether or not the defendant was legally insane at the time the homicide was committed. Relatively how many offenders in criminal homicide are declared insane? What types of interpersonal relationships existed in these cases, between victim and offender? What are the motives recorded for such crimes?

These are some of the questions and major areas of analysis the present research on criminal homicide seeks to examine.

Additional questions and more extensive analysis than originally expected, based on intuitive insights emerging from closer inspection of the data, have resulted in descriptions, observations, and associations beyond those just mentioned. It has been possible, as a by-product of the main body of research, to test empirically several declared and implied suggestions of earlier and contemporary authors. Finally, this study—like most contemporary analyses of complex social phenomena—bears no honorific title and has no pretension of definitiveness. It is hoped that new areas of research potentialities may be opened by reason of the conclusions formulated from the present study. Not only is repetition of several aspects of this research desirable, but suggestions for psychologically deeper and socially wider possibilities are presented.

Use of Police Data

Four major sources of data were available for analysis of criminal homicide: police records, coroners' reports, court or judicial records, and records of prison commitments. Police records have been utilized in the present study because richness of descriptive detail and procedural proximity to the crime eliminate many defects and limitations of other statistical sources.[1]

Most research on criminal homicide has used coroners' reports. On the local county level of inquiry, direct use of coroners' files may be possible, but on the state or national level, the researcher must rely on general mortality statistics submitted by the coroner to state and national offices of vital statistics, and which list homicide as a cause of death. Coroners' reports lack details of the offense and of investigation which police files possess, and generally do not follow a case through to ultimate disposition after the inquest has established the fact of a homicide. Little or no information on the events leading to the homicide, the criminal record of the victim or offender, or other pertinent data are given in coroners' reports. General mortality statistics, in addition to these limitations, did not until 1949 distinguish between

[1] The advantages of police statistics and limitations of other sources of data for criminal homicide research have been discussed in: Thorsten Sellin, "The Basis of a Crime Index," *Journal of Criminal Law and Criminology* (September, 1931), 22: 335–356; T. Sellin, *Crime and the Depression*, New York: Social Science Research Council Memorandum, 1937, Chapter 4; T. Sellin, "Status and Prospects of Criminal Statistics in the United States," *Festskrift tillagnad Karl Schlyter den* 21 December 1949 (Dedicated publication in honor of Karl Schlyter, December 21, 1949), Stockholm, 1949, pp. 290–307; T. Sellin, "The Measurement of Criminality in Geographic Areas," *Proceedings of the American Philosophical Society* (April, 1953), 97: 163–167; Veli Verkko, "Survey of Current Practices in Criminal Statistics," Part I (December 5, 1950) and Part III (December 6, 1950), International Group of Experts on the Prevention of Crime and the Treatment of Offenders, Social Commission, Economic and Social Council, United Nations; V. Verkko, *Homicides and Suicides in Finland and Their Dependence on National Character*, Copenhagen: G. E. C. Gads Forlag, 1951; *Royal Commission on Capital Punishment, 1949–1953 Report*, London: Her Majesty's Stationery Office, 1953, p. 341; *Royal Commission on Capital Punishment, Minutes of Evidence taken Before the Royal Commission on Capital Punishment*, Thirtieth Day, Thursday, 1st February, 1951. Witness: Professor Thorsten Sellin, London: His Majesty's Stationery Office, 1951, pp. 647–678; Max Grünhut, "Statistics in Criminology," *The Journal of the Royal Statistical Society*, Series A (General) (1951), Vol. 114, Part II: 139–162; H. C. Brearley, *Homicide in the United States*, Chapel Hill: The University of North Carolina Press, 1932; Frederick L. Hoffman, "The Increase in Murder," *The Annals of the American Academy of Political and Social Science* (1926), 125: 20–29; Hans von Hentig, "Some Problems Regarding Murder Detection," *Journal of Criminal Law and Criminology* (May, 1938), 29: 108–118; Arthur V. Lashly, "Homicide in Cook County," in *The Illinois Crime Survey*, Chicago: Illinois Association for Criminal Justice and The Chicago Crime Commission, 1929, pp. 589–640.

criminal and non-criminal (justifiable and excusable) homicides; and some accidental deaths due to criminal negligence which appear in criminal records are not classified as homicides in vital statistics practice.[1]

Court records fail to include homicides involving cases where the offender committed suicide and, hence, never came to the attention of the court. Furthermore, cases classified as unsolved in police records, or that involve suspects who are fugitives, are not found in judicial statistics.

Prison records are useful to determine the prison population of those inmates who committed criminal homicide and perhaps to aid in the collection of detailed psychological interviews and case histories. But prison statistics are the procedural residue of homicide cases after a high percentage "loss" by judicial statistics. Some defendants are found not guilty, the legally insane are committed to special institutions, and a few commit suicide after trial and before commitment to a state penitentiary. Differential treatment of races and sexes by the courts means further that prison data on homicides provide the researcher with a select group for which analyses of the total patterns of criminal homicide and of types of victims and offenders are necessarily invalid if not unreliable.

Police statistics used in the present research have several important advantages. They include the initial investigation and thereby provide a more comprehensive and valid description of the crime, the victim, and the offender than any other source of data. All criminal homicides are investigated and recorded, including the unsolved cases and those where the offender has committed suicide or is still a fugitive.

Data used in this research have been collected by the Homicide Squad of the Philadelphia Police Department.[2]

[1] *Mortality Statistics*, Bureau of the Census, United States Department of Commerce, Washington, D.C.; also, *Special Reports*, National Office of Vital Statistics, Public Health Service, Federal Security Agency, Washington, D.C. For more detailed distinction between criminal and non-criminal homicide see Chapter 2.

[2] For an excellent discussion of the tasks of the homicide division, and for fuller insights into the types of data such a unit regularly collects, see Le Moyne Snyder, *Homicide Investigation*, Springfield, Illinois: Charles C. Thomas, 1950.

This unit employs the services of handwriting experts, fingerprint specialists, photographers, ballistics experts, stenographers, photostatic experts, experienced police officers, and often, other specialists. This skilled team of investigators is on the job as soon as it learns of the homicide and divides its functions between (1) apprehension of the suspect and the accumulation of evidence admissible in court; and (2) collection of background information (not necessarily used in court) regarding the crime, facts about the victim, his mode of living, his associates, activities, reputation, and the same type of data concerning suspects. These latter data may provide clues for new inquiries, explain the mode of perpetration, or throw light on obscure motivations. Fingerprints, footprints, tire marks, photographs of the victim and his effects are provided by the homicide squad. Often the locus of the crime is drawn to scale, exhibits are collected, properly marked for identification and secured in the office safe. Photostatic copies of important documents such as letters, receipts, bills, or any papers that may assist in the investigation are made, and the originals are carefully filed in the unit to prevent loss or defacement. Witnesses are located and interviewed, particularly witnesses who can give testimony or who have any knowledge or information about the circumstances surrounding the crime. The captain of the unit makes periodic reports, checks details, reviews the progress of each case, and maintains direct communication with the district attorney's office.[1]

The homicide officer spends the largest portion of his time checking and interrogating witnesses, writing detailed, precise reports of his daily work, and testifying in court. He seeks to discover apparent human motives either for a particular act, or for general conduct, by inducing suspects and witnesses to express and describe motives and inner experiences. Interrogation without intimidation is the rule. Interviewing techniques are employed to ascertain facts, to sift truth from

[1] For more detailed analysis of the homicide squad and liaison relations with the prosecutor, see Frederick T. Doyle, "Marshalling of Proofs in Homicide Cases," *Journal of Criminal Law and Criminology* (March–April, 1946), 36: 473–484.

falsity, to probe cautiously without impairing ultimate validity. After perfunctory explanation of the defendant's constitutional rights and privileges, the investigator assumes the dual role of dynamic and passive observer in order to elicit presentable evidence.[1]

There are several important reasons that the 1948–1952 quinquennium has been used: (1) It is sufficiently removed from the Second World War and early post-war years not to be affected seriously by disturbing social factors of the war. (2) Material from the 1950 census may be used for a base whether applied to the first or last of the five years, or to the entire period, since the race, sex, age, and other data from the census were collected for a year that falls at the midpoint of the whole period. (3) Perhaps most important is the fact that the new form[2] for recording homicides, which was introduced in 1948, was maintained consistently throughout the period under examination, thus making the raw data excellent for analysis. (4) The five years provide 625 homicides, of which 588 are criminal, a sufficiently large group of consecutive criminal homicides for analysis. Data in the voluminous police files include: race, sex, and age of both victim and offender; photographs and diagrams of the deceased, showing bullet, stab, or other wounds which caused death; description of the weapon used; place where the offense occurred; date and time of the slaying; motive, as recorded by police authorities; description of the events leading to the offense; letters, bills, receipts, diaries, suicide and other notes; verbatim accounts of the interrogation of suspects, witnesses, and other persons who can supply background information; summary of the coroner's inquest; report of the medical examiner; the captain's summary; grand jury indictment; brief record of the court trial, including the

[1] The author has had several opportunities to observe the Philadelphia Homicide Squad in action, and attests to the skill with which the criminal investigation division officers function throughout all stages of police procedure. Recently printed for confidential police circulation are two monographs that concisely describe the major ramifications of investigation and interrogation: (1) *On the Job Training Memorandum*, and (2) *Surveillance Training Memorandum*, Philadelphia: Criminal Investigation Division, 1954.

[2] See Appendix II, pp. 388–391 for recording forms used by the Philadelphia Homicide Squad.

15

names of the judge, prosecutor, and defense counsel; court disposition and designation of the degree of criminal homicide.[1]

There is more than a semantic problem involved in use of the term "criminal homicide." Actually, it may be argued, no homicide is technically criminal until it has been so designated by a court of record; no suspect is an offender until convicted; and no person is a victim of criminal homicide until a court so decides. These are logical, sound arguments and may be nearly as good grounds for using court records as for using police statistics. But police statistics are more comprehensive for purposes of this study. Ordinary automobile deaths due to negligence or accident are not included. All slayings not recognized as justifiable, accidental, or excusable by the police and the coroner's inquest, and that normally make, or would make, a suspect subject to arrest and prosecution are listed and labeled in police records as criminal homicides. As previously mentioned, a person who committed homicide and escaped arrest but is known to the police (fugitive), or who killed himself after killing another (homicide-suicide), or whose identity is unknown (unsolved) does not generally come to the attention of the court and therefore is not included in court statistics. Analysis of criminal homicides is made throughout this study on the basis of police data. Information about the court disposition and designation is also based on police records, and it may be that some court dispositions are recorded by the police less accurately (or not at all) than the court itself might report. Partly because of this fact and partly because our concern is with a larger group of offenders than those convicted and sentenced by the court, less attention is given to the disposition of defendants.

[1] Information from each file was transcribed on cards that, in abbreviated form, supply the data used in analysis. A second transcription process occurred when these data were then coded and recorded on McBee punch cards to facilitate tabulation of complex associations. All told, 42 separate "fields" of information were hand-punched or recorded on each McBee card. For a comprehensive discussion of the use of punch cards in scientific research, see R. S. Casey and J. W. Perry, editors, *Punched Cards, Their Application to Science and Industry*, New York: Reinhold Publishing Corporation, 1951.

Thus, in general, criminal homicides known to the police, investigated, recorded, and procedurally followed through to conclusion provide the most valid and comprehensive data for description and analysis, as well as the best index of the amount and nature of this offense.

Statistical Technique and the Interpretation of Data

The data collected from police files and used to analyze suggested associations and questions are expressed in numerical and percentage frequency distributions, in rates per 100,000 population in some cases, and in ratios. In order to safeguard against loose generalizations, the chi-square test of significance has been used. This test compares a particular observed frequency distribution with the frequency distribution to be expected under the condition of no association or complete independence of the categories examined. Chi-square determines the probability that the differences between these two distributions arise entirely out of chance variations. If this probability is less than .05, it is conventional to reject the null hypothesis (namely, no difference between the observed and expected distributions other than those entirely due to chance), and to accept the observed difference as statistically significant. Moroney,[1] among others, points out that the chi-square test is one of the most useful in testing the significance of the difference in proportions. It should be noted, however, as R. A. Fisher points out in *Statistical Methods for Research Workers*, that chi-square "is not designed to measure the *degree* of association between one classification and another, but solely to test whether the observed departures from independence are or are not of a magnitude ascribable to chance."[2]

In most applications of the chi-square test in the present study a fourfold table has been used with one degree of freedom. Where any expected class frequency of less than five existed, the test was not applied; and in each tested

[1] M. J. Moroney, *Facts from Figures*, Harmondsworth, England: Penguin Books, 1951, pp. 249–250.
[2] R. A. Fisher, *Statistical Methods for Research Workers*, 6th ed., London: Oliver and Boyd, 1936, p. 94.

association, a correction for continuity was used, although the difference resulting without it was only slight. In this study a value of P less than .05, or the 5 per cent level of significance, is used as the minimal level of significant association. Thus, whenever the term *significant*, or phrase *significant association*, appears in italics, the reader may assume that a test for statistical *significance* has been made and that the value of P is less than .05.[1]

When an association between a social attribute or variable and criminal homicide is found to be *significant*, an explanation may sometimes be obvious and perhaps monistic. Other times, *a posteriori* dilemmas arise because of the difficulty of determining which of a series of plausible explanations is most likely. Alternative interpretations are presented, therefore, in several chapters throughout this study, although no attempt has been made to exhaust all possible interpretations of the findings. Furthermore, the researcher who works closely with the same data for a long period of time often develops new insight into meaningful associations which were not apparent at the outset of the research. Re-evaluation of the data and reformulated hypotheses develop along with continued and increasingly detailed analysis. Alternative interpretive statements of anticipated and unexpected associations, in turn, provide new hypotheses for future evaluation and testing. Thus science proceeds to build up a body of empirical knowledge, confirmable and later confirmed by ongoing research.

The present analysis of criminal homicide begins with a general perspective of the offense, then moves into broad race and sex differences noted among both victims and offenders. The age variable is then examined relative to the previous race and sex differentials. As analysis proceeds

[1] Other sources used for description of the chi-square test were: M. J. Hagood, *Statistics for Sociologists*, New York: Henry Holt and Co., 1941, pp. 365–373; E. Bright Wilson, *An Introduction to Scientific Research*, New York: McGraw-Hill Book Co., 1952, pp. 197–202; K. A. Brownlee, *Industrial Experimentation*, 4th ed., New York: Chemical Publishing Co., Inc., 1952, pp. 40–47; H. Arkin and R. R. Colton, *An Outline of Statistical Methods*, 4th ed., New York: Barnes and Noble, Inc., 1939, pp. 109–112; G. U. Yule and M. G. Kendall, *An Introduction to the Theory of Statistics*, 14th ed., New York: Hafner Publishing Co., 1950, pp. 459–481.

through methods and weapons, temporal and spatial patterns, alcohol, motives, previous arrest record, etc., the breakdown by specific categories also continues wherever the sub-classifications are sufficiently large in number to permit testing for statistical significance and meaningful relationships. This process of beginning with a broad, general basis and building up to increasing specificity of social attributes and variables related to criminal homicide, requires repetition of many terms, phrases, and ideas in order to maintain clarity and simplicity.

The raw data used in computation of chi-squares, percentages, and rates, appear in the text or, most frequently, in Appendix I. All *significant* associations resulting from computation using the chi-square or another test to determine *significant* differences between observed and expected frequencies, and all statistical facts expressed in the text as percentages, rates, or ratios are substantiated by the tabulated basic data. Numerical distributions of the Philadelphia criminal homicides by race, sex, age, methods and weapons, etc., and their respective sub-classifications are thus available for additional analysis and for comparison of other areas with the Philadelphia scene.

Finally, replication of this research with a larger number of cases, combined with an interdisciplinary approach, could add new dimensions to our understanding and, perhaps, control and prevention of criminal homicide.

2

A GENERAL PERSPECTIVE OF
CRIMINAL HOMICIDE

The Law of Homicide

HOMICIDE legally means death caused by the behavior of someone other than the person killed; hence, the English common law rules purported to distinguish among homicides in terms of those that were murder, those that were manslaughter, and those that were justifiable and excusable. The primary function of these distinctions was to differentiate criminal from non-criminal homicides, and criminal homicides that were capital from those that were not. The American law followed the same general pattern, though it made further distinctions in order to narrow the category of capital homicides and to prescribe and to vary the penalties for non-capital ones.

A general discussion of the law of homicide[1] and of classi-

[1] For historical development of the mores and laws relative to homicide, see: J. F. Stephen, *A History of the Criminal Law*, 3 vols., London: 1883; C. S. Kenny, *Outlines of Criminal Law*, 10th ed., Cambridge, England: The University Press, 1920; Gabriel Tarde, *Penal Philosophy*, Boston: Little, Brown & Co., 1912; Leon Radzinowicz, *A History of English Common Law and its Administration from 1750 (The Movement for Reform, 1750–1833)*, New York: The Macmillan Co., 1948; Roscoe Pound, *Criminal Justice in America*, New York: Henry Holt and Co., 1930.

Contemporary analyses with many socio-psychological implications appear in: Herbert Wechsler and Jerome Michael, *A Rationale of the Law of Homicide*, reprinted from *Columbia Law Review* (May, December, 1937) 37: 701–761, 1261–1325; Rollin M. Perkins, "The Law of Homicide," *Journal of Criminal Law and Criminology* (March–April, 1946) 36: 391–454; Albert J. Harno, "Some Significant Developments in Criminal Law and Procedure in the Last Century," *Journal of Criminal Law, Criminology, and Police Science* (November–December, 1951), 42: 427–467; C. S. Lobinger, "Homicide Concept—A Study in Comparative Criminal Law," *Journal of Criminal Law and Criminology* (November, 1918), 9: 373–377; Keith W. Blinn, "First Degree Murder—A Workable Definition," *Journal of Criminal Law and Criminology* (March–April, 1950). 40: 729–735; D. S. Davies, et al., *The Modern Approach to Criminal Law*, London: Macmillan and Co., Ltd., 1945, especially J. W. C. Turner, Chapter XIII, "The Mental Element in Crimes at Common Law," pp. 242–261. The manual for police originally prepared by the Committee on Uniform Crime Records of the International Association of Chiefs of Police is an attempt to present a standard definition of criminal homicide: *Uniform Crime Reporting*, New York: 1929, pp. 193–194.

fications of offenders[1] by criminologists is not necessary to the main foci of attention in this research, but a brief

[1] Various classifications of homicide offenders, particularly murderers, have appeared in criminological literature. Lombroso included murderers under his classification of atavistic criminals because they were biologically degenerate, and were found to have bloodshot eyes, aquiline noses, curly black hair, strong jaws, long ears, thin lips, and a menacing grin (*Crime, Its Causes and Remedies*, Boston: Little, Brown and Co., 1911, p. 416). Ferri contended that persons born to commit homicide were characterized by moral insensibility, ferocity, apathy, a weak power of resistance to criminal desires, exaggerated sensibility, sanguine or nervous temperament, and observable anthropomorphic differences from the general criminal population (*Criminal Sociology*, Boston: Little, Brown and Co., 1917, pp. 152–153). Garofalo claimed that murderers were totally lacking in altruism, with no sentiment of benevolence or pity, and present exaggerated cases of moral anomaly (*Criminology*, Boston: Little, Brown and Co., 1914, pp. 111–112). Hooton found murderers older, taller, heavier, larger in chest, broader in jaw, narrower in shoulders relative to their stature, and shorter in relative trunk length when compared to total criminals; the former were more dolichocephalic, had excesses of high nasal bridges, bilateral chins, and carious teeth than criminals at large; and even first degree murderers were different in anthropomorphic degree from second degree murderers (*The American Criminal*, Vol. I, Cambridge, Mass.: Harvard University Press, 1939, pp. 290–292). Tulchin noted a difference in the intelligence distribution of murderers according to nativity and race (*Intelligence and Crime*, Chicago: The University of Chicago Press, 1939, pp. 39–41). Berg and Fox reported that when compared with the total prison population, murderers scored significantly lower on tests of school achievement and intelligence, and that this fact may have had an effect on the type of homicide committed ("Factors in Homicide Committed by 200 Males," *Journal of Social Psychology* [August, 1947], 26: 109–119). Schlapp and Smith developed a biological-personality classification of murderers into four types: the insane, the feeble-minded, the epileptic, and the emotionally defective (*The New Criminology*, New York: Boni and Liveright, 1928). The All-Ukranian Cabinet for Research in Criminality and the Criminal claimed that most murderers fell into a classification called "weakling in conflict," and said that a mental conflict was resolved in explosive behavior and annihilation of an adversary (*Social Science Abstracts*, 2: 947). Bjerre also said that murderers were weak and sought to escape from the realities of life by means of self-deception, passive renunciation, and "shamming" (*The Psychology of Murder*, New York: Longmans, Green and Co., 1927, p. 5).

Studies of causation in homicide have led to a variety of classifications based on motivating factors. Frankel discussed excessive emotionality of the murderer ("One Thousand Murderers," *Journal of Criminal Law and Criminology* [1939], 29: 672–688); Brearley emphasized cultural factors (*Homicide in the United States*); Cassidy classified murderers in terms of sexual, social, and economic frustration ("Personality Study of 200 Murderers," *Journal of Criminal Psychopathology* [1941], 2: 296–304); Abrahamsen spoke of "symptomatic" and "manifest" murder, which were the result of guilt feelings, desire for punishment, distorted erotic drives, and physical inferiority (*Crime and the Human Mind*, New York: Columbia University Press, 1944, pp. 161 f.); Bender called attention to the degree of identification in a study of child murderers ("Psychiatric Mechanisms in Child Murderers," *Journal of Nervous and Mental Disease* [1934], 80: 32–47); types of familial relationships were used in a classification by Curran and Schilder ("A Constructive Approach to the Problems of Childhood and Adolescence," *Journal of Criminal Psychopathology* [1940], 2: 125–142); and Raven suggested that degrees of maladjustment to external reality can aid in classification ("Murder and Suicide as Marks of an Abnormal Mind," *American Sociological Review* [1929], 21: 315–333).

21

review of the Pennsylvania statutes on homicide is desirable to provide a legal framework of orientation for detailed sociological analysis of the police data. It is interesting to note that the first statute to divide the crime of murder into degrees was enacted in Pennsylvania on April 22, 1794. Many other states of the union adopted this model with slight changes in the substantive law, but with considerable variations in judicial interpretations.[1] Article VII, "Offenses Against the Person," Sections 701–703, of the Pennsylvania Penal Code, establishes statutory definitions of the degrees of homicide. The following is an adaptation of a synopsis found in William F. Hoffman's *Pennsylvania Criminal Law and Criminal Procedure*, which provides a basis sufficient for purposes of this research and for understanding pertinent legal problems relative to homicide in this commonwealth.[2]

> *Section 701. Murder of the First and Second Degree.* All murder which shall be perpetuated by means of poison, or by lying in wait, or by any other kind of wilful, deliberate and premeditated killing, or which shall be committed in the perpetration of, or attempting to perpetrate any arson, rape, robbery, burglary, or kidnapping, shall be murder in the first degree. All other kinds of murder shall be murder in the second degree. The jury before whom any person indicted for murder shall be tried, shall, if they find such person guilty thereof, ascertain in their verdict whether the person is guilty of murder of the first or second degree.
>
> *Homicide* is the killing of one human being by another. Homicide is classified as follows:
>
> Excusable Homicide
> Justifiable Homicide
> Murder: First Degree Murder
> Second Degree Murder
> Manslaughter: Voluntary Manslaughter
> Involuntary Manslaughter

[1]Edwin R. Keedy, "History of the Pennsylvania Statute Creating Degrees of Murder," *University of Pennsylvania Law Review* (1949), 97: 759; E. R. Keedy, "A Problem of First Degree Murder: Fisher v. United States," *University of Pennsylvania Law Review* (1950), 99: 267–292; E. R. Keedy, "Criminal Attempts at Common Law," *University of Pennsylvania Law Review* (1954), 102: 464–489.

[2] William F. Hoffman, *Pennsylvania Criminal Law and Criminal Procedure*, 4th ed., Wynnewood, Penna.: Wm. F. Hoffman, 1952, pp. 121–122. Judicial interpretations are also reviewed by the same author, *ibid.*, pp. 121–130.

Excusable Homicide is an unintentional killing where no blame attaches to the killer. It may have resulted from negligence on the part of the victim, but if negligence appears in the actions of the perpetrator, it is involuntary manslaughter.

Justifiable Homicide is an intentional killing sanctioned by law, such as the execution of a legal sentence of death; the killing of a felon who cannot otherwise be taken; or in self-defense where one must kill another to save himself from death or great bodily harm.

Murder, as defined by the common law, consists of the unlawful killing of a human being with malice aforethought, express or implied. Com. v. McLaughlin, 293 Pa. Supreme Ct. 218 (1928).

Malice is a legal term which comprehends not only a particular ill will, but every case where there is wickedness of disposition, hardness of heart, cruelty, recklessness of consequences, or a mind regardless of social duty. Com. v. McLaughlin, 293 Pa. Supreme Ct. 218 (1928).

Murder in the First Degree is the wilful, deliberate and premeditated killing of a human being, feloniously and maliciously. It is also murder in the first degree to kill while committing or attempting to commit certain felonies specified in this section. Under section 919 of the Penal Code, death resulting from malicious injury to railroads is murder of the first degree. Section 3.1 of the Sabotage Prevention Act of March 29, 1951, P. L., No. 15, declares that a death resulting from committing any of the acts of sabotage prohibited by sections 2 and 3 of that act shall be murder in the first degree.

Murder in the Second Degree is the killing of a human being, feloniously and maliciously, but without specific intent to take life. Judge Agnew, while Chief Justice of the Pennsylvania Supreme Court, defined second degree murder in the following words: "Murder in the second degree includes all unlawful killing under circumstances of depravity of heart and a disposition of mind regardless of social duty; but where no intention to kill exists, or can be reasonably and fully inferred. Therefore, in all cases of murder, if no intent to kill can be inferred or collected from the circumstances, the verdict must be murder in the second degree."

Voluntary Manslaughter is the unlawful killing of another in a sudden heat of anger, without premeditation, malice or depravity of heart. Com. v. Drum, 58 Pa. Supreme Ct. 9 (1868).

Involuntary Manslaughter consists of the killing of another without malice and unintentionally, but in doing some unlawful act not amounting to a felony nor naturally tending to cause death or great bodily harm, or in negligently doing some act lawful in itself, or by the negligent omission to perform a legal duty. Com. v. Mayberry, 290 Pa. Supreme Ct. 195 (1927).

General Rates of Homicide and the Confusion of Terms

There are several different classifications of homicide that may be used to express its extent in a given population. In addition to statutory, judicial, and statistical differences that make comparative studies difficult, there is often a lack of discriminate use of these units and terms in the literature.

Homicide is the killing of another person, and includes both criminal and non-criminal killings. From 1948 to 1952 the homicide division of the Philadelphia police listed 627 total homicides. For each of the five years respectively there were 119, 127, 124, 122, and 135, which resulted in an average annual number of 125. Using the Philadelphia census of 1950 as a base,[1] rates for each of the years were 5.7, 6.0, 6.0, 5.9, and 6.5, with a mean annual rate per 100,000 of 6.1. The National Office of Vital Statistics reported a homicide rate for the nation in 1950 of 5.2.[2]

Of the 625 homicides closely examined,[3] 588, or 94 per cent, were *criminal* homicides, and 37, or 6 per cent, were non-criminal. The non-criminal homicides included 23 excusable or accidental deaths and 14 justifiable killings. The city had a mean criminal homicide rate per 100,000 of 5.7. A mean annual rate of 6.6 has been computed from annual police reports of 18 select cities over 250,000 population for the

[1] U.S. Bureau of the Census. *U.S. Census of Population: 1950*, Vol. III, *Census Tract Statistics*, Chapter 42, U.S. Government Printing Office, Washington, D.C., 1952.

[2] *Vital Statistics—Special Reports*, "Deaths and Crude Death Rates for Each Cause, by Race and Sex: United States 1950," National Office of Vital Statistics, Federal Security Agency, Vol. 37, No. 6, February 16, 1953, p. 148.

[3] Two of the original homicides were not included in the present count of 625. One was later declared "not a homicide," and one was unavailable for detailed analysis.

years 1948–1952, and the relative position of Philadelphia is shown in Table 1. The *Uniform Crime Reports*[1] for 1950 revealed that the criminal homicide rate (murder and non-negligent manslaughter) for 2,297 cities with a total population of 69,643,614 was 5.1; for 37 cities over 250,000 population, the rate was 6.8; for cities over 250,000 in the Middle Atlantic States, the rate was 4.8; and for Pennsylvania, 3.5. Hence, the Philadelphia criminal homicide rate (5.7) was similar to urban communities through the nation, compared favorably to urban areas of comparable size, but compared unfavorably to its own region and state.

TABLE 1

CRIMINAL HOMICIDE RATES PER 100,000,
FOR 18 CITIES OVER 250,000 POPULATION,
1948–1952 (a)

City	Mean Annual Rate per 100,000	Number of Criminal Homicides 1948–1952	Population 1950
Miami (b)	15.1	188	249,276
Dallas	13.7	298	434,462
Washington, D.C.	11.8	473	802,175
Kansas City, Mo.	10.0	229	456,622
Baltimore, Md.	9.1	433	949,708
Chicago	7.8	1,415	3,620,962
Cincinnati	7.7	193	503,998
Seattle	5.9	69	467,591
Philadelphia	5.7	588	2,071,605
Boston	5.3	211	801,444
Columbus	4.3	81	375,901
Los Angeles	4.0	398	1,970,358
New York	3.7	1,467	7,891,957
Pittsburgh (c)	3.7	126	676,806
Akron	3.1	43	274,605
Buffalo	2.9	84	580,132
St. Paul	2.4	37	311,349
Milwaukee	2.3	73	637,392
Total	6.6	6,435	19,455,384

(a) Rates were computed from annual police reports for each of the five years from 1948 to 1952. (b) Miami with a population just short of 250,000 has been included. (c) Pittsburgh figures are for 1949–1953.

In some studies and reports, homicide is not clearly differentiated from criminal homicide, nor from the more limited term of murder. Non-criminal homicide is never murder,

[1] *Uniform Crime Reports*, Federal Bureau of Investigation, United States Department of Justice, Washington, D.C., Vol. 21, No. 2, 1950.

while criminal or felonious homicide includes all degrees of murder and some types of manslaughter. Failure to distinguish between criminal homicide in a broad sense and murder, which is a particular category of criminal homicide, appears most often in discussions of an increase or decrease in rates and in debates about the efficacy of the death penalty. Reports of the number of murders occurring in a given year have often erroneously included voluntary and involuntary manslaughters as well as first and second degree murder. Faulty translation of European statistics and terms into English has resulted in comparisons of murder in one country with homicide or criminal homicide in another. The primary focus of attention in the present study is with criminal homicide. Except where indicated, future reference is to criminal homicide, and when necessary for clear understanding of the data, refined distinctions of degrees of criminal homicide are made.

Not only is there confusion of terms regarding homicide, criminal homicide, and murder, but many studies fail to distinguish carefully between victims and offenders.[1] When mortality statistics (which refer only to victims) are used in an analysis of methods by which victims met death, for example, authors sometimes confuse the subject-object relationship and refer to a given number of offenders having used a particular weapon rather than to a given number of victims having been killed by that weapon. Contrariwise, when criminal statistics (which sometimes refer only to offenders) are employed, victims are sometimes referred to, when actually offenders constitute the basis for analysis. In the present study there were 625 victims of homicide, of which 588 were considered by the police to be victims of criminal homicide. There were 665 known agents of homicide,

---

[1] The term "offender" has been used in this study to refer to those listed in police files as responsible for a criminal homicide. To relieve monotony, other words, such as "assailant," "slayer," "killer," "agent," "suspect," have been used synonymously. These latter terms may, of course, be applied to accidental, excusable, and justifiable homicides as well, and thus are somewhat weak terms. "Criminal slayer" is too strong a term because of the implication of a court conviction in all cases. The term "offender," therefore, seems to connote best what the police imply in their files on criminal homicide.

26

of which 621 were known offenders and at least 38 were unknown offenders in criminal homicide. It is important to note that when offenders in criminal homicide are used for analysis rather than victims, the numbers and rates are usually greater, despite the absence of information about unsolved cases where it is impossible, usually, to determine whether the homicide was performed by one or more assailants. It is not valid to presume that the number of victims and offenders is the same, for failure to take cognizance of multiple slayers in one homicidal death, or of a double homicide committed by a single offender, introduces errors in such a presumption. Of the 588 victims of criminal homicide, 550 were killed by 621 known offenders. In short, there were 71 more known offenders than victims among the 550 solved cases, although none of the 588 victims was unidentified. The two major groups used for analysis in subsequent discussions are the 588 victims of criminal homicide with a rate per 100,000 of 5.7, and the 621 known offenders with a rate of 6.0. These general rates provide a framework within which intricacies of interrelated data may be examined more minutely.[1]

[1] By adding a minimum of one offender for each unsolved homicide, a total of 703 agents of homicide in general results, or a rate per 100,000 of 6.8. By adding this same minimum to the number of known criminal homicide offenders, a total of 659 offenders results, or a rate of 6.3. These rates are interesting but unfortunately cannot be compared to any rates given in criminal statistics reported elsewhere. Criminal statistics from the *Uniform Crime Reports*, for example, give the number of cases of criminal homicides known to the police and the number of persons arrested for criminal homicide. A definition of unsolved cases and the number of unsolved are not given in these reports. For further discussion of unsolved criminal homicide, see *infra*, pp. 284–294.

II
THE VICTIM AND THE OFFENDER
IN THE HOMICIDE DRAMA

3

RACE AND SEX DIFFERENCES

CRIMINAL homicide is a complex sociological event. It is the purpose of this chapter to begin description and analysis of that complexity, to test several suggested associations, and to present observations which have unexpectedly emerged from the data. An exhaustive review of criminal homicide literature is not intended, but when related subjects are discussed, references to other studies are made. Comparison of the Philadelphia data to other studies is necessarily crude because of the lack of refinement and the confusion of terms that often exist in the latter.

The Philadelphia Data

The most striking feature in the comparison of race and sex distributions in criminal homicide is the extent to which Negroes exceed whites. This excess occurs both among victims and offenders, males and females. Whatever the causal explanation may be—social, psychological, or biological— it is an incontrovertible fact that Negroes contribute disproportionately to the number of criminal homicides both in Philadelphia and throughout the country as a whole.

Table 2 summarizes data on the incidence of criminal homicides in Philadelphia for the period 1948–1952, by race and sex. Of the 588 victims, 73 per cent are Negro; of the 621 offenders, 75 per cent are Negro. In 1950 Negroes comprised 18 per cent of the Philadelphia population, making obvious the fact that Negroes greatly exceed their "quota" of homicides. Negroes have over three times their "share" of victims and four times more offenders than their proportion in the general population. Testing the difference in proportionate distributions of Negroes and whites, either as victims or offenders, reveals that there is a *significant* association between race and criminal homicide.

TABLE 2

VICTIMS AND OFFENDERS, CRIMINAL HOMICIDE,
PHILADELPHIA, 1948–1952, BY RACE AND SEX

Race and Sex	Victims		Offenders	
	Number	Per cent of total	Number	Per cent of total
Negro				
Male	331	56.3	374	60.2
Female	96	16.3	93	15.0
Total	427	72.6	467	75.2
White				
Male	118	20.1	138	22.2
Female	43	7.3	16	2.6
Total	161	27.4	154	24.8
Both Races				
Male	449	76.4	512	82.4
Female	139	23.6	109	17.6
Total	588	100.0	621	100.0

There is also a *significant* association between sex and criminal homicide, since males, as a gross category, proportionately outnumber females. Of total victims, 76 per cent are males, and of total offenders, 82 per cent are males. Since males are but 48 per cent of the Philadelphia population, their share of homicides is plainly excessive. However, a more important generalization may be noted when specified race and sex groups are combined with victim-offender differentials. It is safe to assert that *the difference in the frequency of criminal homicide is significantly greater between the races within each sex than the difference between the sexes within each race.* In short, race differences are more important in contributing to the phenomenon of criminal homicide than are sex differences. When rates per 100,000 specified race and sex groups are analyzed (Table 3), we may note that Negroes and males have *significantly* higher rates than whites and females respectively, but that the difference in the frequency of criminal homicide is *significantly* greater between the races than between the sexes. For example, among victims, the Negro rate (22.5) is twelve times greater than the white rate (1.9), but the male rate (9.0) is slightly less than four times the female rate (2.6). Similarly among offenders, the race differential is greater than the sex differential, for Negro offenders have a rate (24.6) that is approximately

TABLE 3
RATES PER 100,000 POPULATION, VICTIMS AND OFFENDERS
IN CRIMINAL HOMICIDE, PHILADELPHIA, 1948–1952,
BY RACE AND SEX

Race and Sex	Victims	Offenders
Negro		
Male	36.9	41.7
Female	9.6	9.3
Total	22.5	24.6
White		
Male	2.9	3.4
Female	1.0	.4
Total	1.9	1.8
Both Races		
Male	9.0	10.2
Female	2.6	2.0
Total	5.7	6.0

fourteen times greater than the rate of white offenders (1.8), but male offenders have a rate (10.2) that is only five times greater than the rate for female offenders (2.0). For both victims and offenders differential race rates are approximately three times greater than differential sex rates.

A further breakdown by race and sex lends reliability to this generalization regarding the greater significance of race compared to sex. Among victims the rate for Negro males (36.9) is about thirteen times greater than the rate for white males (2.9), and the rate for Negro females (9.6) is nearly ten times greater than the rate for white females (1.0). However, within each race, a comparison of Negro males with Negro females, and of white males with white females shows, in each case, males with rates that are only between three and four times greater than rates for females. Among offenders virtually the same relative differences occur. The rate for Negro male offenders (41.7) is twelve times greater than the rate for white male offenders (3.4) but is only four times greater than the rate for Negro female offenders (9.3). Although the rate for white males is, as just noted, twelve times less than that for Negro males, the white male rate is only eight times greater than the white female rate. Finally, although Negro female offenders have a rate only four times less than that for Negro male offenders, Negro females have a rate (9.3) twenty-three times greater than the rate for white females (0.4). From any perspective, race differences are greater than sex differences.

There is another meaningful conclusion regarding these race and sex differentials which concerns a contrast between the proportionate distribution of victims and offenders. It should be obvious from the foregoing discussion that reports and studies using mortality statistics may be valid for purposes of describing race and sex distributions of victims, and that studies using criminal statistics may be valid for purposes of describing these same distributions for offenders; but that mortality data should not be used to infer information about offenders and that criminal data should not be used to describe characteristics of victims (unless, as in the present study, victim data are available). Where several studies are combined to test a new hypothesis, rates of victims and offenders are sometimes used indiscriminately and interchangeably. "Homicides per 100,000" is a typical table or chart title without appropriate qualification as to whether the rate refers to persons killed or persons who have killed. Although it appears to be true that there is a marked tendency for victims of homicide to be killed by members of their own race,[1] too many liberties are taken with this generalization in refined treatments of homicide material. Several studies report as high as 10 per cent or more of felonious deaths as being interracial. For any broad and general discussion of Negroes and whites related to numbers

[1] See *infra*, pp. 222–236, for detailed analysis of interracial criminal homicide.

and rates of homicide, this 10 per cent difference probably does not seriously affect the description. However, when race rates for victims are correlated with business cycles and other types of social and personal factors as if these same rates applied to offenders, the interracial difference could, if accounted for, jeopardize an otherwise correctly demonstrated correlation. When race distributions by victims are further refined according to sex, and when these race-sex groups are discussed as if they were offenders killing their victims with particular weapons, during certain seasons of the year, times of the day, etc., a double error is involved. Furthermore, the majority of both male and female victims are killed by males; while the majority of female offenders kill males. In short, criminal homicide is not predominantly an offense among members of the same sex, with males killing males and females killing females.

In Philadelphia, for example, Negro males comprise 77 per cent of Negro victims and 80 per cent of Negro offenders. White males comprise 73 per cent of white victims, but 90 per cent of white offenders. Both among male victims and male offenders, Negroes make up a similar proportion (73 per cent). The most striking difference between victims and offenders is found with respect to females. Of all female victims, 69 per cent are Negro and of all female offenders, 85 per cent are Negro, a proportional difference between victims and offenders which is statistically *significant*. The number of white female victims (43) is over twice as great as the number of white female offenders (16), a fact which further means that white females comprise 7 per cent of the total 588 victims compared to only 3 per cent of the 621 offenders. For both races, females have more victims than offenders—a fact not true of males of either race. However, there are 27 more victims than offenders among white females, but only three more victims than offenders among Negro females. This difference accounts for the fact that although 18 per cent of all offenders are women, 24 per cent of all victims are of this sex. (Relative to this low number and proportion of female offenders—particularly of white female

35

offenders—it may be pertinent to point to the plausibility of Pollak's contention that many more females than males escape detection and that this fact invalidates, to a large extent, official criminal statistics.)[1] Thus, since one-third more females are victims than they are offenders in criminal homicide it is particularly important to distinguish properly between victims and offenders in any analysis of the crime. When rates are broken down by race, sex, and other attributes, slight differences in victim-offender rates become magnified. In general, increasing refinement results in greater magnification of the marginal differentiation; and it becomes obvious that it is not valid to infer characteristics of offenders from mortality (victim) statistics, nor to describe a profile of the victim from most criminal (offender) statistics.

A Note Regarding Race and Occupation

Because it does not usually have much bearing on practical police work involved in a case of criminal homicide, the occupation of victim or offender generally is not reported with the careful attention to detail given other aspects of the case. Police investigators are not social science researchers. However, if the police were to include occupational categories in their recording forms, and if an earnest attempt were made to collect accurate information about the occupation of victim and offender, data of considerable value would be available to the research scientist.

For some victims and offenders the category, "laborer," was frequently listed by the police although the designation of "semiskilled" or "skilled" worker appeared to be more warranted. In the absence of a standard police recording procedure for listing occupation, an original desire to include occupation in this study, as an index of social class, had to be abandoned early in the research.

Because there is a heavy concentration of Negroes in the lower part of the occupational hierarchy, and because the

---

[1] Otto Pollak, *The Criminality of Women*, Philadelphia: The University of Pennsylvania Press, 1951. Relative to homicide, see especially pp. 3, 16–18, 79–82. Further discussion of this point appears in the subsequent section, pp. 47–49.

Negro homicide rate has been shown to be extremely high, it might be contended that if social class were controlled, the Negro rate then would not be appreciably higher than the white rate. Students of race relations have long recognized the difficulties inherent in any attempt to equate the relative status of Negroes and whites in the social class structure of a bi-racial community. No contribution to that area of research is made in the present study, and no definitive conclusion is made about occupation, or social class, and homicide. It is, however, safe to assert on the basis of a crude approximation of occupation that 90 to 95 per cent of the offenders of either race were in the lower end of the occupational scale, or from the category of skilled workers down through the unemployed.

The following analysis is presented as a rough estimate of the relationship between homicide, race, and occupation. Although there are undoubtedly differences in the distribution of occupations by victims and offenders, in the absence of refined and precise data, the present analysis refers only to offenders. Victims probably cover a wider occupational range than offenders, and have a slightly higher proportion in the upper half of the occupational scale. Finally, because homicide is predominantly committed by males, the discussion that follows is concerned only with that sex.

Let us assume that all homicides in Philadelphia were committed by persons in the lower end of the occupational scale—i.e., by skilled, semiskilled, unskilled, service, and unemployed workers. We are eliminating, therefore, categories generally designated as professional, proprietary, clerical and sales. The assumption—if biased at all—is biased against whites, for the few cases in which homicide offenders were clerical workers or of higher occupational status, were also white.

According to census reports for 1950,[1] white males

[1] United States Bureau of the Census, *U.S. Census of Population: 1950*, Vol. III, Census Tract Statistics, pp. 57, 205–211. The non-white figures are based on Census Tracts containing 250 or more non-white persons. The white figures include total civilian labor force for Census Tracts containing less than 250 non-whites. Total white males = 502,481, including 4,905 cases in which occupation was not reported. Total non-white males = 92,956, including 1,595 cases in which occupation was not reported.

classified as skilled (22.6 per cent), semiskilled (22.3 per cent), unskilled (4.6 per cent), service (7.0 per cent), and unemployed (6.1 per cent) workers constituted 311,787 or 62.6 per cent of all white males aged 14 years and over in the labor force in Philadelphia. Assuming that all 138 white male offenders in criminal homicide were members of these occupational groups, the mean annual rate of criminal homicide for white males in these occupational groups is 8.8 per 100,000. Obviously, this rate is higher than the rate when the population base used for computation is white males in Philadelphia in all ages and occupations, 3.4; and is higher than the rate when the population base used for computation is white males aged 15 years and over, in all occupations, 4.2.

According to the same census report, non-white males classified as skilled (10.1 per cent), semiskilled (21.5 per cent), unskilled (25.0 per cent), service (17.0 per cent), and unemployed (13.4 per cent) workers constituted 80,872, or 87.0 per cent of all non-white males aged 14 years and over in the labor force in Philadelphia. Assuming that all 374 Negro male offenders were members of these occupational groups, the mean annual rate of criminal homicide for non-white males in these occupational groups is 94. Obviously, this rate is considerably higher than the rate when the population base used for computation is non-white males in Philadelphia, in all ages and occupations, 41.7; and is higher than the rate when the population base used for computation is non-white males aged 15 years and over, in all occupations, 57.7.

It has been observed previously that the rate for Negro male offenders, in general, is about twelve times greater than that for white male offenders. By combining skilled, semiskilled, unskilled, service, and unemployed workers together as the population unit for which rates are computed for each race, we find that the rate for Negro male offenders is still about eleven times greater than that for white male offenders. When the same type of analysis is made, eliminating skilled workers from the population base, and assuming, therefore, that all homicide offenders were members of only the semiskilled, unskilled, service, and unemployed categories, the mean annual Negro male rate is 106.4 and is still about eight times greater than the white male rate of 13.8. Thus, analysis of the relationship between race and homicide by a crude control for the occupation variable produces little change in the differential rate between the races, and the rate for Negroes still exceeds that for whites.[1]

Race Differences Noted in Other Studies and Reports

Computation of data from the 1950 *Uniform Crime Reports*[2] reveals that of every 1,000 arrests throughout the nation, 8 were for criminal homicide. For the same year, there was slightly more than one arrest for criminal homicide per 1,000 arrests in Philadelphia.[3] For the country, 28 out of every 1,000 arrests for Part I offenses[4] were for criminal homicide; for the same group of offenses, the rate in Philadelphia was 19. Among total arrests for whites in the United states, 6 per 1,000 were for criminal homicide; for Negroes the rate was 14. The criminal homicide rate per 1,000 arrests for Part I offenses was 24 for white and 41 for Negroes. Although Negroes comprised only about 10 per cent of the United States' population in 1950, they made up 26 per cent of all arrests throughout the country and 46 per cent of the arrests for criminal homicide. We have noted that Negroes comprised 18 per cent of the Philadelphia population but constituted 75 per cent of arrests for criminal homicide during the 1948–1952 period. Thus, Negroes are arrested for criminal homicide both in the nation as a whole, and in Philadelphia, proportionately four times greater than their proportion in either the national or city population.

[1] Moses also has shown that when the socio-economic differences between Negroes and whites are held constant, the crime rates of the former still exceed those of the latter. Earl R. Moses, "Differentials in Crime Rates Between Negroes and Whites, Based on Comparisons of Four Socio-economically Equated Areas," *American Sociological Review* (August, 1947), 12: 411–420.
[2] *Uniform Crime Reports*, Vol. 21, No. 2, 1950, p. 112.
[3] *Annual Report*, Bureau of Police, Department of Public Safety, City of Philadelphia, 1950, Appendix, Table No. 2.
[4] Part I offenses include: (1) Criminal homicide, (2) rape, (3) robbery, (4) aggravated assault, (5) burglary, (6) larceny, (7) auto theft.

In 1950, approximately 5 per cent of all male felony prisoners received from courts and imprisoned in state and federal institutions were committed for murder or manslaughter. Among whites, only 3 per cent were committed for criminal homicide; but among Negroes, 10 per cent were institutionalized for this offense.[1]

Most criminal homicide research in this country reveals race differentials similar to those in Philadelphia. Emil Frankel, in a study of one thousand murderers in New Jersey between 1925 and 1934, found that "the extent to which Negroes are represented in the general population of the counties, to that extent is the general homicide rate affected. Thus, the percentage of Negroes in the general population of the classified counties follows the same sequences as the homicide rates. . . ."[2] Frederick Hoffman[3] for many years consistently pointed out that cities with the highest homicide rates in the United States were all southern cities with huge Negro populations and that six southern cities led the world in homicides. Dublin and Bunzel[4] in their excellent report, *Thou Shalt Not Kill*, explain the increase of homicide rates in the Original Registration States since 1900 in terms of an increase of Negroes migrating into that area. Unfortunately no homicide figures were classified according to color prior to 1921, but during the five-year period 1926–1930, more than eight times as many Negro as white males were slain per unit of population, and almost seven times as many Negro as white women. However, these same authors point out that it is the high white rate *combined* with a relatively high Negro rate that gives the South its unenviable position; for in the three years, 1929–1931, the white rate in the South was 8.6 as compared with 5.5 for the country as a whole.[5]

[1] *National Prisoner Statistics, Prisoners in State and Federal Institutions, 1950*, Federal Bureau of Prisons, Washington, D.C., 1954, p. 65.

[2] Emil Frankel, "One Thousand Murderers," *Journal of Criminal Law and Criminology* (January, 1939), 29: 676–677.

[3] Frederick L. Hoffman, *The Homicide Problem*, Newark, N.J.: The Prudential Press, 1925. See particularly, "Homicide Record for 1931," *Spectator* (March, 1932), 28: 4–5.

[4] Louis I. Dublin and Bessie Bunzel, "Thou Shalt Not Kill," *Survey Graphic* (March, 1935), 24: 127.

[5] *Ibid.*, p. 129.

A different perspective is presented by Allredge[1] in a study and analysis of court records during 1940 for seven southern sections with high homicide rates: Richmond, Atlanta, Nashville, Memphis, Birmingham, Houston, and five North Carolina centers. The author purports to show that it is the presence of the Negro in the South that makes for a high homicide record, and that southern whites compare favorably with other sections of the country. For example, he says:

> While the Negroes comprise but one-third of the population of these seven sections of the South, they committed more than six times the number of murders and manslaughters that were committed by the whites in the same areas. This means that the murder and manslaughter rate of the Negroes in these seven sections of the South, at present, is more than twelve times that of the whites among whom they live! . . . If we now compare the murder and manslaughter records of the whites in these seven sections of the South with the records of the other sections of the United States, we shall see that the whites of the South compare favorably with any other section of the United States, except New England.[2]

However, it is important to note that this study employed court records of offenders and compared them with arrest records from the *Uniform Crime Reports*, the latter of which is a national compilation of police data. As Guy B. Johnson has demonstrated, conviction rates for Negroes are consistently higher than for whites in these southern states.[3]

Referring to general homicide death rates, Sutherland pointed out that

> the high crime rates in the southern states are generally interpreted as due to the large number of Negroes, but it is evident that homicides, at least, cannot be explained so simply, for the death rate by homicide for white persons in the South is approximately five times as high as in New England.[4]

[1] E. P. Allredge, "Why the South Leads the Nation in Murder and Manslaughter," *The Quarterly Review*, Nashville, Tennessee (April–May–June, 1942), 2: 123–134.
[2] *Ibid.*, p. 132.
[3] Guy B. Johnson, "The Negro and Crime," *The Annals of the American Academy of Political and Social Science* (September, 1941), 217: 93–104.
[4] Edwin H. Sutherland, *Principles of Criminology*, 4th ed., Philadelphia: J. B. Lippincott Co., 1947, pp. 134–135.

41

This same generalization appears to be applicable when the Philadelphia data are compared with material collected by Harlan[1] in a study of 500 criminal homicides in Birmingham, Alabama, between 1937 and 1944. The white offender rate in Birmingham (5.8) was over three times higher than the white offender rate in Philadelphia (1.8).

In a concise analysis of homicide death rates by racial and regional groups, George Vold[2] said that the homicide rates for the New England states are generally low partly because the number of the colored population there is insignificant and the effect of high colored rates on the total rates for the states as a whole is slight. But Vold also refers to the relatively higher homicide rate for southern whites compared to New England whites:

> Lest anyone conclude . . . that regional differences in homicide are equivalent to, or due only to, differences in the proportions of the total population classed as other than white, attention is invited to the similar consistent and large differences in the rates as between regions for the white group alone.
>
> When comparisons are made between the states of Massachusetts and Georgia, the following will be found to obtain: The homicide rate of the white group in Georgia (5.6) is almost exactly four times as high as that of the white group in Massachusetts (1.4); the Georgia 'other than white rate' (47.1) is likewise almost exactly four times the 'other than white' rate (11.8) for Massachusetts. This basic regional or sectional difference must be recognized and taken account of, independent of, and in spite of, the obviously important differences between the several major racial groups.[3]

Although no exhaustive attempt has been made in this present analysis to examine racial and regional differences in homicide, a few additional studies may shed light both on the Philadelphia data and on comparative techniques of

[1] Howard Harlan, "Five Hundred Homicides," *Journal of Criminal Law and Criminology* (March–April, 1950), 40: 736–752. This is one of the very few studies in which both victims and offenders are analyzed, though crudely. Rates were computed from Table 1, p. 737.

[2] George Vold, "Extent and Trend of Capital Crimes in the United States," *The Annals of the American Academy of Political and Social Science* (*Murder and the Penalty of Death*) (November, 1952), 284: 1–7.

[3] *Ibid.*, p. 5.

analysis. Comparisons already made between northern and southern areas by Dublin and Bunzel, Allredge, and Vold have indicated that two comparative approaches exist, and that choice of their use depends upon the analytic perspective. The one approach interprets the Negro's disproportionate contribution to homicide relative to his proportion in the community's general population. The other approach compares the homicide rate per 100,000 Negroes in one community with the Negro rate in another community. There may be justifiable reasons for using either technique, but clarity of analysis should be maintained.

For example, the proportion of Negroes among total criminal homicide offenders in Philadelphia may be compared to the proportion of Negroes among total criminal homicide offenders in Birmingham. During the period from 1937 to 1944, Harlan found that 85 per cent of the 492 offenders were Negro, and that this race comprised 40 per cent of the Birmingham population.[1] In sum, the proportion of Negro offenders in criminal homicide was twice the proportion of Negroes in the general population. We have noted that 75 per cent of the offenders in Philadelphia during the 1948–1952 period were Negro, although this race made up only 18 per cent of the population. Thus, in Philadelphia, Negroes contributed four times their expected share of the offenders. Computing a mean number of criminal homicides for the two cities during each of the examined periods, Birmingham had approximately 61 cases and Philadelphia 125. On the basis of their proportionate population in the southern city, Negroes would have been expected to have committed criminal homicide in 24 of the 61 cases. Instead, they were responsible for 52. Philadelphia Negroes would have been expected to have committed but 23 such homicides, whereas they accounted for 94 out of the 125. This type of comparative analysis describes Negro killings within the context of a northern city on the one hand, and a southern city on the other, and relates the colored population to the total immediate cultural environment, including whites. It

[1] Harlan, *op. cit.*, p. 737.

thus appears that Philadelphia Negroes in their total setting were twice as homicidal as Birmingham Negroes in their total setting.

When rates per 100,000 population are used in the comparison, however, both Negroes and whites in Birmingham appear to have committed criminal homicide more often than the respective races in Philadelphia. The general criminal homicide rate in Birmingham (23.4) was over four times higher than that for Philadelphia (5.7). In the southern city the Negro victim rate (49.0) and the offender rate (48.0) were approximately twice as high as the rates for Philadelphia Negroes (22.5; 25.6). In Birmingham white victim and offender rates (5.8) were three times greater than those for Philadelphia whites (1.8; 1.9).[1]

Such an apparent disparity between the proportionate involvement of Negroes in criminal homicide and their rates is often overlooked by students who compare the relative homicide status of cities and regions of the country. Both comparative techniques are useful. It may be argued, for example, that in the absence of complete racial integration, a northern urban Negro culture is similar to a southern urban Negro culture, that attitudinal and behavioral norms are sufficiently alike so that statistical comparisons of the two groups, exclusive of whites, are justifiable. Hence, in order to determine propensity to commit criminal homicide, the rate per population unit is necessary. On the other hand, it may be contended that each urban Negro group operates within a larger social environment of normative rules that define and interpret behavior, and that a minority group cannot be adequately described in isolation or without consideration of the majority group with which it has physical and occasional social proximity. From this perspective, it is useful to describe the relation between the Negro's proportion in the general population and his proportionate contribution to the type of behavior under examination. For comprehensiveness, probably both comparative analyses should be employed.

[1] *Ibid.* Rates for Birmingham computed from Harlan's work.

A recent study of 212 murders and non-negligent man-slaughters in St. Louis between 1949 and 1951[1] revealed that 73 per cent of these homicides were committed by 18 per cent of the colored population. Thus, both in St. Louis and in Philadelphia, Negroes constituted a proportion among total offenders four times greater than their proportion in the total population. The offender rates per 100,000 in St. Louis for both Negroes (33.0) and whites (2.5) were higher than those for Philadelphia Negroes (25.6) and whites (1.8).[2]

In his study of homicide in Massachusetts, Stearns[3] showed that 10 per cent of the criminal offenders were Negroes, contrasted to a Negro population that constituted about one per cent in the state. Brearley[4] noted that the combined homicide rates per 100,000 during 1920 and 1925 for Pennsylvania were considerably higher for Negroes than for whites both in urban and rural communities. In urban areas whites had a rate of 5.3 and Negroes 47.1; in rural areas, the white rate was 3.4, and the Negro rate was 45.2. DePorte and Parkhurst,[5] in their comprehensive analysis of 1,606 homicides between 1921 and 1930, and using death certificates of 37 upstate New York counties, showed the rate for whites to be 2.8 per 100,000 and for Negroes, 30.4. In the *Illinois Crime Survey*[6] it is noted that although the colored population in Chicago and Cook County in 1926 and 1927 was only 5 per cent of the total population, 28 per cent of the total victims were Negroes. This means that in Chicago, during the two years examined, the proportion of colored victims was nearly six times greater among criminal homicides than was their proportion in the Chicago population.

[1] Arthur C. Meyers, Jr., *Murder and Non-Negligent Manslaughter: A Statistical Study.* Unpublished manuscript in the author's files, submitted by the St. Louis Police Department.

[2] *Ibid.* Rates and proportions for St. Louis offenders computed from these data; see p. 24.

[3] A. W. Stearns, "Homicide in Massachusetts," *The American Journal of Psychiatry* (July, 1924–August, 1925), 4: 733–734.

[4] H. C. Brearley, "The Negro and Homicide," *Social Forces* (1930), 9: 248.

[5] J. V. DePorte and E. Parkhurst, "Homicide in New York State: A Statistical Study of the Victims and Criminals in 37 Counties in 1921–30," *Human Biology* (1935), 7: 55.

[6] *The Illinois Crime Survey*, pp. 607–608.

This is considerably higher than the three times greater proportion of Negroes found among victims in Philadelphia.

A study of 54 juvenile homicides (i.e., juvenile offenders) referred to the Bureau of Juvenile Research in Ohio for study and observation during the years of 1921 to 1947 inclusive,[1] showed similar race differentials. C. H. Growdon, the late research director, reported that

> a lower percentage of whites and a higher percentage of Negroes were found among our homicide cases than was found in the population of the State, or in our group of unclassified delinquents. The data, on the surface, might be interpreted to indicate that . . . Negro children tend to commit homicide more frequently than white children. However, the limited size of the group, and the factors of special selectivity make this conclusion uncertain. The inferences are true when applied to our particular group, not necessarily beyond those limits.[2]

It was revealed in the study that 5.1 per cent of the general population of Ohio, ages 9 to 18 in 1940, was Negro compared to 14 per cent Negro among the 8,323 unclassified delinquents and 22 per cent Negro in the homicide group.

These various studies showing race distributions and rates have been reviewed because original sources of data similar to those of the present study were used. Prison statistics may be equally revealing, but have been omitted because of the incomparability of the data. The *significantly* higher proportion of Negroes than whites involved in criminal homicide both as victims and as offenders in Philadelphia appears to be a general pattern in other communities throughout the country.

Sex Differences Noted in Other Studies and Reports

A brief review of homicide literature reveals sex distributions more similar than dissimilar to the present study. Causal factors making for a variety of sex differentials in crime are not included in this research, but a plethora of explanations may be found in almost any good criminology

---

[1] C. H. Growdon, *A Group Study of Juvenile Homicide*, Columbus, Ohio: State Bureau of Juvenile Research, Department of Public Welfare, 1950.

[2] *Ibid.*, p. 5.

text. Some explanations for sex differences in homicide are implicit in discussions of specific factors, such as place where the offense occurred, weapons employed, etc. Durkheim has suggested that woman

> kills others less, not because of physiological differences from man but because she does not participate in collective life in the same way. Moreover, she is far from having the same antipathy to these two forms of immorality [suicide and homicide]. Indeed we are inclined to forget that there are murders of which she has monopoly, infanticides, abortions, and poisoning. Whenever homicide is within her range she commits it as often or more than men. According to Oettingen, half the total number of domestic murder is attributable to her. So there is no reason to suppose that she has greater respect for another's life because of her congenital constitution, she merely lacks as frequent opportunities, being less deeply involved in the struggle of life. The causes impelling to sanguinary crimes affect her less than men because she is less within their sphere of influence.[1]

In his *Criminality of Women*, Otto Pollak refers to the fact that murder is considered a crime of highly public character, but because women more frequently resort to poison than do men, the female homicide is probably less detectable.[2] The "masked character" of female crime, less likelihood of arrest, conviction, and incarceration, sex differential data from other countries, and a survey of causality are important contributions Pollak has made to the analysis of female homicide as well as of female crime in general. Mabel Elliott disagrees with Pollak's approach, particularly with respect to homicide, and claims that it is doubtful that more women murderers escape detection than men "since their guilt reactions are generally observable and women murderers usually kill either their husbands or their children."[3] That women are "more gullible and naive" than men and

---

[1] Emile Durkheim, *Suicide: A Study in Sociology*, Translated by John A. Spauling and George Simpson, Glencoe, Illinois: The Free Press, 1951, pp. 341–342.
[2] Pollak, *op. cit.*, p. 3.
[3] Mabel Elliott, *Crime in Modern Society*, New York: Harper and Brothers, 1952, p. 200.

live in a "private world in which the virtues of honesty, faith, and trust form the web, woof, and pattern of responsible family life," and that "the average woman experiences less conflict between her ethical values (and mode of life) and the achievement of her goals than does the average man," are additional reasons Elliott advances to explain what she believes is a real rather than an apparent lower criminal and homicide rate for women than for men.[1] Despite the possible validity of Elliott's assertions, quantitative confirmation and empirical tests of her impressionistic evaluations are lacking.

Pollak notes that women arrested for criminal homicide, as reflected in the fingerprint analysis of the Federal Bureau of Investigation, declined during the war years both in absolute incidence figures and in ratio to male arrests.

> In 1942 the proportionate concentrations of arrests . . . were still 1.1 per cent for female and only 1 per cent for male offenders; in 1943, however, the relationship was already reversed, being .8 per cent for female and 1 per cent for male offenders. The trend continued in 1944, resulting in .7 per cent female and 1 per cent male offenders. The decline of female homicides suggested by these changes in the proportionate concentrations of male and female cases is corroborated by the showing of the absolute incidence figures. The female cases numbered 767 in 1942 and 627 in 1944.
>
> In the first full postwar year, 1946, however, we can already notice a reversal of the war trend. The fingerprint records of the FBI show equal proportionate concentrations of male and female arrests for homicide. In 1947 the general prewar relationship of female preponderance in homicide is re-established. One per cent of the female arrests was based on homicide charges while only .9 per cent of the male arrests were based on that charge.
>
> . . . Many of the husbands went away, and their being out of reach seems to have lowered the incidence of women offenders in this type of crime.[2]

In his analysis of the same data, Hans von Hentig claims that criminal homicides committed by females declined

[1] *Ibid.*, p. 201.
[2] Pollack, *op. cit.*, p. 80.

48

during the last war because of an improvement in women's economic condition.[1] Validity of such an explanation would require precise evaluation of the female economic status during pre-war, war, and post-war years. Mabel Elliott takes issue with von Hentig and claims, like Pollak, that the greater amount of separation of women from their husbands and lovers (whom they are more likely to kill than others) during wartime almost automatically precludes murdering the absent party.[2]

In 1950 the sex ratio of persons arrested for all offenses in Philadelphia was ten males to every female.[3] The distribution of persons involved in criminal homicide in Philadelphia from 1948 to 1952 shows a sex ratio among victims of about three males to each female, and among offenders, a ratio of nearly five to one. For both races the sex ratio among victims was about three to one, but among offenders, the sex ratio for Negroes was four to one and for whites nearly nine to one. Sex differences by rates per 100,000 have previously been examined.[4]

National criminal and mortality statistics attest to the greater amount of recorded criminal homicide committed by males. Of 6,336 arrests for this offense in 1950, 5,482 were males and 854 were females—a ratio of six to one. This ratio is less than the nine-to-one ratio for all offenses in 1950. However, of all male arrests, criminal homicide accounted for .8 per cent, and of all female arrests, 1.1 per cent were for criminal homicide.[5]

Although not precisely comparable to the Philadelphia data, national prison statistics reveal higher sex ratios than those for criminal homicide arrests in Philadelphia. In 1950 the sex ratio of all persons received from the courts and imprisoned in state and federal institutions was about twenty-four to one. The ratio for persons who had committed

[1] Hans von Hentig, *Crime: Causes and Conditions*, New York: McGraw-Hill Book Co., Inc., 1947, p. 119.
[2] Elliott, *op. cit.*, p. 208.
[3] *Annual Report*, Bureau of Police, Department of Public Safety, City of Philadelphia, 1950, Appendix, Table 1.
[4] *Supra*, pp. 32–35.
[5] *Uniform Crime Reports*, 1950, p. 106.

criminal homicide was only nine to one. There was a relatively greater preponderance of institutional commitments for criminal homicide among females. About 5 per cent of all male prisoners and nearly 14 per cent of all female prisoners were incarcerated for criminal homicide.[1] General mortality *rates* of victims in specific race and sex groups for 1950 show a white male rate (3.6) approximately three times larger than the white female rate (1.3). The non-white male rate (42.8) was nearly four times larger than the non-white female rate (11.2).[2]

Comparison to other homicide studies discloses sex distributions in some that are similar, and in others that are dissimilar to the Philadelphia distribution.[3]

Homicide victims during 1926–1927 classified by sex and race in Cook County, Illinois, were distributed as follows: 56 per cent white males; 16 per cent white females; 22 per cent colored males; and 6 per cent colored females. For both races, male victims constituted a group over three times greater than females, a sex distribution corresponding closely to that in Philadelphia.[4]

In Harlan's Birmingham study, 78 per cent of the 500 victims and 76 per cent of the 492 offenders were male.[5] This sex ratio of about three to one is similar to the Philadelphia victim data, but is not similar to the offender ratio of five males to every female. Part of this difference lies in the fact that there were only 12 cases during the eight years in Birmingham in which two or more agents were charged with the same crime. In Philadelphia, there were 44 such cases with a total of 71 offenders over the five years, and 95 per cent of the multiple offenders or defendants were male. In both Philadelphia in 1950 and in Birmingham in 1940,

[1] *National Prisoner Statistics, Prisoners in State and Federal Institutions, 1950*, Washington, D.C.: U.S. Government Printing Office, Federal Bureau of Prisons, p. 63.

[2] Vital Statistics—Special Reports, *op. cit.*, p. 148.

[3] Because primary source material used in other studies was not available to the present author, and because other studies have not always used comparable data, it was impossible to compute various statistical facts that would be relative to the Philadelphia findings. May it suffice, in most cases, to present the documented studies as they were reported by the authors.

[4] *The Illinois Crime Survey*, pp. 607–608.

[5] Harlan, *op. cit.*, pp. 739–740.

males comprised 48 per cent of each of the respective populations. Thus, in both cities, male homicide victims and offenders exceeded their expected proportions to about the same degree.

Similarly, the Meyers report in St. Louis revealed that 77 per cent of the 212 victims and 74 per cent of the 207 offenders were male during the three years studied.[1] Information given regarding multiple agents of homicide indicated there were nine cases of two assailants each who were charged with the same crime. Dublin and Bunzel found a still higher male proportion among offenders:

> Since reliable information regarding the murderer is extremely rare, we undertook a few years ago to analyze over 600 records of homicides committed in 1922–1924. In the cases where sex was specified, 93 per cent of the assailants were males. In the vast majority of cases, both the slayer and his victim were men. Among the males, 36 per cent were white and 64 per cent Negro.[2]

This race distribution among males shows a slightly higher white proportion than was true of Philadelphia homicides, where only 27 per cent of the victims and 25 per cent of the offenders were white.

In a highly select group of 200 murderers, Cassidy[3] found males nine times more frequent than females. Calvin Schmid's[4] analysis of homicides, taken from the death records of the coroner's office in Seattle between 1914 and 1924, resulted in a sex ratio similar to that of Philadelphia. In Seattle, 74 per cent of the victims were males. But the homicide death rate per 100,000 in Seattle in 1920 was over twice as high for males (8.9) as for females (3.7), whereas in Philadelphia the male rate was over three times as high as the female rate.

[1] Meyers, Jr., *op. cit.*, p. 26.
[2] Dublin and Bunzel, *op. cit.*, p. 130. Presumably the authors mean "offender" where they have used the term "murderer."
[3] J. H. Cassidy, "Personality Study of 200 Murderers," *Journal of Criminal Psychopathology* (January, 1941), 2: 297.
[4] Calvin F. Schmid, "A Study of Homicides in Seattle, 1914 to 1924," *Social Forces* (September, 1925–June, 1926), 4: 745–756.

Of the 1,606 homicides taken from death certificates recorded in 37 counties in New York State, 1921–1930, DePorte and Parkhurst[1] found that 77 per cent were male, and 23 per cent female. In addition they pointed out that "the risk of a woman being killed was relatively greater among the native-born white than among either the foreign-born or the Negroes. Among the former, one in three of the victims was a woman as compared with one in four among the Negroes and one in seven among the foreign-born."[2] An unbalanced sex ratio of more males among the foreign-born during those years was affected by the age distribution among victims.

In an earlier and more elementary analysis of Birmingham homicides than that by Harlan, Frederick Hoffman referred to the sex distribution of homicide victims recorded on death certificates for the five-year period 1920–1925. Having used the term "murder" within a context indicating that he meant "homicide," the author claimed:

> During that period there were 567 deaths due to murder. . . . The number of deaths of males was 457 . . . while the number of deaths of females was 110. . . . In addition to the foregoing, there occurred 303 deaths from murder in the county of Jefferson, outside the city of Birmingham. . . . In the whole county of Jefferson during the five years under observation there were 870 deaths from murder, of which 701 were deaths of males and 169 were deaths of females.[3]

Computing from Hoffman's figures, 81 per cent of the victims in both Birmingham and in the whole of Jefferson County were male. In a similar treatment of data from New Orleans over a five-year period ending in 1924, the same author reported that of 475 homicide deaths, 83 per cent were male.[4] It should be remembered that these figures refer to mortality data and therefore include non-criminal as well as criminal homicides.

[1] DePorte and Parkhurst, *op. cit.*, pp. 56–57.
[2] *Ibid.*
[3] F. L. Hoffman, "The Increase in Murder," *op. cit.*, pp. 23–24.
[4] *Ibid.*, p. 26.

The Growdon study of 54 juvenile homicide offenders reported a distribution of 46 males and only 6 females. The 9–18 year age group in the Ohio population in 1940 from which the juveniles came had only 50 per cent male, compared to 89 per cent in the homicide group.[1]

In an analysis of national mortality statistics for the period 1924–1926, Brearley found that females made up a smaller proportion of Negro homicides than of white homicides:

For these years there was one female slain among the Negroes for every 4.5 males, while among the whites there was one to every 3.86 males. The ratio of Negro males to white males slain was one to 1.31, while for females it was one Negro to every 1.53 whites. This indicates that a Negro woman is less likely to be slain, considering the high homicide rate for this race, than is a white woman. In other words, provided the three years studied are typical, if the relative rates for the two races be taken into consideration, a women is somewhat less likely to be numbered among the Negro homicide victims than among the white victims.[2]

Elsewhere he raises the same question regarding offenders:

Little evidence is available to show whether white or Negro women are more liable to become slayers. Of 407 persons who committed homicide in South Carolina, where the two races were at the time of the study approximately equal in numbers, 20 were Negro and 13 were white females, while there were 141 Negro and 220 white males and 13 unknown offenders included in the total. Since most of these cases were secured from the files of newspapers, the ratio between the sexes of each race should be approximately the same. Since the Negro women exceeded the white women while the Negro males did not equal the white males in number it might be correctly assumed that Negro women, in South Carolina at least, are more likely to slay an adversary than are white women. This conclusion is rather credible in view of the Negro woman's greater freedom of life, physical vigor, and familiarity with weapons. Nevertheless, this inference may, like so

[1] C. H. Growdon, *op. cit.*, p. 4.
[2] H. C. Brearley, "The Negro and Homicide," *Social Forces* (1930), 9: 251.

many other "common sense observations" concerning racial differences, prove upon further investigation to be erroneous.[1]

Relative to these earlier comments by Brearley, a set of interesting hypotheses have recently been tested by Henry and Short[2] regarding suicide and homicide in the United States. Among other assumptions, these authors assume that males as a gross category rank higher in the American status hierarchy than females. They then tested the hypothesis that homicide rates are higher in the low status category and lower in the high status category. Data collected by the authors on the relation between homicide and sex contradicted their hypothesis, which predicted that homicide rates would be higher for females, the lower status category, than for males. Our Philadelphia material and abundant data from the literature also reject the sex hypothesis. However, because Negroes generally make up a disproportionate share of the total number of homicides, Henry and Short claim that the status differentiation between males and females within this racial group would be worth examining. They suggest that perhaps the Negro female in American society has a status higher than the male. Thus,

> If it is true that the prestige position of the Negro female is higher, on the average, than the prestige position of the Negro male, we would predict from our hypothesis that the Negro female would have a lower homicide *rate* than the Negro male.
>
> Data are not available adequately to test this formulation. If it is correct, however, further research should show that the ratio of male to female *homicide* among Negroes is higher than the *ratio* of male to female homicide among whites.[3]
>
> This hypothesis may be tested by research comparing the ratios of male to female homicide among the white and Negro categories. If our interpretation is correct, we would expect the *ratio* of male to female *murderers* among Negroes to exceed the ratio of male to female murderers among whites.

[1] *Ibid.* See also, H. C. Brearley, *Homicide in the U.S.*, pp. 107–108.

[2] Andrew F. Henry and James F. Short, Jr., *Suicide and Homicide*, Glencoe, Illinois: The Free Press, 1954.

[3] *Ibid.*, p. 88. Emphasis is that of the present author.

Further research on the status position of the female in the Negro family is also needed.[1]

No measurement of the status of the Negro female in American life is intended in the present Philadelphia study. However, when a Negro was killed, a female was less frequently numbered among the victims than when a white was killed. In the five-year period examined, 43 white females made up 27 per cent of all white victims; whereas, 96 Negro females comprised 22 per cent of all Negro victims. This means that, relatively, females made up a proportion of white victims nearly 19 per cent greater than females among Negro victims. The ratio of males to females among whites was 2.7 to 1.0 while among Negroes it was 3.4 to 1.0. Using rates per 100,000 instead of percentage distributions, we have noted that the Negro male had a rate (36.9) about four times greater than the Negro female (9.6), while the white male had a rate (2.9) only three times that of the white female (1.0). Hence, among *victims*, the Henry and Short assumption regarding the relative position of the Negro female is correct.

However, among *offenders* the prediction of these authors is contradicted. Negro females numbered 93, or approximately 20 per cent of all Negro offenders; white females numbered only 16, or less than 12 per cent of all white offenders. A relative percentage difference indicates that Negro females comprised a proportion 66 per cent greater among Negro offenders than did white females among white offenders. Expressed differently, the sex ratio of males to females among white offenders was 8.6 to 1.0, but among Negroes was only 4.0 to 1.0. Using rates per 100,000, the Negro male had a rate (41.7) that was over four times that of the Negro female (9.3), while the white male had a rate (3.4) that was eight times that of the white female (.4).

---

[1] *Ibid.*, p. 124. Emphasis is that of the present author. It should be noted, relative to our earlier discussion of the confusion of terminology, that in the previous reference, authors used the term "homicide" and in the immediate reference the term "murderers." Context again suggests—but does not confirm—that "criminal homicide" was intended in both references. Likewise, in the previous reference both "rate" and "ratio" were used; and in the present reference only "ratio" is found.

If the Henry and Short prediction was meant to apply to offenders rather than victims, it is obvious that the hypothesis is not supported by the Philadelphia data.

It should be clear that *among female homicides*, whether victims or offenders, or both, a Negro was much more likely to be involved than a white. Proportionately, Negro females were twice as frequent as white females among victims, and about six times as frequent among offenders. Rates per 100,000 indicate that a Negro female was ten times more likely to be numbered among the slain and twenty-three times more likely to be a slayer than a white female. Finally, there were 12 cases in which a Negro female was killed by a Negro female, and only 5 cases in which a white female was killed by a white female.

Again it is necessary to point to the striking differences that may exist between victims and offenders. Henry and Short, like many other students of homicide, do not always make clear to which of these two groups, or to both, they intend their hypotheses to apply. Unfortunately, lack of clarity involving such terms as "homicides," "victims," "murderers," "rates," "ratios," etc., prevails even in the most recent literature. Examination of the Philadelphia data relative to the Henry and Short sex hypothesis reaffirms the contention that valid inferences regarding characteristics of offenders cannot be drawn from victim data, or vice versa.

Drawing attention to European literature which discusses the relationship between women and homicide, Pollak[1] shows that:

(1) Austrian statistics for 1899 reveal that while 14 women appeared in every 100 convictions, female participation in murder was reflected by 30 women in each 100 convictions for that offense.

(2) In 1896 in Germany there were 18 female convictions for each 100 male convictions, but that in homicide there were 22 women for each 100 men convicted.

(3) Italian statistics (contrary to the U.S., England, Austria, and Germany) list poisoning as a special offense,

[1] Pollak, *op. cit.*, pp. 80–82.

and reveal a specific sex ratio of 123 females per 100 male offenders convicted; and when poisonings are added to other types of criminal homicide except infanticide, the sex ratio was still 63 women per 100 men for the three years 1885–1889.

Basing his conclusions on both American and Continental material, Pollak suggests that female homicides make up a larger proportion of all female offenses than is true for males, and "that if all types of victims and all methods of killings are included, the relative liability of women for homicide is greater than that of men."[1]

A study of suicide and homicide in Ceylon by Jacqueline and Murray Straus,[2] using data taken from the registrar-general's report for 1946, shows rates of homicide victims similar to those in Philadelphia. In Ceylon, the rates were 9.7 per 100,000 for males and 2.1 for females. This is a male rate between four and five times higher than the female rate, and is a slightly greater differential than that in Philadelphia where the male rate was about three times higher than that for females. It is interesting to note that in a number of ways (to be considered later), other than that of sex ratios, the pattern of homicide in Ceylon is in striking agreement with what is known of this phenomenon in the West.

An exceptionally high male proportion among homicide offenders was found in Ching-yueh Yen's *A Study of Crime in Peiping*,[3] covering the period from 1919 to 1927. Unfortunately, data for this study were collected from the Peiping prisons and result, as the author has pointed out, in a highly select group, especially in view of his reference to much police inefficiency, differential treatment in the courts, etc. Comparisons with American data, and with Philadelphia police records in particular, must be made cautiously. Keeping in mind these differential sources, computation

---

[1] *Ibid.*, p. 82.
[2] Jacqueline and Murray Straus, "Suicide, Homicide, and Social Structure in Ceylon," *American Journal of Sociology*, Vol. 58 (March, 1953), pp. 461–469.
[3] Ching-yueh Yen, *A Study of Crime in Peiping*, Peiping, China: Yenching University, Department of Sociology and Social Work, Series C, No. 20, December, 1929.

from the author's basic statistics shows that of the 14,309 male criminals incarcerated during the nine years studied, 3 per cent had been imprisoned for homicide, and that of the 1,286 females, 1.7 per cent had been committed for homicide.[1] Of the 459 persons imprisoned for criminal homicide, therefore, approximately 95 per cent were male and only 5 per cent female. The proportion incarcerated for homicide within each sex appears to be different from the general proportions usually found in the United States. This much higher proportion of male homicide offenders in Peiping suggests the correctness of Sutherland's statement that

the sex ratio in crime varies widely from one nation to another, with the female rate showing some tendency to approach closest to the male rate in countries in which females have the greatest freedom and equality with males, such as Western Europe and the United States, and being most remote from the male rate in countries in which females are very closely supervised. . . .[2]

Criminal homicide appears to be an offense detectably committed more often by males regardless of time or space. Ethnological descriptions of primitive societies seem to support this contention although a general review of anthropological literature on homicide yet remains to be written.[3] Cultural rather than biological reasons are invariably given to explain these sex differentials, however varied the social environments may be. One example might be used merely to show that a like phenomenon (officially recorded high proportion of males committing homicide) may have unlike causes. In an especially enlightening summary of homicides and suicides in a primitive Asiatic Indian society, Elwin says:

[1] Based on *ibid.*, pp. 7–9. The author uses the term "murder," but context suggests he means "criminal homicide," as these terms are defined in this research.
[2] E. H. Sutherland, *Principles of Criminology*, p. 100.
[3] A review and comparative analysis of the law of homicide and of whatever statistics might be available from non-literate societies, similar to the review of law in general by E. Adamson Hoebel in *The Law of Primitive Man* (Cambridge, Mass.: Harvard Univ. Press, 1954), would be highly desirable and might add much to our understanding of the variables associated with homicide.

The reason for the low incidence of homicide among Maria women is possibly connected with the strong aboriginal belief that it is supernaturally dangerous for a woman to take life. This is the ultimate reason why there are no women priests, for the priest has to offer sacrifice. Maria women are not supposed to kill goats or even chickens. They are not permitted to join in hunting. The only pursuit of the kind which is not taboo to them is fishing—but fish are cold-blooded creatures.[1]

Criminal statistics in the United States for 1950 indicate that the number of male offenders was six times higher than that of females, and mortality rates show that males were counted among victims approximately four times more frequently than females. However, sex ratios in England disclose a higher proportion of females than in the United States. Basing some of his speculative remarks on Calvert's article on "Murder and the Death Penalty,"[2] and incorrectly comparing homicide with murder, Brearley says:

> . . . the slaying of women is much less frequent in the United States than in England. During the period 1924–1926, there were in the United States registration area states 24,949 *homicides*. In 4,874 of these, females were the victims, 19.5 per cent of the total. Slightly more than four times more males than females were homicide victims. In England, however, women are more often slain than are men. Although nine out of every ten *murders* are committed by men, "two out of every three persons murdered are women".[3]

Referring to this statement by Brearley, von Hentig says:

> In discussing the sex of his homicide victims Brearley has wondered why in the United States more than four times as many males as females were homicide victims, whereas in England "two out of every three persons murdered are women".
>
> This apparent discrepancy can easily be explained. The legal concept of murder differs widely in England, Germany, France and all of Europe from the American notion. It corresponds

[1] V. Elwin, *Maria Murder and Suicide*, London: Oxford University Press, 1943, p. 162.
[2] E. Roy Calvert, "Murder and the Death Penalty," *Nation*, 129: 405–407, quoted by Brearley, *Homicide in the U.S.*, p. 81.
[3] H. C. Brearley, *Homicide in the U.S.*, p. 81. Emphasis is that of the present author.

somewhat to the first degree murder of our statutes and is even more restricted than that. We erroneously, therefore, try to draw a parallel between two incomparable magnitudes.[1]

As the latter author points out, however, where legal notions coincide, similar results occur, for 56 per cent of 135 murder victims who were slain during 1928, 1929, and 1930 in Germany were females.[2]

Computation from data in the recent report of the Royal Commission on Capital Punishment discloses that the percentage of female *victims* in Germany coincides with that in England and Wales. During a twenty-year period ending in 1905, 313 or 57 per cent were female victims from a total of 551 criminal homicides for which the offenders were convicted.[3] With respect to *offenders*, tables of "persons arrested for murder," supplied by Templewood in *The Shadow of the Gallows*, reveal a grand total between 1900 and 1948 of 4,077, of whom 1,318, or 32 per cent, were women.[4] This is a sex ratio among offenders of approximately two males to each female, as compared to a five-to-one ratio in Philadelphia. However, it is most important to segregate clearly Negroes from whites when making this type of international comparison. In Philadelphia, *among white victims*, 27 per cent were female, a ratio just short of three males for each female and considerably different from the reversed ratio of victims in England and Wales, where there was only one male for each 1.3 females. *Among white offenders* in Philadelphia, 10 per cent were female, but in England 32 per cent of all "persons arrested for murder" were female. This means that more women were counted among both victims and offenders in England than in Philadelphia when like races are compared. No striking differences in comparative results occur, however, when Negroes are included, for 24 per cent of the total victims and 18 per cent of all offenders in Philadelphia

[1] Hans von Hentig, "Remarks on the Interaction of Perpetrator and Victim," *Journal of Criminal Law and Criminology* (1940–1941), 31: 305.
[2] *Ibid.*
[3] Computed from *Royal Commission on Capital Punishment, 1949–1953 Report*, Table 1, Appendix 6, p. 329.
[4] Viscount Templewood, *The Shadow of the Gallows*, London: Victor Gollancz, Ltd., 1951, pp. 132–137.

were female. Finally, it may be that the proportion of females arrested for murder in England is approaching the American proportion. In the 1910–1919 period, 39 per cent of all persons arrested for the offense in England were female; in 1920–1929, 36 per cent; in the 1930–1939 decade, 30 per cent, and in the nine years from 1940 to 1948, 22 per cent were women.[1] This last period shows a female proportion among offenders similar to those in the United States and in Philadelphia.

Veli Verkko has discovered some interesting historical changes in the sex ratio of victims in Finland. During the last period included in his analysis, which is somewhat comparable to the Philadelphia material, he says that between 1939 and 1944, 23 women were killed in Finland for every 100 men, and that the rates per 100,000 of the population were 7.1 for men and 1.6 for women.[2] Swedish data by sex of victims of crimes against life are available from 1881 and reveal that from this time up to 1940 the ratio of women killed per 100 men has increased considerably. In the twenty-year period from 1881–1900 only 25 per 100 males were female victims, between 1901–1920 the ratio was 37 to 100, and in 1921–1940, their ratio climbed to 63 per 100 males.[3]

This brief review of some of the homicide literature related to sex cannot fail to report Verkko's "laws" regarding regular sex sequences in crimes against life. He claims that fluctuations in crimes against life have been mainly in the numbers of male victims, and he has established the following rule: "Distribution by sexes of victims of crimes against life in any country is always dependent on the frequency level of the crime concerned."[4] This general rule is illustrated

[1] Computed from *ibid.*

[2] Veli Verkko, *Homicides and Suicides in Finland and Their Dependence on National Character*, p. 42. "Finland is the only country in the world able to present a curve of nearly 200 years showing the development in the number of male and female victims of crimes against life" (*ibid.*, p. 44).

[3] *Ibid.*, p. 47.

[4] *Ibid.*, p. 51. Brearley must be given credit for pointing out this same relationship. He says: "There is the possibility that the relative danger to women increases when the homicide rate is low. In England, for example, where very few persons are killed, two out of every three victims are women, but in the United States with a much higher homicide rate the proportion is one female to approximately four male victims" (*Homicide in the United States*, p. 108).

in greater detail by two laws, he contends, one of which is static and the other dynamic. The static law is: "In countries of high frequency of crimes against life the female proportion of those killed is small; and vice versa: in countries of low frequency of crimes against life the percentage of female victims is perceptibly greater than in countries of high frequency of crimes against life."[1] He includes Finland, Serbia, Bulgaria, Italy, Chile, and the United States in his first group of high frequency of homicides where female victims are below 10 per cent of the total. It is interesting to note that because the United States provides "an erroneous picture of the distribution of the victims of crimes by sexes,"[2] he excludes this country from his presentation of ratios. In countries of low frequency of homicides, including Sweden, Norway, Denmark, Prussia, England and Wales, and Switzerland, the proportions of female victims fluctuate between 18 and 48 per cent. His dynamic law of victims is: "If frequency of crimes against life in a country is on the increase, the increase affects mainly the number of male victims of crimes against life, and vice versa: if the statistics of crimes against life in a country reveal a declining trend, the reduction affects primarily the number of men killed."[3] Using the historical method, abundant evidence is presented by the author to help prove his contentions. For example, he says, "The figures for Sweden incidate an even decline during the period 1881–1940. The total killed per 100,000 inhabitants declined from 0.90 to 0.49. The ratio for men was reduced from 1.46 to 0.60 while that for women was at the beginning 0.37 and at the end 0.38."[4]

Verkko establishes a static and a dynamic law for *offenders* as well, and treats them similarly:

> The static law reads as follows: In countries of high frequency of crimes against life the participation of women in these crimes is small; and vice versa: in countries of low frequency of crimes against life the participation of women in

[1] *Ibid.*
[2] *Ibid.*
[3] *Ibid.*, p. 52.
[4] *Ibid.*, p. 54.

these crimes is perceptibly larger than in countries of high frequency of crimes against life. . . .

The dynamic law reads: If the frequency of crimes against life in a country tends to increase, the increase primarily affects the number of male criminals, and vice versa: if the frequency of crimes against life in a certain country is on the decline, the decline primarily affects the number of male criminals.[1]

Data on men and women prosecuted for, and found guilty of, crimes against life collected from an earlier investigation by the author tend to support his hypotheses.

Five years may be too short a period to test Verkko's hypotheses, although in some of his own data as few as three years are used. We have already noted the relatively higher proportion of female victims and offenders in England and Wales (a low frequency area) compared to the proportion of that sex in Philadelphia (a high frequency area), thus indicating support for his two "static laws." However, the various United States urban studies included in this review show no consistent relationship between the general victim and offender rates and proportions of females in either group. Special tabulations and computations were made for the Philadelphia data to test his "dynamic laws." For example, the distribution of 139 female victims throughout the five years under review is as follows:

Year	Number of Victims	Number of Female Victims	Per cent Females of Total
1948	113	23	20.4
1949	117	32	27.4
1950	117	23	19.7
1951	110	28	25.5
1952	131	33	25.2

Inspection of female percentages shows an inconsistent fluctuation, with little or no apparent relationship to the total number of homicides. It might also be mentioned that these annual female percentages correspond very closely to the percentage distributions Verkko lists among the countries

[1] *Ibid.*, pp. 55–56.

of *low* frequency of homicide rather than to the countries of *high* frequency to which he claims the United States belongs. Similarly the Philadelphia data lend no support to his "dynamic law" with respect to 109 females among the 621 total offenders when examined for each of the five years. A longer time period, however, may produce different results.

Despite the fact that the regularities which Verkko discusses are based on relatively reliable criminal statistics for the various countries, national differentials of conduct norms, of legal definitions, and of judicial treatment of the sexes are not given cognizance in his analysis. Perhaps even if these difficult impediments to valid international comparisons were removed, conclusions would be virtually the same. At any rate, Verkko's explanation for his "static and dynamic laws," namely that "it is obvious that the different biological qualities of men and women are the fundamental cause of this phenomenon,"[1] is hardly palatable to the socio-psychological emphases in American criminology.

[1] *Ibid.*, p. 57.

4

AGE DIFFERENCES

The Philadelphia Data

DESPITE the seemingly fortuitous nature of criminal homicide, there are, nonetheless, manifest age patterns with respect to both victims and offenders. In general, those who kill are younger than those who are killed. Analysis of persons involved in the homicide drama is made by five-year age classifications according to the mean annual rate per 100,000 specified age groups. Such analysis in general shows (Table 4) that offenders have their highest rate (12.6) between ages 20 and 24, and their second highest rate (11.9) between ages 25 and 29. However, among victims in general, the highest rate (10.4) appears in two age groups, 25–29 and 30–34, while the second highest rate (9.0) is in the age class 35–39. Offenders as a group, therefore, evidence highest incidence between five and ten years younger than victims. Furthermore, under age 50 the statistical chance of being an offender in criminal homicide is slightly greater than that of being a victim; while over age 50 the chance of being a victim is two times greater than that of being an offender. The mean annual rate for offenders 50 years of age and over is only 2.3, but the rate for victims in this same age category is 4.7. The same conclusion is observed when frequency distributions, as well as rates, are analyzed among the 620 offenders[1] and the 588 victims for whom age data are available: only 9 per cent of all offenders are 50 years of age or older compared to 20 per cent of all victims. Finally, the median age for all offenders is 31.9 years compared to 35.1 years for victims.

A more detailed picture of age differences requires a further breakdown by specified race and sex groups. Generally

---

[1] In one case, age of offender is unknown.

65

TABLE 4
RATES PER 100,000 POPULATION, CRIMINAL HOMICIDE VICTIMS
AND OFFENDERS, BY RACE, SEX, AND AGE, PHILADELPHIA,
1948–1952

	Both Races			Negro			White		
Victims	Total	Male	Female	Total	Male	Female	Total	Male	Female
Age									
Under 15	1.2	1.7	.7	2.8	4.4	1.2	.8	1.0	.6
15–19	3.8	5.8	1.8	15.8	29.3	4.4	1.0	.8	1.1
20–24	7.3	12.5	2.6	29.2	54.6	10.2	2.1	3.8	.6
25–29	10.4	14.1	6.9	41.0	56.8	28.2	2.3	3.7	.8
30–34	10.4	15.1	6.1	39.6	63.3	20.4	3.1	4.0	2.3
35–39	9.0	15.7	3.0	38.0	69.4	12.0	1.7	2.8	.6
40–44	7.5	11.9	3.3	28.6	48.5	10.6	2.6	3.7	1.6
45–49	6.2	10.2	2.5	26.2	45.6	7.6	1.6	1.9	1.4
50–54	7.3	12.7	2.1	30.0	53.3	5.8	2.9	4.5	1.4
55–59	4.6	8.0	1.4	19.7	30.7	8.5	2.4	4.6	.4
60–64	4.0	7.7	.4	19.8	35.6	4.0	2.0	4.1	—
65 and over	3.3	5.4	1.7	10.7	18.3	4.4	2.5	3.9	1.4
All ages	5.7	9.0	2.6	22.5	36.9	9.6	1.9	2.9	1.0
Offenders(*a*)									
Under 15	.3	.3	.1	.2	.4	.4	.2	.3	—
15–19	9.4	18.3	.9	38.0	79.2	2.9	2.5	4.6	.4
20–24	12.6	22.7	3.1	46.6	92.5	12.4	4.6	8.2	1.2
25–29	11.9	18.9	5.4	47.4	77.8	22.3	2.5	4.6	.6
30–34	11.1	18.4	4.5	44.3	75.1	19.3	2.8	5.2	.6
35–39	9.7	17.5	2.7	35.4	65.5	9.8	3.3	6.0	.9
40–44	7.6	12.5	3.0	30.0	47.1	14.6	2.4	4.7	.3
45–49	7.8	12.0	4.0	30.8	44.0	18.2	2.5	4.4	.7
50–54	3.0	5.9	.3	15.9	29.4	1.9	.5	1.1	—
55–59	3.2	5.9	1.2	19.7	30.6	8.5	.8	1.7	—
60–64	2.0	3.2	.9	5.9	7.9	4.0	1.5	2.6	.5
65 and over	1.3	2.7	.2	6.0	10.5	2.2	.8	1.8	—
All ages	6.0	10.2	2.0	24.6	41.7	9.3	1.8	3.4	.4

(*a*)The age of one offender is unknown. Throughout the age tables relative to offenders, the universe is 620 instead of 621.

when discussing offenders it is unwise to include the age group under 15 years, because most persons under 15 years of age are either physically incapable of killing others or socially unlikely to do so, and, therefore, analysis of rates only for those offenders 15 years of age and over is justified and necessary. The mean annual rate for all criminal homicide offenders in Philadelphia is 6.0. By excluding persons under 15 years of age, the rate is raised to 7.7 per 100,000. Specified race and sex rates result in the following changes when this young age group is eliminated: the rate for Negro male offenders changes from 41.7 to 57.7; that for white males rises from 3.4 to 4.2; for Negro females, from 9.3 to 12.4; and for white females, from .4 to .5.

There is an obvious and *significant* difference in the rates of commission of criminal homicide by age groups—a difference, that is, between the relative rates according to Negro and white male offenders. Both Negro and white males appear to have the strongest proclivity for committing criminal homicide between ages 20 and 24. Regardless of race, males in this age group have the highest rates among offenders. The two age groups with highest rates among Negro male offenders are 20–24, for which the rate is as high as 92.5; and 15–19, for which the rate is 79.2. No other specified race and sex group has such extremely high rates, or high rates so young as those of Negro males. The highest rate for white male offenders is also found in the 20–24 age group, but is only 8.2; and the second highest rate is found in a considerably older group aged 35–39, for which the rate is 6.0. *Significant* differences in the age-specific rates between Negro and white male offenders is again obvious when it is observed that the lowest rate for Negro males (7.9) is for ages 60–64 and is only .3 per 100,000 lower than the highest rate for white males (8.2), which is for ages 20–24. Thus, Negro males in their early sixties kill as frequently as white males in their early twenties.

The age pattern among female offenders is somewhat different from that of male offenders, although *significant* race differences are also found. Among Negro females who commit homicide, there is concentration of the two highest rates between the ages of 25 and 34. Their highest rate (22.3) is for ages 25–29, and their second highest rate (19.3) is for ages 30–34, a total span in which Negro female offenders are ten years older than the span of ages 15–24 in which highest rates for Negro male offenders are concentrated. The two top rates for white female offenders are separated by fifteen years, with the highest rate (1.2) in the age class 20–24, and the second highest (.9) in the age class 35–39.

Because white female offenders number only 16 for the whole period studied, there are several age groups not represented. As a final note regarding age differences among female offenders, it may be observed that the lowest rate by five-year age groups for Negro females, which is 1.9 for ages 50–54, is .7 per 100,000 *higher* than the highest rate for white females, which is 1.2 for ages 20–24.

Turning attention from offenders to victims, there are several interesting age differences according to race and sex, which indicate that Negroes are liable to homicide victimization not only more often, but considerably earlier in life than are whites. The highest rate for Negro male victims (69.4) occurs during the ages 35–39. Although this age group is fifteen years older than that in which Negro male offenders have their highest rate, it is twenty years younger than the 55–59-year age group in which white male victims have their highest rate (4.6). The age difference between Negro and white female victims is not so great as this, but still exists: the highest rate for Negro females (28.2) is in the age group 25–29, and for white females the highest rate (2.3) is in the age group 30–34.

Comparison of the lowest age-specific rate for Negro victims with the highest such rate for white victims again makes obvious the greater victimization of Negroes in every age group (excluding victims under 15 years of age). Despite the fact that the lowest rate for Negro male victims (18.3) is in the age category 65 years and over, their lowest rate is four times greater than the highest rate for white male victims (4.6), which is in the age group 55–59 years. Similarly, the lowest rate for Negro female victims (4.0) is for ages 60–64 and is almost twice as high as the highest rate for white female victims (2.3) which is in the 30–34 age group.

Another interesting pattern emerges from this analysis of age: the highest age-specific rate for all victims, offenders, or any race, sex, or race-sex specific group of victims or offenders, is approximately twice as high as the rate for all persons in these same respective categories. For example, we have noted that the highest age-specific rate for all offenders regardless of race or sex is 12.6 (ages 20–24), while the rate for offenders of all ages is just 6.0. The highest age-specific rate for Negroes is 47.4 (ages 25–29), and the rate for Negroes of all ages is 24.6. The following table clearly reveals this "twice-as-high pattern" for offenders:

	Both Races			Negro			White		
	Total	Male	Female	Total	Male	Female	Total	Male	Female
Five-year age group with highest rate per 100,000	12.6	22.7	5.4	47.4	92.5	22.3	4.6	8.2	1.2
Rate per 100,000 for all ages	6.0	10.2	2.0	24.6	41.7	9.3	1.8	3.4	.4

This same pattern is revealed among victims too, for the highest rate by five-year age categories for Negroes, whites, males, and females is generally about twice as high as the rate for all ages in each race and sex group. For example, the highest rate for Negro victims is 41.0 (ages 25–29), whereas the rate for Negroes of all ages is only 22.5. For white victims, the highest rate is 3.1 (ages 30–34), while the rate for whites of all ages is only 1.9. For male victims, the highest rate is 15.7 (ages 35–39), while the rate for males of all ages is 9.0. Finally, the highest rate for female victims is 6.9 (ages 25–29), while the rate for females of all ages is only 2.6.

Thus, this same rate differential between the rate for the age group having the highest rate and the rate for all ages of the category to which the age group is compared, roughly applies to both offenders and victims, to gross race and sex categories, and to specified race-sex groups. It appears, therefore, that knowledge of the highest rate for any race and sex group by five-year age categories makes possible a good estimate of the general rate for all ages of these same race and sex groups. Contrariwise, knowledge of the general rate allows us to estimate with considerable accuracy the highest five-year age-specific rate.

We have previously noted that, in general, victims are older than offenders. The following list of median ages for each specified race-sex group makes this fact abundantly clear:

Race and Sex	Median Age		
	Victims	Offenders	Difference
Negro male	35.5	31.1	4.4
White male	40.5	33.4	7.1
Negro female	31.1	32.6	−1.5
White female	36.3	32.5	3.8
Total	35.1	31.9	3.2

All told, victims have a median age that is 3.2 years older than that of offenders. The only exception occurs among Negro females, for whom the victim's median age is 1.5 years younger than that of the offender. The median age of the white female victim is 3.8 years older than her counterpart among offenders, and the median age of the Negro male victim is 4.4 years older than that of the Negro male offender. But the greatest age differential is found among white males, for the median age of the white male victim is 7.1 years older than that of the white male offender.

The foregoing discussion should again make obvious the necessity always to distinguish carefully between victims and offenders in any study of criminal homicide. A later chapter in which the specific interrelationships between victims and offenders are more closely examined, provides some suggested explanations for several of these victim-offender age differentials.

Age Differences Noted in Other Studies and Reports

Most of the homicide literature describes age distributions similar to those revealed in the Philadelphia data. Sutherland's general statement that "the crime rate is about five times as great for persons twenty to twenty-four years of age as for those over fifty"[1] is applicable both to the country as a whole and to Philadelphia in particular with respect to criminal homicide. Furthermore, comparison of the age distribution of offenders in Philadelphia to that of persons

[1] Sutherland, *Principles of Criminology*, p. 95.

70

arrested for criminal homicide in the United States in 1950 shows striking similarities. Among the latter, the highest rate—like that in Philadelphia—was for ages 20–24 (10.3), and the second highest was for ages 25–29 (9.8). Also like Philadelphia, the percentage of arrests for the country was highest for the age group 25–29, and second highest for ages 20–24.[1]

Brearley[2] has shown that for both races and both sexes the ages of greatest frequency of death by homicide are from 25 to 30 years. He refers to a study in South Carolina for the period 1920–1924, which indicated that the median age for victims was 30.6, and for offenders 19.2, the latter of which was a considerably younger age than that for offenders in Philadelphia (31.9). In his study, white victims had a median age of 36.0 and offenders 20.5; Negro victims were younger, having had a median age among victims of 29.0 and among offenders 18.1. In South Carolina the white victim had a median age seven years older than the Negro victim; in Philadelphia, he was five years older. No data appeared for the offender in the southern state, but in Philadelphia the white agent was only 1.8 years older than the Negro offender.

In the United States registration area for the period 1908–1912, Hoffman[3] found that the highest percentage of homicides was for ages 20–29 for both males (33.8 per cent) and females (32.6 per cent). This author used death-certificate data, which, it must be remembered, included non-criminal as well as criminal homicides. Nonetheless, as Hoffman points out, the largest proportion of persons are killed during "the period when human life has its highest economic value and when willful destruction involves the greatest loss to the community."[4]

Von Hentig claims that the homicide offender shows up

---

[1] Computed from *Uniform Crime Reports*, 1950, p. 110. Unfortunately the age distribution herein reported includes negligent manslaughter as well as murder and non-negligent manslaughter. Furthermore, the ages are not broken down by race or sex.

[2] Brearley, *Homicide in the U.S.*, pp. 78–79.

[3] F. L. Hoffman, *The Homicide Problem*, p. 23.

[4] F. L. Hoffman, "The Homicide Record for 1929," *Spectator* (March 22, 1930).

71

most frequently in the younger ages, usually between 20 and 30, but that caution must be exercised when prison statistics are used for analysis. He reports that of all female murderers admitted to Michigan prisons between 1936 and 1938, 34 per cent were 40 years and over at the time of their admission.[1] Of all male prisoners in the United States during the years 1936–1940, those incarcerated for murder had a rate of 3.5, but for ages 20–30, a rate of 6.0.[2] However, as he makes clear, these rates were for murderers, not offenders in all types of criminal homicide. He indicates that use of prisoner data may be invalid by referring to two studies made by Albert Stearns, psychiatrist of the Massachusetts State Prison, one of which was published in 1921, and the other in 1925. The earlier study presented a much younger set of homicide offenders, 42 per cent of whom were 25 years of age or younger, whereas four years later the frequency was only 22 per cent. This change was presumably the direct result of new, non-institutional methods of treating the youthful killer.[3]

Durkheim[4] reported that the highest rates for offenders per 100,000 population in France during 1887 were between the ages of 25 and 30. For both premeditated and unpremeditated murder, the rate for this age group was 15.4. The rate for premeditated murders alone was highest for ages 30–40 (15.9), although unpremeditated dropped (11.0). He concludes that "while suicide increases regularly until old age, premeditated and unpremeditated murder reach their

[1] Hans von Hentig, *Crime: Causes and Conditions*, p. 115.
[2] *Ibid.*, p. 137.
[3] *Ibid.*, p. 135.
[4] Durkheim, *op. cit.*, p. 143. In Chapter XVII the age differences between murderers and other homicide offenders found in the Philadelphia data are shown. Relative to Durkheim's dichotomy, the editor of this new translation of Durkheim's famous study says: "Durkheim uses several technical, French legal terms for the varieties of homicide. These terms are somewhat different from those employed in English and American law. In French law there are five varieties of what is called *homicide volontaire*; they are *assassinat, meurtre, parricide, infanticide, empoisonnement*. The two most important for Durkheim's analysis are *assassinat* and *meurtre*. *Assassinat* is intentional homicide with aggravating circumstances such as premeditation or prearrangement. *Meurtre* is simple intentional homicide (*homicide volontaire simple*) without aggravating circumstances such as premeditation or prearrangement. *Assassinat* has been translated, therefore, as 'premeditated murder', while *meurtre* has been translated as 'unpremeditated murder'" (*ibid.*, p. 342, note 34).

height in maturity, at about 30 or 35 years of age, and then decrease."[1]

In his analytical treatment of female crime, and after having pointed out that "women reach the peak of their criminal activities at a later stage than do men," Pollak says that "since in our culture, with its premium on youth, women are apt to understate their age after they have passed the mid-twenties, this phenomenon of delay in female crime is even more pronounced that the available figures suggest."[2]

Pollak's statement regarding "delay" in female crime refers to *offenders*, and the Philadelphia data do show that the maximal rate for females is in an age span (25–29) five years older than the age span of maximal rate for males (20–24). Moreover, the median age for female offenders is 32.6, while that for males is 31.7. However, generalizations about the later age of female offenders become more meaningful when race-sex differentials are examined. While among whites, both males and females have exactly the same two maximal five-year age spans (20–24 and 35–39), Negro females have highest rates (25–34) ten years later than do Negro males (15–24).

Although women are more likely to be *offenders* at *later* ages than men, women have a higher liability of becoming *victims* at *earlier* ages than men. The highest rate for male victims is in an age span (35–39) ten years older than that for females (25–29). Regardless of race, female victims are younger: the maximal rate for Negro females is in an age span (25–29) ten years younger than that for Negro males (35–39), and the former has a median age 4.4 years younger than the latter. The maximal rate for white females occurs in an age span (30–34) twenty-five years younger than that for white males (55–59), and the former has a median age 4.2 years younger than the latter.

Both Mabel Elliott[3] and Hans von Hentig[4] emphasize the

[1] *Ibid.*
[2] Pollak, *op. cit.*, p. 156.
[3] Elliott, *op. cit.*, pp. 301–303.
[4] Hans von Hentig, "The Criminality of the Negro," *Journal of Criminal Law and Criminology* (January–February, 1940), 30: 662–680.

fact that youth and male sex are the *dynamic* factors in crime. Elliott says that "the Negro population evidences certain disturbances in sex and age ratios. These disturbances also may well account for at least part of the disparity between native-white and Negro crime rates because they promote the factor of jealousy."[1] She indicates, in a discussion of Negro murder, that a large percentage of young colored males in a population results in greater intensity of inter-personal relationships within their age group, and hence increases the rates as well. The author's causal hypothesis remains in its *a priori* stage, but Negroes in Philadelphia do have a slightly larger proportion of their population in the young adult ages than do whites. This fact may partially account for the higher homicide rates for Negroes, should Elliott's contention be correct. Comparison of each specified race and sex group 15 to 39 years of age in the Philadelphia population with the respective group among criminal homi-cide offenders reveals the following: Among Negro males, 41 per cent of their population and 75 per cent of their offenders may be contrasted to white males, for whom 38 per cent of their population and 65 per cent of their offenders are in this same age class. The number of white female offenders is too small to produce meaningful results for this age group, but it is interesting to note that as high as 45 per cent of the Negro female population is 15 to 39 years of age, while only 38 per cent of the white female population is in this age class. This greater difference between females may partially contribute to the greater difference in their homicide rates than exists between males. In any case, it is obvious not only that rates are highest for ages 15 to 39, but that this age class contributes considerably more than its share to the number of criminal homicide offenders. Although the difference between the races aged 15–39 years may seem slight (3 per cent for males and 7 per cent for females), it

[1] Elliott, *op. cit.*, p. 302. This "dynamic" factor resulting from a heavy concentration of population in a given age group may be somewhat related to Durkheim's belief that a density and increase of population intensifies competition. (Emile Benoit-Smullyan, "The Sociologism of Emile Durkheim and His School," in H. E. Barnes, *An Introduction to the History of Sociology*, Chicago: The University of Chicago Press, 1948, p. 508.)

swells the ranks of the potential homicidal group among Negroes.

Henry and Short[1] were forced to reject one of their hypotheses which posited higher homicide rates in the older (65 and over) and lower status age category. They use their own computation of arrest rates per 100,000 age-specific groups from the 1950 *Uniform Crime Reports* and a study of murder (which these authors refer to as "homicide") by Frankel in New Jersey to test the hypothesis. The Philadelphia data on age confirms their rejection. Henry and Short describe homicide and suicide data within a frustration-aggression causal framework, and, as has been pointed out, the biologically required and culturally prescribed passivity for persons over 65 years of age contrasts sharply with the youthful premium on aggressiveness and physical strength. It may be that with increasing age there is a gradual diminution of aggressive overt manifestations of frustration regardless of status.

Many homicide studies fail to provide comprehensive age data suitable for comparison with the Philadelphia findings. The age data that are comparable appear to correspond closely. In his Birmingham study, Harlan[2] found the mean age of Negro victims (32.8 years) younger than that of white victims (38.0 years) as is the case in Philadelphia for median ages (Negroes, 34.3 years; whites, 39.3 years). Female victims, he noted, had a mean age (29.4 years) six years younger than that of male victims (35.5 years), which corresponds closely to the four-year difference between the median age for females (32.3 years) and males (36.3 years) in Philadelphia.

Like Harlan, Meyers in his 1949–1951 study of criminal homicide in St. Louis does not provide age-specific rates, but does say: "Fewer teenagers are victims than assailants. The greatest number of persons among the victims is found in the 30 to 40 age group while the 20 to 30 age group produces the greatest numerical offenders. . . ."[3] Without computed rates, a numerical distribution merely points a weak

[1] Henry and Short, *op. cit.*, pp. 88–89.
[2] Harlan, *op. cit.*, p. 740.
[3] Meyers, Jr., *op. cit.*, p. 25.

finger of inference at the age groups most likely to commit homicide or to be victimized. No consideration of race and sex differentials by age appears in the report. Moreover, on the basis of only sixteen offenders and twelve victims 60 years of age or older, Meyers contends that "not as many old folks seem to be victims as are assailants."[1] This statement is in direct contradiction to the Philadelphia findings. Unfortunately, Meyers does not analyze those aged 60 years and older by race and sex, but the Philadelphia data show that persons in this age category are much more likely to be victims than offenders.

Briefly, other studies referring to age differentials include the following: Dublin and Bunzel[2] pointed out, on the basis of death certificates between 1926 and 1930, that female victims had highest rates for ages 20–24, while males had highest rates for ages 25–34. Hoffman[3] reported that the average male victim age in a study of 475 homicides in New Orleans, during a five-year period ending in 1924, was 31.6 years compared to 30.1 for females. The same author reported in a study of 567 homicides in Birmingham, 1920–1925, that the average male victim age was 31 years, and that of females, 25.5 years.[4] Frankel's[5] analysis of 1,000 murderers in New Jersey revealed an average age of 32.5 years, 29.5 years for native-born whites, 35 years for the foreign-born, and 32.4 years for Negroes. The highest per cent was in the 25–29 age group. Banay,[6] in a study of a select group of twenty-two men convicted of murder in the first degree, revealed that nineteen were between 20 and 35 years of age. Cassidy's[7] personality study of two hundred murderers showed that the highest proportion was between 20 and 30 years. Kilpatrick's[8] analysis of homicide in the Deep South

---

[1] *Ibid.*
[2] Dublin and Bunzel, *op. cit.*, p. 128.
[3] F. L. Hoffman, "The Increase in Murder," *op. cit.*, p. 26.
[4] *Ibid.*, p. 24.
[5] Frankel, *op. cit.*, p. 684.
[6] R. S. Banay, "A Study of 22 Men Convicted of Murder in the First Degree," *Journal of Criminal Law and Criminology* (July, 1943), 34: 110.
[7] Cassidy, *op. cit.*, p. 297.
[8] J. J. Kilpatrick, "Murder in the Deep South," *Survey Graphic* (October, 1943), 32: 396.

indicated that 70 per cent of the deaths were caused by persons between the ages of 16 and 37. Gillin's[1] research on 92 male murderers in Wisconsin revealed that, compared with the male population 15 years of age and over in the state, the murderers had a disproportionately large share in the age groups 20 to 24, 25 to 29, 45 to 54, and 65 to 74. MacDonald, who analyzed murder in England and Wales, revealed that "a large majority commit their crime between the ages of 21 to 40 years, when they are strongest. About 59 per cent of all of them convicted between 1886 and 1905 were between these ages."[2] In their carefully analyzed survey of 37 counties in New York, DePorte and Parkhurst, reported:

> The curve of homicides according to age is bell-shaped, having a maximum in young adult life, 25–34 years, the rate falling off in the younger and older ages. Somewhat more than half of the persons murdered were between 25 and 45, the median age for the entire group being 35.3 years. The median age of the males, 35.7 years, was greater than that of the females, 33.8 years. The highest rate among the males was 9.3; among females, 2.5—both in the age group 25–34 years.[3]

Because of variations in technique analyzing age and homicide, and because some authors refer to convicted offenders, or to a select group of murderers, not all the above studies can be equated with the Philadelphia material. Furthermore, in none of these studies has the age factor been minutely examined relative to race and sex of *both* victims and offenders. Unfortunately, Veli Verkko provides no age standardization in his analysis; the recent report of the Royal Commission gives only a crude distribution of

[1] J. L. Gillin, "Social Background of Sex Offenders and Murderers," *Social Forces* (December, 1935), 14: 233. See also, by the same author, "The Wisconsin Murderer," *Social Forces* (May, 1934), 12: 550–556; and *The Wisconsin Prisoner*, Madison: University of Wisconsin Press, 1946, p. 226.

[2] Arthur MacDonald, "Death Penalty and Homicide," *American Journal of Sociology* (July, 1910), 16: 96.

[3] DePorte and Parkhurst, *op. cit.*, p. 57. Presumably the authors do not use the term "murdered" in the precise sense in which it is used in the present study.

males convicted for murder by age groups;[1] and the Illinois Crime Survey does not include age in relation to homicide at all.

Analysis of the Philadelphia data thus far tends to support the contention that criminal homicide is manifested by certain regularities or patterns associated with race, sex, and age of both victims and offenders. These gross traits provide additional reference frames within which more extensive and intensive analysis can now be made.

[1] *Royal Commission on Capital Punishment, 1949–1953 Report*, Table 6, pp. 308–309. Computation from this table by the present author showed that the frequency of males convicted of murder was highest for ages 20–29. The following data resulted:

Males Convicted of Murder, England and Wales, 1900–1949, *by Age*

Age	Number	Per cent of total
Under 20	65	6.0
20–29	453	41.9
30–39	272	25.2
40–49	172	15.9
50–59	82	7.6
60–69	31	2.9
70 and over	5	.5
Total	1,080	100.0

78

5

METHODS AND WEAPONS OF
INFLICTING DEATH

IN an issue of *The Annals*, C. W. Topping asks: "What factors in the total situation stood out in a study of seventy years of murder in Canada? The most significant factor was the presence of a suitable weapon—a revolver, a shotgun, a rifle, a hunting knife, a butcher knife, a heavy bottle, or a club."[1] Although there are many factors which must converge before homicide occurs, there can be little doubt that accessibility of a weapon, cultural traditions of carrying and employing certain types of weapons, and individual perspectives associated with various means of inflicting death are important factors. We shall later see that the relationship between the offender and his victim often plays a significant role in the type of weapon used. It is probably safe to contend that many homicides occur only because there is sufficient motivation or provocation, and that the type of method used to kill is merely an accident of availability; that a gun is used because it is in the offender's possession at the time of incitement, but that if it were not present, he would use a knife to stab, or fists to beat his victim to death. On the other hand, the small physical size of the offender relative to that of his potential victim, or the offender's physical repugnance to engaging in direct physical assault by cutting or stabbing his adversary, may mean that in the absence of a firearm no homicide occurs. A cultural tradition that encourages, or at least does not discourage, carrying a penknife for protection may make the difference between

---

[1] C. W. Topping, "The Death Penalty in Canada," *The Annals of the American Academy of Political and Social Science* (November, 1952) (*Murder and the Penalty of Death*), 284: 156.

aggravated assault and criminal homicide. As Gabriel Tarde early pointed out, many homicides among the nobility during the sixteenth century were "due to a great extent to that monopoly of the right of wearing a sword which was so fatal to them."[1] Similarly, as a recent witness before the Royal Commission on Capital Punishment, Sellin commented:

> I would say that there are patterns of behaviour there [in the Deep South] that favour homicide, just as the high homicide rate in Finland is probably favoured by the custom of the population of carrying knives. If you get into a fight the likelihood of a fatal result is greater if you have a piercing weapon or a firearm handy, than if you have only brass knuckles. Irish immigrants in the United States used to get into all sorts of fights, but their homicide rate was always low because they fought with their fists and brass knuckles, and not with knives or revolvers.[2]

The world around us abounds in available means to inflict death. Everyone has access to many cutting and piercing instruments or to solid, heavy objects that can be used to bludgeon a victim. From the Philadelphia police files such common household items as an electric iron, a floor lamp, and a pencil were uniquely listed as homicide weapons. Yet, our cultural prescriptions dictate a relatively narrow range of weapons from which an individual offender makes his choice. Portability of some weapons, as well as speed, efficiency, and economy are important. The murderer who carefully plans his felonious, willful, and malicious assault is more likely to employ a weapon that performs his intended task quickly and efficiently. In such a situation a pistol or revolver probably will be used. During a drunken

[1] Gabriel Tarde, *Penal Philosophy*, p. 333. In a footnote, the author adds: "There were gentlemen of the Old Regime, like the Corsicans of today, who were turning to murder owing to the habit of carrying weapons, so much so that by forbidding them to do so their criminality was suddenly diminished by three fourths under the Second Empire. To the habit of wearing a sword was related that of going on horseback in the streets, which, given up toward the end of the sixteenth century, had also (see Voltaire) a great homicidal influence" (*ibid.*).

[2] *Royal Commission on Capital Punishment, Minutes of Evidence Taken Before the Royal Commission on Capital Punishment*, Thirtieth Day, Thursday, 1st February, 1951, Witness: Professor Thorsten Sellin, p. 678.

brawl, or in the white heat of passion, an offender uses whatever weapon is available—a brick in an alley, a stick on the sidewalk, a butcher knife on the kitchen table, or his bare fists if necessary. At any rate, homicide in fact is quite different from murder in fiction. As other writers also have pointed out, no mysterious South American poisons, African insects, jeweled Indian letter openers, nor any other strange means by which the murderers of whodunit writers kill their victims appear in most empirical data. Homicide is usually quick, brutal, direct; the weapons employed are simple and relatively commonplace.

The Philadelphia Data

In the present study, methods by which death was inflicted are categorized as: (*a*) stabbing or cutting, (*b*) shooting, (*c*) beating, and (*d*) others. In the classification of weapons, an attempt has been made to keep items together which have some generic homogeneity. Similar places where the weapons may be located and like degrees of access were criteria used in demarcation of the following groups: (*a*) penknife, switchblade knife,[1] or razor, (*b*) kitchen knife, icepick, (*c*) pistol or revolver, (*d*) shotgun or rifle, (*e*) fists or feet, (*f*) blunt instrument, (*g*) other. The "other" classification includes such things as asphyxiation by means of gas, use of poison, causing death by arson, etc.

Several students of homicide have tried to show that the high number of, or easy access to, firearms in this country is causally related to our relatively high homicide rate. Such a conclusion cannot be drawn from the Philadelphia data. Material subsequently reported in the present study regarding the place where homicide occurred, relationship between victim and offender, motives, and other variables, suggest that many situations, events, and personalities that converge

[1] A switchblade knife is the type most commonly carried and used by a large number of lower-class Negroes. The blade is often curved, averages about six inches in length, and springs out of its case when a small button at the top of the case is depressed. As the knife is drawn from the pocket, it can be brought into swift preparation for assault by means of one hand. The sale and carrying of such knives have been declared illegal in Philadelphia since 1952.

in a particular way and that result in homicide do not depend primarily upon the presence or absence of firearms. While it may be true both that the homicide rate is lower in Europe and that fewer homicides abroad involve use of firearms, it does not necessarily follow that the relatively high homicide rate in this country is merely due to greater accessibility of such weapons.

Comparison of a general homicide rate with percentage use of firearms is not an adequate comparison. Unless all methods and weapons used in homicide are compared between two areas or communities, the proportionate use of firearms compared in isolation is not convincing evidence of a causal relation between a high homicide rate and the number of shootings. Moreover, comparison of like cultural areas having similar homicide rates but vastly dissimilar proportions of deaths caused by firearms would tend to reject an hypothesis of a causal nexus between the two phenomena. By way of example, Brearley[1] noted for the years 1924–1926 that Pennsylvania had a homicide rate of 5.9 per 100,000 population. Using Philadelphia victim data to correspond to Brearley's use of mortality statistics, we see that the rate during 1948–1952 for criminal homicide deaths was 5.7, and for all homicides—criminal and non-criminal—the rate was 6.1. Despite the closeness of these Philadelphia rates with the Pennsylvania rate reported by Brearley, use of firearms in Pennsylvania amounted to 68 per cent of all methods, while use of firearms in Philadelphia was only 33 per cent. The fact that Brearley's figures are for an earlier period of time has no effect on the conclusion. Thus, while the homicide rates for these two population units are similar, the proportionate use of firearms is quite dissimilar, being over twice as high for the state as for the city. The hypothesis of a causal relationship between the homicide rate and proportionate use of firearms in killing is, therefore, rejected.

More than the availability of a shooting weapon is involved in homicide. Pistols and revolvers are not difficult to purchase—legally or illegally—in Philadelphia. Police inter-

[1] Brearley, *Homicide in the United States*, p. 69.

rogation of defendants reveals that most frequently these weapons are bought from friends or acquaintances for such nominal sums as ten or twenty dollars. A penknife or butcher knife, of course, is much cheaper and more easily obtained. Ready access to knives and little reluctance to engage in physical combat without weapons, or "to fight it out," are as important as the availability of some sort of gun. The type of weapon used appears to be, in part, the culmination of assault intentions or events and is only superficially related to causality. To measure quantitatively the effect of the presence of firearms on the homicide rate would require knowing the number and type of homicides that would not have occurred had not the offender—or, in some cases, the victim—possessed a gun. Research would require determination of the number of shootings that would have been stabbings, beatings, or some other method of inflicting death had no gun been available. It is the contention of this observer that few homicides due to shootings could be avoided merely if a firearm were not immediately present, and that the offender would select some other weapon to achieve the same destructive goal. Probably only in those cases where a felon kills a police officer, or vice versa, would homicide be avoided in the absence of a firearm.

There appears to be a cultural preference or selection for particular types of methods of inflicting death and of weapons used to kill. The terms "preference" and "selection" are used here in a general sociological sense and do not necessarily and literally mean that deliberate, volitional, and rational choices are made for particular types of methods or weapons to inflict death. The implication is that individuals are socialized positively or negatively toward special objects, that the culture-bound personality is by race, sex, age, social class, and other gross social attributes oriented to react in amazingly uniform ways. From this perspective we may speak of *significant* race and sex preferences for weapons employed in criminal homicide. As can be seen from Table 5, 39 per cent of the 588 criminal deaths were due to stabbings, 33 per cent to shootings, 22 per cent to beatings, and 6 per cent to other and miscellaneous methods. The leading method experienced by Negro victims was stabbing (47 per cent), while that experienced by white victims was beating (42 per cent). Proportionately, the frequency of each of these two methods is reversed for the two races, for Negroes were beaten to death only one-third as often as they were stabbed,

TABLE 5
METHOD AND WEAPON USED IN CRIMINAL HOMICIDE, BY RACE AND SEX OF VICTIM, PHILADELPHIA, 1948–1952

(In per cent)

METHOD	VICTIM								
	Both Races			Negro			White		
	Total	Male	Female	Total	Male	Female	Total	Male	Femal
Stabbing	38.8	40.3	33.8	46.8	48.3	41.7	17.4	17.8	16.3
Shooting	33.0	33.9	30.2	34.0	35.4	29.1	30.4	29.7	32.6
Beating	21.8	21.4	23.0	14.1	12.4	19.8	42.3	46.6	30.2
Other	6.4	4.4	13.0	5.1	3.9	9.4	9.9	5.9	20.9
Total	100.0	100.0	100.0	100.0	100.0	100.0	100.0	100.0	100.0
	(588)	(449)	(139)	(427)	(331)	(96)	(161)	(118)	(43)
WEAPON									
Penknife, switchblade knife	20.9	22.9	14.4	25.8	27.8	18.8	8.1	9.3	4.6
Kitchen knife, ice pick	16.3	16.1	17.3	19.4	19.0	20.8	8.1	7.6	9.3
Pistol, revolver	27.9	28.7	25.2	28.3	29.6	24.0	26.7	26.3	27.9
Rifle, shotgun	5.1	5.1	5.0	5.6	5.7	5.2	3.7	3.4	4.7
Fists, feet	14.9	13.8	18.7	8.7	7.0	14.6	31.7	33.1	27.9
Blunt instrument	8.0	8.0	7.9	6.6	6.0	8.3	11.8	13.6	7.0
Other	6.8	5.4	11.5	5.6	4.8	8.3	9.9	6.8	18.6
Total	100.0	100.0	100.0	100.0	100.0	100.0	100.0	100.0	100.0
	(588)	(449)	(139)	(427)	(331)	(96)	(161)	(118)	(43)

and whites were stabbed with a piercing instrument only one-third as often as they were beaten. Sex differentials are primarily related to stabbings and beatings too, for over two-fifths of the males and only one-third of the females died from stabbings. Furthermore, the difference between victim data and offender data once more looms large with respect to methods of slaying. (Compare Table 5 with Table 6.) Nearly twice as many female offenders stabbed (64 per cent) as were killed by stabbing (34 per cent); and only 3 per cent of the female offenders committed criminal homicide by beating, whereas 23 per cent of female victims were slain in this manner.

These observed race and sex differences relative to the methods of killing or of being killed become more clear as we examine particular weapons employed. Cultural prefer-

TABLE 6

METHOD AND WEAPON USED IN CRIMINAL HOMICIDE, BY RACE AND SEX OF OFFENDER, PHILADELPHIA, 1948–1952

(In per cent)

	OFFENDER								
METHOD	Both Races			Negro			White		
	Total	Male	Female	Total	Male	Female	Total	Male	Female(a)
Stabbing	37.5	31.8	64.2	44.1	37.7	69.9	17.5	15.9	—
Shooting	32.9	35.6	20.2	34.1	38.2	17.2	29.2	28.3	—
Beating	23.5	27.9	2.8	17.3	21.1	2.1	42.2	46.4	—
Other	6.1	4.7	12.8	4.5	3.0	10.8	11.1	9.4	—
Total	100.0	100.0	100.0	100.0	100.0	100.0	100.0	100.0	100.0
	(621)	(512)	(109)	(467)	(374)	(93)	(154)	(138)	(16)
WEAPON									
Penknife, switchblade knife	20.3	20.3	20.2	25.3	25.9	22.6	5.2	5.1	—
Kitchen knife, ice pick	15.8	10.1	42.2	17.8	11.0	45.2	9.7	8.0	—
Pistol, revolver	27.2	28.7	20.2	28.0	30.8	17.1	24.7	23.2	—
Rifle, shotgun	5.6	5.9	4.6	6.0	6.1	5.4	4.6	5.1	—
Fists, feet	16.1	18.9	2.7	10.0	12.3	1.1	34.4	37.0	—
Blunt instrument	8.9	10.6	.9	8.8	10.7	1.1	9.1	10.1	—
Other	6.1	5.5	9.2	4.1	3.2	7.5	12.3	11.5	—
Total	100.0	100.0	100.0	100.0	100.0	100.0	100.0	100.0	100.0
	(621)	(512)	(109)	(467)	(374)	(93)	(154)	(138)	(16)

(a) Category too small for breakdown by percentage distribution.

ences for certain weapons and plausible explanations for such preferences may be made when it is noted that the association between race or sex and the distribution of weapons employed is highly *significant*. Although socio-economic class could not be reliably and precisely determined from police files, it would be safe to assert on the basis of extensive review of the raw data that over 90 per cent of the victims and offenders were members of the lower social class stratum. Carrying a pocket knife or some other type of cutting or piercing instrument is believed to be a cultural tradition among lower-class Negroes. This belief is partly substantiated by the predilection of this race for such a weapon in committing homicide. The use of a penknife or switchblade knife is five times more frequent among Negroes (25 per cent) than among whites (5 per cent). More specifically, five times more Negro males (26 per cent) than white males (5 per cent) and nearly four times more Negro females (23 per cent) than white females (1 out of 16) use this type of weapon.[1] Finally, some type of kitchen instrument for stabbing or cutting is used almost twice as often by Negroes (18 per cent) as by whites (10 per cent).

If these data support the contention that there is a cultural selection made by Negroes for stabbing weapons, they also point to the fact that whites (or more particularly, white males) tend to choose beating by fists, feet, or blunt instruments as their principal means of inflicting death. A direct physical assault with fists or feet is over three times more frequent among whites (34 per cent) than among Negroes (10 per cent). A *significantly* higher proportion of white males (37 per cent) than of Negro males (12 per cent) directly assault their victims with their bare hands, usually in a pugilistic encounter. Many of these beatings appear to have been the result of fighting with no intention on the part of the offender to kill. However, a victim frequently fell from his assailant's blows and fractured his skull on the sidewalk or curb, a condition which, nonetheless, resulted in the assailant's being charged with homicide.[2]

Lack of physical strength relative to the male means that the female must, in most cases of violent encounter with a male, resort to weapons that remove this disadvantage. Because, as is shown later, 84 per cent of all female offenders killed males, these women sought some means to overcome

[1] The use of a razor in any form was so rare that it made no important contribution to the penknife and switchblade knife category.

[2] Snyder describes such circumstances in detail in *Homicide Investigation*, Chapter 15, "Deaths Due to Direct Violence," pp. 277–280.

the greater physical prowess of the men with whom they engaged in physical violence. The fact that only 3 per cent of female offenders committed homicide by beating, compared to 23 per cent of the female victims who were slain in this manner, confirms the suggestion that females find it difficult to slay males without some weapon beyond their naturally endowed but physically inferior fists and feet. Males, either with a blunt instrument or with their fists alone, beat their victims to death nine to ten times more often than do female offenders. But females employ a piercing or cutting instrument (usually a butcher knife) over four times more frequently than do males. Because such a large proportion of female offenders kill as a result of domestic quarrels which frequently occur in kitchens while they are preparing meals, it is not unlikely that females should use cutting and stabbing weapons for the purpose of slaying. Mealtime is one of those family rituals often used for discussion of the family budget and emotional problems affecting individual members of the familial group.[1] Rising tensions and marital discord may find more opportunity for overt—both verbal and physical—expression during mealtime when family members are usually in contact with one another. In a later chapter the Philadelphia data are examined in more detail relative to the different places where criminal homicides occur. Since our present concern is with methods and weapons (Table 6), it is perhaps sufficient to note that 42 per cent of all female offenders committed homicide by means of a kitchen knife although only 17 per cent were killed with this weapon. Negro females, especially and more often than white females, used a pocket knife or butcher knife. About 23 per cent of Negro females used a pocket knife and another 45 per cent used a kitchen knife. Only one white female used a pocket knife and four of the 16 white female offenders used a butcher knife. Six white females resorted to a pistol or revolver, a frequency about twice as great as the 17 per cent of Negro female offenders who used such weapons.

[1] James H. S. Bossard and Eleanor Boll, *Family Ritual*, Philadelphia: University of Pennsylvania Press, 1950, p. 99.

Although not indicated in any of the tables, it should be noted that when more than one defendant is involved in a single criminal homicide, the slaying is most likely to have been a beating rather than a stabbing, shooting, or any of the miscellaneous methods of inflicting death. There were 44 killings, in each of which more than one offender participated. Altogether there were 71 multiple offenders or defendants of whom 34 were involved in beatings, 22 in shootings, 14 in stabbings, and only one in another method. This generalization regarding the high proportion of beatings in multiple-defendant killings is particularly applicable to white males, among whom were 12 multiple offenders who committed homicide by beating, 6 by shooting, and only one by stabbing.

A general and crude relationship exists between age of the offender and predilection for certain types of weapons. (Table 7.) It appears that the use of a pistol or revolver is highest in the younger and in the older age groups, for the incidence of homicide by small firearms is high (36 per cent) for offenders under 20 years of age, then decreases between ages 20–49, and reaches another high (37 per cent) for ages 50–59. It may be that offenders under 20 years of age and

TABLE 7
WEAPON EMPLOYED IN CRIMINAL HOMICIDE,
BY AGE OF OFFENDER, PHILADELPHIA, 1948–1952
(In per cent)

| WEAPON | Total | AGE | | | | | |
		Under 20 years	20–29 years	30–39 years	40–49 years	50–59 years	60 years and over(a)
Penknife, switchblade knife	20.3	24.2	22.0	19.4	19.6	15.8	—
Kitchen knife, ice pick	15.8	7.6	15.8	16.6	18.8	18.4	—
Pistol, revolver	27.1	36.4	23.4	28.6	24.1	36.8	—
Rifle, shotgun	5.7	6.1	6.2	7.4	.9	5.3	—
Fists, feet	16.1	12.1	18.2	16.0	17.0	10.5	—
Blunt instrument	8.9	9.1	11.5	5.7	8.0	10.5	—
Other	6.1	4.5	2.9	6.3	11.6	2.6	—
Total	100.0	100.0	100.0	100.0	100.0	100.0	100.0
	(620)	(66)	(209)	(175)	(112)	(38)	(20)

(a) Category too small for breakdown by percentage distribution.

those over 50 require (as do women who slay men) some weapon to maintain distance between themselves and their victims, and to offset their limited physical power when involved in an episode of violence. Commensurate with this probable explanation is the fact that beatings (with blunt instruments or with fists alone) show highest frequency for ages 20–29 when most males are in their physical prime.

In a stabbing, offenders under 20 years of age seem most often to select a pocket knife and those over 40 to select a kitchen knife. Use of a pocket knife ranges from a high frequency (24 per cent) among offenders under 20 years of age, and gradually decreases to a low frequency (10 per cent) among those 60 years of age and over. Use of a kitchen instrument generally rises with age, from a low frequency (8 per cent) among offenders under 20 years of age, to a high frequency (18 per cent) among those aged 50–59 years. These age differentials according to the methods of inflicting death further suggest that the younger age groups are not home as often as older age groups when they commit homicide (butcher knives are in the kitchen); and that their victims, therefore, are less likely to be close family members. Further analysis of these variables is made in subsequent chapters.

We may summarize the data on methods and weapons presented thus far by pointing out that the order of frequency of methods used in criminal homicide is the same for victims and offenders within each race-sex category save one. Both victims and offenders among Negroes of either sex are involved, according to frequency, first, in stabbings, secondly, in shootings, and thirdly, in beatings. Stabbings among Negro males involve penknives or switchblade knives, while stabbings among Negro females involve kitchen (almost invariably, butcher) knives. White male victims and offenders are involved, first, in beatings, secondly, in shootings, and thirdly, in stabbings. Only for the white female is there a difference in the distribution of victims and offenders according to methods used to inflict death. As an offender she uses a pistol most frequently, then a butcher knife, and, lastly, gas or poison to asphyxiate her victim. As a victim, the white female is most likely to be beaten, shot, and put to death by one of the miscellaneous methods, in that order of frequency.

Methods and Weapons Noted in Other Studies and Reports

Mortality data and general homicide literature show considerable diversity from the Philadelphia data with respect to the distribution of methods and weapons used in criminal homicide. Classifications of methods are not always comparable to that used in the present study. However, comparisons that can be made indicate that the use of firearms is more extensive for the nation as a whole than for Philadelphia, and that Philadelphia has a higher incidence of felonious deaths caused by cutting and piercing instruments. A vital statistics report for the nation in 1950 lists 7,567 victims of homicide.[1] Of this total, less than one per cent were killed by non-accidental poisoning, 55 per cent were victims of assault by firearms and explosives; 25 per cent by cutting or piercing instruments, and 19 per cent by other means. Thus, shootings were, in absolute terms, 22 per cent higher and stabbings 14 per cent lower for the nation than for Philadelphia. As was true in Philadelphia, so in the United States, more Negroes than whites were killed by stabbings. In the country as a whole, 14 per cent of white males and 10 per cent of white females were killed by cutting or piercing instruments, while 36 per cent of Negro males and 31 per cent of Negro females were killed in this manner. Nonetheless, for each of the race and sex groups, nationally, over 50 per cent were killed by shooting.

Information derived from the police files of ten cities[2] in the United States, each with a total population over 250,000, reveals a distribution of methods of inflicting death that is

[1] *Vital Statistics—Special Reports*, National Summaries, 1950, 37: 148. Not included in this total are deaths caused by "injury by intervention of police" or "executions."

[2] Co-operation from the police departments of the following cities made this tabulation possible: Los Angeles (Calif.), Kansas City (Mo.), Milwaukee (Wisc.), Baltimore (Md.), St. Paul (Minn.), Columbus (Ohio), Akron (Ohio), Buffalo (N.Y.), Seattle (Wash.), Jersey City (N.J.). Unfortunately, most annual police reports do not include a detailed summary of criminal homicide by race, sex, age, method, etc.

more similar to the Philadelphia data than to national mortality reports. For the period 1948–1952, these ten cities listed a total of 1,514 criminal homicides. Of these, 31 per cent were persons killed by stabbings, 45 per cent were victims of shootings, 20 per cent were beaten to death, and 4 per cent were killed by some other means. Comparison with the present study indicates that Philadelphia had approximately 8 per cent more stabbings, 13 per cent fewer shootings, about the same amount of beatings and of miscellaneous methods.

Hoffman early emphasized the high rates of homicide by firearms. For a three-year period ending with 1912, he showed that 62 per cent of males and 53 per cent of females were killed by firearms.[1] Combining mortality returns for the registration area during 1910–1914, out of 20,465 homicide deaths, 61 per cent were caused by firearms.[2] Extensiveness of the use of firearms is further indicated by the fact that in 1921 the homicide rate for all methods was 8.5 per 100,000, of which 6.2 per 100,000 were due to deaths from firearms. In England and Wales out of 85 male homicide deaths in 1922, only 5 were caused by firearms, and out of 117 female deaths, 11 were due to this method.[3] Hoffman concluded that this type of data "conclusively proves that the murder problem in the United States is essentially a problem of the wrongful use of firearms, the sale and possession of which require to be made more effectively a matter of control and punishment on the part of the authorities."[4] Like Elliott,[5] who discusses the relationship between the use of guns and our frontier mores, Abrahamsen claims that "this necessitated having a gun at hand at all times, a habit which is somewhat prevalent today, and which is reflected in the many homicides by firearms."[6]

Later evidence from other sources confirms Hoffman's earlier reports on the excessive use of firearms in this country.

[1] F. L. Hoffman, *The Homicide Problem*, p. 24.
[2] *Ibid.*, p. 34.
[3] *Ibid.*, p. 74.
[4] *Ibid.*, p. 70. Obviously, the author means "homicide" instead of "murder" as these terms are employed in this study.
[5] Mabel Elliott, "Crime and the Frontier Mores," *American Sociological Review* (April, 1944), 9: 185–192.
[6] Abrahamsen, *Crime and the Human Mind*, p. 149.

Dublin and Bunzel, using death registration data from years 1926–1930, point out:

> In marked contrast to the situation in other countries, about two thirds of American deaths from homicide are due to the use of firearms. In England and Wales in 1932, only 13 per cent were caused by firearms. In Germany prior to the present regime, about 27 per cent of the homicides were so caused; in New Zealand, about a third. Fifteen per cent of the homicides in this country are due to the use of cutting and piercing instruments and the remaining 17 per cent are divided among other miscellaneous methods. . . . During the years 1925 to 1929, 73 per cent of all rural homicides were caused by firearms, as against 64 per cent in the cities of the country. . . .[1]

The higher proportion of rural homicides caused by firearms is due, claimed Brearley, to the country dweller's experience and skill in the use of firearms or to his greater tendency to carry weapons, especially concealed ones. He further revealed that at the time of his study (1924–1926), and contrary to common belief, the Negro was more often slain with firearms than was the white, or 73 per cent of the Negro homicidal deaths were caused by firearms, while only 68 per cent of the slayings among the whites were due to this means. For Negro females the percentage of firearms slayings was 63, while for the white females it was only 47.[2] These proportions are clearly diverse from the Philadelphia distributions. The same author also presents evidence to show that "there is a fairly close relationship between the high homicide rate and a large percentage of firearms slayings."[3] He compares the mean homicide rates of each of forty-two states during 1924–1926 with the percentage of homicides resulting from the use of firearms. The range was from Florida, with a mean rate of 38 per 100,000 population, of which 74 per cent were shootings, to Vermont, whose mean rate was only 1.2 and the percentage of firearms, 42. We have previously criticized Brearley's assumptions of a causal relationship between high rates of homicide and frequency of shootings.

[1] Dublin and Bunzel, op. cit., pp. 128–129.
[2] Brearley, Homicide in the U.S., p. 69.
[3] Ibid., p. 71.

Homicides classified by mode of killing according to the *Illinois Crime Survey* can be compared only crudely with the present study. In the Cook County survey, "causes of death in murder, 1926–1927" are related to color and sex. Shootings were much higher and stabbings much lower than in Philadelphia. Summarizing this material, Arthur Lashly says:

> Exactly the same percentage of the total colored males and colored females murdered were shot, and the same is approximately true of deaths by stabbing, being 27 per cent in the case of colored males and 25 per cent in the case of colored females. This is contrasted with 71 per cent deaths by shooting of white males, which is due to the large number of gang killings of white men. Of the total number of murders in 1926, 63.68 per cent were shot and 11.84 per cent cut or stabbed, as against 61.84 per cent shot in 1927 and 13.68 per cent stabbed.[1]

Closer to the distribution of methods in Philadelphia was that in Birmingham. Harlan reports:

> Firearms prove to be the most popular weapon with the 492 agents, 49.2 per cent of them employing this type of weapon; but the various cutting and piercing instruments run a close second, being used by 40.4 per cent of the agents.
>
> . . . it is nonetheless plain that cutting and piercing instruments are employed far more commonly by Negro than by white murderers. Of the 418 Negro agents, 45.7 per cent used such weapons while only 10.8 per cent of the 74 white agents used them. Firearms are much more popular with white murderers than with Negroes; 71.6 per cent of the white agents using them as compared with only 45.2 per cent of the Negro agents. . . .
>
> The most notable sex difference is the greater predilection of women for knives and ice picks than is true of men, and their lesser reliance on firearms. Thus, 54 per cent of the female agents employed cutting or piercing instruments while the proportion of male agents is but 36 per cent; and 40 per cent of the women used firearms as compared to 52 per cent of the men.[2]

The proportion of women who cut or stabbed their victims was even higher in Philadelphia (64 per cent) than in

[1] *The Illinois Crime Survey*, p. 608.
[2] Harlan, *op. cit.*, pp. 743–744.

Birmingham, and their reliance on firearms less (20 per cent). Like Philadelphia, stabbings ranked highest among the methods employed by Negroes in Birmingham.

Of the 212 criminal homicides in St. Louis, 1949–1951, nearly 60 per cent resulted from gun wounds and 24 per cent from stabbings or cuttings.[1] This distribution is relatively close to the national pattern according to mortality data. The greater use of knives by Negroes is again confirmed by the St. Louis report, for out of 50 cases in which such a weapon was used, a white was the agent in only five.

For Upper New York State, DePorte and Parkhurst reported that "by far the most common means of homicide was fire-arms, 64 per cent of the deaths of males and 59 per cent of the deaths of females being caused by this agency."[2] Although firearms ranked highest for Negroes as well as whites, the proportion of cases in which cutting and piercing instruments were used was, as in Philadelphia, strikingly high among Negroes—38 per cent as against 13 per cent for whites.[3] In his study of 252 homicides during the decennial period, 1914–1923, in Seattle, Calvin Schmid noted an unusually high proportion of 191 resulting from the use of firearms, while fracturing of the skull claimed 26, and stabbing, 19 victims.[4] In his special study of 870 homicides in Jefferson County, Alabama, 1920–1925, Hoffman also found 75 per cent caused by firearms.[5] On the basis of his analysis of 22 first degree murderers, Banay said that the chances of the murderer's weapon being a gun were three to one.[6] Summarizing his material on 92 murderers, Gillin claims: "As to the weapon he used there were three chances out of five that he used a revolver; over one out of ten a rifle or shotgun; almost one out of ten any instrument at hand, such as club, axe, or pocket-knife; one out of twelve his own hands in strangulation; one out of sixteen a dagger or

[1] Based on Meyers, Jr., *op. cit.*, p. 29.
[2] DePorte and Parkhurst, *op. cit.*, p. 52.
[3] *Ibid.*
[4] Calvin Schmid, "A Study of Homicides in Seattle, 1914 to 1924," *Social Forces* (September, 1925–June, 1926) 4: 754.
[5] F. L. Hoffman, "The Increase in Murder," *op. cit.*, p. 24.
[6] Ralph Banay, *op. cit.*, p. 111.

long-bladed knife; and only one out of a hundred, poison."[1]
In the Growdon study, 33 of the 54 juvenile homicide offenders had used firearms, 6 a cutting or stabbing instrument, 9 had beaten their victims to death, 9 used miscellaneous methods.[2] Finally, Frankel was unusually excited by the proportionate use of firearms when he reported that "homicides by firearms is one of the alarming phenomena in present-day social life. In more than one-half of the 1,816 homicide cases reported to the New Jersey health authorities during 1925–1934, firearms were the means employed."[3]

A large number of women may be able to conceal the felonious nature of the homicide they commit, as Pollak[4] suggests, due to their employing poison rather than one of the more violent and obvious methods. Using data from a Russian source and a French source[5]—the first 100 cases from Tarnowsky's monograph on female murderers, and an investigation of all poison cases which came to the attention of the French courts from 1825 to 1880 by Lacassagne— Pollak says, "There seems to be almost unanimous agreement among criminologists that the woman who kills uses poison more often than any other means."[6] The present writer suspects that such may be the case for the white female in Philadelphia, but if so, she has been exceptionally clever in escaping detection. Only three cases of poisoning were recorded for the entire five-year period, and one of these was committed by a male offender. Furthermore, only 54 of the 7,567 homicide deaths in the United States in 1950 were listed as due to non-accidental poisoning by another person, and it is interesting to note that proportionately more females of both races were killed by poisoning than were males.[7]

[1] Gillin, "The Wisconsin Murderer," *op. cit.*, p. 552.
[2] Growdon, *op. cit.*, p. 11. Multiple slayings may account for 57 total.
[3] Frankel, *op. cit.*, p. 672.
[4] Pollak, *op. cit.*, pp. 3, 16–19.
[5] Pauline Tarnowsky, *Les Femmes Homicides*, Paris: Felix Alsar, 1908; and A. Lacassagne, "Notes statistiques sur l'emprisonnement criminel en France," *Archives D'Anthropologie Criminelle*, I, 1886, 260–264, referred to by Pollak, *op. cit.*, p. 16.
[6] Pollak, *op. cit.*, p. 16.
[7] *Vital Statistics—Special Reports*, National Summaries, 1950, 37: 148.

6

TEMPORAL PATTERNS

By Months

STUDY of the effects on man's individual and social behavior of factors such as temperature, humidity, seasonal changes, and the like has been relegated, for almost half a century, to a minor position in criminological literature. It may be desirable, therefore, to review very briefly some of the early works and types of associations reported by pioneers in this field before analyzing the Philadelphia data for possible associations between homicide and monthly variations.

Theorists have long promulgated impressionistic speculations about the effects of meteorological conditions upon human behavior. Among the earliest to apply these theories to the problems of criminology was M. de Guerry, who found that from 1825 to 1830, for every 100 crimes against the person in the northern part of France, there were 182 crimes against property, whereas in southern France, for every 100 crimes against the person, there were only 49 crimes against property.[1]

Quetelet was led to formulate his "thermic law of delinquency" according to which violent crimes against the person were more prevalent in the south of France and in warm seasons, while crimes against property were more prevalent in the north and in colder weather. He believed that the number of crimes in a geographical unit could, therefore, be predicted with a fair degree of accuracy.[2] Quetelet's thesis was substantiated somewhat by Mayo-Smith, who stated that crimes against the person were more numerous in warm

---

[1] Cited by Maurice Parmelee, *Criminology*, New York: The Macmillan Company, 1919, p. 45.
[2] See Bernaldo De Quiros, *Modern Theories of Criminality*, Boston: Little, Brown and Co., 1911, p. 10.

weather, whereas economic crimes against property were more frequent in winter.[1]

Lombroso reported that 54 per cent of the murderous attacks in England and Wales occurred in spring and summer and only 46 per cent in the autumn and winter.[2] Similar observations made by Lombroso and Ferri[3] for Italy and France, and by Aschaffenburg[4] for Germany added weight to these contentions. De Quiros quotes a mathematical formula provided by Kropotkin (*Prisons*, 1890), who said that one could predict the number of homicides for any month in any European country by multiplying the average temperature of the month by 7, adding the average humidity, and multiplying again by 2.[5]

Albert Leffingwell, in two essays published in 1892, said that 55 per cent of homicides and murderous assaults in England and Wales between 1883 and 1887 occurred in the spring and summer months, but that only 45 per cent occurred in the autumn and winter months.[6] Referring to such types of human conduct as suicide, duels, insanity, illegitimate births, and crimes of violence, this American physician said that "either by the gradual increase of solar light or of solar heat, or else in some other manner quite mysterious at present, the breaking up of winter and the advent of spring and summer seasons produces upon all animated nature a peculiar state of excitement or exaltation of the nervous system."[7]

[1] Richard Mayo-Smith, *Statistics and Sociology*, New York: The Macmillan Company, 1907, pp. 271–272.

[2] Cesare Lombroso, *Crime: Its Causes and Remedies*, Boston: Little, Brown and Co., 1911, pp. 12–15.

[3] Enrico Ferri, *Criminal Sociology*, Boston: Little, Brown and Co., 1917, p. 210.

[4] Gustav Aschaffenburg, *Crime and its Repression*, Boston: Little, Brown and Co., 1913, pp. 16–17.

[5] Cited by De Quiros, *op. cit.*, p. 10. As Barnes and Teeters point out, however: "This is manifestly absurd, as there is no factor in the formula to represent the population of the country; in other words, the formula would give identical results for two areas with the same temperature and same humidity but with populations related as one to fifty." (H. E. Barnes and Negley Teeters, *New Horizons in Criminology*, New York: Prentice-Hall, 1945, p. 133.)

[6] Albert Leffingwell, *Illegitimacy and the Influence of the Seasons Upon Conduct*, New York: Scribner's, 1892, cited by H. C. Brearley, *Homicide in the U.S.*, p. 166. See also, Franklin Thomas, *The Environmental Basis of Society*, New York: D. Appleton = Century, 1925, p. 100.

[7] Quoted by Brearley, *Homicide in the United States*, p. 165.

Edwin Dexter's[1] study of certain criminal cases in New York City and in Denver, correlated with weather records of the two cities, is of interest to the criminologist. He found that cases of assault and battery in New York, 1891–1897, were most numerous in the warmest months of the year, during periods of low barometer and low humidity, on calm, clear days, and during least precipitation; and that murders in Denver were most frequent during periods of warm weather, low barometer and low humidity, during winds, upon cloudy days, and during periods of some precipitation.[2] Primary concern here is with his reference to homicide, and it is at this point that one of the chief objections to the Dexter study may be found. Although he included some 40,000 cases of New York assault and battery and 3,891 cases of prison discipline, only 184 slayings in Denver were studied, and these were scattered over a period of thirteen years. Therefore, he had an inadequate sample with insufficient data to lend much confidence to his results since chance factors could have seriously affected his findings.

These studies, though not concerned primarily with homicide, and antedating what may be called our contemporary, more sophisticated scientific research, nonetheless set the stage for examination of a possible relationship between seasonal and other temporal variations of criminal homicide.

The Philadelphia Data

The monthly distribution of criminal homicides for each of the years from 1948 to 1952 shows a considerable amount of capricious oscillation and no consistent pattern. (Table 8.) The five years combined show two major peaks, one in May, with 11 per cent of all homicides, and the other in September, with 10 per cent. However, on the basis of a theoretically expected equitable distribution of homicides for each of the twelve months, the observed frequencies do not differ to a sufficient degree of statistical significance that chance and

[1] Edwin Dexter, *Weather Influences: An Empirical Study of the Mental and Physiological Effects of Definite Meteorological Conditions*, New York: Macmillan Co., 1904.
[2] *Ibid.*, pp. 141–165.

TABLE 8
MONTHLY DISTRIBUTION OF CRIMINAL HOMICIDE, BY RACE
AND SEX OF VICTIM, PHILADELPHIA, 1948-1952

(In per cent)

Month	Both Races			Negro			White		
	Total	Male	Female	Total	Male	Female	Total	Male	Female
January	6.3	6.0	7.2	5.9	5.7	6.2	8.5	6.8	9.3
February	5.8	5.4	7.2	6.1	6.0	6.2	5.0	3.4	9.3
March	8.2	8.5	7.2	7.9	7.6	9.4	8.7	11.0	2.3
April	8.5	8.5	8.6	9.1	9.1	9.4	6.8	6.8	7.0
May	10.5	10.7	10.1	9.4	9.4	9.4	13.7	14.4	11.6
June	8.5	9.1	6.5	9.4	10.0	7.3	6.2	6.8	4.6
July	7.3	7.6	6.5	8.2	8.5	7.3	5.0	5.1	4.6
August	9.9	8.7	13.7	9.4	8.5	12.5	11.2	9.3	16.3
September	10.4	10.5	10.1	11.5	12.1	9.4	7.4	5.9	11.6
October	8.3	8.7	7.2	7.7	7.9	7.3	9.9	11.0	7.0
November	8.0	8.0	7.9	7.7	7.9	7.3	8.7	8.5	9.3
December	8.3	8.5	7.9	7.7	7.6	8.3	9.9	11.0	7.0
Total	100.0	100.0	100.0	100.0	100.0	100.0	100.0	100.0	100.0
	(588)	(449)	(139)	(427)	(331)	(96)	(161)	(118)	(43)

Note: Calendar shift corrections using original data failed to show any significant associations.

other variables could be eliminated as responsible for their distribution. Using a winter, spring-autumn, and summer trichotomy[1] for the twelve months, we note that more homicides occur during the hot months of May, June, July, and August (36 per cent); followed closely by the relatively warm spring and autumn months of March, April, September, and October (35 per cent); and that the lowest frequency is in the winter months of January, February, November, and December (28 per cent). Thus, there is a slight but insignificant association between seasons and the number of criminal homicides. The number of multiple suspects arrested for criminal homicide shows a closer association to a meaningful seasonal distribution. Of 71 such suspects, 33 were involved in homicides that occurred during the summer months, 26 during the spring-autumn months, and only 12 during the

[1] This trichotomy results from a logical grouping of months according to their mean temperatures. Material supplied to the author by the United States Weather Bureau in Philadelphia shows that the mean temperatures for the three four-month periods between 1910 and 1953 were: (1) January–February–November–December: 37.8; (2) March–April–September–October: 55.2; (3) May–June–July–August: 71.7. (*Local Climatological Data*, U.S. Department of Commerce, Weather Bureau, Philadelphia, Pennsylvania, 1953.)

winter months. We have previously indicated that the largest proportion of multiple suspects participated in beatings, so that the association between homicides involving more than one offender, beating to death, and summer months becomes clear.

More Negroes (12 per cent) are killed during September than any other month, and it is this race which contributes most to the fact that a very high frequency for all victims occurs in September. May is the highest month for whites (14 per cent) and for males in general (11 per cent), while August is the month of highest frequency for females (14 per cent). Specified race and sex groups among victims show the following months of highest frequency:

Negro males in September (12 per cent);
White males in May (14 per cent);
Negro females in August (13 per cent); and
White females in August (16 per cent).

Negro homicides appear to oscillate less frequently than white homicides. Slayings among Negroes gradually build up from a January low of 25 homicides to a September high of 49, then maintain a stable number (33) throughout the last three months. The highest incidence is twice as great as the lowest incidence. Whites, on the other hand, show no consistent increase or decrease, and the May high of 22 deaths is nearly three times greater than the February and July lows of 8 cases each. Vacillations such as these, with no significant or positive association noted, require us to reject an hypothesis which suggests a relationship between monthly or seasonal changes and variations in criminal homicide.

Months and Seasons Noted in Other Studies and Reports

A brief review of homicide literature in this country shows that the tendency in Philadelphia for homicides to rise slightly during the summer months and to decline during winter months is similar to previous research findings. There are exceptions and differences in the literature, however. Sutherland says that "statistical studies show very uniformly that crimes against property reach a maximum in winter months, and crimes against the person and against morals in the summer months."[1] He believes these differences can be explained in social terms, for crimes against the person reach a maximum in the summer months "when the contacts between persons are most frequent and the consumption of alcohol in group relationships is greatest."[2] Dublin and Bunzel, to the contrary, claim that "the frequency of homicide does not vary with the seasons."[3]

The *Uniform Crime Reports* for 1950 shows that for urban areas in general, as for Philadelphia, September is a high month (12 per cent), while January and February are the low months (9 per cent each). The annual report says:

> The effect of the seasons on the volume of crime is clearly indicated in the data presented. . . . It is apparent that felonious assaults and murder occur with greatest frequency during the summer months and that crimes against property as a group show a tendency to increase in frequency during the winter. . . . Murders, rapes and assaults during the peak summer months exceeded by approximately one-third the frequency of such crimes during the low months in the cooler seasons.[4]

Dividing the year into quarters, the report further reveals that the daily average number of murders and non-negligent manslaughters known to the police was 9.92, exceeded only by the July-September quarter, having a daily average of 10.95. The lowest daily average of 9.03 was in the January-March quarter. It is interesting to observe that two other major offenses of personal violence, aggravated assault and rape, also had their peaks (for the nation as a whole) in the July-September quarter, the former offense reaching a high in July, the latter in August.[5]

Analyzing the monthly distribution of 51,798 homicides (including non-criminal) reported for the registration area

[1] Sutherland, *Principles of Criminology*, p. 82.
[2] *Ibid.*
[3] Dublin and Bunzel, *op. cit.*, p. 130.
[4] *Uniform Crime Reports*, 1950, 21: 85–86.
[5] *Ibid.*, p. 86.

during the years 1923–1928, Brearley found that summer had more homicides than any other season, although winter months were slightly higher than spring. On the other hand, the individual years showed clearly (as in Philadelphia) that there was little uniformity in the results secured. The author concluded that

> the criminologist is forced to suspend judgment. Temperature trends may affect the seasonal distribution of homicide in the United States, and, again, they may not. The relationship may actually exist, obscured by interfering factors, but the evidence already present does not lend much support to this conclusion.[1]

Mortality statistics by homicide for 77 large cities in the United States (1924) were analyzed by Hoffman[2] to discover the extent of seasonal variations. The distribution of 2,798 cases showed that the greatest number in any one month occurred in December (258), closely followed by July (251). However, the three summer months (736) exceeded the winter months (647). Consequently, though December had the highest record for homicides, the report as a whole indicated a slight association between high temperatures and homicide.

The *Uniform Crime Reports* for 1930 seems to indicate that the present monthly pattern is quite similar to that of twenty years ago. After defective and incomplete returns had been excluded for that first year of national reporting, and when more definite information on the subject of murder and non-negligent manslaughter for about 80 per cent of the cities of 25,000 or more population had been tabulated, criminal homicide comprised a relatively larger proportion of the offenses of importance during the late summer and early autumn than at any other period. For 58 cities of 100,000 or more inhabitants, the gross number of slayings reached its maximum in August and September, the minima being in February and November.[3]

Reviewing and analyzing the *Uniform Crime Reports*,

---

[1] Brearley, *Homicide in the U.S.*, pp. 189–190.
[2] F. L. Hoffman, *The Homicide Problem*, pp. 101–103.
[3] *Uniform Crime Reports*, 1930, 1: 1–6.

1935–1940, Joseph Cohen[1] tabulated by months the number of total homicides known to the urban police. Once more the summer months were highest—for this period, July and August—while January retained its usual low number.

The distribution of 1,606 homicide deaths in New York State, exclusive of New York City, for the 1921–1930 period showed similar results. Of the total, 478 were in the summer and only 343 in the winter. As DePorte and Parkhurst point out:

> The highest number of homicides was recorded in the summer months, July–September; the lowest, in the winter months, January–March. When correction is made for an unequal number of days in the months, it is found that the summer excess of homicides over the winter minimum equalled 40 per cent for males and 25 per cent for females.[2]

Murder and non-negligent manslaughter in St. Louis for 1949–1951 were highest in August, during which month 24 of the total 212 offenses occurred. Although there was also a slight peak in March as well, a seasonal distribution shows that the quarter, July–September, with 64 cases, was the highest for the combined three years.[3]

Not all the studies in this country reveal distributions that follow the pattern usually reported for the nation, or that for Philadelphia. Three studies—one in the Southeast, another in the Northwest, and a third in the Midwest—indicate that there is a lack of complete uniformity to the general prevailing seasonal pattern of homicide. First, in his own analysis of the seasonal distribution of 1,601 homicides from mortality data in South Carolina during the years 1920–1926, Brearley found no consistent pattern. Comparing the lowest with the highest number for each month during the period he clearly demonstrated this inconsistency. He says,

> For example, July varies from 12 to 33 and September from 10 to 33. It is also worthy of note that in ten of the twelve months

---

[1] Joseph Cohen, "The Geography of Crime," *The Annals of the American Academy of Political and Social Science* (September, 1941), 217: 33–34.
[2] DePorte and Parkhurst, *op. cit.*, p. 52.
[3] Meyers, Jr., *op. cit.*, p. 20.

the range from lowest to highest number in any one year is greater than the minimum. December is appreciably higher than either July or August, the two warmest months. When corrected so that each month's total would represent the equivalent of 31 days each, the lowest months were found to be February, May and October, and the highest were December, November, and July.[1]

Second, Calvin Schmid analyzed 252 homicides in and near Seattle, Washington, for the years 1914–1923, and found, as Brearley had in South Carolina, that December was the month of greatest frequency, closely followed by January and April. In the winter months there were 84 homicides, while only 47 were reported for the summer months. This excess of homicides during the winter, according to Schmid, was due to the distress and disorder among the large number of migratory seasonal workers who made the city their headquarters during cold weather.[2]

Third, Lashly surveyed the murders of Cook County classified by months in *The Illinois Crime Survey* (1926–1927). For both years, December was the month of highest incidence, during which 88 of the total 760 killings occurred. Dividing all murders into "gang killings" and "non-gang killings," the high months for the former were July and March, and for the latter, October and December.[3]

These three studies show seasonal inconsistencies and monthly peaks in criminal homicide that are the direct antithesis of the usual pattern reported in this country, in the present study, in Europe, and elsewhere.[4] In passing,

[1] Brearley, *Homicide in the U.S.*, pp. 177–178.
[2] Schmid, *op. cit.*, pp. 750–751.
[3] *The Illinois Crime Survey*, pp. 612, 615.
[4] The anthropological literature has not been reviewed in connection with the present study, but there are indications that seasonal variations are observable among relatively stable, primitive groups as well. For example, in discussing Maria homicide in India, Elwin points out that there is a definite increase in homicides in the hottest months, April and May, as well as in September and October, the enervating months. June and July have rates only half September and October, but the former are the months when everyone is exceptionally busy and hard at work in the fields. April and October are high months and festival periods, "which are not only occasions for heavy drinking, but by providing opportunities for people to meet together make it possible for disputes to arise and old grievances to be remembered" (Elwin, *op. cit.*, p. 142).

one study from abroad may be added to the weight of inconsistency. In his review of the monthly variations of the different forms of homicidal criminality in France between 1827 and 1870, Durkheim found that premeditated and unpremeditated murder oscillate from month to month most capriciously:

> . . . Not only is the general development different, but neither the maxima nor the minima coincide. Unpremeditated murders have two maxima, one in February and the other in August. Premeditated murders also have two, one being the same, February, but the other is in November. . . . If the seasonal, not the monthly variations are calculated, the divergencies are equally striking. Autumn has almost as many unpremeditated murders as Summer (1,968 as against 1,974) and Winter has more than Spring. For premeditated murder, Winter leads (2,621), Autumn follows (2,596), then Summer (2,478) and finally Spring (2,287).[1]

Such facts as these from Brearley, Schmid, Lashly, and Durkheim make manifest the necessity to use caution in discussing seasonal variations and homicide. Despite differences in the sources of data, levels of statistical treatment, historical periods and operational definitions, these studies throw some doubt on simplified generalizations. Furthermore, use of general mortality data which may include noncriminal homicide, and inclusion of negligent manslaughter (mostly automobile deaths) in police statistics of criminal homicide make research comparisons difficult. For example, the *Uniform Crime Reports* consistently reveals that negligent manslaughters are highest in December. These offenses consist almost entirely of traffic fatalities where gross negligence is present, and occur with greatest frequency during the winter months when driving conditions are less favorable. In 1950 it was reported that the daily average in December was nearly three-fourths greater than that during the month of June.[2] Thus, unless proper distinctions are made of the types of homicide under review, inconsistencies in seasonal distributions are inevitable.

[1] Durkheim, *op. cit.*, p. 344.
[2] *Uniform Crime Reports*, 1950, 21: 86.

That the seasons and their temperatures, indirectly at least, affect human conduct, and that criminal homicide appears generally to follow seasonal patterns, can hardly be denied. Physical and biochemical reactions to heat and cold can be measured, and these in turn may affect our inter-personal relationships as well as the nature of collective group life. But little is known about emotional and psycho-logical effects from thermometric (or barometric) variations; and until these factors can be quantitatively analyzed in isolation from other variables, we must still conclude with Brearley that "the positive relationship between temperature changes and variation in the number of homicides is not established."[1]

By Days and by Hours: The Philadelphia Data

Daily and hourly patterns of criminal homicide are defi-nitely discernible in Philadelphia. There is a *significant* asso-ciation between criminal homicide and days of the week, as well as hours of the day when the offense occurs. On the basis of a theoretically equal distribution of these 588 cases throughout the week, striking variations noted are the high frequency of criminal homicides on Saturday (32 per cent), and the relatively low frequency on Tuesday (7 per cent). (Table 9.) In short, nearly five times as many criminal homicides occur on the day of highest frequency as occur on the day of lowest frequency. Friday and Sunday each claim 17 per cent, or almost half that of Saturday. There is neither a build-up to the Saturday high, nor a gradual decline to the Tuesday low, for frequency during the remain-ing days of the week varies only slightly.

Of the high number of 187 victims on Saturdays, Negroes contribute 152, or 81 per cent. Moreover, it is largely Negro males who produce a high incidence on Saturdays. They comprise 68 per cent of all persons slain on Saturdays but are only 56 per cent of the total group of 588 victims. The other specified race and sex categories share less in the Saturday toll: white males make up 16 per cent of those

[1] Brearley, *Homicide in the U.S.*, p. 199.

TABLE 9

DAILY DISTRIBUTION OF CRIMINAL HOMICIDE, BY RACE
AND SEX OF VICTIM, PHILADELPHIA, 1948–1952

(In per cent)

Day	Both Races			Negro			White		
	Total	Male	Female	Total	Male	Female	Total	Male	Female
Monday	9.7	8.2	15.1	8.9	7.6	13.5	12.4	10.2	18.6
Tuesday	6.9	6.9	7.2	6.1	5.7	7.3	9.3	10.2	7.0
Wednesday	9.4	8.5	12.2	9.1	7.9	13.5	9.9	10.2	9.3
Thursday	8.2	5.1	18.0	5.9	3.6	13.5	14.3	9.3	27.9
Friday	17.0	17.6	15.1	16.9	16.9	16.7	17.4	19.5	11.6
Saturday	31.8	35.2	20.9	35.6	38.7	25.0	21.7	25.4	11.6
Sunday	16.8	18.5	11.5	17.6	19.6	10.3	14.9	15.3	13.9
Total	100.0	100.0	100.0	100.0	100.0	100.0	100.0	100.0	100.0
	(588)	(449)	(139)	(427)	(331)	(96)	(161)	(118)	(43)

killed on Saturday, and account for 20 per cent of all victims; Negro females comprise 13 per cent of Saturday homicides but 16 per cent of all homicides; and white females make up 3 per cent of Saturday killings but 7 per cent of all homicides.

Except for white females, who were killed more frequently and inexplicably on Thursdays, all the other groups were more frequently killed on Saturday than on any other day of the week. Thirty-nine per cent of Negro males, 25 per cent of both white males and of Negro females became victims on a Saturday. Only 12 per cent of white females were victimized on this day, but 28 per cent were killed on Thursday.

Because the Negro male is the largest contributor to the high frequency of homicides on a Saturday, and because his group is positively associated with stabbings, it is to be expected that Saturdays have more stabbings than any of the other methods of inflicting death. Of all homicides, 39 per cent were caused by stabbing, but this method accounts for 46 per cent of Saturday slayings. Sixty shootings account for one-third of all Saturday killings, which is the same proportion as that among all homicides. Thirty-four beatings took place on Saturday (18 per cent), an amount slightly less than the proportion among all deaths (22 per cent). Finally, the Negro male's contribution to Saturday's high is more readily evident by the fact that of the 85 stabbings on this day, 71, or 84 per cent, were inflicted on him.

TABLE 10
DISTRIBUTION OF CRIMINAL HOMICIDE BY FOUR SIX-HOUR
PERIODS OF THE DAY, AND BY RACE AND SEX OF VICTIM,
PHILADELPHIA, 1948–1952

(In per cent)

Hours	Both Races			Negro			White		
	Total	Male	Female	Total	Male	Female	Total	Male	Femal
8:00 P.M.– 1:59 A.M.	49.7	50.6	46.7	53.6	53.5	54.2	39.1	42.4	30.2
2:00 A.M.– 7:59 A.M.	16.5	16.2	17.3	15.0	15.1	14.6	20.5	19.5	23.3
8:00 A.M.– 1:59 P.M.	9.2	7.6	14.4	8.0	6.6	12.5	12.4	10.2	18.6
2:00 P.M.– 7:59 P.M.	24.7	25.6	21.6	23.4	24.8	18.7	28.0	27.9	27.9
Total	100.0 (588)	100.0 (449)	100.0 (139)	100.0 (427)	100.0 (331)	100.0 (96)	100.0 (161)	100.0 (118)	100.0 (43)

Distribution by hours of the day (Table 10) has been
tabulated for quarter periods, or four six-hour divisions.[1]
The observed distribution is a highly *significant* one, and cannot be attributable to chance variations. The most lethal
hours are between 8:00 P.M. and 2:00 A.M. which contain
50 per cent of all criminal homicides. The second most
dangerous period, 2:00 P.M. to 8:00 P.M., has only half as
many homicides as the first period, or 25 per cent. The
period between 2:00 A.M. and 8:00 A.M. ranks third with
17 per cent; while the least dangerous period, between
8:00 A.M. and 2:00 P.M., has only 9 per cent, or less than one-
fifth the number of homicides during the highest period.
Although half of all felonious deaths occurred between the
hours of 8:00 P.M. and 2:00 A.M., a larger proportion of Negroes
of either sex (54 per cent each) than of whites (42 per cent

[1] It has been necessary, in the process of gathering data, to take account
of Daylight Saving Time, which begins 2:00 A.M. on the last Sunday in April
and ends 2:00 A.M. the last Sunday in September of each year in Philadelphia.
When the city is observing advanced time, officers of the Homicide Squad
record the time on some forms according to Eastern Standard Time, but on
others according to Daylight Saving Time. Because the social habits of most
of the population follow the same temporal sequences during Daylight as
during Standard Time, the decision to use the former when recording the
time of the offense for purposes of this study is apparent. Only in this way
can the working, sleeping, eating, and leisure-time hours be the same for the
whole year.

males and 30 per cent females) were slain during these hours.

Cognizance should be taken of the fact that a division of criminal homicides into days of the week and six-hour periods of the day are purely arbitrary delineations. They fail to take account of the fact that a set of circumstances (such as a drinking party that ends with a drunken brawl and a killing) that has been put in motion during the late hours of one day but which results in homicide about 12:30 A.M. the following day, does not, when officially recorded, give credit to events of the first day. Usually a homicide occurring during the first few hours of a day is the culmination of factors begun the previous evening. From this point of view, and in terms of social and personal interrelationships, the very early morning hours are merely an extension of the preceding day. A thorough reading of 588 cases leads to the conclusion that the 97 homicides which occurred between 2:00 A.M. and 8:00 A.M. may logically be added to the 292 cases that were committed between 8:00 P.M. and 2:00 A.M., resulting in a total of 389 homicides that occurred during an important "social time span."

As will be discussed later, drinking is a common accompaniment of crimes of personal violence, and Friday and Saturday nights are traditional periods for social drinking and drinking sprees. Homicide is generally committed against persons who are relatively close friends or relatives, and the opportunities for such personal contacts are probably much greater during the leisure hours of evenings and week-ends. These facts, combined with others to be shown below, make the week-end the most dangerous period of a week. It is interesting to note that out of 100 homicides on Friday, for instance, 50 took place within the four-hour period between 8:00 P.M. and midnight. Between 8:00 P.M. Friday and midnight Sunday there were, during the five years under review, 380 criminal homicides, but from the beginning of Monday morning to 8:00 P.M. Friday, there were only 208. Thus, on the average, 65 per cent of all homicides occurred during the shorter time span of 52 hours, while only 35 per cent occurred during the longer time span of 116 hours.

Days and Hours Noted in Other Studies and Reports

In almost all studies, distributions of criminal homicide by days and hours are similar to the pattern for Philadelphia. Unfortunately, detailed analyses by race and sex are not generally provided, so that comparisons and contrasts with Philadelphia must be made on the basis of total cases.

Harlan's study of Birmingham (1937–1944) shows that the incidence of criminal homicide reaches its peak there on week-ends and at night, as is true in Philadelphia:

> Of the 500 homicides 123 (24.6 per cent) occur on Saturdays and 136 (27.2 per cent) occur on Sundays. No other day of the week shows any such concentrations, the range for the remaining days of the week being from 44 (8.8 per cent) on Mondays to 56 (11.2 per cent) on Fridays. Most of the murders occur during the night hours; thus 53.4 per cent take place between the hours of 8:00 P.M. and 2:00 A.M. Twenty-five per cent of the murders are perpetrated between 6:00 P.M. Saturday and 6:00 A.M. Sunday morning, making this the most lethal twelve hour period during the week.[1]

For 212 criminal homicides in St. Louis (1949–1951), Meyers reports a similar distribution, except that Wednesday is the day of lowest frequency instead of Tuesday, as in Philadelphia:

> St. Louis murder and non-negligent manslaughter had a definite pattern of occurrence on certain days of the week. . . . Wednesday invariably was the low day and produced the low aggregate for the three years, Saturday was the peak day. There was a build up to the Saturday peak and a tapering down to the Wednesday trough. It is interesting to note that the days Monday, Tuesday, Thursday and Friday produce more than double Wednesday's offenses while Sunday has four times as many offenses and Saturday more than five times as many offenses as Wednesday.
>
> There is a very marked pattern in the occurrence of this offense through the twenty-four hours of the day. This is most strikingly illustrated if the day be divided into four 6-hour periods. The three year total of offenses indicates that

[1] Harlan, *op. cit.*, p. 742.

in the four o'clock in the morning to ten o'clock in the morning period, the fewest offenses were committed, the total being only 15. In the next six hour period, from 10 o'clock in the morning to 4 o'clock in the afternoon about twice as many offenses occurred as in the lowest six hour period. The total here was 32 offenses. The 4 o'clock to 10 o'clock 6-hour period saw 71 offenses or almost five times as many as occurred in the 6-hour period with the fewest offenses. Finally, the 10 o'clock in the evening to 4 o'clock in the morning produced exactly six times as many offenses as did the period with the fewest. Murder is clearly established to be an offense that occurs during the night hours rather than the daylight hours.[1]

Porterfield and Talbert report briefly on a "study of 222 cases of homicide which occurred in a city of the Southwest during the years 1946–1950."[2]

Two thirds of our 222 victims met their doom between 7:00 P.M. and 1:00 A.M., which constitutes but one fourth of the complete round of the clock. Nobody died at lunch, though several did yield up the ghost just before time for breakfast. Most victims (54 per cent) also managed to get killed on Saturday and Sunday. . . .[3]

For a select group of 208 murderers sentenced to death in England and Wales between 1886 and 1905, MacDonald found a temporal pattern: "The highest number (39) was on Saturday, the lowest (23) on Sunday. About one-fifth of the murders were committed between 10 P.M. and midnight and nearly half between the hours of 8 P.M. and 2 A.M."[4] All types of criminal homicides in Philadelphia were combined for purposes of showing temporal associations so that only a crude comparison can be made with the time during which homicides were committed by MacDonald's group of "murderers sentenced to death." Only 7 offenders from Philadelphia were sentenced to death. At any rate, the author's reference to a high incidence of murder on Saturdays and

---

[1] Meyers, Jr., *op. cit.*, pp. 19–23.
[2] A. L. Porterfield and R. H. Talbert, *Mid-Century Crime in Our Culture*, p. 47. No other information is given by these authors regarding the specific location of this study.
[3] *Ibid.*
[4] MacDonald, *op. cit.*, p. 95.

111

during the hours between 8:00 P.M. and 2:00 A.M. indicates a pattern similar to Philadelphia. However, MacDonald noted that Sundays had the lowest incidence for murder. This fact suggests that the high percentages usually recorded for week-ends (Friday, Saturday, and Sunday) reflect, primarily, the high incidence of unpremeditated offenses. A partial confirmation of this suggestion may be found in an analysis of homicide in Finland. Verkko[1] carried out an investigation covering a period of thirty-seven years (1895–1931), which included persons sentenced to capital punishment and to imprisonment by the courts for crimes against life (excluding infanticide and negligent manslaughter), and, in addition, those sentenced to prison for "battery resulting in grievous bodily harm." Offenses were divided into: murders (1,025), and "other outrageous crimes of violence (6,268 cases)."

> The percentages . . . provide striking evidence of the differences between murder and other crimes against life and outrageous crimes of violence. Murder is fairly evenly divided between the days of the week, the daily percentages varying between 10 and 15 only. The case is different with other crimes lacking the premeditated character of murder. Nearly a third of these crimes, or 31.5 per cent, were committed on a Sunday. If we add to this percentage those committed on a Saturday and a Monday, the percentage of crimes committed during the week-end jumps up to 61.2 per cent, or roughly three-fifths of all the cases. . . .[2]

Because Philadelphia folkways consider Friday evening the beginning and Sunday night the ending of a week-end, and because 50 of the 100 homicides recorded for Friday took place between 8:00 P.M. and midnight, it is logical to use Friday, Saturday, and Sunday combined as the basis for comparison of the incidence of homicide during week-ends. In Philadelphia 66 per cent of the homicides occurred during a period beginning Friday and ending Sunday midnight. Most

---

[1] Verkko, *Homicides and Suicides in Finland and Their Dependence on National Character*, p. 82.
[2] *Ibid.*

of this percentage would be classified under Verkko's group of "other crimes against life," and not under "murder." An inspection of Verkko's tables shows that 58 per cent of the offenses in the former category occurred over the week-end, whereas 44 per cent of the murders in England and Wales were perpetrated during this period, and even fewer, 37 per cent, of such offenses were committed in Finland over the week-end. It appears, therefore, that "the difference between murder, on the one hand, and other crimes against life and crimes of violence on the other, is, if possible, still more distinctly clarified if we consider the day of the week on which the crime was committed."[1]

Time Between Assault and Death

The previous discussion of temporal distributions has been concerned with the months, days, and hours during which homicidal assaults occurred. But the victim may not die for several hours, days, or even weeks after an assault. If he does not die within a year and a day, according to common law, charges of homicide cannot be brought against the perpetrator.[2]

The "long form" used by the Philadelphia Homicide Squad makes it possible to measure the amount of time that elapsed between commission of the homicidal assault and death of the victim. The data are probably as reliable as can be expected, considering the different personnel and circumstances involved in recording precise time designations. In most cases, a fairly accurate determination of the time when the assault was committed is possible. The victim may live long enough to give some information, and witnesses are usually able to corroborate one another sufficiently so that a precise time of assault can be determined. The suspect may confess his responsibility for the homicide and has, therefore, little reason to falsify the moment of assault. If he does not

---

[1] *Ibid.*

[2] "The rule that death must occur within a year and a day of the act that caused it does not apply to involuntary manslaughter. Com. v. Evaul, 5 D and C. 105 (1924)" (William F. Hoffman, *Pennsylvania Criminal Law and Criminal Procedure*, p. 131).

confess to the crime, the suspect often admits to some degree of participation in the struggle and is aware of the time of assault. In some cases the police are at the scene of the crime, and in these greater accuracy is possible. Death is usually pronounced in the hospital to which the victim is taken, but in many cases he is dead on arrival. Usually the police are informed several minutes after the assault, and the victim is immediately transported to a hospital. When some time elapses between assault and notification to the police, the victim may have been dead several hours, days, or even weeks. Under such circumstances, medical examination is necessary to provide a general range of time within which the victim probably died as a result of the assault. When a victim dies at the scene of the crime before the eyes of the perpetrator, and if the defendant admits his responsibility, a precise time is usually available. If a victim dies in a hospital bed, the time of death recorded is considered very accurate. A bullet or stab wound directly through the heart or head usually causes instantaneous death. Obviously, errors in determining either the time of the assault, or the exact moment of death, or both, find their way into police reports. But (*a*) because of the importance of these time factors in police investigation, (*b*) because the medical examiner must record such information, (*c*) because the time of death may be important to insurance companies, and (*d*) because these items become matters of public record and are included in the proceedings of the court trial, we may assume that diligent efforts are made to achieve accuracy.[1] At any rate, the following analysis of the time that elapses between commission of the crime and death of the victim is presented with cautious acceptance of the available data. (Table 11.)

[1] For further details on determining the time of assault and of death, see *The Medicolegal Necropsy* (symposium held at the 12th Annual Convention of The American Society of Clinical Pathologists, June 9, 1933), edited by Thomas B. Magath, Baltimore: The Williams and Wilkins Company, 1934; also, LeMoyne Snyder, *Homicide Investigation*, pp. 29–42; and Richard Ford, "Critical Times in Murder Investigation (Time of Assault, Incapacitation, and Death)," *Journal of Criminal Law, Criminology, and Police Science*, 43: 672–678.

TABLE 11

PER CENT OF TOTAL VICTIMS WHO DIED WITHIN VARIOUS
PERIODS OF TIME BETWEEN ASSAULT AND DEATH,
ACCORDING TO METHOD BY WHICH VICTIM MET
DEATH, PHILADELPHIA, 1948–1952

Time Period	Method Per Cent of Total				
	Total	Stabbing	Shooting	Beating	Other
Less than 10 minutes	30.8	28.5	47.9	6.3	39.5
10 minutes to 1 hour	25.7	39.5	22.7	7.8	18.4
Less than 1 hour	56.5	68.0	70.6	14.1	57.9
1 hour to 1 day	21.4	18.0	17.5	32.8	23.7
Less than 1 day	77.9	86.0	88.1	46.9	81.6
More than 1 day	16.8	8.0	11.3	42.2	13.2
Uncertain	5.2	6.1	.5	10.9	5.3
	(588)	(228)	(194)	(128)	(38)

Within ten minutes after being assaulted, the victim died
in 48 per cent of the homicides caused by shooting, in 40 per
cent caused by one of the miscellaneous methods, in 29 per
cent due to stabbing, and in only 6 per cent due to beating.
Within an hour after a homicidal attack, the victim was dead
in 71 per cent of the cases if he had been shot, in 68 per cent
of the cases if he had been stabbed, in 58 per cent if one of the
miscellaneous methods had been used, and in only 14 per
cent of the cases if beaten.

By the end of the first day after his encounter with the
perpetrator, the victim assaulted by shooting was deceased
in 88 per cent of the cases, by stabbing in 86 per cent of the
cases, by one of the miscellaneous methods in 82 per cent of
the cases, and by beating in 47 per cent of the cases. More
victims of beating lived beyond the first day than was true
for victims of any other type of assault. For all classes, about
one-third of the victims were dead within ten minutes after
assault, nearly three-fifths before the first hour had passed,
and four-fifths within a day. Of the 17 per cent who lived
beyond the first day, 12 per cent died within ten days after
the homicidal attack, while the remaining 5 per cent lived
more than ten days.[1]

[1] For 31 of the 588 criminal homicides the precise time of assault and/or
death was unknown or not reported.

A Final Note Regarding Time

Examination of the time span between assault and death raises an interesting question: How many aggravated assaults, assaults with intent to kill, and other violent assaults, are today prevented from becoming classified as criminal homicides because of quicker communication with the police, more rapid transportation to a hospital, and more effective medical care for the victim?

General homicide rates for the nation and for Philadelphia are lower today than a quarter of a century ago.[1] Hoffman[2] reported that for 28 cities the homicide mortality rate per 100,000 in 1923 was 10.2, and in 1924, 10.3. For Philadelphia in 1923 there were 180 homicides, or a rate of 9.4 compared, for example, to a mean number of 125 homicides for the period 1948–1952, and a mean annual rate of 6.0. In a recent article on the extent of capital crimes in the United States, George Vold[3] reviews the comparative trends of (*a*) murder and non-negligent manslaughter recorded by the Federal Bureau of Investigation in *Uniform Crime Reports*, and (*b*) homicide rates recorded by the Office of Vital Statistics in *Special Reports*. From 1933 to 1951 there was a gradual decrease in both rates, the former moving from 7.1 in 1933 to 4.9 in 1951, and the latter declining from 9.7 in 1933 to 4.5 in 1951. The author concludes: "The general tendency

[1] Sutherland, comparing rates in the area covered by registrations in 1905, found the rate of 2.22 for 1905–1909 had increased only to 2.86 in 1920–22. Moreover, he found that in 1922 twenty-nine out of sixty-one cities with a population of 100,000 or more in the death registration area had lower homicide rates than in 1912, while twenty-nine had higher rates and three had just the same. In the same year, of twenty-three states that were in the registration area in 1912, one had the same rate, eleven had higher rates, and eleven had lower rates. Thus, homicide rates had not appreciably increased in these sixty-one cities and twenty-three states. In addition it must be remembered that in the later years the statistics of homicide were more complete and accurate than in the earlier years because doctors were becoming more familiar with registration practice and therefore were more likely to report homicides accurately. The apparent increase of homicide rates in the census mortality figures may be due to the fact that the death registration area had increased by addition of territory in the West and South, where homicide is more frequent than in the East. Hence, while it is possible that there has been an increase in criminal homicide in this country, it cannot with our present knowledge be proved. (E. H. Sutherland, "Murder and the Death Penalty," *Journal of Criminal Law and Criminology* [February, 1925] 16: 522.)

[2] F. L. Hoffman, *The Homicide Problem*, pp. 96–100.

[3] Vold, *op. cit.*, pp. 1–7.

to a downward trend during this period of uniform reporting is unmistakable. There was a brief upturn in both indexes in 1945 and 1946, with continuous decreases since that time. The rates for 1951 are again at the all-time low levels."[1]

Do these comparisons indicate that we place a higher value on human life today than a quarter of a century ago? It is probably impossible to answer such a question quantitatively, but a negative answer is suspected, primarily because of the great increases in such offenses against the person as aggravated assault and rape that have been officially recorded in the last decade or so. For example, the *Uniform Crime Reports* for 1948 compare the amount of aggravated assault and rape reported from 373 cities, each with a population of 25,000 or more that year, with the 1938–1941 prewar levels, and show an absolute increase of 69 per cent in the former and 50 per cent in the latter offense.[2] These data combine to suggest that something other than a greater repugnance to commit crimes of personal violence has entered our mores. Of course, many variables are involved in changing rates of homicide, such as the changing age composition of the population, business cycles, etc. But because crimes of violence against the person, excluding homicide, appear to have increased during the last two decades, it is logical to assume that if these gross social variables affect homicide, they should affect other crimes of violence in the same way. Perhaps the following explanation, which remains on the level of an *a priori*, untested assumption, provides a partial explanation of the lower homicide rates in recent years.

We have noted that the time between assault of the victim and pronouncement of death varies according to the method by which death was inflicted. It would be interesting to have this same type of information for a period twenty or twenty-five years ago. It would also be valuable to know the recovery rate for those who are today grievously assaulted but who would have probably died under medical and other conditions of a generation ago.

[1] *Ibid.*, p. 2.
[2] *Uniform Crime Reports*, 1948, 19: 79.

It may be that three major factors present in our culture today, and absent a generation ago, make it possible for many victims of aggravated assault and other serious offenses against the person to recover from their wounds, to continue living and thereby swell the police statistics of major assaults, while simultaneously reducing the number of criminal homicides. These three factors are:

(1) quick communication with the police by telephone and radio shortly after a homicidal attack;
(2) rapid transportation to a hospital after a serious stabbing, shooting, beating, etc.; and
(3) advanced medical technology, such as the development of the many "wonder drugs" since 1935.

A complete analysis of these three factors goes beyond the confines of the present study, but the importance of these factors today hardly can be denied. In most cases of assault crimes, either the police are notified almost immediately, or someone is available to transport the victim to a nearby hospital. The motorized police in most urban communities are thus capable of getting an assault victim to the hospital within a very short period of time. (Upon notification, the police in Philadelphia arrive at the scene within an average of two minutes.) Such speed of communication and transportation was undoubtedly less possible twenty-five years ago.

Once in the hospital, a victim of an assault probably has a much better chance of recovery and survival today than earlier. Development during the middle thirties and more extensive use since 1940 of sulfonamids and antibiotics are partially responsible for the differential recovery rate. Since 1950 cortisone is used as a standard shock treatment in many acute stages of stress, in cases of severe body damage, and as a means of providing a general supportive effect to the body. Within the past fifteen or more years there has been a virtual revolution in preventing blood and other fluid loss. Fluid replacement therapy today means that probably many lives are saved that would have been lost before because of our ability to maintain fluid and electrolyte balance in proper chemical relationships. Today, there are better emergency teams in our hospitals, capable of preventing and controlling infection and shock after a stabbing or shooting or other assault. Techniques in surgical repair, whereby whole sections of blood vessels and nerve sheaths are replaced, are amazing developments that have matured within the past ten years or less. Heart manipulation and chemical or electrical stimulation after cardiac arrest are now almost common practice in our major hospitals. The alcoholically debilitated victim can now be supported with vitamins, hormones, and other means so that life is often sustained when such would not have been possible previously. Studies of the changes in mortality rates resulting from combat wounds during World War I, World War II, and the Korean War,[1] add convincing evidence to the assumed importance that these medical advances have had in reducing homicide rates in the civilian population.

Thus, quick communication, rapid transportation, and such medical technological advances as those mentioned above as well as many others, may mean that many cases of physical assault are kept in the column of aggravated assault statistics and are thereby prevented from being listed as criminal homicides. At any rate, empirical research testing the hypothesis suggested by these factors might be useful in explaining the decrease in homicide.

[1] Warner F. Bowers, Frederick T. Marchant, and Kenneth H. Judy, "The Present Story on Battle Casualties from Korea," *Surgery, Gynecology, and Obstetrics* (November, 1951), 93: 529–542.

7

SPATIAL PATTERNS

THE number of criminal homicides by police districts or by census tracts is of local interest only to Philadelphia.[1] As interesting as ecological analyses have been in past criminological research, and as useful as such an approach may be for the study of homicide, it is not the purpose of this chapter to analyze the present data by means of an ecological approach.

The primary focus of attention in the present chapter concerns a spatial factor in criminal homicide almost entirely overlooked by previous research: the specific place where the fatal assault is sustained. This factor, as is shown below, may play an important role in the homicide drama. There are spatial minutiae of social living to which the victim and offender in criminal homicide are intimately related.[2] In

[1] Tabulation of the number of homicides by police districts was difficult because of several district mergers that occurred during the five years under examination. These mergers are brought up to date (as of April, 1955), and the number of criminal homicides according to the present police districts may be found in Appendix II. The distribution of criminal homicides by census tract areas is shown in Appendix II, p. 387. Also see Appendix II, p. 386 for a map showing police districts in Philadelphia. For precise determination of the number and letter of each census tract see Map P.C.P.C. 451.2–50. Five census tracts contain more than 20 criminal homicides each. They are: 32-A with 27 homicides; 30-A with 22 homicides; 20-B with 22 homicides; 20-D with 21 homicides; and 7-B with 21 homicides. These 5 areas have a combined population of 56,511 inhabitants; 48,669 Negroes and 7,842 whites. Although the combined population comprises less than 3 per cent of the total Philadelphia population, the 113 homicides committed in these 5 areas make up over 19 per cent of the 588 of the whole city. Moreover, while the city has a rate of 5.7 per 100,000 population, these 5 areas have a rate of 40, or 7 times greater.

[2] The decision to analyze the specific place where the homicide occurs was based upon a section in J. H. S. Bossard, *The Sociology of Child Development*, New York: Harper and Brothers, 1948, Chapter XVII, "Families Under Stress," pp. 377–380, where the author discusses the physical bases of home life and refers to some of the factors included in the present study. For a recent ecological analysis of homicide, see H. A. Bullock, "Urban Homicide in Theory and Fact," *Journal of Criminal Law, Criminology, and Police Science* (January–February, 1955), 45: 565–575.

the personal microcosm of his immediate environment, the individual usually eats in a kitchen or restaurant, sleeps in a bedroom, visits friends in a living room, meets drinking companions in a taproom, goes to a third-floor apartment by a stairway, and walks along a public street. Regardless of the poverty or wealth of the individual, the modernity or antiquity of his home, these places are usually part of his most immediate environment. Because notation of places where homicides occur is made by the police, it has been possible to classify the places and to note whether an act of homicide is more likely to occur in one place rather than in another. Police files yield more such data than any other original source because descriptions of the premises, and inclusion of diagrams, maps, or detailed photographs of the crime scene are part of the dossier for each case.

Units of analysis used in the present discussion include the following:

(*a*) bedroom,
(*b*) kitchen,
(*c*) living room,
(*d*) stairway,
(*e*) highway (public street, alley, or field),
(*f*) taproom,
(*g*) commercial place other than a taproom, and,
(*h*) other.

It is sometimes difficult to determine exactly where the crime occurred. For example, in a small apartment, the eating, sleeping, and living quarters may be in one or two rooms. In such cases, the functional use of space at the time of the onset of assault was determined. If a stabbing occurred during a meal or while the wife was cooking, and the entire living area was only a one-room flat, a "kitchen" designation was given. If a husband, under the same living conditions, beat his wife while they were in bed, the place of the crime was designated as having occurred in the bedroom. If a man shot his wife in the bedroom and she staggered down the steps to the living room, where she died, again the bedroom was used because the assault occurred in that place. In short, the locale used in this analysis of distribution by place was that where the major wound was inflicted. It may be that the victim and offender began fighting in one place, but the fatal shot, stab, or blow occurred in another. Reliance upon the medical examiner's report as to which was the fatal wound was then necessary. If the victim was slightly cut in the kitchen, but fatally stabbed in the living room, the latter place was used. If the victim survived an assault for several days or weeks before dying, if he had been stabbed in the kitchen, shot in the living room, and beaten on the front stairway, the report of the medical examiner giving the immediate cause of death due to one of these methods determined the designation. In a few cases the victim was assaulted in the doorway between two rooms, as, for example, between a kitchen and a bedroom. The direction and reason for his movement were criteria used to determine the particular place in the house where the homicide occurred. If he was preparing to sit down to an evening meal while passing through the doorway, the kitchen was used. If he was about to retire for the night and was facing the bedroom, the designation was obvious. If the homicide occurred in an hotel room, there was usually no doubt, judging by the relationship between victim and slayer, that a bedroom should be the designation. If the assault occurred directly outside a taproom and if either the victim or the offender had just patronized the bar, a "taproom" category was used. The "other" classification refers to such places as a cellar, an abandoned house, a bathroom, and other unusual places of occurrence.

Although a few examples of relatively unique circumstances have been given to illustrate the problems of precise categorization, most cases are sufficiently clear so that no doubt arises regarding the place where the homicide occurred, or what events took place prior to the slaying. As is shown below, spatial distributions reveal much about the nature of the homicide: the race and sex of victim and offender, the weapon used to inflict death, the hour of the day, the inter-

122

personal relationship between the slayer and the slain, the motive, and other variables.

The following analysis is based on the frequency distribution of total victims, and does not actually measure the chances of being killed in one place rather than another, relative to the amount of time victims spend in these places. This latter type of information is not available. The amount of time spent in different places outside the home, and in different rooms in the home probably varies by race and sex, time of the day, day of the week, etc.

There is a *significant* association between place where the crime occurred and the race and sex of both victims and offenders. (Tables 12 and 13.) In terms of total cases, the most dangerous single place is on the highway (public street, alley, or field) where 30 per cent of all victims met death.

TABLE 12

PLACE OF OCCURRENCE OF CRIMINAL HOMICIDE,
BY RACE AND SEX OF VICTIM,
PHILADELPHIA, 1948–1952

(In per cent)

PLACE		RACE		SEX	
	Total	Negro	White	Male	Female
Bedroom	19.0	19.0	19.3	14.3	34.5
Kitchen	12.1	13.1	9.3	11.1	15.1
Living Room	12.1	12.9	9.9	12.3	11.5
Stairway	6.8	8.7	1.9	6.9	6.5
Highway	30.1	31.4	26.7	33.2	20.1
Taproom	8.2	7.5	9.9	9.6	3.6
Other Commercial Place	8.0	4.9	16.2	8.5	6.5
Other	3.7	2.6	6.8	4.2	2.2
Total	100.0	100.0	100.0	100.0	100.0
	(588)	(427)	(161)	(449)	(139)
In the Home of:					
Both	40.9	40.2	43.3	34.5	54.7
Victim	26.9	24.8	34.3	26.7	27.4
Offender	16.9	18.4	11.9	21.4	7.4
Another	15.3	16.6	10.5	17.5	10.5
Total	100.0	100.0	100.0	100.0	100.0
	(301)	(234)	(67)	(206)	(95)
In the Home	51.2	54.8	41.6	45.9	68.3
Not in the Home	48.8	45.2	58.4	54.1	31.7
Total	100.0	100.0	100.0	100.0	100.0
	(588)	(427)	(161)	(449)	(139)

123

TABLE 13

PLACE OF OCCURRENCE OF CRIMINAL HOMICIDE,
BY RACE AND SEX OF OFFENDER,
PHILADELPHIA, 1948–1952

(In per cent)

PLACE	Total	RACE		SEX	
		Negro	White	Male	Female
Bedroom	17.7	18.0	16.9	16.0	25.7
Kitchen	11.1	11.6	9.7	7.2	29.4
Living Room	12.6	13.1	11.0	13.3	9.2
Stairway	6.9	7.7	4.5	6.4	9.2
Highway	31.4	33.2	26.0	35.3	12.8
Taproom	8.1	7.1	11.0	9.0	3.7
Other Commercial Place	8.7	7.5	12.3	9.0	7.3
Other	3.5	1.9	8.4	3.7	2.8
Total	100.0	100.0	100.0	100.0	100.0
	(621)	(467)	(154)	(512)	(109)
In the Home of:					
Both	39.9	37.8	47.8	32.3	59.8
Victim	27.9	26.9	31.3	33.6	12.6
Offender	17.4	18.1	14.9	16.2	20.7
Another	14.9	17.3	6.0	17.9	6.9
Total	100.0	100.0	100.0	100.0	100.0
	(316)	(249)	(67)	(229)	(87)
In the Home	50.9	53.3	43.5	44.7	79.8
Not in the Home	49.1	46.7	56.5	55.3	20.2
Total	100.0	100.0	100.0	100.0	100.0
	(621)	(467)	(154)	(512)	(109)

The distributions of victims and offenders who are involved in highway killings are similar for all race and sex groups except females. For example, a little over 30 per cent of Negroes, both as victims and as offenders, were involved in criminal homicides that took place on a public street. Similarly, slightly over one-fourth of all whites both killed and were killed in that place; and approximately one-third of males, in general, participated in a killing there. But women show a divergency from this pattern, for one-fifth of them were victims on the highway while only an eighth committed the offense there.

On the highway, most Negro males were stabbed or shot, while most white males were victims of beatings. White males were more often victimized by beatings (47 per cent) than by any other method and more often killed on the highway (31 per cent) than in any other single place. Furthermore, when a white male was slain on the highway, he was beaten in 23 out of the 37 cases. Like the Negro male, the Negro female was most likely to be stabbed if killed on the highway. (See Appendix I, Tables 7 and 8.)

The higher proportion of males killed on the highway probably is accounted for by the greater number of men on the streets at night, particularly during the time period of highest frequency of homicide—between eight o'clock in the evening and two in the morning. Most women are reluctant and unlikely to venture out alone into the dark impersonal anonymity of the late hours in a large metropolitan community. Such is not the case with males. As groups of young fellows moving erratically (and in many cases, erotically) from one place of amusement, adventure, or misadventure, to another, they roam the streets late at night and early in the morning. Male groups of this sort are especially likely to congregate on the streets Friday and Saturday evenings when, as we have seen, homicides have highest frequency. The female is escorted home and deposited there, while her male companion still must travel the streets to his own domicile, and on his way frequently meets other men— friends or strangers—with whom he may get drunk, exchange derogatory remarks, and become involved in violent combat. If married, the woman is the one more likely to stay home to take care of the children while the husband goes to the local taproom either to escape domestic boredom and conflict or to enjoy the conviviality of associates at the bar—and, according to the statistics, to be killed there three times more frequently than women.

The bedroom has the dubious honor of being the most dangerous room in the home and the place of second highest frequency of criminal deaths. Nearly a fifth of all victims were killed in the bedroom. But the most striking fact about bedroom slayings is the *significantly* higher proportion of women who were slain there compared to men. As a matter of fact, more women were killed in the bedroom than in any other designated place. Only 14 per cent of male victims in this study were killed in the bedroom, while 35 per cent—proportionately over twice as many—of females were killed there. Furthermore, the converging factors that result in homicide appear to occur more often in the bedroom when women *commit* homicide too, because 26 per cent of all women killed their victims in this room compared to only 16 per cent of the men who killed. Second only to the kitchen, women were offenders most frequently in the bedroom. We may note again a differential between victims and offenders, for although a quarter of all women committed homicide in the bedroom, over a third were slain in this place. It is striking that white females constitute only 7 per cent of total victims killed in all places, but make up 15 per cent of the 112 persons killed in a bedroom.

This high proportion of bedroom slayings among females is associated with the fact that 87 per cent of all female victims were slain by males and 84 per cent of all female offenders slew males, and that the predominant motives inciting these interrelationships, as will be described in detail later, were those involving arguments concerned with sex, love, and family matters. Arguments, emotional conflicts, tensions that arise before a couple enters the bedroom are ordinarily resolved in order to enjoy the primary purposes of the room. The primary purposes of the bedroom—sleep and sexual intimacies—appear to become secondary, however, for a high proportion of women who are criminally killed. In those cases where the interpersonal conflicts are carried into the bedroom, or that arise there in the first place, the sleep or sex drive which conducted the couple there becomes subordinated to the tension issues between them. Thus, the physical proximity required largely by institutional expectation in the case of sleep, and of biological necessity in the case of sex, provides a setting in the bedroom for unresolved conflicts. Most women who kill, kill their mates or loved ones, and since they are not generally in direct contact with their husbands during the working hours of the day, it is likely that when domestic quarrels, pangs of jealousy, or desire for revenge arise they occur during the evening hours, and, if unresolved, are taken to the bedroom.

Finally, either because there is no expectation of the need or desire to commit homicide in the bedroom and, hence, no necessity for having a deadly weapon available there; or because a physical assault without such weapons more readily suggests itself to the perpetrator, beatings have higher frequency among female victims in the bedroom than in any other place. Of course, as has been alluded to elsewhere, the normally greater physical power with which men are endowed compared to women means that men generally need nothing more than their bare hands to subdue, either temporarily or permanently, women with whom they have a physically violent encounter. When a Negro female was killed in a bedroom, for example, in one-third of the cases she was beaten to death; and when a white female was killed in a bedroom, she was the victim of a beating in over half the cases.

The kitchen and living room share equally (12 per cent each) in ranking third among the places where homicide occurs. Once more, sex differences are *significant*, and patterns of homicidal behavior are obvious particularly with respect to kitchen slayings. Among female victims, 15 per cent were killed in the kitchen compared to 11 per cent among male victims. But most striking is the fact that 29 per cent of female offenders slew their victims in the kitchen compared to only 7 per cent of male offenders. Thus, women used the kitchen to kill four times more frequently than did men and more often than any other single place. The fact that proportionately twice as many women killed than were killed in this room should not be overlooked as a victim-offender differential. The foregoing discussion regarding the inter-sex nature of most homicides involving a female is also applicable to the present concern with the kitchen. As a frequent family meeting place, as a place for family discussion during which tempers may rise and frustrations accumulated during the day may find vent among primary group members; as a place where wives raise questions about the family budget

127

and suggest that their husbands are spending too much money on liquor and perhaps other women; and as a place where deadly weapons are handy, the kitchen more often than any other room provides a setting for women who commit criminal homicide. When a homicide occurs in a kitchen, it is likely to be a stabbing in two-thirds of the cases, due undoubtedly to the ready accessibility of a butcher knife or other such kitchen instrument. When a Negro male was killed in a kitchen, he was never beaten, but in 33 out of 41 cases he was stabbed to death. Of the 15 Negro females killed in a kitchen, 10 were stabbed.

The frequency distributions, by race and sex, of persons who are killed or who kill in the living room are quite similar, and for all groups the living room comprises about 12 per cent of the various places where homicide occurs. The most important thing that may be said about living-room deaths is that shooting was the usual method, and was almost twice as frequent as stabbing and over four times as common as beating.

Although only 7 per cent of all homicides occur on a stairway, this proportion is probably high relative to the amount of time people spend going up and down steps and relative to the amount of time spent in various rooms in the house. In almost all cases, these were indoor stairways used in multiple-dwelling units. Proportionately, many more Negroes (9 per cent) than whites (2 per cent) were killed on a stairway. This difference may be due to the fact that more Negroes than whites live in multiple-dwelling units. Moreover, the typical Negro multiple-dwelling unit, it is believed, has a greater amount of inter-apartment traffic than does a similar white dwelling. More frequent, direct, and interpersonal contacts seem to occur among Negro than among white inhabitants of these dwellings. This apparent fact does not mean that the more open type of living relationship "causes" Negro slayings to be higher than white, but it may give some clue to an explanation of the higher proportion of stairway killings among Negroes. The stairway is a place of transition and as such ordinarily lacks the emotional content that the kitchen and bedroom possess. People on a stairway are in the process of going to or coming from a room in one apartment to a room in another apartment, or, within a house, from one floor to another. One who is a victim of homicide on a stairway is almost undoubtedly caught by his adversary while moving from one emotionally loaded room to another. A roomer on the third-floor rear who has been engaging in amorous intimacies with the wife of a dweller on the second floor may be suspected and seen by the husband one night as he returns home. Caught on the stairway between the two apartments, the victim is fatally stabbed by the irate husband. Such a case was common among stairway deaths.

Some of the stairway deaths occurred on steps or landings leading into one of the multiple-dwelling buildings. Here again, a culture trait suspected of being more prevalent (and perhaps more necessary) among Negroes than whites adds to the explanation of a greater proportion of Negro homicides on stairways; i.e., the tendency to congregate in dense groups during the hot summer months on the steps just outside row apartments in order to catch an occasional passing breeze. Analysis indicates, finally, that death occurring on a stairway means primarily the killing of a Negro male, who was killed by stabbing twice as often as by shooting and three times as often as by beating.

About 8 per cent of all homicides took place inside or directly outside a taproom. An hypothesis suggesting and testing the relationship between alcohol and homicide is examined in a later chapter. Suffice it to say at present that the only striking difference noted in the race-sex distributions is that approximately and proportionately between two and three times as many men as women killed and were killed in a taproom. Taproom deaths resulted from stabbings in two-fifths of all such cases. Of the 29 Negro males killed in taprooms, 13 were stabbed, 10 were shot, and 6 were beaten. However, 9 of the 14 white males killed in taprooms were victims of beatings.

The other two racial distributions that show great diversity with respect to place of occurrence indicate that from three to four times as many whites as Negroes are killed in commercial places other than taprooms, and in miscellaneous places. A commercial place is often the scene of a robbery during which a felon kills the owner or patron, and since whites have a larger number of such establishments to burglarize, or patrons to rob, than do Negroes, the chance of a felony murder[1] occurring in these places owned by whites is greater. Half the homicides occurring in commercial places other than taprooms involved white male victims (24 of the 47), and of these, half were by shooting.

Although it has been observed that the highway is the most dangerous single place for all victims of criminal homicide, the home is slightly more dangerous than outside the home. (Tables 12 and 13.) The place where homicide occurred may be dichotomized according to whether it occurred "in the home," or "outside the home."[2] Of all victims, 51 per cent were killed in the home, and 49 per cent outside the home. This relatively equal distribution is disturbed, however, by the introduction of *significant* race and sex differences, for more Negroes (55 per cent) than whites (42 per cent) and more females (68 per cent) than males (46 per cent) were slain in the home. The striking association between white males killed outside the home and white females in the home is obvious from the following distribution of victims according to specified race and sex groups who met death in the home:

> Negro males—52 per cent
> Negro females—66 per cent
> White males—30 per cent
> White females—74 per cent

Subdividing the home into that of (1) the victim, (2) the offender, (3) both, and (4) another, some important associations are noted according to the race of the offender. For both Negroes and whites the distributions are similar, although a slightly higher proportion of Negroes (48 per cent) than of whites (38 per cent) committed homicide in the home

[1] For definition and description of felony murder, see Chapter XIII.
[2] In the future, sometimes referred to as home/not-home.

of both the slayer and the slain. By sex of offender there is a *significant* association, for nearly twice as frequently, females (60 per cent) as compared to males (32 per cent) were perpetrators in the home of both the victim and the offender. On the other hand, males (34 per cent) were between two and three times more frequently than females (13 per cent) perpetrators in the home of the victim. Similarly, in a home that was neither the victim's nor the offender's, males (18 per cent) committed homicide over twice as often as females (7 per cent).

When the home/not-home dichotomy is applied to total victims and offenders by specified race and sex groups according to months, days, and hours, some interesting differences emerge. It has been previously noted that Negro males had their highest number of homicides in September. During this high month they had 20 cases in the home and 20 outside the home, a distribution which is similar to the general distribution of Negro male homicides in general (171 in the home/160 not in the home). Only for white males were there more homicides outside the home (35/83), a pattern which occurs for every month of the year. During the high month of May for white males, the home/not-home ratio is still higher, or 14 cases occurring outside the home out of a May total of 17. The home/not-home ratios of two to one for Negro females (63/33), and three to one for white females (32/11) are consistently maintained throughout the year.

In general, there is a slight tendency for homicides to occur outside the home more frequently during the summer months when collective life generally is more frequent outdoors than during the winter months. From July to September, 54 per cent, and from January to March, 46 per cent of the homicides took place outside the home. The most striking differences are in December (31/18) and in February (24/10) when approximately twice as many killings occurred in the home, due largely to the fact that female victims during February had a nine-to-one ratio for the home/not-home division. These are, after all, cold winter months when most social relationships occur indoors. During these two months

131

the number of homicides occurring in the home and those occurring outside the home are separated by 13 and 14 cases respectively, while the other ten months have an average difference of only 4 cases and no more than 7 in any one month.

There is no significant association between the home/not-home dichotomy and days of the week during which homicide occurs, but there are several important divergencies by specified race and sex groups. Sunday killings considerably disturb the relatively equal division of the Negro male group, for on this day nearly twice as many Negro males become victims in the home as outside the home (43/22). It is of further interest to note that 21 of the 43 home deaths on Sunday among Negro males are stabbings. Evidence presented later leads to the inference that these are mostly husbands stabbed or cut by their wives after a long week-end of excessive drinking. Furthermore, taprooms, bars, and similar commercial places are closed on Sunday in Philadelphia. White males by days of the week follow their usual pattern of having well over twice as many deaths outside the home, but on Saturday the ratio is unusually high, or about one slaying in the home to six outside the home (4/26). Cell size becomes exceedingly small when the numbers of Negro and white females are refined to this same degree, but, in general, the higher proportion of deaths occurring in the home tends to prevail throughout the days of the week for these two groups.

Finally, the same home/not-home division relative to four six-hour periods of the day reveals no significant distributions either by race or by sex. However, although the majority of males were killed outside the home (206/243), there is one time period when such is not the case, and that is during the hours between 2:00 A.M. and 8:00 A.M. when more males were killed in the home (43/31). This one time-period exception when more males were killed in the home than outside it must be due partially to the fact that bars are required by law to close at 2:00 A.M. during the week and at 12:00 midnight on Saturday. For females the same excess of homicides occurring in the home during the 2:00 A.M.–8:00 A.M.

132

period may be noted. The relationship is not statistically significant, but the twelve hours between 2:00 P.M. and 2:00 A.M. have a two-to-one ratio of homicides in the home compared to those outside the home (62/33), while the twelve hours between 2:00 A.M. and 2:00 P.M. have a three-to-one ratio (33/11).

In only one major homicide study in this country has reference been made to the types of places mentioned above. In Birmingham, Harlan found that the home had a higher incidence of homicide than did public places, and, as in Philadelphia, that more Negroes (62 per cent of all Negroes) were killed in a home than were whites (42 per cent of all whites). In his study, a larger proportion of highway homicides occurred among males of both races (Negro, 28 per cent; white, 23 per cent), than among females (Negro, 15 per cent; white, 10 per cent). Although he noted that more females than males were killed in a private home, in Birmingham this fact was more true of Negro females (81 per cent) than of white females (55 per cent), and is the reverse of the situation in Philadelphia.[1]

This analysis regarding the specific places where homicides occur has been presented to show patterns of spatial distribution. It is hoped that additional studies in other communities will examine similar data to determine the extent to which the distributions in Philadelphia, by race, sex, and other attributes and variables are similar to those elsewhere. The particular room or general place where homicide occurs does not "cause" the offense, and the offender may not "choose" one place in preference to another, but the data indicate that the place where the victim is assaulted may play an important role in the circumstances associated with the whole homicide drama. Study of the amount of time during the average daily life experiences of Negroes, whites, males, and females spent in specific places where they engage in social relationships, or participate in varying degrees in collective life, would throw considerable light on the relative frequency of homicide occurring in these same places.

[1] Harlan, *op. cit.*, p. 743.

8

ALCOHOL AND VIOLENCE

BECAUSE the relationship between alcohol and crimes against the person has long been asserted,[1] and because previous research on homicide has noted such a relationship, the Philadelphia data have been examined and tested for such an association.

It is the purpose of this chapter (*a*) to determine whether there is any relationship between alcohol and criminal homicide, (*b*) to describe the difference between violent and non-violent homicides and to determine whether any *significant* variables are associated with the violent manner in which homicide is committed, and (*c*) to determine whether the two factors, alcohol and violent homicide, are associated.

ALCOHOL

The Philadelphia Data

Unfortunately, a record of the amount of alcohol in the blood stream, liver, brain, or urine of neither the victim nor the offender is supplied in the police files of the Homicide Squad; and without precision, it is possible only to record the presence or absence of alcohol. It is regrettable that the presence and especially the degree of presence of alcohol is not more often confirmed by the police or some other agency by means of actual tests for alcohol. Obviously in the case of offenders apprehended after a lapse of time such a test would be useless. But in those offenders arrested soon after the offense, the failure of some authority to make tests is unfortunate. Tests for the presence of alcohol are possible at

---

[1] See, for example, Arthur Fink, *Causes of Crime*, Philadelphia: University of Pennsylvania Press, 1938, Chapter IV, "Alcohol and Drugs," pp. 76–98.

least in the case of victims, for the *corpus delicti* is almost always available soon after the assault and is in the hands of the authorities for purposes of testing.[1]

For each criminal homicide in Philadelphia, police description of events prior to the crime, reports from witnesses and defendants, and observations by the police that the defendant was too intoxicated to make a coherent statement immediately after the crime, yielded sufficient information to record whether the victim and/or the offender had been drinking directly before the homicide. Standard practice of the Homicide Squad is to record such information, and in many cases the exact type of beverage (wine, whisky, gin, beer, etc.) is recorded. When alcohol is present, a general description of the circumstances leading to the homicide indicates in most cases that drinking was excessive and occurred over a prolonged period of time.[2] Unless the police specifically mention in a case file the presence of alcohol, the absence of alcohol is assumed. Therefore, if there is recorded bias in any direction, it is in favor of the absence of alcohol.

The data have been grouped as follows (Table 14):

(*a*) alcohol present in both the victim and the offender,
(*b*) alcohol present in the victim only,
(*c*) alcohol present in the offender only,
(*d*) alcohol present in the homicide situation,
(*e*) alcohol absent from the homicide situation.

[1] Several studies in which actual tests for alcohol in victims have been made include: K. M. Dubowski and L. M. Shupe, "Improved Semimicro Distillation Apparatus," *American Journal of Clinical Pathology* (1952), 22: 147–149; R. S. Fisher, "Alcohol, Accidents and Crime," *Current Medical Digest* (1952), 19: 37–41; A. O. Gettler and S. Tiber, "Quantitative Determination of Ethyl Alcohol in Human Tissues," *Archives of Pathology* (January, 1927), 3: 78–83; L. M. Shupe, "Alcohol and Crime. A Study of the Urine Alcohol Concentration Found in 882 Persons Arrested During or Immediately After the Commission of a Felony," *Journal of Criminal Law, Criminology, and Police Science* (January–February, 1954), 44: 661–664; L. M. Shupe and K. M. Dubowski, "Ethyl Alcohol in Blood and Urine," *American Journal of Clinical Pathology* (1952), 22: 901–910; D. M. Spain, V. A. Bradess, and A. A. Eggston, "Alcohol and Violent Death. A One-Year Study of Consecutive Cases in a Representative Community," *Journal of the American Medical Association* (1951), 146: 334–335; W. C. Wilentz, "The Alcohol Factor in Violent Deaths," *American Practitioner and Digest of Treatment* (1953), 4: 21–24.

[2] There is no necessity, nor is this the place, to describe the physiological and psychological effects of alcohol.

TABLE 14

CRIMINAL HOMICIDE AND THE PRESENCE OF ALCOHOL,
BY RACE AND SEX OF VICTIM, PHILADELPHIA, 1948–1952

(Per Cent of Total)

Alcohol	Both Races			Negro			White		
	Total	Male	Female	Total	Male	Female	Total	Male	Femal
Alcohol Present in Both Victim and Offender	43.5	45.0	38.8	48.2	49.5	43.8	31.0	32.2	27.9
Alcohol Present in the Victim Only	9.2	11.1	2.9	9.4	11.2	3.1	8.7	11.0	2.3
Alcohol Present in the Offender Only	10.9	8.7	18.0	11.7	9.4	19.8	8.7	6.8	14.0
Total: Alcohol Present in the Homicide Situation	63.6	64.8	59.7	69.3	70.1	66.7	48.4	50.0	44.2
Total: Alcohol Absent from the Homicide Situation	36.4	35.2	40.3	30.7	29.9	33.3	51.6	50.0	55.8
Grand Total	100.0 (588)	100.0 (449)	100.0 (139)	100.0 (427)	100.0 (331)	100.0 (96)	100.0 (161)	100.0 (118)	100.0 (43)

In 214, or 36 per cent, of the 588 homicides alcohol was entirely absent and could have played no role in the commission of the crime. In these cases there was no evidence uncovered or recorded by the police that either the victim or the offender had been drinking prior to the crime. Generally, this means that during the day of the slaying or during the day preceding the crime there was no evidence of drinking. In no sense may we say that the persons involved in these 214 cases were abstainers, for drinking habits were not reported unless they could be shown to bear some relationship to the crime.

In only 54, or 9 per cent, of the 588 homicides alcohol was present in the victim only.

In 64, or 11 per cent, of the 588 homicides alcohol was present in the offender only.

In 256, or 44 per cent, of the 588 homicides alcohol was present in *both* the victim and the offender.

For purposes of measuring the association of alcohol and homicide, the most important classification is that which combines all categories involving the presence of alcohol. Thus, reference to "the presence of alcohol in the homicide situation" means that either the victim, or the offender, or both, had been drinking immediately prior to the crime, and combines categories (*a*), (*b*), and (*c*) in the grouping mentioned above. When this combination is made we observe that in 374, or 64 per cent, of the 588 cases alcohol was present in the homicide situation, or that at least one of the persons directly involved in each of the 374 homicides had been drinking. It is *significant* that of these 374 cases in which alcohol was a present factor nearly seven-tenths were those involving the presence of alcohol in *both* the victim and the offender.

To determine whether the presence of alcohol is associated with important attributes, numerous fourfold tables were constructed and a test of the significance of association was made for each. Various relationships between alcohol and the race and sex of both the victim and the offender were then tested. The *significant* associations summarized below may seem at first confusing and overlapping, but careful examination should disclose the refinements required by the grouping of data used in this study. Most previous studies have analyzed the presence of alcohol in *either* the victim of a violent death by homicide, *or* the presence of alcohol in the offender. Because an attempt is made in the present research to measure significance of the frequency of *both* victims and offenders, together and separately, who had been drinking immediately prior to the homicide, many combinations of these data are available for analysis. When these groupings relative to the presence of alcohol are then compared with the various race and sex categories of victims and offenders, the combinations obviously increase in number. Seven associations with race, sex, and alcohol emerge to the level of statistical *significance*. They are as follows:

(1) Alcohol in the homicide situation and race of the offender.[1] Alcohol was present (in the victim, offender, or both) as a factor in the homicide situation in 311, or 67 per cent, of the cases when a Negro was an offender but in only 89, or 58 per cent, of the cases when a white was an offender.

(2) Alcohol in the homicide situation and race of the victim. Alcohol was present as a factor in the homicide situation in 70 per cent of the cases when a Negro was killed, but in only 49 per cent of the cases when a white was slain.

(3) Alcohol in the homicide situation and race of the male victim. Alcohol was present as a factor in the homicide situation in 70 per cent of the cases when a Negro male was killed, but in only 50 per cent of the cases when a white male was killed.

(4) Alcohol in the homicide situation and race of the female victim. Alcohol was present as a factor in the homicide situation in 67 per cent of the cases when a Negro female was slain, but in only 44 per cent of the cases when a white female was slain.

(5) Alcohol in the offender (in the offender only and in both victim and offender) and race of the offender. Alcohol was present in 271, or 58 per cent, of Negro offenders and present in 72, or 47 per cent, of white offenders.

(6) Alcohol in the victim (in the victim only and in both victim and offender) and race of the victim. Alcohol was present in 58 per cent of Negro victims but in only 40 per cent of white victims.

(7) Alcohol in the victim and sex of the victim. Alcohol was present in 56 per cent of male victims but in only 42 per cent of female victims. If the presence of alcohol in the victim only is separately considered, a *significant* relationship also exists with the sex of the victim. Alcohol was present in

[1] It should be remembered that there were 71 multiple defendants, in addition to the principal defendants, who were involved as two or more offenders in one slaying. Therefore, if two offenders attacked one victim, for example, and only one of the offenders had been drinking prior to the crime, alcohol was considered to have been present in the homicide situation. Both the numerical and percentage frequencies are given for the two associations described above which involve alcohol and offenders since the table that appears in the text is broken down by race and sex of victims.

the victim only in but three of the 96 Negro female victims, and was present in the victim only in just one of the 43 white female victims. Thus, alcohol was present only in the victim in as few as four, or less than 3 per cent, of the 139 criminal homicides involving female victims. Contrariwise, alcohol was present only in the victim in 50, or over 11 per cent, of the 449 criminal homicides involving male victims.

These associations with the presence of alcohol should not be construed as causal connections. Significant relationships only point a finger of inference at the presence of alcohol as a cause. As Taft[1] has pointed out, a genuine causal relationship often does exist between alcohol and homicide, for "occasionally, as when a man kills his best friend over a trivial situation, drunkenness appears as a direct and almost sole factor." On the other hand, although many serious crimes may be committed by men who are drunk, more often drunkenness is rather a complicating factor, and most men who drink or who are drunk do not commit serious crimes, and especially not homicide.

It should be borne in mind that the connection in which we have used the chi-square test has been to shed light on the question of the differences in observed behavior between the races (and the sexes) in the homicide situation with respect to the absence or presence of alcohol. Such differences have a meaning only when the races (or sexes) are compared to each other. This comparison, of course, leaves unanswered the much larger question of the relationship between drinking and homicide. In order to discuss this latter question, the researcher would have to possess information about the drinking norms within each race (or sex) group, and then compare these drinking norms with the sample which persons involved in homicide could then be said to represent. The drinking mores of males and of Negroes—the two groups that appear to be most significantly associated with homicide and the presence of alcohol—may be such that a larger share of the male and Negro population in general compared to the female and white population is engaged in social interaction

[1] Donald Taft, *Criminology*, New York: Macmillan, 1952, p. 252.

involving alcohol ingestion at any time. Hence, the higher incidence of alcohol present in males and Negroes among persons involved in criminal homicide may simply be a reflection of the higher incidence of drinking among these two groups in the general population. The relationship of alcohol to homicide involves one factor (homicide) which is presumably unique for the individual, whereas the other factor (presence of alcohol) *might* be unique but is probably as common for many individuals as various other types of behavior. It should be kept in mind that "presence of alcohol" and "homicide" are not equivalent behaviors. Finally, if drinking alcoholic beverages is part of the mores of over a majority of a given race or sex population group, then the absence of alcohol in a third of the homicide situations involving this same race or sex group might prove to be an inversely significant association. Analysis, however, must proceed on the basis of the frequency distributions of victims and offenders in whom alcohol was present. Such distributions do not, of course, tell us what the chances are of killing or being killed while drinking, relative to the chances of the same phenomena occurring while not drinking. The relative amounts of time spent drinking, where, when, with whom, and under what circumstances are data about the general population not presently available, but these factors probably vary by race, sex, age, and other social attributes.

When alcohol is present in the offender alone or in both the offender and the victim, implications of a causal relationship are undoubtedly stronger than for those cases involving the presence of alcohol in the victim only. Alcohol in the victim only does not necessarily mean, however, that alcohol is an inconsequential factor in the events leading up to the crime. In many cases, as will be described in detail in Chapter 14, the victim is a major precipitator of the homicide and the fact that he had been drinking prior to his own death is of no small consequence in causing the offender to strike out against him.

In addition to the relationships of race, sex, and alcohol, there is also a *significant* association between alcohol in the homicide situation and the method of inflicting death (Appendix I, Table 10). More stabbings (72 per cent) than any other assault method occurred with alcohol present during the act of homicide. The presence of alcohol appeared in the homicide situation in fewer cases (45 per cent) when one of the miscellaneous methods was used than when any other method was used. Several interesting race differences may be noted in these relationships. It has already been observed that stabbing is the most typical method by which Negroes meet death, while beating is most typical among whites. Of the 200 Negro stabbings, alcohol was present in 74 per cent, and of 68 white beatings, alcohol was present in 60 per cent. Among Negroes, alcohol was more likely than not to be present regardless of the method by which they were killed, but among whites, only beatings had a higher proportion with alcohol present. White stabbings were almost equally divided between the presence and absence of alcohol, so that it is not stabbings and alcohol that are associated, but Negro stabbings and alcohol. For each race, however, homicide by beating had a higher proportion with alcohol present than homicide by any other method (alcohol present in 77 per cent of Negro beatings and in 60 per cent of white beatings), which leads us to conclude that, regardless of race, beatings and alcohol involve a socially meaningful association. Many of the beatings with alcohol present were the result of drunken brawls during which the offender had intention to harm but not to kill his adversary.

It is generally suspected that week-ends have a disproportionately high number of homicides partly because of the greater consumption of alcohol during this period. Analysis shows that there is a *significant* association between the presence of alcohol and days of the week during which homicide occurred. (Table 15.)

This relationship may be a spurious one that fails to account for other, and perhaps more important, factors. Nonetheless, a causal nexus is implied, based on a thorough reading of police files. A *significantly* higher proportion of week-end homicides, than of homicides occurring during the remainder

141

TABLE 15

PRESENCE OF ALCOHOL DURING CRIMINAL HOMICIDE
BY DAY OF THE WEEK, PHILADELPHIA, 1948–1952

Alcohol	Monday		Tuesday		Wednesday		Thursday		Friday		Saturday		Sunday		Total	
	No.	%	No.	%	No.	%	No.	%	No.	%	No.	%	No.	%	No.	%
Present	24	41.4	17	41.5	34	61.8	28	58.3	66	66.0	136	72.7	69	69.7	374	63.6
Absent	34	58.6	24	58.5	21	38.2	20	41.7	34	34.0	51	27.3	30	30.3	214	36.4
Total	58	100.0	41	100.0	55	100.0	48	100.0	100	100.0	187	100.0	99	100.0	588	100.0

of the week, had alcohol present (in either the victim, offender, or both). Alcohol was present in seven-tenths of the 386 homicides committed on Friday, Saturday, and Sunday, but in only half of the 202 homicides committed between Monday and Thursday. Moreover, the incidence of homicide in general is highest on Saturday and lowest on Tuesday; and the incidence with alcohol present is also highest on Saturday (73 per cent) and low on Tuesday (42 per cent).

In the absence of adequate data to test the assumption, it is only suggested that the high number of week-end slayings is due to (a) the greater amount of leisure-time during the week-end, for (b) engaging more fully in collective life, where (c) alcohol is more abundantly consumed, because (d) the Friday pay day provides greater financial ability to purchase alcohol. It may be difficult to quantify some of these factors, to measure the relative weight of each, and, consequently, to determine the share of each in contributing to the high week-end toll. Probably only the last of these factors, (d), is subject to some social control in the absence of prohibition.

Occupation was not reliably reported in the sources examined for this study, but the data suggest that a high proportion of both victims and offenders were semiskilled or unskilled laborers. Most of these workers were employed by industrial and construction firms that pay wages on a weekly basis. In Philadelphia approximately 31 per cent of these occupational groups, of which most agents and victims of criminal homicide are members, are paid on Thursday, and 55 per cent are paid on Friday.[1]

[1] Written communication from the Chamber of Commerce of Greater Philadelphia, 17th and Sarsom Streets, Philadelphia, Pa.

142

Furthermore, examination of the volume of daily sales by dollar value in state liquor stores throughout Pennsylvania consistently shows Friday and Saturday leading all other days. In 1950, for example, liquor sales were highest on Saturday (23 per cent), second highest on Friday (21 per cent), and lowest on Monday (13 per cent).[1]

These facts are more heuristic than conclusive, but it seems logical to assume that mass payment of wages on Thursday and Friday results in heavy purchases of liquor (in state stores and taprooms) on Friday and Saturday, and, together with week-end leisure and increased social intercourse, may produce the week-end pattern of homicide noted in Philadelphia. On the other hand, it should be remembered that the presence of alcohol might well be about as common for many individuals as wearing a tie, taking a bath, or going to the movies—each of which may be a Saturday night or almost an every night occurrence. Greater purchasing power on Friday does not "cause" more homicides, but when the socio-economic group most likely to commit homicide almost simultaneously receives its weekly wages, purchases alcohol, and socially interacts, it is not unlikely that the number of homicides should also rise.

Alcohol Noted in Other Studies

There is a considerable amount of contradiction and inconsistency among the homicide studies in which the presence of alcohol is examined. Unfortunately, few other studies can be compared with the present analysis because sources of data or types of homicide examined are different. Some studies refer only to murders, some to both criminal and non-criminal homicide. Generally, when murder rather than criminal homicide is analyzed, the proportion of cases involving alcohol is less than the 64 per cent found in total cases of criminal homicide recorded by the Philadelphia police.

In a description that sounds almost contemporary, Garofalo claimed:

[1] *Store Sales Analyses, Calendar Year, 1953, Special Summaries,* Commonwealth of Pennsylvania, Liquor Control Board, Bureau of Accounting and Service, Statistics Division.

143

Comparative statistics prove drunkenness to be uncommon in the countries which show the highest percentage of homicide and, on the other hand, very common in countries where homicides seldom occur. Without doubt, drunkenness easily excites the mind and is often the cause of quarrel. But in these quarrels it is only the drunkard with a criminal temperament who seeks to use the knife or revolver. The non-criminal drunkard, on the contrary, fights with his bare hands. His object is to lay his opponent prostrate, to "knock him out" as the English say. When he has succeeded, he will himself perhaps aid his fallen foe to regain his feet.[1]

Lewis Lawes[2] repeatedly contended that assault and homicide are offenses associated with alcohol, and Verkko claims that "where unpremeditated crimes against life are in the majority, we may always assume that the influence of alcohol on the criminality is of decisive importance."[3] Snyder says that "about 50 per cent of persons homicidally slain had been drinking, according to the case records of the Department of Legal Medicine of Harvard Medical School. Consequently, it is exceedingly important to know whether the perpetrator or the victim of violence was under the influence of alcohol. . . . "[4] Theron Kilmer[5] estimated that 40 per cent of victims are intoxicated at the time they are killed. Sutherland contradicts himself somewhat when he says in one place that "intoxication is involved in *many cases* of homicide," and, in another, "probably a relatively *small* proportion of the serious crimes result directly from intoxication. A *few* homicides are committed as the result of drunken quarrels. . . . "[6]

In an article on "Alcoholism and Crime," Banay claims that assault is the most frequent crime of the alcoholic, and

[1] Baron Raffaele Garofalo, *Criminology*, Boston: Little, Brown, and Co., 1914, p. 117.
[2] Lewis Lawes, *Life and Death in Sing Sing*, p. 42.
[3] Verkko, *Homicides and Suicides in Finland*, p. 30.
[4] Snyder, *op. cit.*, p. 269.
[5] Theron W. Kilmer, "Alcoholism, Its Relation to Police Work and Jurisprudence," *Correction* (New York Department of Correction) (August, 1933), 3: 11–12.
[6] Edwin Sutherland, *Criminology*, p. 25 and p. 113. Emphasis is that of the present author. Perhaps the contradiction is eliminated if emphasis is placed on the extent to which homicides are directly or indirectly the result of intoxication.

that the immature alcoholic prefers certain behavior patterns of childhood that, if followed, would result in lost community status. Under the influence of alcohol, this particular type of individual, he says, may revert to his tabooed earlier behavior patterns. Banay found that hostility and lessened anticipation of punishment were both increased by alcohol and that the alcoholic's aggression may be manifested either as sadistic cruelty leading to a serious assault crime or to masochistic self-accusation, in which case he may commit a crime in order to be punished.[1] Howard[2] estimates that at least 60 per cent of the "graver homicides," about 82 per cent of the minor assault crimes, and at least half of the crimes of lust are chiefly due to alcohol. Aschaffenburg[3] quotes statistics from Copenhagen, showing that among delinquents who had committed crimes of violence the percentage of drunkenness was about 65 per cent compared to only 14 per cent of the thieves who were drunk at the time their offenses were committed. He further points out that most of the student criminality in German university towns before World War I was due to the abuse of alcohol and that most of the crimes of students were insults, aggravated assault and battery, and resisting an officer. Aschaffenburg believes that these crimes of violence were due to excessive alcoholic indulgences. Bonger,[4] in discussing crimes of vengeance, attempts to show that there probably is a correlation between assault crimes and the acute stage of alcoholism. He quotes Fornasari di Verce, who pointed out that in Italy, Great Britain, Ireland, and New South Wales, crimes of violence increase and decrease in direct ratio with the consumption of alcohol. The Dutch criminologist also says that studies generally indicate that of serious crimes of violence

---

[1] Ralph Banay, "Alcoholism and Crime," *Quarterly Journal of Studies on Alcohol* (March, 1942), pp. 686–716. See also D. B. Rotman, "Alcoholism and Crime," *Federal Probation* (July–September, 1947), pp. 31–35.

[2] George E. Howard, "Alcohol and Crime: A Study in Social Causation," *American Journal of Sociology* (July, 1918), 24: 71. This article is a strong call for Prohibition.

[3] Gustav Aschaffenburg, *Crime and Its Repression*, Boston: Little, Brown and Co., 1913, pp. 75–78.

[4] W. A. Bonger, *Criminality and Economic Conditions*, Boston: Little, Brown and Co., 1916, pp. 639–643.

the percentage committed while drunk ranges from 33 per cent to as high as 67 per cent, and probably on the basis of these figures it could be contended that from one-half to three-fourths of the crimes of violence are committed while the offender is drunk. Returning once more to the alcoholic, research by M. A. Gray and Merrill Moore[1] on the type of offenses committed under the influence of alcohol showed a much higher percentage of assault and violence among alcoholic than among non-alcoholic offenders.

Although unable to get sufficiently adequate data on alcohol for his study of 500 homicides in Birmingham, Harlan was impressed by the importance of alcohol in his reading of the coroner's records and said that "it would be no exaggeration, certainly, to guess that it [alcohol] is significantly involved in more than 50 per cent of the cases."[2] He believed that Saturday night and Sunday Negro killings were associated with alcohol because "the Saturday night spree is probably even more of a tradition among lower class Negroes than among whites."[3]

In a comparison of indices of deaths from homicide taken from mortality statistics for each of the states, with indices of alcoholism reported by E. M. Jellinek, Porterfield and Talbert[4] found a relatively high correlation. In their detailed analysis of homicide and the business cycle, Henry and Short tried to separate the relation between alcoholism, the business cycle, and homicide among whites and Negroes:

> These data show that the negative relation between homicide and alcoholism of whites and the positive relation between homicide and alcoholism of Negroes both "wash out" when the effect of the business cycle is held constant. When business prosperity is accompanied by an increase of alcoholism for both whites and Negroes, it is also accompanied by a decrease in homicide of whites and an increase in homicide of Negroes.

[1] M. A. Gray and Merrill Moore, "Incidence and Significance of Alcoholism in the History of Criminals," *Journal of Criminal Psychopathology*, (October, 1941), 3:316.

[2] Harlan, *op. cit.*, p. 748.

[3] *Ibid.*, p. 742.

[4] A. Porterfield and R. H. Talbert, *Crime, Suicide and Social Well-Being*, p. 106.

But the variation in alcoholism has little or no relationship with the variation in homicide either of whites or Negroes. Since both vary independently with the business cycle, the spurious relationship they have with each other disappears when the effect of business fluctuation is removed.[1]

It is important to note that both in the Porterfield and Talbert study and in the Henry and Short study, rates of homicide are correlated with rates of alcoholism, and that such correlations do not indicate the number of homicides committed under the influence of alcohol nor the number of victims intoxicated at the time of the offense.

Examination of 100 consecutive cases of homicide convictions in Massachusetts led Stearns to conclude that "alcohol appears as a very prominent factor. Twenty per cent were drunk when the crime was committed; seven so drunk that they have little recollection of the act. Fourteen others had been drinking and the remaining 66 deny alcohol at the time of the murder."[2] It should be noted that these were all cases of *convicted males*, whereas the Philadelphia data include suspects known to the police. The Massachusetts proportion with alcohol present in 44 per cent of the males is not entirely comparable, therefore, to the 58 per cent of male offenders in Philadelphia who had been drinking prior to the offense.

An even smaller proportion of the 92 Wisconsin murderers examined by Gillin showed the presence of alcohol. He says that "more than 30 per cent of these murderers were drunk at the time of the crime or at least had been drinking."[3] However, in his study of 200 murderers, Cassidy found alcohol present in approximately 50 per cent at the time of the crime.[4] Both of these studies also constituted very select groups compared to the Philadelphia offenders.

In several valuable studies, competent observers have measured the amount of alcohol in the victim by conducting post-mortem examinations. In 1949, Spain and his associates

[1] A. F. Henry and J. F. Short, Jr., *op. cit.*, pp. 49–50.
[2] Stearns, *op. cit.*, p. 736.
[3] Gillin, *The Wisconsin Prisoner*, p. 87.
[4] Cassidy, *op. cit.*, p. 297.

147

analyzed 246 cases of violent death. "Necropsy," they claimed, "was foregone only when it was absolutely clear that no alcohol was involved, when 24 hours had elapsed between the time of the accident and death and when circumstances beyond our control were present."[1] Either brain or liver analysis was used, depending on various circumstances, and the method of Gettler and Tiber was employed.[2] Unfortunately, only 8 homicides were included in their study of violent deaths, 7 of which involved victims with alcohol present. The average alcohol content of the brain or liver for these homicide victims was 0.18 per cent compared, for example, to 0.15 per cent for suicide and auto deaths, although non-industrial accidents also showed 0.18 per cent. Presumably these homicides were criminal, although there is only implicit indication of such by the authors. All told, of the 246 violent deaths, ethyl alcohol was considered "a contributory or responsible factor" in 68, or 27 per cent. Although the number of homicides in this study is very small, the fact that seven of the eight victims had been drinking prior to the crime compared to other types of violent deaths is suggestive of the association found in the Philadelphia study. Something regarding the nature of the seven homicides appears in the following comments by the authors: "Investigation revealed that in practically all instances there was no obvious premeditation or malicious intent. Very often after the influence of alcohol had subsided there was no real recollection of what had occurred."[3]

In a study of 136 homicides, Wilentz reported that 42, or 31 per cent, "showed an alcoholic factor (19 were intoxicated and 23 had been drinking)."[4] It is not possible to determine whether these were only criminal homicides, or whether some non-criminal homicides were also included. The author also noted that the New York Medical Examiner's Office reported that in 1948 an alcoholic factor was present in 155 instances, or 44 per cent, of the 351 autopsies of homicide

[1] Spain, *et. al., op. cit.*, p. 334.
[2] Gettler and Tiber, *op. cit.*
[3] Spain, *et. al., op. cit.*, p. 335.
[4] Wilentz, *op. cit.*, p. 23.

148

cases. This article by Wilentz contains sweeping generalizations on the basis of meager data and no supportive documentation.

The Columbus (Ohio) Police Department since 1945 has maintained a program of surveying a number of individuals who were caught in the act of committing a crime and analyzing their blood or urine for the per cent of alcohol present at that time. An interesting study by Lloyd Shupe,[1] Police Chemist of Columbus, reports the urine alcohol concentration of 882 persons picked up during or immediately after commission of a felony during the period from March, 1951, to March, 1953. This is one of the few studies which gives data on the precise amount of alcohol in the offender rather than in the victim. The author reports 30 murder cases among the 882 felony cases examined. Unfortunately again, whether these are all actually murder cases, or whether some are murder and others manslaughter cases is not indicated. At any rate, of the 30 "murder" cases, 17 per cent of the arrested offenders showed no alcohol concentration whatever compared to an average of 27 per cent for all felons arrested. Relative to his findings on crimes of violence Shupe says:

> The figures show that crimes of physical violence are associated with intoxicated persons. Cuttings (11 to 1 under the influence of alcohol), the carrying of concealed weapons (8 to 1 under the influence of alcohol) and other assaults (10 to 1 under the influence of alcohol) are definitely crimes of alcoholic influence, even crimes of true intoxication. Although a fewer per cent of persons involved in shootings and murders are under the influence of alcohol, and a greater percentage are actually sober, than those committing similar crimes of cutting, concealed weapons, and other assaults, the chances are still better than 4 to 1 that these crimes are committed by persons under the influence of alcohol.[2]

The 30 cases reported by Shupe is a relatively small number from which to generalize about so specific a factor as the presence of alcohol. However, the precise measurement of

[1] Shupe, *op. cit.*, pp. 661–664.
[2] *Ibid.*, p. 663.

alcohol in the homicide offender in Columbus, showing only 17 per cent of the slayers with no alcohol concentration whatever compared to 45 per cent of the Philadelphia offenders may indicate that in the absence of accurate tests of alcohol concentration there has been a recorded bias towards underreporting of alcohol in the offender in Philadelphia.

Norwood East, a former Commissioner of Prisons in England, described a series of 100 "unselected cases of men and youths" who had been tried for murder, and claimed that alcohol was a predominant or contributing "cause" in only 19 cases. East concluded from this and from a study of other investigations that there appears to be no reason to consider alcohol as "more than an occasional factor in the causation of crime in England. Every practical criminologist," he says, "will attach some importance to the association of alcoholism and crime. It is, however, very easy to over-emphasize the connection."[1]

However, a different perspective is noted in George Catlin's article on "Alcoholism" in the *Encyclopedia of the Social Sciences*, where he refers to a survey in England by W. C. Sullivan and says that "of 200 convicts guilty of homicide, Sullivan found the act in 60 per cent of the cases to be due to alcoholism. . . ."[2] (Alcoholism, not merely the presence of alcohol, was presumably the major factor among these offenders.)

Another investigation in England into the influence of alcohol on homicide was reported by J. C. M. Matheson, then Governor of Holloway Prison for Women. In an analysis of all women received into the prison charged with homicide from 1935 to 1939, he found that in only 3 out of 55 cases did alcohol appear as a direct factor.[3]

Dr. East's conclusion about the relative unimportance of alcohol in England may not be applicable to the more heterogeneous American population. Moreover, East and Matheson

---

[1] Norwood East, "The Problem of Alcohol in Relation to Crime," *The British Journal of Inebriety* (1939), 37: 55 ff.

[2] George Catlin, "Alcoholism," *Encyclopedia of the Social Sciences*, Vol. I, p. 626.

[3] J. C. M. Matheson, "Alcohol and Female Homicides," *The British Journal of Inebriety* (1939), 37: 87 ff.

refer to alcohol as a "cause" of homicide. No attempt was made in analyzing the Philadelphia data to label alcohol as a "cause." Alcohol as a factor present in the homicide situation, whether as a direct and precipitating factor or merely as a subsidiary factor, was sufficient for inclusion in the analysis.

Distinction of the types of offenders, or between offenders and victims, is sometimes made in the homicide literature. Of interest are the conclusions of Hartvig Nissen, who reports that in Norway, "Of those accused of negligent manslaughter, 92 per cent were found to be intoxicated. Of those who committed murder, 60 per cent were intoxicated."[1] Abrahamsen believes a further distinction should be made between the offender with no previous criminal record and one who has a record, for he says:

> It must be stressed that the importance of alcohol as contributive or causative factors in first-time murderers and recidivists differs. A first-time homicide may be attributed to alcohol if it is found that the perpetrator was intoxicated. Quite different is the situation with recidivists. Individuals with a previous criminal career who commit homicide on an alcoholic spree may have murdered without being intoxicated.[2]

A Ukranian investigation of 216 homicides by Tersiev[3] several years ago indicated that of those persons prompted by the "hooligan motive," 74 per cent were intoxicated when the crime was committed, and of the murderers classed as "weaklings in conflict," only 25 per cent were intoxicated.

An investigation in Finland in 1931 under the direction of Bruno Salmiala revealed important differences in the amount of intoxication and lesser quantities of alcohol consumed on the day of the crime among persons convicted of murder and those convicted of manslaughter. The proportion of alcohol

[1] Cited by Abrahamsen, *op. cit.*, p. 168.
[2] *Ibid.*, p. 169. See *infra.*, Chapter 9, for further discussion of alcohol and previous record.
[3] N. Tersiev, "The Evaluation of Their Deeds on the Part of Condemned Murderers," reported in *Social Science Abstracts*, Vol. II (October, 1930), pp. 1661–1662.

in the *victim* was also described. Referring to the survey, Veli Verkko reports:

The investigation comprises the crimes between 1904 and 1913, and 1920 and 1929, that were taken to the Courts of Appeal, and covers both the culprits and the victims. It reveals, firstly, whether the culprit or the victim at the moment of the crime were intoxicated, and secondly, if not, whether they had consumed a lesser quantity of alcohol on the day of the crime.

As regards *murders*, it is found that, of the committers of this crime, only 7.1% were intoxicated at the moment of the crime in 1904–1913, and 7.3% in 1920–1929. The corresponding percentages regarding the victims of murder were quite negligible: 1.41 in 1909–1913, and 2.41 in 1920–1929. The cases in which the murderer, on the day of committing the crime, had consumed a lesser quantity of alcohol, or taken a so-called "stiffener," before his evil deed, amounted to 9.0% in 1904–1913, and 14.1% in 1920–1929. Very few victims had consumed a lesser quantity of alcohol on the day of the crime; 1.9% in the former period, and 2.4% in the latter.

The vast difference between murders and other crimes against life is revealed when the corresponding information on *intentional manslaughter and wounding occasioning death* is recorded. In 1904–1913 58.7 per cent of these culprits were intoxicated, the figure for 1920–1929 being 62.1%. It is remarkable that, of the victims of the crimes too, 44.8% in the former period and 49.5% in the latter were intoxicated at the moment of the crime. The percentages for those who had consumed a lesser quantity of alcohol on the day of the crime were, in 1904–1913, 11.3% of the culprits and 11.0% of the victims, and in 1920–1929 14.9% of the culprits and 12.9% of the victims.[1]

This investigation by the Salmiala Committee is of interest not only because it reports the relationship between alcohol and homicide in general, but also because it is one of the few studies indicating a victim-offender differential, and in this respect is similar to the present analysis of Philadelphia homicides. Differences between persons convicted of murder and those convicted of manslaughter are most striking.

[1] V. Verkko, *Homicides and Suicides in Finland*, pp. 79–80.

Von Hentig[1] reports on a similar survey conducted by the Belgrade Institute of Legal Medicine in 1935. No information is given about the offender, but data are supplied for two types of victims: those killed by murder, and those killed by manslaughter. Not intoxication, but "signs of alcoholism" in the victims are reported. Of 214 individuals killed in Belgrade between 1924 and 1933, 55 were murdered and 159 were victims of manslaughter. Of the former, 9 per cent showed signs of alcoholism; and of the latter, 70 per cent had such signs. Combined, 55 per cent of the victims revealed "the presence of alcoholism" in a post-mortem examination. The influence of the victim's alcoholic condition relative to manslaughter von Hentig considered obvious and important.

Finally, this review of the relationship between alcohol and criminal homicide cannot fail to take cognizance of some of the legal problems this relationship raises. Courts in this country and in Great Britain, particularly, have often mitigated penalties in criminal homicide on grounds that the person was intoxicated when he committed the crime. As Norwood East points out:

> On occasion the intoxication of the defendant may be taken into consideration as a circumstance to show that the act was not premeditated. And as in murder the killing must be committed with malice aforethought—that is to say, with a deliberate mind and formed design—the intoxication may disprove the act was premeditated and intended, and suffice to reduce the crime to manslaughter.[2]

In Pennsylvania, intoxication is not an excuse for crime, but if it deprives the intellect of power to think and to weigh the nature of the act, it may prevent a conviction of first degree murder. Moreover, even though the defendant may have been intoxicated at the time of the crime, there may have been deliberation and premeditation. If evidence shows these elements of first degree murder to have been present,

[1] Hans von Hentig, *The Criminal and His Victim*, p. 413.
[2] Norwood East, *op. cit.*, p. 401.

153

the intoxication will not reduce the murder to second degree.[1]

Court records were not examined for purposes of the present study, so that the extent of such mitigation is not known. But many homicides in Philadelphia were the result of drunken brawls, and juries are purportedly unlikely to convict a defendant of first degree murder under such circumstances. The socio-psychological implications involved in mitigation of the seriousness of a typical case of homicide committed during a drunken brawl are succinctly revealed by Charles Arado in the following account:

> In such a killing, where both the defendant and the deceased are drunk at the time, there is not present that usual bitter feeling on the part of the family of the deceased. Very often there are no witnesses to the tragedy. Where the defendant is an elderly man, the father of a family, or a man who has something in his background peculiarly in his favor, he is bound to attract the sympathy of the jury. The dead man will not be brought back by a verdict of guilty. The defendant very often does not know that he has killed the deceased until some hours later. In some instances he would be the last man to perpetrate such a deed in his right mind. Sympathy is not as readily extended to the deceased because he, himself, was at fault and contributed to his own death. On the slightest showing of self defense the accused has an excellent chance to be acquitted of the charge of murder. Where he can produce witnesses to describe the tragedy so that it appears clearly that the homicide was the outcome of a drunken brawl there are few juries which will take the case so seriously that they will condemn a man to the penitentiary for at least fourteen years. . . . The atmosphere in the trial in such a case is not as tense as in the ordinary murder case. The sympathy of the onlooker is frequently extended to the man who survives such a brawl.[2]

[1] Wm. F. Hoffman, *Pennsylvania Criminal Law and Criminal Procedure*, p. 125. To support these principles of law, the author cites the following cases: "Jones v. Comm., 75 Pa. Supreme Ct. 403 (1874) . . . . Com. v. McGowen, 189 Pa. Supreme Ct. 641 (1899); Keenan v. Com., 44 Pa. Supreme Ct. 55; Com. v. West, 204 Pa. Supreme Ct. 68 (1902); Com. v. Dudash, 204 Pa. Supreme Ct. 124 (1902)" (*Ibid.*).

[2] Charles C. Arado, "Homicides Committed in Drunken Brawls," *Journal of Criminal Law and Criminology* (September, 1932), 23: 477–478.

The legal ramifications of adjudication of an intoxicated offender are greater than a sociological analysis of homicide permits. Suffice it to say that, in general, the great weight of authority in states where two degrees of murder obtain is that intoxication in such degree that the accused is incapable of forming the premeditated design to kill will serve to reduce a murder from first to second degree but not to manslaughter. Among those jurisdictions allowing a reduction to second degree murder, only a few vary the general rule and permit the intoxication, in extreme cases, to reduce the homicide to manslaughter. When so reduced it is usually under particular statutory requirements regarding the intent necessary for second degree murder. As noted earlier, the distinction between second degree murder and manslaughter is the element of malice, which is a necessary constituent of the former but is entirely lacking in the latter.[1]

It appears, therefore, that given a set of circumstances leading to homicide, a defendant is in a more favorable position if he can demonstrate his intoxication at the time of the crime. Despite the fact that drunkenness is itself an offense and that juries are usually instructed by the courts not to permit intoxication to excuse the homicide offender, mitigation of the degree of homicide is common. A recent review of such cases clearly points out this apparent discrepancy:

> Almost all courts instruct the jury that intoxication is not to be considered for the purpose of excusing or mitigating the killing but only for the purpose of determining whether the defendant was capable of entertaining the necessary purpose, malice, or intent which is an indispensable ingredient of the crime charged. But such talk is sophistry: how intoxication may be a circumstance to be considered by the jury in determining intent and yet not be an excuse for the crime is a distinction for lawyers, not lay jurors, to draw. See *Evers v. State*, 31 Tex. Crim. Rep. 318, 20 S.W. 744 (1892). Obviously the distinction is designed to disguise the odious position of allowing a citizen already violating public morals by being drunk to escape the same offense by a lighter punishment than

[1] "Recent Criminal Cases," *Journal of Criminal Law and Criminology* (May, 1940), 31; 72–74.

a sober person. Such highly legalistic reasoning, as is often the case, leads to confusion and was the cause of the erroneous instruction in the instant case. If, as the Supreme Court held, the first part of the instruction that drunkenness cannot excuse, justify, or mitigate the commission of crime was correct, it can easily be understood why the trial judge went on to say that intoxication cannot be taken into consideration at all in determining guilt. For if drunkenness is taken into consideration at all it is difficult to understand how it can act any way other than in mitigation. It would seem more sensible if the courts would face the facts and, rather than say intoxication cannot be considered in one part of an instruction and yet hold it cannot be ignored in another part, instruct that drunkenness *may* mitigate murder—but only if it is so severe that the defendant is rendered incapable of forming the necessary felonious intent.[1]

Alcohol and criminal homicide are related in various ways, some of which have been shown in the present section. Additional associations between alcohol and the homicide situation, the victim, and the offender are included in analyses that follow.

VIOLENCE

All criminal homicide has an element of violence in that one person feloniously takes the life of another. But inspection of police files, including photographs of the deceased, the medical examiner's reports, statements by the defendant, witnesses, and sometimes by the victim, leads to an observation of discernible degrees of violence.

Garofalo is one of the few writers to refer to the degree of violence as a means of classifying murderers, and, in what he calls "Second Category: Mode of Execution as Index," he points out:

A second category of murderers is characterized by the manner in which the crime is committed. Where the murder is attended by torture, where the criminal intentionally prolongs the suffering which he is inflicting, we may always be sure of his innate cruelty—for no normal man could withstand the

[1] *Ibid.*, p. 74.

sound of the victim's groans, or the sight of his agonized writhing. The fact of torture is in itself sufficient proof of the complete absence of the sentiment of pity, even where the intention to take life does not clearly appear. For this reason the French Code is right when it applies the term "murder" ("assassinat") to any species of crime which in its execution has involved the deliberate infliction of physical cruelty ("services sur le corps de la victime").[1]

Our conclusion, then, is that the cruelty with which the murder has been committed and the absence of grave provocation on the part of the victim, are the two criteria which ought to be substituted for that of premeditation. By their means, we shall be enabled to distinguish from other homicidal criminals, those whom we have called murderers, that is to say, the extreme, instinctive, or typical criminals who may be regarded as beings morally degenerate in the last degree, and permanently incapable of sociability.[2]

There is no implication in the present study that Garofalo's suggestion of replacing the present element of premeditation with that of cruelty should be adopted. Nor is it implied that his categorization of murderers is valid, that a violent murderer is morally more degenerate than any other type of murderer, nor that anyone who kills another is "permanently incapable of sociability." But Garofalo has described an important difference in the extent of violence by which death is inflicted.

In *Crime and the Human Mind*, Abrahamsen also refers to degrees of violence in different types of homicide, and claims that "several cases of murder as expressions of jealousy have been characterized by the thoroughness with which the victim is killed. Stab upon stab may follow, even after the victim is dead. Such total destruction may even extend to all that symbolizes the victim."[3]

More precise comments regarding violence and homicide have been made by Irwin Berg and Vernon Fox[4] in their

[1] Garofalo, *op. cit.*, p. 374.
[2] *Ibid.*, p. 376.
[3] Abrahamsen, *op. cit.*, p. 163.
[4] Irwin A. Berg and Vernon Fox, "Factors in Homicides Committed by 200 Males," *The Journal of Social Psychology* (August, 1947), 26: 109–119.

analysis of 200 males convicted of first and second degree murder and sentenced to the State Prison of Southern Michigan between 1939 and 1943. Their statement has been used as the basis for analysis in the present research.

> There is a difference in degree of violence in a murderous assault where one blow is struck compared with an assault where numerous blows are rained upon the victim. Similarly, a murder by gunshot was considered to be less violent if one shot was fired than, for example, if the pistol were fired until empty and the victim riddled. While admittedly somewhat arbitrary, the classification used was that where one shot was fired or one blow was struck or one stab wound was inflicted or where the murder was more or less accidental, as in the case of slain bystanders, the offense was considered *non-violent* in manner of commission. Since all the other offenses were committed by methods requiring more prolonged effort on the part of the murderer, they were classified as *violent* in manner of commission.[1]

These authors believe that the extent to which the offender's ego is involved in his relationship with the victim is importantly related to the degree of violence with which the murder is committed. This point is partially discussed in a later chapter.

The Berg-Fox definition of violence used in the present study is definitely arbitrary. Determination of violence would seem to depend upon more than merely the number of stabs, gunshot wounds, or blows inflicted on the victim. The emotional and psychic state of the offender, the extent to which the victim resists an assault, a prevailing culture pattern of violent and aggressive behavior, and other such factors should probably be included; but the only data available at present are those indicating the number of observable physical movements. Debatable as the terms ("violence" and "non-violence") and their definitions may be, they have the virtue of having been used with consistency.

Police reports and those of the medical examiner make possible a record of the number of assaultive acts in each

[1] *Ibid.*, p. 111.

criminal homicide, on the basis of which the following classification of violence was made:

(a) two acts;
(b) three to five acts;
(c) more than five acts;
(d) severe beating;
(e) severe beating followed by one stab;
(f) severe beating followed by one shot.

The first three divisions refer to stabbings and shootings, while "severe beating" invariably means a series of blows by fists, feet, or blunt instruments. It may be argued that two stabs or two gunshots are not necessarily violent. However, in terms of both our prevailing idealized and behavioral norms governing human interrelationships, it may be contended just as strongly that an individual who can fire a gun a second or more times after having once pulled a trigger, heard the blast, and seen his victim stagger, or who can raise his knife a second time after having felt his weapon cut or puncture flesh, and after having seen blood flow, has engaged in behavior somewhat more violent than one act involves. To label a severe beating "violent" may be more subject to criticism than labeling a stabbing or shooting as violent, for in some beatings the victim died from a fractured skull because his head hit the pavement during a fight that might otherwise never have come to the attention of the authorities. Such cases are usually identifiable and have been classified as "non-violent." The majority of severe beatings culminating in homicide are bitter physical battles during which many blows are rained on the victim by means of fists, feet, blunt instruments, or any combination of these three.

For purposes of testing association between violence of the homicide and race or sex, all categories of violence have been combined into one. As in previous analyses, victims and offenders are separately considered.

Offenders are almost equally divided in terms of violence and non-violence of the homicides which they perpetrated.

159

TABLE 16

VIOLENCE AND DEGREE OF VIOLENCE IN CRIMINAL HOMICIDE,
BY RACE AND SEX OF OFFENDER, PHILADELPHIA, 1948–1952

(In per cent)

	Both Races			Negro			White		
	Total	Male	Female	Total	Male	Female	Total	Male	Female (a)
Violence	50.7	54.5	33.0	49.9	53.5	35.5	53.2	57.2	—
Non-Violence	49.3	45.5	67.0	50.1	46.5	64.5	46.8	42.8	—
Total	100.0 (621)	100.0 (512)	100.0 (109)	100.0 (467)	100.0 (374)	100.0 (93)	100.0 (154)	100.0 (138)	100.0 (16)
Degree of Violence									
2 acts	19.4	18.6	25.0	20.2	19.5	24.2	17.1	16.5	—
3–5 acts	30.2	29.4	36.1	33.0	32.5	36.4	21.9	21.5	—
More than 5 acts	15.6	15.8	13.9	16.7	17.0	15.2	12.2	12.7	—
Severe Beating	29.5	31.9	11.1	25.3	27.5	12.1	41.5	43.0	—
Severe Beating prior to one stab	4.1	3.2	11.1	3.9	2.5	12.1	4.9	5.1	—
Severe Beating prior to one shot	1.3	1.1	2.8	.9	1.0	—	2.4	1.2	—
Total	100.0 (315)	100.0 (279)	100.0 (36)	100.0 (233)	100.0 (200)	100.0 (33)	100.0 (82)	100.0 (79)	100.0 (3)

(a) Category too small for breakdown by percentage distribution.

(Table 16.) Of the 621 offenders, 315 committed violent homicide, and 306 committed non-violent homicide. A *significant* association exists between sex of the offender and violence of the homicide. Only 33 per cent of the females compared to 55 per cent of the males committed homicide in a violent manner. This higher proportion of males than females who killed with violence is not surprising in view of the greater overt expression of hostility and aggressiveness either expected or permitted males in our culture.

Whites were slightly, but not significantly, more violent than Negroes in the commission of homicide. Race, therefore, is not associated with the violent or non-violent character of the homicide, for Negroes (50 per cent) and whites (53 per cent) committed homicide with a similar frequency of violence. It is the white male who contributed to the higher white violence record, for 79, or 57 per cent, of the

160

138 white male offenders killed violently, but only 3 of the 16 white females did so. Negro males were violent offenders in 54 per cent of the cases. Negro females are nearly twice as violent as white females, for 36 per cent of the former killed in this manner.

Analyses of the varying degrees of violence indicate that among those who killed violently (a) three-tenths of the offenders committed homicide by inflicting three to five stab or gunshot wounds; (b) another three-tenths assaulted their victims by severe beatings; (c) a fifth engaged in two acts of stabbing or shooting; (d) and only one in twenty severely beat his victim prior to one stab or shot.

No statistically significant association is discernible between age of offender and violence of the killing:

	Age						Total
	10–19	20–29	30–39	40–49	50–59	60 and over	
Violence	30	98	97	62	18	10	315
Non-Violence	36	111	78	50	20	10	305
Total	66	209	175	112	38	20	620

The greater aggressiveness of youth leads to the assumption that younger age groups might be more violent than older age groups in the manner of inflicting death. Such is not the case—at least, not for the 620 offenders for whom age was recorded. For slayers under 30 years of age, non-violent killings (54 per cent) exceed violent ones. The only age groups with a higher incidence of violent than of non-violent homicide are those between 30 and 49 years (55 per cent violent). Between ages 50–59, non-violent homicides again predominate (53 per cent non-violent), and for over 60 years of age an equal division occurs. None of these differences is statistically significant. Cell size on the polar ends of the age scale, particularly, is too small for detailed refinement.

Turning attention from offenders to victims, we see, according to Table 17, that exactly the same number (294) were killed violently as non-violently. There is no significant

TABLE 17

VIOLENCE AND DEGREE OF VIOLENCE IN CRIMINAL HOMICIDE,
BY RACE AND SEX OF VICTIM, PHILADELPHIA, 1948–1952

(In per cent)

	Both Races			Negro			White		
	Total	Male	Female	Total	Male	Female	Total	Male	Female
Violence	50.0	46.1	62.6	50.6	45.0	69.8	48.4	49.2	46.5
Non-Violence	50.0	53.9	37.4	49.4	55.0	30.2	51.6	50.8	53.5
Total	100.0	100.0	100.0	100.0	100.0	100.0	100.0	100.0	100.0
	(588)	(449)	(139)	(427)	(331)	(96)	(161)	(118)	(43)
Degree of Violence									
2 acts	22.1	24.6	16.1	24.1	28.9	13.4	16.7	13.8	(a)
3–5 acts	29.6	30.4	27.6	31.0	33.5	25.4	25.6	22.4	—
More than 5 acts	17.7	15.5	23.0	19.9	16.8	26.9	11.5	12.1	—
Severe Beating	24.5	22.7	28.7	19.0	14.7	28.3	39.8	43.1	—
Severe Beating prior to one stab	4.4	4.4	4.6	4.2	3.4	6.0	5.1	6.9	—
Severe Beating prior to one shot	1.7	2.4	—	1.8	2.7	—	1.3	1.7	—
Total	100.0	100.0	100.0	100.0	100.0	100.0	100.0	100.0	100.0
	(294)	(207)	(87)	(216)	(149)	(67)	(78)	(58)	(20)

(a) Category too small for breakdown by percentage distribution.

difference in the proportionate distribution of violence and
non-violence among Negro and white victims. Analysis by
sex of victim, however, does reveal *significant* differences,
for 46 per cent of the men, but 63 per cent of the women were
killed violently. Because almost invariably women kill men
and are killed by men, it is possible to combine our knowledge of victims and offenders and safely assert that: (1) men
are killed by men in an almost equal ratio of violence and
non-violence; (2) when men are killed by women it is with
violence in only one-third of the cases; and (3) when women
are killed by men it is with violence in nearly two-thirds of
the cases.

We have previously noted that most women are killed by
men, that beating is the usual method, and the bedroom the
most common place where such cases occur. Perhaps, as
Berg and Fox contend, ego-involvement is greater in violent
homicides, and, we might add, where victim-offender rela-

tionships cross the sex line. It may be that quarrels between the sexes are more likely to center around personal deficiencies and defects than issues; and that frustrations, tensions, conflicts impeding an accommodative functional relationship between members of the opposite sex are likely to reach higher levels of intensity and conscious development than those between members of the same sex. These hypotheses may explain why so many women are killed violently. Furthermore, when women kill men it is most commonly done by stabbing or shooting—methods that do not require as much repetition of action to kill as does beating. To beat someone to the point of death almost of necessity requires severity of the method as well as considerable repetition of the action. Differential physical strength possessed by the sexes means that it is virtually impossible for a female to beat a male to death (except in cases where the male victim is an infant or a child). If one stab or shot does not kill her male adversary, the female probably is likely to desist because in our culture she is less given or expected to engage in physical violence than the male, and the trauma of actually having engaged in a physical assault—of having cut, stabbed, or shot another human being—may produce a quicker and more negative reaction in her than in the male. Finally, even a female life is not easily snuffed out by one or two blows struck by a male fist, and, since most female victims are beaten to death by males, it follows that more females are killed violently than are males.

Few race differences are observable according to the degree of violence and the method by which death occurred, but by every method except the "other" category, females were more violently killed than males. (Appendix I, Table 13.) Twenty-three of the 47 females who were stabbed were stabbed three or more times compared to 49 of the 181 males. In general, as we have just noted, 63 per cent of female victims and 46 per cent of male victims were killed violently. Among stabbings, 72 per cent of the females were killed violently contrasted to 46 per cent of the males. Among shootings, two-thirds of the females were killed with more than one shot compared to only 44 per cent of the males. Among beatings, 63 per cent of the females met death violently compared to half of the males. To summarize the data on methods and violence by sex, we may say that: (1) men were killed violently and non-violently in almost equal proportions, regardless of the particular method—stabbing, shooting, or beating—by which they were assaulted; (2) women were killed violently more frequently than non-violently regardless of the particular major method by which they were assaulted, but women who were stabbed were more likely to be killed violently than women who were shot or beaten.

It is interesting to note that for each race and sex group among victims, more beatings took place in the home than outside the home. For example, two-thirds of Negroes beaten to death in the home were beaten violently, contrasted to 47 per cent violently beaten outside the home. Corresponding figures for whites were 62 per cent violently beaten in the home and 40 per cent outside the home. Important sex similarities are noted for violent or severe beatings when the home/not-home dichotomy is applied: 19 males out of 27 were violently beaten in the home, but only 30 out of 69 outside the home; and 18 females out of 27 were violently beaten in the home, compared to 2 out of 5 outside the home.

Finally, it should be noted that the most excessive degrees of violence during a stabbing or shooting, or those in which more than five acts were involved, were more likely to have occurred in the home than outside the home. Fifty-two deaths from more than five stabs or gunshot wounds were recorded for the five-year period. Of these, 34 occurred in the home and only 18 outside the home. Hence, although there was only a slight and insignificant tendency for violent homicides in general to occur in the home than outside the home, and although no differences were noted in the home/not-home dichotomy for two acts or three to five acts, the most violent stabbings and shootings in which more than five acts occurred were much more likely to take place in the home. This proportion of very violent homicides (more than five acts) occurring in the home contrasted to those outside the home is a fifth again as great as the proportion of all violent homicides that occur in the home.

As is pointed out in Chapter 11, husband-wife slayings have a much higher incidence of excessive violence than any other type of interpersonal relationship between victim and offender. Since most mate slayings occur in the home, we are provided with the major reason for explaining why homicides that occur in the home show a higher proportion of excessive violence (more than five acts) than homicides outside the home.

Only the Berg and Fox study can be used for comparison with the Philadelphia data on violence. Their universe was composed entirely of male offenders, hence no information is available for comparison with female offenders. Furthermore, differential degrees of violence were not included in their study. Although no important racial differences in terms of violence of the homicide were observed for Philadelphia, these authors found that Negro males killed violently in 65 per cent of the cases, while white males did so in 58 per cent of their homicides. Like the findings for Philadelphia, female *victims* were more likely to be slain violently than males, for 79 per cent of the former and 52 per cent of the latter were classified as violent homicides.[1]

Alcohol and Violence

Because presence of alcohol has been found associated with crimes of violence, and because the Philadelphia data suggest a relationship between alcohol and homicide among certain groups, it seems logical to inquire whether presence of alcohol in the homicide offender makes for a greater degree of violence in the manner by which he inflicted death. By combining the previous alcohol and violence data, a series of null hypotheses was established to determine whether any relationships exist between alcohol, violence, race, and sex. One association was found to be *significant*: that between violent homicide and presence of alcohol in the offender. (Table 18.) Alcohol in the offender of either sex is associated with violent

[1] *Ibid.*, p. 115.

TABLE 18

PRESENCE OF ALCOHOL IN THE OFFENDER IN
VIOLENT AND NON-VIOLENT CRIMINAL HOMICIDE,
BY RACE AND SEX OF OFFENDER, PHILADELPHIA, 1948–1952

(In per cent)

	Both Races			Negro			White		
	Total	Male	Female	Total	Male	Female	Total	Male	Female(a
Violence									
Alcohol									
Present	60.0	60.2	58.3	62.7	63.5	57.6	52.4	51.9	—
No Alcohol	40.0	39.8	41.7	37.3	36.5	42.4	47.6	48.1	—
Total	100.0	100.0	100.0	100.0	100.0	100.0	100.0	100.0	100.0
	(315)	(279)	(36)	(233)	(200)	(33)	(82)	(79)	(3)
Non-Violence									
Alcohol									
Present	50.3	52.4	43.8	53.4	55.2	48.3	40.3	44.1	—
No Alcohol	49.7	47.6	56.2	46.6	44.8	51.7	59.7	55.9	—
Total	100.0	100.0	100.0	100.0	100.0	100.0	100.0	100.0	100.0
	(306)	(233)	(73)	(234)	(174)	(60)	(72)	(59)	(13)

(a) Category too small for breakdown by percentage distribution.

homicide. Approximately 60 per cent of all offenders who committed homicide violently had been drinking prior to the crime, while 40 per cent had not been drinking. On the other hand, among those who killed non-violently, half had been drinking and half had not been drinking before the crime.

Although by inspection of the table, Negro offenders with alcohol present may appear to be associated with violent homicide, the number of Negro offenders with alcohol present and who committed non-violent homicide was sufficiently great to prevent the former association from being significant. For each specified race-sex group among violent offenders, the proportion who had been drinking is higher than the proportion who had not been drinking. However, a higher percentage of Negro male offenders than any other race-sex category who killed violently had been drinking. Furthermore, for each specified race-sex group (except Negro males) among non-violent offenders, the proportion who had *not* been drinking is higher than the proportion who had been drinking. Thus, only among Negro male offenders was alcohol more likely to be present than absent whether the homicide was violent or non-violent.

A null hypothesis was not rejected by testing any of the other possible combinations of alcohol, violence, race, and sex. It appears, therefore, that although alcohol, on the one hand, and violence, on the other, are associated with several variables, they are not together related to these same variables. Only the general association between violence and alcohol among offenders reaches the level of *significance* accepted by the present study.

9

PREVIOUS RECORD

Types of Previous Records

MANY scholars in criminology and administrators in penology contend that the typical person who commits criminal homicide is a first offender. They sometimes confuse persons who commit any of the varying degrees of criminal homicide with those who have committed murder in the first degree. Moreover, the type of record a particular offender has is not always clearly designated. He may have any or all three of the following: (1) an arrest, or police record; (2) a conviction, or court record; (3) a commitment, or prison record. It follows, therefore, that a graduated decrease in the proportion of offenders with previous records will be noted as the analyst moves from arrest to commitment data. An individual may have a police record without having a criminal record, for the latter is a legal term implying conviction of a crime. Obviously then, a man with a previous prison or conviction record has a criminal record, whereas a previous arrest without conviction must be denoted as arrest or police record.

In much of the literature on homicide it is claimed that most offenders have no previous record of *any* type. A typical comment is the following by Bernaldo de Quiros:

> . . . Both before and after a murder, the perpetrator thereof is usually quite an ordinary human being, personable or commonplace as the case may be, a dullard, a genius, a scholar, a gentleman or even a hero. . . . A wife doesn't poison her husband for the joy of seeing him die. She does it for his money, for a lover, to be free of his cruelty. Beyond this slight defect in her social scheme, she may be a loving mother, a good housewife and an excellent cook, except upon the day that she puts in the arsenic.[1]

[1] Bernaldo de Quiros, *Modern Theories of Criminality*, p. 60.

It is questionable, of course, whether any person who commits the type of murder this author describes is "quite an ordinary human being" and free from a pathological condition.

Lewis Lawes frequently commented on the typical murderer and referred to him as generally law-abiding. "When we examine the records of men convicted of murder," he said, "we become impressed by the preponderance of those who are 'one-crime men'. Most of those who come into Sing Sing death house have committed the crime as a first offence."[1] The former Sing Sing warden claims, in one place, that 90 per cent of those committed to Sing Sing for homicide were (as of 1927) first offenders,[2] and, elsewhere, that "seventy per cent of all killers who have come to Sing Sing during my twenty years as Warden were never in previous conflict with the law. Does it not seem strange that murder, invariably attributed only to the most depraved individuals, should be committed by people with blameless pasts?"[3] The group Lawes refers to is a select one that was convicted and incarcerated in a select institution. Furthermore, it appears that his reference to the fact that they were "never in previous conflict with the law" *may* mean absence of an arrest record, although it is impossible to be certain he did not mean, instead, absence of court record of conviction.

Like Lawes, who claimed that the murderer was invariably a model prisoner, Jerome Sacks in *Troublemaking in Prison* found, in a study of fifty prisoners at the reformatory in Lorton, Virginia, that none of the homicide offenders were among what he called "resistant prisoners," whose behavior was often a serious administrative problem, but that all such offenders were to be found in the "good prisoner" classification.[4]

In a statement more cautious, but with similar conclusions to those of Lawes, Dublin and Bunzel point out:

[1] Lewis Lawes, *Life and Death in Sing Sing*, Garden City, New York: Garden Publishing Company, Inc., 1928, p. 153.

[2] *Ibid.*, p. 46.

[3] Lewis Lawes, *Meet the Murderer*, New York: Harper and Brothers, 1940, p. 77.

[4] Jerome Gerald Sacks, *Troublemaking in Prison*, Washington, D.C.: The Catholic University of America, 1942, p. 148.

Even more significance attaches to the question: Is the murderer a first offender or has he had a long career of crime, passing from one offense through a series of successively more and more serious acts of lawlessness? Again we are confronted with very faulty data. The best information comes from the publication of the Census Bureau, Prisoners in State and Federal Prisons and Reformatories. As this bulletin points out, methods of identification are inadequate and many prisoners classified as first offenders may have had previous criminal records which were not detected, or they may have been arrested and convicted previously without having been sentenced to a penal institution. Considering the records that are complete, we find that 75 per cent of those admitted on a charge of homicide are classified as first offenders. Homicide, apparently, had been the first criminal act of 74 per cent of the men and 90 per cent of the women. In contrast, first offenders formed only 57 per cent of those admitted on all charges.[1]

Likewise, Tulchin, in his study of prisoners in Joliet penitentiary, found that among those imprisoned for murder, 72 per cent of the native whites of native-born parents had no record of previous commitment, 14 per cent had one previous commitment, 10 per cent two commitments, and 4 per cent three or more. Seventy per cent of southern-born Negroes had no previous commitments, 21 per cent had one, 5 per cent two, and 5 per cent three or more. About half of the northern-born Negroes had no prior commitments, 32 per cent one, 7 per cent two, and 12 per cent three or more.[2] Such a racial breakdown of offenders, as we shall shortly observe, is an important refinement of homicide data with respect to previous record of an offender.

Cassidy's personality study of 200 murderers showed that 38 per cent had previous records (presumably criminal). No racial division was reported for this factor of a previous record although 34 per cent of the total murderers was Negro.[3] Kilpatrick reported that 37 out of the 44 murders committed in

[1] Dublin and Bunzel, op. cit., p. 130.
[2] Simon H. Tulchin, Intelligence and Crime, University of Chicago Press, 1939, pp. 100–101.
[3] Cassidy, op. cit., p. 297.

Richmond in 1942 were by Negroes, and that all but one of the 44 offenders had a previous criminal record.[1] Reviewing the census report on prisoners in state and federal prisons in 1926, Brearley[2] reported that of all persons committed in that year, 56 per cent were first offenders, but of those committed during the same period for charges involving homicide 71 per cent were first offenders. In this case, being a first offender meant no previous commitment record. Of the 29 per cent who were recidivists, 8 per cent had never been in a prison or reformatory but had been in jail once, 2 per cent had been in jail twice, and less than 1 per cent had been in jail three or more times. Fourteen per cent had been in prison or reformatory once, 4 per cent twice, and less than 2 per cent three or more times. The author concludes, on the basis of these reported facts, that "the typical slayer is not, therefore, a person who has been 'hardened' by years of anti-social behavior —he is far more likely to be a first offender."[3]

C. W. Topping[4] describes the convicted Canadian murderer as typically a first offender, and shows that 30 out of 32 were first offenders in 1946, 11 out of 18 in 1947, and 15 out of 15 in 1942. DePorte and Parkhurst comment briefly on previous convictions and sentences of 388 persons convicted of homicide in New York. Although making no reference to the important race variable, these authors do point out that sex differences exist: "Of the male criminals, 196 or 54.0 per cent had no record of a previous conviction, one previous conviction was shown in 85 cases, two in 29, three in 15, and four in 16 cases. All of the females belonged to the first category."[5]

Contrary to most of the previous studies mentioned, Banay found that a high percentage of the very small and select group he analyzed had a previous record. Reporting in 1943 his analysis of 22 persons convicted of murder in the first degree and imprisoned during the period while he was chief psychiatrist in the classification clinic at Sing Sing, he found

[1] Kilpatrick, *op. cit.*, p. 397.
[2] Brearley, *Homicide in the United States,* p. 85.
[3] *Ibid.*, p. 86.
[4] Topping, *op. cit.*, p. 157.
[5] De Porte and Parkhurst, *op. cit.*, p. 65.

a much higher proportion of previous criminal records than Lawes before him reported. "A previous criminal history was present," he says, "in all but four cases which were emotional killings and a murder committed in the course of another felony. The remaining 18 had been convicted from 2 to 30 times on misdemeanors or felonies. . . . In summing up these findings one would be inclined to feel that a man who has been convicted of murder in the first degree . . . will have been convicted before on some felony and have committed a crime of an acquisitive nature."[1] Banay's generalization about the first degree murderer differs considerably from most other reports as does Sellin's comment in *The Criminality of Youth* that commitments to prisons and reformatories for homicide with previous commitments (not necessarily for the same type of crime) were about 62 per cent.[2] Sellin's statement refers to criminal homicide in general and not to murder alone.

Thus, in terms of research concerning the previous conviction or commitment record of persons incarcerated in penal institutions, there is some contradictory evidence, but a general prevailing attitude that at least the murderer (and probably any homicide offender) is more likely than not to be a first offender.

One other type of previous record remains to be analyzed: police, or arrest record. This is the type record used in the present analysis of Philadelphia victims and offenders. There are several reasons justifying use of arrest records rather than conviction or commitment records: (*a*) Fingerprint arrest cards are available for both the victim and the offender in each homicide case. For some records, the disposition of a previous arrest is not known or not recorded, particularly if the arrest had been completed in some jurisdiction other than in Philadelphia. In many cases the individual previously arrested was discharged by the minor judiciary because of insufficient evidence, only to be returned several months later

[1] R. S. Banay, "A Study of 22 Men Convicted of Murder in the First Degree," *op. cit.*, p. 111.
[2] Thorsten Sellin, *The Criminality of Youth*, Philadelphia: The American Law Institute, 1940, pp. 73, 85.

and convicted in a court of record for similar or more serious offenses. It should be noted at this point that there is some inconsistency in the use of conviction records. Some authors presumably use only conviction in a court of record, and, thereby, exclude conviction in any other court and for any criminal case not eligible for adjudication in a court of record. Other authors use conviction for any criminal act, regardless of the court of jurisdiction. It is a matter of conjecture which of the three types of records—arrest, conviction, or commitment—should be used for purposes of analysis, but it is the belief of the present observer that the arrest record is more valid for determining previous contact with the law. Strongly supportive of this position is the fact that, almost invariably, when one of the offenders in the present study had a police record for an offense not culminating in conviction, he had a conviction record for other offenses as well. Rarely did an arrest record stand alone, despite an occasional unknown disposition in some cases.

(*b*) Wallerstein and Wyle,[1] Porterfield,[2] Murphy,[3] and others contend that a large proportion of our normally law-abiding citizenry have committed acts for which they could have been incarcerated or heavily fined had they been detected. It is probably logical, therefore, to assume that the majority of persons arrested by the police did in fact violate the law, that their conduct was sufficiently flagrant to attract attention of the authorities, and that the absence of conviction often was due primarily not to lack of evidence that a crime was committed, but to lack of sufficient evidence necessary to convict in court.

(*c*) Vicissitudes of arrest from one period of time to another, and from one community to another, are probably less than those connected with court and sentencing procedures.

---

[1] James S. Wallerstein and Clement J. Wyle, *Our Law Abiding Law Breakers*. Reprint from *Probation* (April, 1947).

[2] Austin L. Porterfield, *Youth in Trouble*, Fort Worth: Leo Potishman Foundation, 1946.

[3] Fred J. Murphy, Mary M. Shirley, and Helen L. Witmer, "The Incidence of Hidden Delinquency," *American Journal of Ortho-Psychiatry* (October, 1946), 16: 686–696.

(*d*) Some previous homicide research that has used arrest records makes possible comparisons with new research. Furthermore, beginning with their *500 Criminal Careers*,[1] the Gluecks effectively used police as well as court and prison records to determine success or failure during and after parole experience.

(*e*) Although comparison of homicide offenders to other types of criminal offenders has not been included in the present study, it may be, as examination of the data suggests, that the felonious slayer with a past record has graduated from minor assaults against the person to relatively more serious and aggravated offenses against the person, and culminates his career of violence by committing homicide. Quoting from remarks by Sir John Macdonell, the recent Royal Commission Report on Capital Punishment points out: "The short history of a large number of the cases which have been examined might be summed up thus:—Domestic quarrels and brawls; much previous ill-treatment; drinking, fighting, blows; a long course of brutality and continued absence of self-restraint. *This crime* [criminal homicide] *is generally the last of a series of acts of violence.*"[2] To gain insight about the beginning of "a series of acts of violence," and the development of a life pattern of violent behavior, arrest records are more valid than other types of available records.

(*f*) "Loss" of the number of cases in which homicide offenders have a past record increases from arrest to conviction to commitment records.

[1] Sheldon Glueck and Eleanor Glueck, *500 Criminal Careers*, New York: Alfred A. Knopf, 1930. Among other criteria, "success" meant no police record; "partial failure" included arrest for not more than three minor offenses and cases in which there had been arrests for not more than two serious offenses not followed by conviction, or arrest for one serious offense not followed by conviction and for not more than two minor offenses not followed by conviction; and "total failure" included, among other criteria, cases in which there had been arrests for three or more serious offenses not followed by conviction, or arrests for more than three minor offenses not followed by conviction. In some cases offenses known to have been committed but for which arrests were not made were included in their analysis. For an excellent summary of the "success-failure" criteria employed by these authors in several researches, see their *After-Conduct of Discharged Offenders*, London: Macmillan and Co., Ltd., 1946, pp. 21–22.
[2] *Royal Commission on Capital Punishment, 1949–1953 Report*, p. 330. Emphasis is that of the present author.

For these main reasons, then, arrest records provide the best index for measuring previous unfavorable contact with the law, as well as the best index for early detection of some potential homicide offenders.

The Philadelphia Data

Contrary to past impressions and some research, analysis of the offenders in criminal homicide in Philadelphia reveals a relatively high proportion who have a previous police or arrest record. (Table 19.) Analysis of the victim's previous record with possible implications such may have regarding the victim's role in the crime of which he is a part is a new contribution to the field of criminology. Although the proportion of victims with such a record is not so high as that of offenders in this study, a large percentage of victims also have a previous police record—as high as, or higher, in fact, than is reported for offenders in some other studies.

Of the 621 offenders, 400, or 64 per cent have a previous arrest record, and of the 588 victims, as many as 277, or 47 per cent have a previous arrest record. There is a *significant* association between previous arrest record and race of the offender, for 68 per cent of Negro offenders compared to 53

TABLE 19

VICTIMS AND OFFENDERS WITH A PREVIOUS
ARREST RECORD, BY RACE AND SEX, PHILADELPHIA, 1948–1952

(In per cent)

	Both Races			Negro			White		
VICTIMS	Total	Male	Female	Total	Male	Female	Total	Male	Female
No Record	52.7	46.1	74.8	45.7	38.7	69.8	72.0	67.0	86.0
Record	47.3	53.9	25.2	54.3	61.3	30.2	28.0	33.0	14.0
Total	100.0	100.0	100.0	100.0	100.0	100.0	100.0	100.0	100.0
	(588)	(449)	(139)	(427)	(331)	(96)	(161)	(118)	(43)
OFFENDERS									
No Record	35.6	32.0	52.3	31.9	27.8	48.4	46.8	43.5	—(a)
Record	64.4	68.0	47.7	68.1	72.2	51.6	53.2	56.5	—
Total	100.0	100.0	100.0	100.0	100.0	100.0	100.0	100.0	100.0
	(621)	(512)	(109)	(467)	(374)	(93)	(154)	(138)	(16)

(a) Category too small for breakdown by percentage distribution.

175

per cent of white offenders have a previous record. The race differential is also *significant* and even greater among victims, for 54 per cent of Negro victims and only 28 per cent of white victims have a record. The predominance of Negroes with a previous arrest record is strikingly obvious when it is observed that a higher percentage of Negro *victims* than of white *offenders* have a previous record.

Having a previous arrest record is also *significantly* associated with sex of both offenders and victims. Of male offenders, 68 per cent have a previous record compared to 48 per cent of female offenders. As is true of the race differential, so the sex differential with respect to a police record is greater among victims than among offenders, for 54 per cent of male victims have a previous record compared to 25 per cent of female victims. Furthermore, the greater likelihood of males having an official record of past arrest is obvious from the fact that more male *victims* have a previous arrest record than do female *offenders*. In general, therefore, we may assert that Negro and male victims have a previous record in proportions twice as high as do white and female victims respectively.

Among the 400 offenders with a previous police record, 106 have a record of one offense only, 87 of two offenses, 40 of three offenses, and 123 of five or more offenses. The mean number of offenses previously committed by these offenders is 4.1. (Table 20.)

Besides asking whether victims and offenders have a previous police record, it is also important to ask what types of offenses they committed. We may hypothesize that: (*a*) when an offender has a prior record he is more likely to have a record of offenses against the person than against property; moreover, (*b*) if he has a record of offenses against the person he is more likely than not to have a record of having committed a serious offense such as aggravated assault or intent to kill. Some social insight into a possible program of prevention of criminal homicide may be acquired from empirical data that supports these two hypotheses. An individual who commits a serious crime of assault against the person, such as aggravated assault connotes, should not be treated lightly.

Table 20

NUMBER OF OFFENSES FOR WHICH OFFENDERS HAD BEEN
ARRESTED PRIOR TO INSTANT OFFENSE OF CRIMINAL
HOMICIDE, BY RACE AND SEX, PHILADELPHIA, 1948–1952

(In per cent)

Number of Previous Offenses	Both Races			Negro			White		
	Total	Male	Female	Total	Male	Female	Total	Male	Female (a)
One	26.5	25.3	34.6	27.0	26.3	31.2	24.4	21.8	—
Two	21.8	20.4	30.8	22.6	20.7	33.3	18.3	19.2	—
Three	10.0	10.6	5.8	10.1	10.7	6.3	9.8	10.3	—
Four	11.0	11.5	7.7	9.4	9.6	8.3	17.1	17.9	—
Five	9.2	9.5	7.7	8.8	9.3	6.3	11.0	10.3	—
Six to Ten	14.0	14.7	9.6	15.1	15.9	10.4	9.8	10.3	—
More than Ten	7.5	8.0	3.8	6.9	7.4	4.2	9.8	10.3	—
Total	100.0	100.0	100.0	100.0	100.0	100.0	100.0	100.0	100.0
	(400)	(348)	(52)	(318)	(270)	(48)	(82)	(78)	(4)

(a) Category too small for breakdown by percentage distribution.

This comment does not imply that such an offender should be
punished severely according to harsh and classical penological methods, but it does imply more serious and concentrated concern regarding the future behavior of such an
offender. Perhaps if more socio-psychological attention,
supervision, and follow-up by appropriate authorities were
given the person who commits aggravated assault, assault
with intent to kill, or a series of less serious personal assaults,
the rate of criminal homicide might be further reduced.

As the following analysis makes clear, the two hypotheses
just mentioned are confirmed by the Philadelphia data on
previous record of offenders. Future research should compare the proportion of criminal homicide offenders having a
previous record of assaults with the proportion of offenders
of other types of crime who have a record of assaults. Such a
comparison could prove of considerable value for quantitatively measuring what logically appears to be, from inspection
of the frequency distributions, a significantly high proportion
of homicide offenders with a previous record of assaults; for
it may be that the individual develops a habit of reacting
violently to certain stimuli, and grows more set in the habit
when these stimuli re-occur.

TABLE 21

TYPE OF PREVIOUS ARREST RECORD, BY RACE AND SEX
OF VICTIM AND OFFENDER IN CRIMINAL HOMICIDE,
PHILADELPHIA, 1948–1952

(In per cent)

	Race			Sex	
VICTIM	Total	Negro	White	Male	Fema
Previous Arrest Record					
Offenses Against the Person	54.2	52.6	62.2	55.0	48.6
(Aggravated Assault)	(36.5)	(37.5)	(31.1)	(39.7)	(14.3)
Offenses Other Than Those					
Against the Person	45.8	47.4	37.8	45.0	51.4
(Offenses Against Property)	(14.4)	(15.1)	(11.1)	(14.9)	(11.4)
Total Previous Arrest	100.0	100.0	100.0	100.0	100.0
	(277)	(232)	(45)	(242)	(35)
OFFENDER					
Previous Arrest Record					
Offenses Against the Person	66.0	66.4	64.6	68.4	50.0
(Aggravated Assault)	(48.0)	(50.6)	(37.8)	(49.1)	(40.4)
Offenses Other Than Those					
Against the Person	34.0	33.6	35.4	31.6	50.0
(Offenses Against Property)	(9.3)	(15.7)	(8.5)	(10.9)	(36.5)
Total Previous Arrest	100.0	100.0	100.0	100.0	100.0
	(400)	(318)	(82)	(348)	(52)

Note:

The category, "Offenses Against the Person," includes those individuals whose previou arrest record comprises *at least* one offense against the person, but does not exclud individuals who have a record of other types of offenses as well as offenses again: the person. Although included in "Offenses Against the Person," the category "Aggravated Assault," is also separately considered for purposes of discussio The percentage with a previous arrest record of aggravated assault is compute from the total number of persons having a previous record. The category, "Offense Other Than Those Against the Person," excludes all individuals who have an previous record of an offense against the person. "Offenses Against Property" means that the individual has a record of property offense only and has no record c any other type of offense. The percentages in parentheses are computed on th basis of the total number in each specific race and sex category.

A summary analysis of Tables 19–21 reveals the following interesting conclusions about the types of offenses committed by persons (victims and offenders) involved in criminal homicide. (See also Appendix I, Table 15.)

(1) Of 400 *offenders* with a previous arrest record, 66 per cent have a record of at least one or more offenses against the person, 34 per cent against property only or other types of offenses, and 48 per cent, aggravated assault. Of the 264 offenders with a record of one or more offenses against the

person, 73 per cent have a record of aggravated assault. (Because aggravated assault is included among offenses against the person, these percentages obviously do not add up to 100 per cent.)

(2) Of 277 *victims* with a previous arrest record, 54 per cent have a record of at least one or more offenses against the person, 46 per cent against property only or other types of offenses, and 37 per cent aggravated assault. Of the 150 victims with a record of one or more offenses against the person, 67 per cent have a record of aggravated assault.

(3) A greater proportion of Negro males have a previous arrest record than any other specified race and sex group.

(4) White females have the lowest previous arrest record.

(5) Negro males have the highest record for offenses against the person, offenses against property, and aggravated assault both among offenders and victims.[1]

(6) Negro male *victims* (61 per cent) have a higher arrest record than white male *offenders* (57 per cent); and Negro female *victims* (30 per cent) have a higher arrest record than white female *offenders* (25 per cent).

(7) The proportionate difference between offenders and victims with previous arrest records increases as one moves from Negro males (offenders have a record 18 per cent greater than victims) to Negro females and white males (offenders in both groups have a record 71 per cent greater than victims) to white females (of 16 offenders 4 have a record, and of 43 victims 6 have a record).

(8) Both among offenders and victims with a previous arrest record, a greater proportion have a record of offenses against the person than offenses against property. This conclusion applies to every specified race and sex group.[2]

(9) A larger proportion of offenders with an arrest record have a record of aggravated assault than of all types of property offenses combined. While 176 have a record of property offenses (property only, or both person and property), 192 have a record of aggravated assault. This fact supports the

[1] This generalization excludes white female offenders, who numbered only 16.
[2] Except white female offenders, whose number is too small for such refinement.

179

contention that criminal homicide offenders have a strong proclivity for engaging in crimes of violence or of personal assault rather than in crimes of an acquisitive nature. It is important to take cognizance of the fact that when offenses against the person are compared to offenses against property, not an equal number of potential crimes are compared. According to the Pennsylvania Penal Code, there are 33 sections of offenses against the person for which an individual may be arrested.[1] On the other hand, there are 157 sections of offenses against property for which an individual may be arrested.[2] However, it must be admitted that the "cleared by arrest" rate is higher for offenses against the person than for offenses against property. But this clearance differential is probably unimportant when comparison is made between *one* offense of personal violence (aggravated assault) and *all* types of property offenses. Therefore, since more offenders have a previous arrest record of aggravated assault than of all types of property offenses combined, this fact provides a valid index of the homicide offender's propensity for offenses of personal violence. It appears that Sir John Macdonell's statement is correct; namely, that criminal homicide is the culmination of a previous pattern of violent behavior.

(10) Nearly half of the total *victims* have a previous arrest record; and among victims with a record, over half have a record of one or more offenses against the person, and over a third have a record of aggravated assault. Such evidence leads to the suggestion that in many cases the victim is a homicide-prone person; i.e., one who either is placed, or puts himself, in situations conducive to violent physical assault. Because in nearly half the criminal homicides the victim has a previous record, he is probably often more than a passive, submissive player in the homicide drama.[3]

(11) Two additional variables—presence of alcohol and age

---

[1] William Hoffman, *Pennsylvania Criminal Law and Criminal Procedure*, Article VII, "Offenses Against the Person," 1952, pp. 121–143.

[2] *Ibid.*, Article VIII, "Offenses Against Personal Property and Fraudulent Dealing Therewith," and Article IX, "Offenses Against Real Property and Malicious Mischief," pp. 143–187.

[3] For detailed analysis of the victim's contribution to the crime, see Chapter 14.

of the offender—were tested using the null hypothesis to determine whether they were associated with offenders having a previous arrest record. Analysis reveals that there is a *significant* relationship between presence of alcohol in the offender and the offender with a previous arrest record. Of 400 offenders with an arrest record, two-thirds (263) had been drinking at the time of their offense, and of 221 offenders with no previous record, only one-third (80) had been drinking. By reversing the perspective it may be noted that of 343 offenders with alcohol present, 77 per cent have an arrest record, but of the 278 with no alcohol at the time of homicide, less than half have an arrest record.

Offenders in criminal homicide who have violated the law previously are probably more readily led, or driven, to violate the law again (especially to assault others) than those who have no such record. Lowered inhibitions due to the presence of alcohol may mean that the offender with a previous record even more quickly follows a response-pattern adopted in past experiences. Moreover, because a higher proportion of Negroes and males than of whites and females, in general, have a previous arrest record as well as having had alcohol present, we should expect to find previous record and the presence of alcohol associated. A life pattern of heavy drinking may be related to the crimes for which these offenders were previously arrested, and the homicide committed by those with a record also may be related to their present ingestion of alcohol. Perhaps, however, persons with a police record are more likely than persons with no record to commit homicide, regardless of whether or not they had been drinking. In any case, the *significant* association between the two attributes (previous police record and presence of alcohol in the offender) requires an explanation which is only partially satisfied by the interpretations just given.

(12) Finally, no association is noted between age of offender and arrest record. For purposes of testing the null hypothesis, the offender group was dichotomized at age 35.[1]

[1] Division at this age was an arbitrary choice, but other divisions, when tested for a relationship to previous arrest record, yielded similar results.

Of the 369 offenders under 35 years of age, 231 or 63 per cent have a record, and of 251 offenders aged 35 and over, 169, or 68 per cent, have a record.

Perhaps there is some significance in the absence of a statistical association between age of the homicide offender and a previous arrest record. Clearly, the older the individual, the longer has been his past association with other persons and social situations that could have resulted in his violating the law at one time or another. Contrariwise, the younger the individual, the shorter has been such association and the fewer are his experiences in social intercourse. Hence, the older the offender is, all other things being equal, the greater the likelihood of a previous police record. The person aged 35 when he commits criminal homicide may have been arrested when he was 19, or 21, or even 34 years of age (or at each of these ages), so that the total span of time during which an arrest could have occurred is considerably greater than that of a person aged 21 when he commits criminal homicide. Since offenders aged 35 and over have a previous arrest record in a proportion similar to offenders under age 35, despite the differential number of years in which to acquire such a record, there may be variables in operation not easily discernible. It may be that the time period between the last (or perhaps only) arrest prior to the homicide and the homicide itself is similar for both age groups. If this time period is short and the offense preceding homicide is aggravated assault, or something similar, then these variables relegate the question of age to a subordinate role, and the *lack* of a statistically significant association between age and previous record becomes an important corollary of the positive association of homicide and a previous record of assault within a given period of time prior to the slaying. If we could say that given a person with an aggravated assault charge, the chances are such and such that he will, within a definite period of time, commit homicide —then the responsibility and right of society to take necessary measures to prevent such a killing could be more firmly established.

Previous Arrest Record Noted in Other Studies

Homicide literature that analyzes offenders and/or victims in terms of a previous arrest record rather than a conviction record is meager and uses material not always comparable to the Philadelphia data. In his study of 92 Wisconsin murderers, Gillin[1] noted that less than 30 per cent had a previous commitment record, slightly less than half had a previous court record, and 53 per cent had a previous arrest record. Erroneously referring to "criminal record" when actually meaning arrest record, Stearns[2] claimed that 50 out of 100 consecutive murderers admitted to the Massachusetts State Prison in 1921 had a previous arrest record. Berg and Fox pointed out that the previous history of the offender contained a record of behavior which represented a kind of preparation or training for the current offense. Examining previous arrest records, they noted that of the 200 males incarcerated in the Michigan prison for homicide, 12 per cent of the whites and 22 per cent of the Negroes had a previous police record for one or more assaultive legal offenses.[3] In his study of the habitual offender law in Kansas, Sam Carter[4] found that of 20 murderers committed to the Kansas State Penitentiary between June 30, 1930 and the following June, 1931, 11 had been arrested prior to their present murder offense.

With the caution in mind that sources of data in other studies differ, Philadelphia offenders (and probably victims) in criminal homicide appear to have previous arrest records in greater proportion than elsewhere reported in the literature. Finally, it is important to note that more criminal homicide offenders in Philadelphia are recidivists than are offenders of all types of crime in the nation as a whole. In 1950, 60 per cent of all arrest records examined, represented persons who already had fingerprint cards on file in the Identification Division of the F.B.I.[5] This is a proportion slightly less than the 64 per

---

[1] Gillin, "Social Backgrounds of Sex Offenders and Murderers," *op. cit.*, pp. 234–235. See also, "The Wisconsin Murderer," *op. cit.*, p. 551.

[2] Stearns, *op. cit.*, p. 239.

[3] Berg and Fox, *op. cit.*, p. 117.

[4] Sam Carter, *The History of the Habitual Offender Law in Kansas*, Unpublished M.A. thesis, 1935, pp. 70–73.

[5] *Uniform Crime Reports*, 1950, p. 111.

cent of Philadelphia offenders in criminal homicide who have a previous arrest record. In terms of police or arrest records, therefore, we must conclude that the criminal homicide offender in Philadelphia is *not* typically a first offender, that in over six cases out of ten he has a previous record of contact with the law, and that Negroes and males are much more likely than whites and females to have such a record.

10

MOTIVES

Classification of Motives

VARIATIONS in the classification of homicide motives assume vast proportions in the literature. In *Penal Philosophy*, Gabriel Tarde[1] provides an interesting review of different classifications concluding that motive is more important than the presence or absence of premeditation in homicide. Garofalo[2] contends that every homicide is committed for a purely egoistic end and proves the offender's "exceptional perversity or utter lack of the altruistic sentiments." Jesse[3] believes that murder motives fall into six classifications, including murder for gain, revenge, elimination, jealousy, the lust of killing, and from conviction. Abrahamsen[4] classifies murder into (1) "symptomatic," including (a) murder due to a distorted erotic drive, which can be divided into jealousy murder and murder in the course of a sexual offense, and (b) murder due to an aggressive drive, which can be divided into alcoholic murder, surrogate murder, and murder due to physical inferiority; and (2) "manifest (essential)" murder, which includes (a) profit murder and (b) murder from motives unknown. In psychoanalytic literature, emphasis is on the frustration-aggression thesis,[5] unconscious hostilities against the

[1] Tarde, *op. cit.*, especially pp. 464–466.
[2] Garofalo, *op. cit.*, p. 373.
[3] F. Tennyson Jesse, *Murder and Its Motives*, London: George G. Harrap and Co., Ltd., 1952 edition, p. 13.
[4] Abrahamsen, *op. cit.*, p. 162.
[5] For example, see: John Dollard, L. W. Doob, Neal E. Miller, O. H. Mowrer, and Robert R. Sears, *Frustration and Aggression*, New Haven: Yale University Press, 1939; Anna Freud, *The Ego and the Mechanisms of Defence*, translated by Cecil Baines, New York: International Universities Press, Inc., 1946; and the recent study which summarizes much of the frustration-aggression research related to homicide, A. F. Henry and J. F. Short, *Suicide and Homicide*, 1954.

father- or mother-image,[1] the unconscious desire for punishment,[2] etc., as motives in homicide. Helene Frenkel[3] provides an interesting account of homicide not motivated by personal gain. Rupert Vance and Waller Wynne[4] ably discuss the unwritten law that permits a husband motivated by revenge to kill his wife's paramour under certain circumstances.

The fact that motives for killing another must be interpreted in terms of the culture value system and goals within which the offender operates is clear from even a cursory examination of anthropological and historical literature. Elwin,[5] for example, shows that homicide among the Maria in India may result from what he calls a "social rather than an anti-social instinct." Colonel Sleeman's[6] classic account of the Thugs of India reveals that, although robbery and plunder were often involved in their deliberate killings, the Thug was a murderer by hereditary profession and sincerely believed he had a divine right to kill. The British report on Basutoland medicine murder shows that premeditated crimes were committed for the specific purpose of obtaining medicines from the bodies of victims in order to promote fertility of crops and to enhance the personality of important persons.[7] A review

[1] See, for example: James E. Greene, "Motivations of a Murderer," *The Journal of Abnormal and Social Psychology* (1948), 43: 526–531; Hervey Cleckley, *The Mask of Sanity*, St. Louis: C. V. Mosby Co., 1941; Robert M. Lindner, *Rebel Without a Cause*, New York: Greene and Stratton, 1944; Frederick Wertham, *Dark Legend: A Study in Murder*, New York: Duell, Sloan, and Pearce, 1941, and *The Show of Violence*, New York: Doubleday and Company, 1949; Alice Raven, "A Theory of Murder," *The American Sociological Review* (April, 1930), 22: 108–118.

[2] See, for example: Franz Alexander, "The Need for Punishment and the Death-Instinct," *International Journal of Psycho-Analysis* (1929), 10: 256–269; Franz Alexander and W. Healy, *Roots of Crime*, New York: Alfred A. Knopf, 1935; O. Fenichel, "The Clinical Aspect of the Need for Punishment," *International Journal of Psycho-Analysis* (1928), 9: 47–70; B. Karpman, "Criminality, the Super-ego and the Sense of Guilt," *Psychological Review* (1930), 17: 280–296; H. Nunberg, "The Sense of Guilt and the Need for Punishment," *International Journal of Psycho-Analysis* (1926), 7: 420–433; D. Abrahamsen, *Crime and the Human Mind*.

[3] Helene Frenkel, "The Murderer Who Is Not Motivated By Personal Gain," *Social Science Abstracts* (May, 1930), 2: 947.

[4] R. B. Vance and W. Wynne, Jr., "Folk Rationalizations in the Unwritten Law," *The American Journal of Sociology* (January, 1934), 39: 483–492.

[5] Elwin, *op. cit.*, p. 53.

[6] Colonel James L. Sleeman, *Thug, or a Million Murders*, London: Sampson Low, Marston and Co., Ltd., 1933.

[7] *Basutoland Medicine Murder*, A Report on the Recent Outbreak of "Diretlo" Murders in Basutoland, London: H.M. Stationery Office, April, 1951.

of crimes and punishments in Renaissance Florence by the author illustrates complex political, economic, religious, and other motives that dominated an earlier historical period in our own Western civilization.[1]

It is obvious, therefore, as Ralph Banay points out, that "classifications of murder lend themselves to such variety that the nature of homicide and the motives for killing can be assigned to an infinity of divisions."[2]

The present analysis of motives is necessarily rudimentary and relies upon terminology used by the police to describe those factors which prompt one individual to take the life of another.[3] As the term is used in the present analysis, it should not be confused with intent. Intent is an essential legal element of crime and refers to the actor's intellectual ability to comprehend the nature of his act; motive is not an essential of any crime. Intent is the resolve to commit an act, whereas motive is the inducement which stimulates a person to commit it. The fact that one's act may have been motivated by some particular type of ill will or even by kindness does no more than contribute to circumstantial evidence of intent. The Homicide Squad in Philadelphia uses the term "motive" in descriptive summaries, but is well aware of the fact that most underlying "causes" and unconscious motivations usually lie beyond the realm of even the most competent or necessary police investigation. The term used in the present study refers to the ostensible and police-recorded motive. It does not necessarily imply conscious design or planning, nor does it mean underlying socio-psychologic or psychoanalytic "cause." Although several motives may be involved in the same homicidal act, the predominant motive observed and reported by the police is used for purposes of statistical analysis. There

[1] Marvin E. Wolfgang, "Political Crimes and Punishments in Renaissance Florence," *Journal of Criminal Law, Criminology, and Police Science,* (January–February, 1954), 44: 555–581.

[2] Ralph Banay, "Study in Murder," (*Murder and the Penalty of Death, The Annals of the American Academy of Political and Social Science*), (November, 1952), 284: 26.

[3] If the present study were a deeply probing psychologic or psychoanalytic description of the homicide offender, this probably would be the most important chapter. Such an analysis of the Philadelphia offenders awaits future research involving, among other methodological techniques, interviews in prison with convicted and sentenced slayers.

are many problems, including semantic ones, involved in establishing a classification of motives. As Le Moyne Snyder says in his handbook on homicide investigation, "Motivations and passions which may finally be activated to the point of murder are complex and varied. Establishing a motive such as revenge, robbery, or jealousy may greatly facilitate an investigation, but many of the most brutal homicides seem to be without incentive of any kind."[1]

The classification of motives used in the present analysis is found in Table 22. Not always has it been possible to select easily the predominant motive from a *mélange* of circumstances and motives. Homicides resulting from altercations and family quarrels constitute the two largest groups, perhaps partly because of the very general nature of these categories. Despite diligent efforts to discern the exact and precise factors involved in an altercation or domestic quarrel, police officers are often unable to acquire information other than the fact that a trivial argument developed, or an insult was suffered by one or both of the parties. Intensive reading of the police files and of verbatim reports of interrogations, as well as participant observation in these interrogations by the author suggest that the significance of a jostle, a slightly derogatory remark, or the appearance of a weapon in the hands of an adversary are stimuli differentially perceived and interpreted by Negroes and whites, males and females. Social expectations of response in particular types of social interaction result in differential "definitions of the situation."[2] A male is usually expected to defend the name and honor of his mother, the virtue of womanhood (even though his female companion for the evening may be an entirely new acquaintance and/or a prostitute), and to accept no derogation about his race (even from a member of his own race), his age, or his masculinity. Quick resort to physical combat as a measure of daring, courage, or defense of status appears to be a cultural expecta-

---

[1] Snyder, *op. cit.*, p. 8.
[2] W. I. Thomas, "The Persistence of Primary-Group Norms in Present-Day Society and Their Influence in Our Educational System," in Herbert S. Jennings and others, *Suggestions of Modern Science Concerning Education*, New York: Macmillan and Co., 1917.

tion, especially for lower socio-economic class males of both races. When such a culture norm response is elicited from an individual engaged in social interplay with others who harbor the same response mechanism, physical assaults, altercations, and violent domestic quarrels that result in homicide are likely to be relatively common. The upper-middle and upper social class value system defines and codifies behavioral norms into legal rules that often transcend sub-cultural mores, and considers many of the social and personal stimuli that evoke a combative reaction in the lower classes as "trivial." Thus, there exists a cultural antipathy between many folk rationalizations of the lower class, and of males of both races, on the one hand, and the middle-class legal norms under which they live, on the other. The fate of 206 victims and the 227 offenders responsible for their death, whose motive has been classified as "altercation," can be partially interpreted in terms of the foregoing remarks.

The "other" classification found in the tables listing motives refers to a miscellaneous collection that could not be properly grouped elsewhere, and was used rather than force a motive into one of the more precise classifications. A Negro male who sexually assaulted an unknown white female, a mentally diseased offender who felt a compulsion to kill, a sniper who used a victim for target practice, and so forth, make up the "other" category. The categories "self-defense" and "accidental" are so listed by the police because the defendants' accounts of the homicides for which they were charged, and police investigations of the cases, seem to indicate no other ostensible reason for the acts. However, sufficient doubt remained concerning the validity of the defendants' adamant contentions so that the coroner's inquest did not exonerate the defendants; thus a court trial was still required for final adjudication. The "unknown" category includes many of the unsolved homicides, as well as some cases involving a victim killed by an offender who committed suicide at the scene of the crime and left no indication of the motive behind either or both acts. Some overlapping probably occurs in the "jealousy" and "revenge" categories. A jealous suitor seeking revenge for his having been emotionally rejected is difficult to classify, but full description of such cases has usually led to a "revenge" classification. An offender motivated by jealousy and seeking to resolve an emotional problem by means of a physical assault usually attacks his rival. A jealous offender who kills his love object is most often motivated by revenge for the alienation he has had to suffer.

To kill purposefully a newly born infant is a criminal homicide, but the primary difficulty for the police and other judicial agencies is to prove that a live birth occurred. The mother may have committed self-abortion, or may have carelessly disposed of a miscarried fetus, which, upon coming to the attention of the police authorities, may result in an investigation charging her with homicide. In six cases the coroner's office failed to exonerate females who had been responsible for disposing of fetuses.

A homicide occurring during the commission of another felony is separately tabulated. Such homicide may actually have resulted from an accidental firing of a robber's gun, or from any other type of unintentional action, but the law classifies homicide committed during certain types of felonies as murder in the first degree. In some cases a "revenge" or "jealousy" motive was dominant although the homicide occurred during the commission of another felony. For example, in a few cases the offender set fire to a house inhabited by his rival and the woman who spurned his love. The defendant committed arson from which homicide resulted, but the primary motive was revenge and arson was the means to achieve the end.

The Philadelphia Data

Only with respect to a few motives are there important differences in the distribution of motives according to victims and offenders. (Table 22.) The discussion that follows, therefore, refers to homicide cases (victims) except where important differences exist between victims and offenders. Striking and *significant* race and sex differences may be noted for the distributions according to motive.

190

TABLE 22

MOTIVE IN CRIMINAL HOMICIDE, BY RACE AND SEX OF
VICTIM AND OF OFFENDER, PHILADELPHIA, 1948–1952

(In per cent)

MOTIVE	VICTIM								
	Both Races			Negro			White		
	Total	Male	Female	Total	Male	Female	Total	Male	Female
Altercation of relatively trivial origin; insult, curse, jostling, etc.	35.0	40.8	16.6	35.8	40.5	19.8	32.9	41.5	9.3
Domestic quarrel	14.1	10.5	25.9	15.5	12.1	27.1	10.6	5.9	23.3
Jealousy	11.6	8.9	20.1	14.1	11.5	22.9	5.0	1.7	14.0
Altercation over money	10.5	12.0	5.8	13.1	15.1	6.3	3.7	3.4	4.7
Robbery	6.8	8.0	2.9	2.3	2.4	2.1	18.6	23.7	4.7
Revenge	5.3	5.1	5.8	5.4	5.4	5.2	5.0	4.2	7.0
Accidental	3.9	3.6	5.0	4.0	3.6	5.2	3.7	3.4	4.7
Self-defense	1.4	1.6	.7	1.9	2.1	1.0	—	—	—
Halting of felon	1.2	1.6	—	1.6	2.1	—	—	—	—
Escaping arrest	1.0	1.6	.7	.5	.6	—	2.5	2.5	2.3
Concealing birth	1.0	.5	2.9	.7	.6	1.0	1.9	—	7.0
Other	3.4	2.5	6.5	1.4	.9	3.1	8.7	6.8	14.0
Unknown	4.8	4.0	7.2	3.8	3.0	6.3	7.5	6.8	9.3
Total	100.0	100.0	100.0	100.0	100.0	100.0	100.0	100.0	100.0
	(588)	(449)	(139)	(427)	(331)	(96)	(161)	(118)	(43)

	OFFENDER								
Altercation of relatively trivial origin; insult, curse, jostling, etc.	36.6	38.5	27.5	35.3	36.4	31.2	40.3	44.2	(a)
Domestic quarrel	13.4	9.0	33.9	13.7	9.1	32.3	12.3	8.7	—
Jealousy	11.1	10.2	15.6	12.9	12.0	16.1	5.8	5.1	—
Altercation over money	10.3	10.7	8.3	12.6	13.6	8.6	3.2	2.9	—
Robbery	7.9	9.6	—	6.6	8.3	—	11.7	13.0	—
Revenge	4.8	5.3	2.8	4.9	5.4	3.2	4.6	5.1	—
Accidental	4.5	4.7	3.7	4.3	4.3	4.3	5.2	5.8	—
Self-defense	1.3	1.2	1.8	1.7	1.6	2.2	—	—	—
Halting of felon	1.1	1.4	—	1.3	1.6	—	.7	.7	—
Escaping arrest	1.0	1.2	—	.4	.5	—	2.6	2.9	—
Concealing birth	.8	—	4.6	.4	—	2.2	1.9	—	—
Other	4.2	4.9	.9	3.6	4.6	—	5.8	5.8	—
Unknown	3.1	3.5	.9	2.1	2.7	—	5.8	5.8	—
Total	100.0	100.0	100.0	100.0	100.0	100.0	100.0	100.0	100.0
	(621)	(512)	(109)	(467)	(374)	(93)	(154)	(138)	(16)

(a) Category too small for breakdown by percentage distribution.

191

Criminal homicides due to general altercations are the most frequent type (35 per cent) and involved 206 victims. Regardless of race, 41 per cent of all males were killed as a result of an altercation and thus more often than for any single reason. However, female victims of these general altercations are proportionately twice as great among Negroes as among whites, and Negro female *offenders* nearly five times more frequently than white female offenders committed homicide during altercations.

The 83 family or domestic quarrels (14 per cent) constitute the second largest category among all victims, but make up proportionately twice as many of the cases involving Negro males (12 per cent) as white males (6 per cent). Domestic quarrels were responsible for more deaths among females (26 per cent) than any other motive, and proportionately over twice as frequently as among males (11 per cent). An interesting victim-offender difference may be noted among white females in this category: less than a fourth were victims, while nearly a half were offenders in cases involving family disputes.

The third largest motive category is jealousy (12 per cent), and is recorded to have been responsible for 68 deaths. Nearly three times as many Negroes (14 per cent) as whites (5 per cent) were victims of a jealous assault. But equally striking is the fact that only 9 per cent of the men compared to 20 per cent of the women were killed because of jealousy. This smaller proportion of men killed as a result of a jealousy motive is indicative of the fact that men more frequently than women are involved in interpersonal relationships with other men with whom they become embroiled in heated argument. Men in our culture participate in a greater number of interactive relationships with a greater number of people each day than do women—hence, the opportunities or possibilities of situations likely to precipitate or incite a physical assault are commensurately increased. Durkheim, as previously quoted, frequently referred to the greater amount of social participation in collective life by men than by women and incorporated this point into his general interpretation of suicide and homicide.[1] As a result of this greater amount of social interaction, proportionately more men than women are slain due to motives other than jealousy. Jealousy, as an affective trait, may be equally distributed between the sexes. Yet, because men are outside the home engaging in a multitudinous variety of collective life activities to a greater degree than women, the probability of their becoming victims of homicide due to many other and varied motives reduces their chances of becoming victims of a jealous rage.

In addition to this sex differential, race appears to be a *significant* factor in homicides due to jealousy. Proportionately almost twice as many Negro females (23 per cent) as white females (14 per cent), and six times as many Negro males (12 per cent) as white males (2 per cent) were killed due to jealousy.

These cases invariably involved a victim and offender of opposite sex. Could it be that more Negro males felt uncertain of the strength of the emotional bond between them and their mates or lovers than did white males of their mates or lovers? Were more of these Negro females felt to be unfaithful than white females to their husbands or lovers? An affirmative answer to both questions is indicated by what is known about the shifting liaisons or cohabitation patterns of lower-class Negroes in general in Philadelphia. Inability of the Homicide Squad to vouch for the accuracy of reported information regarding marital status of Negroes involved in homicide—either as victims or offenders—combined with a general presumption of the prevailing culture trait of successive common-law marriages among lower-class Negroes, plus reported high rates of desertion and separation among Negroes[2]—all point to the conclusion that the incidence of infidelity and alienation of affection either by mates or

[1] Durkheim, *op. cit.*, pp. 341–342.
Relative to this discussion of personal interrelationships see James H. S. Bossard, "The Law of Family Interaction," *American Journal of Sociology* (January, 1945), 50: 293; the same author's *The Sociology of Child Development*, p. 146; and William M. Kephart, "A Quantitative Analysis of Intragroup Relationships," *American Journal of Sociology* (May, 1950), 55: 546.
[2] William M. Kephart and Thomas P. Monahan, "Desertion and Divorce in Philadelphia," *American Sociological Review* (December, 1952), 17: 725–726, for desertion and separation figures.

cohabiting persons is higher among Negroes than among whites. Hence, more Negroes—both male and female—than whites are likely to be killed because of a jealousy motive.

Altercations over money, the fourth largest category, were responsible for 62 deaths (11 per cent). Three times as many Negroes (13 per cent) as whites (4 per cent), and twice as many males (12 per cent) as females (6 per cent) were killed in this type of altercation. Probably underlying socio-psychological factors are involved in any attempt to explain why five times as many Negro males (15 per cent) as white males (3 per cent) were killed during arguments over money. In over 95 per cent of these altercations, which usually occurred during a dice or card game, the amount of money involved was less than ten dollars and often was as little as twenty-five cents.

Robbery was a motive in the death of 40 persons (7 per cent) and manifests a *significant* race difference, since nine times as many whites (19 per cent) as Negroes (2 per cent) were victims of homicide involving robbery. Even more glaring is the fact that 24 per cent of white males, compared to only 2 per cent of Negro males were killed when robbery was a primary motive leading subsequently to felonious death. Presumably white males either have, or are suspected of having, more monetary and other personal property than Negroes, and/or white males are more frequently in situations (such as night watchmen) where they are likely to be victimized as a result of robbery.

Beyond these five leading motive categories, the number of cases is too small to analyze by race and sex groups for any meaningful statements.

Analysis of the home/not-home division reveals some interesting differences where cell size is sufficiently large to permit generalizations. It has been previously observed that almost an equal number of homicides occurred in the home as occurred outside the home (301/287). This ratio is maintained by race and sex groups throughout most of the motive categories. However, although nearly an equal number of Negro males during altercations were killed in the home as outside the home (68/66), seven times as many white males were killed

194

outside the home as in the home (6/43). It is, therefore, largely white male altercations outside the home that contribute to the fact that among all victims nearly 60 per cent of the altercations occurred outside the home. As might be expected, more cases of jealousy (62 per cent) and domestic quarrels (86 per cent) occurred in the home. Finally, in cases involving altercation over money, about half of the men compared to three-quarters of the women were killed in the home.

No significant differences of motives are noted according to age of offender. (Appendix I, Tables 18, 19.) However, there is some relationship between motive and violence with which the victim was slain. (Table 23.) Homicides most likely to be

TABLE 23

MOTIVE IN CRIMINAL HOMICIDE BY VIOLENCE,
PHILADELPHIA, 1948–1952

Motive	Total	Non-violence	Violence
Altercation of relatively trivial origin; insult, curse, jostling, etc.	206	112	94
Domestic quarrel	83	33	50
Jealousy	68	30	38
Altercation over money	62	33	29
Robbery	40	16	24
Revenge	31	10	21
Accidental	23	21	2
Self-defense	8	4	4
Halting felon	7	5	2
Escaping arrest	6	4	2
Concealing birth	6	5	1
Other	20	10	10
Unknown	28	11	17
Total	588	294	294

non-violent are those classified as accidental, disposing of a fetus, and killing of a suspected felon. Homicides most likely to be violent are those classified as due to revenge, unknown motives, family quarrels, and robbery.

Comparable Motives Noted in Other Studies

Discussion of homicide motives in the literature usually involves either a case-study analysis of particular types of offenders, or frequency distributions of incomparable categorizations. Uniform data are lacking, and police departments rarely tabulate homicides by motive.

Von Hentig was able to gather information on murder and manslaughter for New York City during 1936-1940, and with a five year average found that, like Philadelphia, the two leading reported motives were altercations (34 per cent) and domestic disputes (26 per cent).[1] The classification of motives in *The Illinois Crime Survey* is not very comparable, for a phenomenon existed in Chicago during the time of the survey which is foreign to present Philadelphia homicides; i.e., the large number of gang killings occurring during the days of Prohibition in 1926 and 1927. For each of these years, 380 criminal homicides were recorded by the Cook County authorities, and in 1926, 90 were altercations and brawls, 74 were gang killings, 37 were committed during holdups, and 32 were domestic quarrels. The distribution for 1927 was similar.[2] Internecine gang wars have been considerably reduced throughout the country since the repeal of Prohibition and the development of regional syndicates of organized crime.[3] As a result, Lawes' statement in *Meet the Murderer* seems generally applicable today: "On the contrary, most murders are not committed by members of the underworld. Many more people are killed as the result of domestic, lovers', or financial quarrels, marital incompatibility, and drunkenness than in gang wars or holdups."[4]

A review of 500 homicides reported by the Metropolitan Life Insurance Company in 1939 indicated that approximately 30 per cent were due to domestic quarrels and jealousy, and that "practically all killings arise under the stress of emotions of fear, hatred, anger, jealousy, or greed . . . about trifles."[5] Cassidy[6] claimed that over 30 per cent of the 200 murders he examined were what he called "surface murders," due to

---

[1] H. von Hentig, *The Criminal and His Victim*, p. 397.

[2] *The Illinois Crime Survey*, p. 610.

[3] Burt Turkus and Sid Fedor, *Murder, Inc.*, Garden City, New York: Permabook Division of Doubleday and Company, Inc., 1952, pp. 86–119.

[4] Lawes, *Meet the Murderer*, p. 76.

[5] "Domestic Quarrels Deadlier than Gangster Slayings," *Science News Letter* (March, 1939), 35: 152.

[6] Cassidy, *op. cit.*, p. 297.

impulsive behavior during arguments and personal affronts. As might be expected, Gillin[1] found a higher proportion of the Wisconsin murderers serving life sentences had committed homicide in connection with another crime (44 per cent), but even among this group, nearly a third killed as a result of a "long-standing feud or grudge," involving marital difficulties and seeking revenge on persons other than a spouse, while another fourth were due to "immediate quarrels." In his study of 54 juvenile homicides, Growdon[2] reported that no motive was clearly established in 11 cases, that 12 were due to revenge, 10 occurred during robbery, and the rest were miscellaneous motives. In Massachusetts, Stearns[3] found that, among 100 homicides intensively analyzed, major motives included 33 due to a "quarrel over a woman," 30 due to "miscellaneous quarrels," 21 as "murder secondary to some other crime," and 9 the result of "quarrels over money." In one of the few studies in which data on motives are broken down by specified race and sex groups, Harlan[4] found that among Negro male offenders and victims, quarrels of relatively trivial origin, including an insult, curse, jostling, etc. (33 per cent), comprised the largest proportion of cases, and that quarrels over money ranked second (29 per cent). A sex triangle, with infidelity of a spouse or lover, made up 60-70 per cent of Negro homicides. Among white male offenders and victims, a drunken quarrel was involved in 53 per cent of the homicides, and when a white male killed a white female, a sex triangle predominated in 72 per cent of the cases.

Reports on motives from abroad are scanty, but von Hentig[5] examined German data (1931) which permitted a breakdown by sex of 135 victims. The major single motivating factor was robbery for both male (31 per cent) and female (23 per cent) victims. The next leading motives among female deaths were "aversion and weariness (meaning sex weariness, and the wish to escape a legal or social norm)" (22 per cent),

[1] Gillin, *The Wisconsin Prisoner*, p. 57.
[2] Growdon, *op. cit.*, p. 11.
[3] Stearns, *op. cit.*, p. 740.
[4] Harlan, *op. cit.*, pp. 746–752.
[5] Von Hentig, *The Criminal and His Victim*, p. 398.

and "fear of denunciation" (19 per cent). Among males, "aversion, weariness," "fear of denunciation," and "to escape arrest or confinement" each comprised 12 per cent. About these German statistics the author said: "Males kill other males chiefly to rob them or to escape arrest and confinement. Murder seems highly personalized in so far as it is directed against females, much less so when men are killed."[1]

After examining German data of a different sort, and recognizing that a classification of crimes based on purely legal criteria is rudimentary, Radzinowicz pointed out: "On examining the motive for murder in a very interesting inquiry published in 1931 in German criminal statistics, which analyzed the cases of 124 murderers condemned to death by German courts, we reached the conclusion that the motive for murder was economic in as many as 48 per cent of cases, erotic in only 14 per cent, and hatred and revenge in 17 per cent."[2]

In France during the same year (1931) it was reported[3] that over 70 per cent of the murders were due to quarrels, three-quarters of which were over money, while the rest were domestic. In only 12 per cent of the total was jealousy established as the motive; approximately 7 per cent were due to robbery; and the remaining 11 per cent were for miscellaneous motives such as revenge, despair, and the disposal of illegitimate children. In England and Wales, however, it appears that murder arising out of jealousy and revenge is more frequent than in France. Both Margery Fry[4] and Arthur MacDonald[5] refer to an analysis by Sir John Macdonell of "motives or causes of the murders committed by all persons convicted of murder in England and Wales during the twenty years ending in 1905." Of 551 murders during this period, the five leading motives or causes listed were: jealousy and

---

[1] *Ibid.*
[2] L. Radzinowicz, *The Modern Approach to Criminal Law*, Chapter XII, "English Criminal Statistics—A Critical Analysis," London: Macmillan and Co., Ltd., 1945, p. 185.
[3] "Murder in France," *Literary Digest* (April 16, 1931), 109: No. 16.
[4] Margery Fry, *Arms of the Law*, London: Victor Gollancz, Ltd., 1951, p. 189.
[5] MacDonald, *op. cit.*, p. 95.

intrigue, 92; drink, 90; miscellaneous causes or not known, 81; revenge, 77; and quarrels or violent rage, 68. Unfortunately, an incomparable list in the Royal Commission's Report on Capital Punishment[1] includes the following five leading factors in an analysis of 1,210 murders during the years 1900-1949: domestic quarrels involving a wife or husband (19 per cent); murder of children (16 per cent); quarrels involving a mistress or lover (15 per cent); in connection with robbery (13 per cent); quarrels involving a sweetheart (10 per cent).

This cursory examination of homicide literature that classifies police-recorded motives, makes obvious the lack of and need for uniform reporting. Not only are international comparisons difficult to make, but interstate and interurban comparisons are equally incomparable. There appears to be sufficient evidence to assert that most criminal homicides in this country involve vaguely defined altercations, domestic quarrels, robberies, jealousy, and revenge. Beyond these major categories, motives become too diverse among the available studies to generalize.

[1] *Royal Commission on Capital Punishment, 1949–1953 Report*, p. 330.

III

THE VICTIM-OFFENDER RELATIONSHIP

I I

THE INTERPERSONAL RELATIONSHIP
BETWEEN VICTIM AND OFFENDER

CRIMINAL homicide is probably the most personalized crime in our society. Because motives do not exist in a vacuum, the subject-object, doer-sufferer relationship is of prime importance in this particular crime. The static, structural analysis of homicide thus far presented has been necessary for a complete picture of the phenomenon in its varied ramifications. But homicide is a dynamic relationship between two or more persons caught up in a life drama where they operate in a direct, interactional relationship. More so than in any other violation of conduct norms, the relationship the victim bears to the offender plays a role in explaining the reasons for such flagrant violation. In most crimes the personal relationship between victim and offender plays a less significant role than in homicide. In other offenses, external precipitating factors that operate upon the motivation of an offender do not require a highly personalized victim. Defalcation of funds by an embezzler usually involves an impersonal, secondary institution as victim. The confidence man seeks a likely "mark," but all of us are potential victims. A burglar generally is not motivated to burglarize because of his personal association with the victim, and the auto thief rarely comes into contact with the owner of the car. All offenses against the person involve direct contact between victim and offender, but homicide usually means a greater degree of intensity or longer duration of this contact than is true for any other offense.

The victim and the offender have been examined more or less as separate entities in previous chapters. Further analysis suggests the necessity to set in motion the dynamic interaction of the two principal players in the homicide drama—to examine the relationship between the one who kills and the one who is killed. On the basis of the foregoing, we may postulate that the distribution of interpersonal relationships existing between victim and offender in criminal homicide evidences highest frequency for those relationships characterized as relatively close, intimate, personal, and direct— in short, primary contacts. This statement implies that stranger relationships are least frequent in homicide. Furthermore, accepting Durkheim's contention that males participate in collective life more fully than females, we are led to hypothesize that the frequency of primary group relationships existing between female victims and their slayers is greater than the frequency of primary group relationships existing between male victims and their slayers.

The Philadelphia Data

The classification of victim-offender relationships used in this study includes the following:

(a) close friend;
(b) family relationship;
(c) acquaintance;
(d) stranger;
(e) paramour, mistress, prostitute;
(f) sex rival;
(g) enemy;
(h) paramour of offender's mate;
(i) felon or police officer;
(j) innocent bystander;
(k) homosexual partner.

Because there are 38 homicides for which no known offenders have been discovered, a total of 550 relationships are provided for detailed analysis.[1]

In most cases, study of the police dossiers has made possible what is believed to be a relatively valid appraisal of the

[1] These 550 associations include the relationship between victim and principal slayer.

association. Usually no subjective evaluation of the type of personal association between victim and offender was necessary for such cases as a family relationship, or those in which the victim was an innocent bystander, a police officer, a sex rival, or a paramour of the offender's mate. Judgment of the degree of personal association was not always easy, however, when differentiation between relatively close friend and acquaintance was necessary. Duration of time that victim and offender knew one another aided in the designation but was not an adequate single criterion. Usually police investigation, including interrogation of the defendant and witnesses, or other persons involved in the total relationship, supplied information regarding the length of time the victim and offender were acquainted, as well as the frequency and degree of intimacy in their personal contacts. Probably the specific designations are as valid as can be expected. Terms employed in the present study are, in most cases, those also used by the police to describe relationships. A "close friend" refers to one with whom frequent, direct, personal, and intimate contacts were consistently maintained until the time of the crime. These are primary group relationships on the *Gemeinschaft* level of interaction. An "acquaintance" generally implies more than recognition, but less than fellowship or friendship. It refers to direct contact as a result of personal knowledge, but devoid of intimacy or frequency. A "stranger" is one with whom no known previous contact existed. A "paramour" refers to one who is the love-object of the offender, a lover, sweetheart, or regular sex partner other than a spouse. Although the term often carries connotations of illicit relationships, it is not used here in this limited sense. A "family relationship" includes relationships by consanguinity or legal affinity. In almost all cases, the family relationship was sufficiently close (husband, wife, parent, child, sibling) that cousins and other comparatively distant family association did little to reduce the close personal contact this category implies. A "known enemy" means that hostility characterized the victim-offender relationship for a considerable period of time before the homicide, that they looked upon one another as traditional foes and avoided normal social relations. Of course a "paramour of the offender's mate" or a "sex rival," in cases involving the unmarried, may mean much enmity between the victim and offender, but in these latter categories the particularized nature of the hostility is of special significance in motivating the homicide agent and has been separately tabulated. The same logic applies to those few cases where the victim was a homosexual partner.

In general, the data support our first assumption regarding victim-offender relationships and a high proportion of primary group contacts. (Table 24.) Categories which involve primary contacts (close friend, family member, paramour, and homosexual partner), when combined, constitute 65 per cent of all victim-offender relationships. Categories which involve non-primary contacts (acquaintance, stranger, sex rival, enemy, felon or police officer, innocent bystander), when combined, comprise the remaining 35 per cent.

Relatively close friends (28 per cent) and family associations or relatives (25 per cent) are the two relationships with highest frequency, and account for over half the 550 known associations. Acquaintances (14 per cent), strangers (12 per cent), and paramours (10 per cent) account for a third of all relationships. Where numbers are sufficiently large to allow analysis according to race, some important differences emerge. For example, white victims were most likely to be slain by a relative (27 per cent) and Negro victims by a close friend (31 per cent). A close friend relationship ranks third in frequency among whites (21 per cent). Approximately three times as many whites were strangers to those who killed them (25 per cent) as was true of Negroes (8 per cent). Except for these differences, the distribution of victim-offender relationships is similar for both races.

The hypothesis which suggests a higher proportion of primary group relationships for female victims is also supported by the data. The frequency distribution of victim-offender relationships according to sex reveals *significant* differences. Categories which involve primary group con-

TABLE 24

TYPE OF INTERPERSONAL RELATIONSHIP BETWEEN VICTIM
AND PRINCIPAL OFFENDER, BY RACE AND SEX OF VICTIM,
CRIMINAL HOMICIDE, PHILADELPHIA, 1948–1952

(In per cent)

Interpersonal Relationship	Both Races			Negro			White		
	Total	Male	Female	Total	Male	Female	Total	Male	Female
Close Friend	28.2	34.0	9.3	30.7	35.9	13.0	20.7	28.1	—
Family Relationship	24.7	16.4	51.9	23.9	17.3	46.7	27.1	13.6	64.9
Acquaintance	13.5	15.7	6.2	14.4	16.0	8.7	10.7	14.6	—
Stranger	12.2	14.2	5.4	7.8	9.1	3.3	25.0	30.1	10.8
Paramour, Mistress, Prostitute	9.8	6.4	20.9	10.5	7.6	20.7	7.9	2.9	21.6
Sex Rival	4.0	4.8	1.6	4.9	6.0	1.1	1.4	1.0	2.7
Enemy	2.9	3.6	.8	2.9	3.5	1.1	2.9	3.9	—
Paramour of Offender's Mate	2.0	2.1	1.6	2.7	2.8	2.2	—	—	—
Felon or Police Officer	1.1	1.4	—	.5	.6	—	2.9	3.9	—
Innocent Bystander	1.1	.7	2.3	1.2	.6	3.3	.7	1.0	—
Homosexual Partner	.6	.7	—	.5	.6	—	.7	1.0	—
Total	100.0 (550)	100.0 (421)	100.0 (129)	100.0 (410)	100.0 (318)	100.0 (92)	100.0 (140)	100.0 (103)	100.0 (37)

Note: Because there are 38 criminal homicides for which no known perpetrators have been identified, only 550 interpersonal relationships are known. Percentages are based on this universe of 550.

tacts, when combined, constitute 59 per cent of all victim-offender relationships among males, but 84 per cent among females. Moreover, specific differences in the type of primary relation are noted for males and females. If we may assert that family and paramour relationships are indicative of closer, more intimate primary relationships, generally, than the relationship of close friend, then we find additional confirmation of the hypothesis. The data show that over a third of the males (34 per cent), but less than a tenth of the females (9 per cent) were close friends of their slayers. Although a family relationship is of second highest frequency among males (16 per cent), it constitutes only a sixth of all male relationships. Among females, on the other hand, this single type of association is of highest frequency and accounts for over half of all female relationships (52 per cent). Similarly, only a small proportion of male victims were paramours (6 per cent), while this category characterizes a fifth (21 per cent) of all female victims. As one author suggests, "We must say that when a man is found murdered we should first look for his acquaintances; when a woman is killed, for her relatives, mainly the husband, and after that her paramour, present or past."[1]

Some interesting differences emerge when the data are refined according to specified race and sex groups. The major difference between Negro and white male victims is that white males were much more likely to be strangers to their slayers than Negro males. Less than a tenth (9 per cent) of Negro victims were strangers, while three-tenths (30 per cent) of white males were unknown to their slayers. This difference is attributable to the fact that 24 per cent of white males and only 2 per cent of Negro males were killed during the commission of robbery, which usually involves a stranger relationship. More Negro males (36 per cent) than white males (28 per cent) were close friends of their slayers, and slightly more Negro males (17 per cent) than white males (14 per cent) were relatives of their slayers.

While 13 per cent of Negro females are classified as having had a close friend relationship with their slayers none of the white females fall into this category. Like white males, white females were more likely to be strangers (11 per cent) to their slayers than Negro females (3 per cent). About a fifth of both white and Negro female victims were paramours, but nearly two-thirds of white females compared to less than half of Negro females were relatives of their slayers.

The previous analysis of violence and non-violence in criminal homicide leads to the suggestion that the closer the relationship between victim and offender, the greater will be the proportion of violent deaths. The distribution of victim-offender associations according to the violence/non-violence dichotomy indicates that variables—some of which already have been analyzed—are involved in violent homicide other

[1] Von Hentig, *The Criminal and His Victim*, p. 392.

208

than the type of relationship between victim and offender. Among the 550 identified relationships, 271, or approximately half of the victims were subjected to a violent death, as defined in this study. The highest proportions of violence are among known enemies, homosexual partners, and family members. (Table 25.) Bystanders constitute the smallest

TABLE 25

TYPE OF INTERPERSONAL RELATIONSHIP BETWEEN
VICTIM AND PRINCIPAL OFFENDER BY VIOLENCE OF
CRIMINAL HOMICIDE, PHILADELPHIA, 1948–1952

Interpersonal Relationship	Non-Violence		Violence	
	Number	Per Cent	Number	Per Cent
Close Friend	89	31.9	66	24.3
Family Relationship	57	20.4	79	29.2
Acquaintance	36	12.9	38	14.0
Stranger	37	13.3	30	11.1
Paramour, Mistress, Prostitute	30	10.8	24	8.9
Sex Rival	11	3.9	11	4.1
Enemy	4	1.4	12	4.4
Paramour of Offender's Mate	7	2.5	4	1.5
Felon or Police Officer	3	1.1	3	1.1
Innocent Bystander	4	1.4	2	.7
Homosexual Partner	1	.4	2	.7
Total	279	100.0	271	100.0

group killed violently, as might be expected, but in all these types of relationships except that of relatives, total cases are probably too small to be statistically meaningful. Certainly the hypothesis regarding violence and relationships would suggest that close friends comprise a larger proportion of violent cases than strangers. Such is not the case, however, for slightly more strangers (45 per cent) than close friends (43 per cent) were killed violently. Further rejection of the hypothesis is found in the fact that a larger proportion of acquaintances were killed violently than were close friends, and strangers and paramours were killed in almost equal proportions of violence and non-violence. In general it appears that the assumption must be rejected and the degree of intimacy of personal relationships has little direct association with the violence or non-violence of the homicide. Some

209

qualification and an exception to this general conclusion appears, however, when spouse slayings are analyzed.[1]

Comparison has been made of the age of each victim with that of the offender responsible for his death. All told, 620 age relationships have been identified. Eleven victims were infants under one year of age, and 26 victims were the same age as their slayers. Among the 583 relationships having an age difference, not counting those cases where the victim was an infant, 342 (59 per cent) of the offenders were younger than their respective victims. No more than five years difference in age occurs for over a third of all victim-offender relationships (37 per cent). (See Appendix I, Table 21.) Beginning with this first five-year age difference, there is a consistently gradual decrease in the number of victim-offender relationships as the age difference increases, so that in the last category where the victim and offender are separated by fifty years or more, there are only three relationships.

The personalized nature of homicide has already been indicated by the types of police-recorded motives and specific victim-offender relationships. Husbands, wives, close friends, acquaintances, paramours—these are the most common relationships, and these are relationships usually found between individuals of the same or similar ages. The majority of criminal homicides involve, therefore, victims and offenders whose ages are similar, because most normal social interaction of any close, personalized relationship (with the exception of parent-child relations) probably occurs among persons of the same age status, the same generation of life experiences, attitudes, value judgments, and social striving. Age is a determining factor in status and role, and consequently a factor in the position the individual possesses and the role he assumes in a homicide situation.

In every category representing five-year age differences between victims and offenders, more offenders are younger than their respective victims. Up to and including the age differential of 25 years, the total number of cases in which the

[1] *Infra.*, pp. 212–217.

offenders are younger than their victims is 276, compared with 221 cases in which the offenders are older than their victims. The following table makes this point clear:

| | Age Differential | | | | | |
| | 25 years or less | | More than 25 years | | Total | |
	No.	%	No.	%	No.	%
Offender Younger than Victim	276	55.5	66	76.7	342	58.7
Offender Older than Victim	221	44.5	20	23.3	241	41.3
	497	100.0	86	100.0	583	100.0

Note: Eleven additional victims were infants under one year of age, and 26 additional victims were the same age (according to last birthday) as their respective slayers.

Thus, of the 497 cases in which the age differential is 25 years or less, 56 per cent of the offenders are younger than their victims. Beyond the age differential of 25 years, however, the number of offenders who are younger than their victims increases within each category. Moreover, the total number of cases in which offenders are younger beyond the age differential of 25 years is 66; compared with only 20 cases in which the reverse occurs. Thus, of the 86 cases representing an age differential between victims and offenders of more than 25 years, 77 per cent of the offenders are younger than their victims. Although all categories evidence a greater number of offenders who are younger than their victims, we may conclude that:

(1) if the victim-offender age differential is 25 years or less, offenders are younger or older than their victims in almost equal proportions;

(2) if the victim-offender age differential is more than 25 years, offenders are younger than their victims in over three-fourths of the relationships;

(3) the difference between the distributions found in (1) and (2) above is *significant*.

In many of the cases where the difference in age between

211

victim and offender is greater than 25 years, robbery was involved in the homicide. As noted elsewhere, victims of a robbery-homicide are likely to be in the older age groups. Robbery is an offense committed usually by young adult males. It is the coming together of these two groups in a homicide situation that results in a *significantly* high proportion of offenders younger than their respective victims when the age difference between them is greater than 25 years. Moreover, a robbery motive in homicide almost always means a stranger relationship between victim and offender; and such a relationship is less likely than most to involve persons of similar ages.

Husband-Wife Homicides. The difficulties involved in determining marital status of victims and offenders were almost insurmountable; hence, no attempt has been made in this study to analyze rates or frequency distributions according to marital status. Police officers, clerks, and other personnel who recorded marital status on the homicide reporting forms admitted inaccuracy primarily due to the cultural prevalence of common-law marriages among Negroes arrested on homicide charges. It was often impossible to determine whether the liaison or cohabitation of a man and woman was sufficiently permanent to be recognized as common-law marriage. Since Negroes constitute over three-fourths of all persons involved in the cases studied, it was deemed unwise to pursue analysis of victims and offenders in terms of how many were married, single, divorced, etc. However, when an agent killed a person of the opposite sex, every possible effort was made by the police to determine precisely the victim-offender relationship. Therefore, the 100 criminal homicides involving a husband-wife relationship may be considered quite accurately identified.

Of the 136 victims who had a familial relationship to their slayers, there were 100 husbands or wives, 9 sons, 8 daughters, 3 mothers, 3 brothers, 2 fathers, one sister, and 10 other types of associations. Of the 100 marital relationships, 53 wives were slain by their husbands, and 47 husbands by their

212

TABLE 26
HUSBAND-WIFE CRIMINAL HOMICIDE, BY RACE, METHOD,
PLACE, MOTIVE, AND VIOLENCE, PHILADELPHIA,
1948–1952

	Total	Husband killed by wife	Wife killed by husband
Both Races	100	47	53
Negro	80	40	40
White	20	7	13
Method			
Stabbing	46	30	16
Shooting	34	15	19
Beating	15	–	15
Other	5	2	3
Place			
Bedroom	35	11	24
Kitchen	29	19	10
Living room	11	4	7
Stairway	9	6	3
Highway	8	4	4
Taproom	3	2	1
Commercial	4	1	3
Other	1	–	1
Motive			
Family quarrel	64	33	31
Jealousy	23	10	13
Revenge	2	1	1
Altercation	2	1	1
Self-defense	2	1	1
Unknown	7	1	6
Violence	62	18	44
Non-violence	38	29	9

wives. (Table 26.) *Significantly*, the number of wives homicidally assaulted by their husbands constituted 41 per cent of all women who were killed, whereas husbands homicidally assaulted by their wives made up only 11 per cent of all men who were killed. Among those killed by a spouse, Negro husbands numbered 40, Negro wives 40, white husbands 7, and white wives 13.

When a man was killed by a woman, he was most likely to be killed by his wife. Of 75 Negro males slain by Negro females, 40, or 53 per cent, were husbands slain by their mates; and of 9 white males killed by white females, 7 were slain by their mates.

When a woman committed homicide, she was more likely than a man to kill her mate. Of 89 Negro female offenders (for whom a victim-offender relationship has been identified),

40, or 45 per cent, killed their husbands; and of 15 white female offenders, 7 killed their husbands. On the other hand, of 321 Negro male offenders, only 40, or 12 per cent, killed their wives; and of 118 white male offenders, only 13, or 11 per cent, killed their wives.

All told, when the 105 identified female offenders committed homicide, they killed their husbands in 45 per cent of the cases; but when the 445 identified male offenders committed homicide, they killed their wives in only 12 per cent of the cases.

Although among the 588 cases there is no positive association between the intimacy of interpersonal relationship and violence of the homicide in general, there is a *significant* association between violence and spouse slayings. Husbands killed their wives violently in *significantly* greater proportion than did wives who killed their husbands. Among the 53 husbands who killed their wives, 44 did so violently, but among the 47 wives who killed their husbands, only 18 did so violently.

It has been shown elsewhere that the more excessive degrees of violence during a stabbing or shooting occur in the home rather than outside the home, and that severe degrees of violence in which more than five acts are involved are most likely to have a home for the scene. The distribution of degrees of violence of husband-wife homicides is similar to the distribution of other types of relationships, except for the fact that a larger proportion of "more than five acts" occurs among mate killings. For all victims (588), "more than five acts" ranks fourth among the violent homicide categories, preceded by "three to five acts," "severe beatings," and "two acts" respectively. Of all violent homicides, 18 per cent involve more than five acts of stabbing or shooting. However, among husband-wife homicides, the category of "more than five acts" ranks second, and constitutes 24 per cent of all the violent mate slayings. Thus, husband-wife homicides are violent to a greater degree than violent homicides in general. To this extent, violence and intimacy of personal relationship are associated.

The distribution of husband-wife homicides according to police-recorded motives shows an expectedly high proportion due to domestic quarrels. Sixty-four per cent of the slayings were the result of such quarrels. Twenty-three per cent were due to jealousy, compared to only 11 per cent of all homicides.

The single place where most husband-wife killings occurred was in the bedroom. Sex differentials are important to this generalization, however. Whereas 24 (45 per cent) of the 53 wives were killed in a bedroom, only 11 (23 per cent) of the 47 husbands were killed there. Thus, proportionately, the bedroom is a more lethal place for wives than for husbands. For the kitchen the reverse appears to be true, for only 10 wives were slain there, compared to 19 husbands. Finally, with respect to place of occurrence, 85 per cent of husband-wife slayings occurred in the home and only 15 per cent outside the home, a relative proportion that is true for both husbands and wives.

Wives usually stabbed their mates, as indicated by the fact that 30 wives used this method to kill their husbands and only 15 shot them. Husbands were less discriminating, and killed their wives in almost equal proportions of the leading methods. In 19 cases they shot their mates, in 16 they stabbed them, and in 15, beat them to death. Of the 45 wives killed in the home, 17 were shot and 15 were beaten; of the 40 husbands killed in the home, 23 were stabbed.

When a husband was killed in the kitchen, his wife usually used a kitchen instrument (a butcher knife or paring knife was most common) which was easily accessible. This fact indicates that most kitchen slayings were committed in the heat of passion, during a quarrel, and on the spur of the moment. Of the husbands killed in a kitchen, 17 were stabbed with a kitchen knife, and only 2 were shot. Of the wives killed in a kitchen, 5 were stabbed with a kitchen knife, 3 were shot, one was beaten to death with a broomstick, and one was severely cut with a hatchet. Of 11 husbands killed in a bedroom, 4 were stabbed with a kitchen knife, 4 were shot with a pistol, one with a shotgun, one was cut with a jagged

215

drinking glass, and one was soaked with kerosene and burned to death. Of 24 wives killed in a bedroom, 9 were beaten or strangled, 6 were stabbed with a kitchen knife, 4 were shot, and one each was slain by a mop handle, an electric iron, an iron pipe, an overdose of barbiturates, and a push from a third-floor apartment. All told, among the wives killed in a bedroom there were 12 beatings, 6 stabbings, 4 shootings, and 2 by miscellaneous methods. When a husband was killed in any place in the home other than the kitchen or bedroom, his wife used a pistol in 4 cases, a shotgun in one, a penknife in 3, a kitchen knife in 2. When a wife was slain any place in the home other than the kitchen or bedroom, her husband used a pistol in 9 cases, a shotgun in one, and a penknife in one.

Court designation and disposition of criminal homicides known to the police are separately analyzed in Chapter 17, but brief mention might be made now of the adjudication of husband-wife slayings. The following breakdown shows disposition according to marital status of offender:

	Husband	Wife	Total
Guilty	34	26	60
Not Guilty	2	16	18
Nolle Prosequi	2	2	4
Pending	3	2	5
Suicide	10	1	11
Died Before Trial	1	—	1
Fugitive	1	—	1
Total	53	47	100

The following table shows the court designation of the homicide according to marital status of defendant:

	Husband	Wife	Total
First Degree Murder	10	—	10
Second Degree Murder	10	4	14
Voluntary Manslaughter	10	15	25
Involuntary Manslaughter	4	7	11
Total	34	26	60

These court dispositions reveal that:

216

(1) a higher proportion of husbands (64 per cent) than wives (55 per cent) were found guilty;

(2) a higher proportion of wives (34 per cent) than husbands (4 per cent) were acquitted;

(3) more husbands (19 per cent) than wives (2 per cent) committed suicide after having killed their mates;

(4) husbands were convicted of more serious degrees of homicide than were wives.[1] The majority of husbands were convicted of murder while five-sixths of wives were convicted of manslaughter. None of the wives, but about a third of the husbands, were convicted of first degree murder. Less than a sixth of the wives, contrasted to three-fifths of the husbands, were convicted of either of the degrees of murder. An immediate and common conclusion from these data suggests that the courts treat wives with greater leniency than they do husbands. Such an interpretation of differential treatment assumes that all other things are equal—i.e., there is no major difference in the actual types of homicides committed by wives and husbands. Close examination of these mate slayings reveals, however, that it is not necessarily true that the courts treated wives with unjustifiably greater leniency than they did husbands, for in 28 cases of female defendants, the husband had strongly provoked his wife to attack; and, although she was not exonerated on grounds of self-defense, there had been sufficient provocation by the husband (as the victim) to reduce the seriousness of her offense. In contrast, provocation recognized by the courts occurred in only 5 cases in which husbands killed their wives.

Victim-Offender Relationships Noted in Other Studies

The usual difficulties of incomparable classifications are met when the distribution of victim-offender relationships is compared with other research. If the relationships are identified at all, classifications are rarely the same from one

[1] If the 10 husbands who killed their wives and committed suicide had killed themselves in the same proportion as did wives, the number of husbands convicted of first degree murder would have been much higher. Judgment of these 10 homicide-suicides of husbands by competent observers places them in the first degree murder category; and should the cases have gone to trial, likelihood of conviction for murder would have been great.

study to another. Nonetheless, the present review attempts to indicate the extent of similarity to, or divergence from, the distribution of relationships described for Philadelphia victims and offenders.

The types of interpersonal relationships between victims and their slayers in Philadelphia contradict Tarde's rhetorical question: "Now, is it not especially in the great cities, where more often than not the murderer and his victim are unacquainted with each other, that greed is what inspires murder or assassination?"[1] It *may* be true that more homicides due to "greed" occur in the city than in rural areas, but even in the city, other types of motives, involving a known, and often long-established relationship between victim and offender, predominate.

More intensive analysis of victim-offender relationships was suggested by Pollak when he said that "the type of victim particularly exposed to female homicides deserves further attention for an evaluation of criminal statistics."[2] The present research has given attention to this particular type of victim, and supports Pollak's belief that "persons to whom women offenders are related or with whom they are in otherwise close contact loom largely among their victims."[3] The Philadelphia data clearly show that close and intimate relationships—particularly those of a spouse—are much more common among the victims of female offenders than of male offenders.

In his review of 100 males committed to the Massachusetts State Prison on conviction of homicide, Stearns found that 40 of the victims had been friends or associates, 12 had been victims of robbery as well as of homicide, and 8 had been wives.[4] In New Jersey, Frankel pointed out that "this study of 1,000 murderers . . . has found that personal animosities are most often the causative factors culminating in murder."[5] Among the relationships between victim and

[1] Tarde, *op. cit.*, p. 355.
[2] Pollak, *op. cit.*, p. 18.
[3] *Ibid.*
[4] Stearns, *op. cit.*, p. 740.
[5] Emil Frankel, *op. cit.*, pp. 686–687. Percentages have been computed from Frankel's raw data.

offender that Frankel reported was a "relative" category, which is comparable to the one used in the present analysis. Twenty-one per cent of the victims of 713 identified associations were relatives of these male offenders, a proportion similar though slightly larger than the 16 per cent who were relatives of Philadelphia male offenders. In Frankel's study, sex rivals were victims in 4 per cent of the cases, a proportion comparable to the 5 per cent who were sex rivals in the present study. In Growdon's survey[1] of 54 juvenile offenders, a larger proportion had killed family members and total strangers than was the case among adults in Philadelphia. Among the Ohio juveniles, 17, or 32 per cent, of their victims were relatives compared to 25 per cent in Philadelphia; and 12, or 22 per cent, were strangers to the juvenile offenders compared to only 12 per cent in Philadelphia. *The Illinois Crime Survey* sometimes confuses motives and relationships, so that comparisons to Philadelphia are difficult. However, it is interesting to note that during 1926 and 1927 the Chicago police recorded 55 husband-wife slayings. Of these, only 13 victims, or 24 per cent, were husbands, which is a proportion considerably smaller than that of husbands (47 per cent) who were victims of mate slayings in Philadelphia.[2]

Arthur MacDonald pointed out that in England and Wales a large number of the victims of male murderers were women. Of 487 murders committed by men between 1886 and 1905, 50 per cent of the victims were women who had had an intimate relationship with their slayers: 26 per cent were wives, and 24 per cent were mistresses or sweethearts.[3] Comparison with the Philadelphia data must be qualified because the British statistics refer to persons convicted of murder, whereas the Philadelphia statistics refer to offenders in criminal homicides known to the police. At any rate, of 445 homicides committed by men in Philadelphia, only 18 per cent of the victims were women who presumably had had an intimate relationship with their slayers: 12 per cent were wives, and

---

[1] C. H. Growdon, *op. cit.*, pp. 9–10. Percentages have been computed from Growdon's raw data.
[2] *The Illinois Crime Survey*, p. 610.
[3] Computed from MacDonald, *op. cit.*, pp. 96–97.

6 per cent were mistresses, sweethearts, or similar types of associates. In order to provide a group of male offenders comparable to the British group just mentioned, it is necessary to consider only the 171 males in Philadelphia convicted of murder in the first or second degree. Of this select group, 12 per cent had killed their wives. Thus the proportion that wives slain by their husbands bears to the total number of homicides committed by males is similar to the proportion that wives *murdered* by their husbands bears to the total number of *murders* committed by males. In either case, the proportion is only half that reported in England and Wales.

More recent statistics from England and Wales may be found in the Report of the Royal Commission on Capital Punishment, which reveals that between 1900 and 1949, 20 per cent of the 1,080 males convicted of murder in England and Wales had murdered their wives.[1] This proportion still constitutes a group much larger than that in Philadelphia. In contrast, only 13, or 10 per cent, of the 130 females convicted of murder in England and Wales had murdered their husbands. In Philadelphia, 47, or 45 per cent, of the 104 female offenders (for whom personal interrelationships have been identified) killed their husbands, and 6 of the 19 females convicted of murder in the second degree (none were convicted of murder in the first degree) had *murdered* their husbands. Using comparable data, the ratio of British males convicted of having murdered their wives, to Philadelphia males convicted of the same type of offense, was nearly 2 to 1. But the ratio of British to Philadelphia females convicted of the same offense was about 1 to 3.[2]

German statistics (1931) cited by von Hentig[3] supply some information regarding husband-wife slayings. Of all male relatives who were victims of murder, 14 per cent were husbands killed by their wives; and of all female relatives who were victims of murder, 62 per cent were wives killed

[1] Computed from *Royal Commission on Capital Punishment, 1949–1953 Report*, p. 330.
[2] It should be noted, however, that in Philadelphia these females, convicted of *murdering* their husbands, were all Negro.
[3] Von Hentig, *The Criminal and His Victim*, p. 392.

220

by their husbands. For Philadelphia it may be said that of all male relatives who were victims of criminal homicide, 68 per cent were husbands killed by their wives; and of all female relatives who were victims of criminal homicide, 79 per cent were wives killed by their husbands.

Interesting but largely incomparable evidence from a Ukrainian study[1] of 216 homicides "not motivated by personal gain," showed that persons who were strangers to their slayers constituted 50 per cent of all victims, a proportion much larger than the 12 per cent of Philadelphia victims who were strangers to their slayers.

[1] Helene Frenkel, *op. cit.*, p. 947.

12

RACE AND SEX RELATIONSHIPS

IN most homicide research, analysis is based on either victims *or* offenders. In the present study, both victims *and* offenders have been separately examined. Significant differences noted between victims and offenders have indicated that many generalizations about homicide should not be made from analysis of the one alone, and that inferences about the one should not be derived from analysis of the other. The preceding chapter and the present one add to our knowledge of the nature and pattern of criminal homicide by describing important factors in the dynamic interaction between the victim and the offender. When each victim is specifically related to his slayer, a kind of chiaroscuro is provided, which is lacking in an analysis of the victim or offender alone.

The Philadelphia Data

The distribution of victims by race and sex, relative to the same distribution of their respective slayers, provides some interesting patterns of interrelationships. (Tables 27 (A), (B).)

In 94 per cent of the 550 identified relationships, the victim and offender were members of the same race: 72 per cent of the total were Negro and 22 per cent white. Of these 516 homicides involving members of the same race, 77 per cent were Negro and 23 per cent white. Hence, in only 34, or 6 per cent, of the homicides did an offender cross the race line: 14 were Negro/white and 20 were white/Negro slayings.[1] (See Appendix I, Table 22.)

[1] In the present discussion of race and sex relationships, the victim shall (unless otherwise indicated) precede the offender. Thus "Negro/white" refers to a Negro victim and a white offender. The diagonal line denotes "killed by."

222

TABLE 27 (A)

RACE AND SEX OF VICTIM BY RACE AND SEX OF OFFENDER,
CRIMINAL HOMICIDE, PHILADELPHIA, 1948–1952

(A) (Per cent of total)

OFFENDER	VICTIM								
	Both Races			Negro			White		
	Total	Male	Female	Total	Male	Female	Total	Male	Female
Both Races	(550) 100.0	(421) 100.0	(129) 100.0	(410) 100.0	(318) 100.0	(92) 100.0	(140) 100.0	(103) 100.0	(37) 100.0
Male	81.0	79.1	86.8	78.3	75.8	87.0	88.6	89.3	86.5
Female	19.0	20.9	13.2	21.7	24.2	13.0	11.4	10.7	13.5
Negro	75.6	77.0	71.3	96.6	96.5	96.7	14.3	16.5	8.1
Male	59.5	58.7	62.0	75.4	73.0	83.7	12.9	14.6	8.1
Female	16.1	18.3	9.3	21.2	23.6	13.0	1.4	1.9	—
White	24.4	23.0	28.7	3.4	3.5	3.3	85.7	83.5	91.9
Male	21.5	20.4	24.8	2.9	2.8	3.3	75.7	74.8	78.4
Female	2.9	2.6	3.9	.5	.6	—	10.0	8.7	13.5

TABLE 27 (B)

RACE AND SEX OF VICTIM BY RACE AND SEX OF OFFENDER,
CRIMINAL HOMICIDE, PHILADELPHIA, 1948–1952

(B) (Per cent of total)

VICTIM	OFFENDER								
	Both Races			Negro			White		
	Total	Male	Female	Total	Male	Female	Total	Male	Female (a)
Both Races	(550) 100.0	(445) 100.0	(105) 100.0	(416) 100.0	(327) 100.0	(89) 100.0	(134) 100.0	(118) 100.0	(16) 100.0
Male	76.5	74.8	83.8	77.9	75.5	86.5	72.4	72.9	—
Female	23.5	25.2	16.2	22.1	24.5	13.5	27.6	27.1	—
Negro	74.5	72.1	84.8	95.2	94.5	97.8	10.4	10.2	—
Male	57.8	54.1	73.4	73.8	70.9	84.3	8.2	7.6	—
Female	16.7	18.0	11.4	21.4	23.6	13.5	2.2	2.6	—
White	25.5	27.9	15.2	4.8	5.5	2.2	89.6	89.8	—
Male	18.7	20.7	10.4	4.1	4.6	2.2	64.2	65.3	—
Female	6.7	7.2	4.8	.7	.9	—	25.4	24.5	—

(a) Category too small for breakdown by percentage distribution.

The predominant intra-racial nature of homicide means
that only a slight error results from the use of mortality
statistics to describe merely the racial distribution of offenders, or from the use of criminal statistics to describe the
racial distribution of victims.

However, the distribution by sex of victims and offenders results in a different pattern. In 64 per cent of the 550 identified relationships, the victim and offender were members of the same sex: 61 per cent were male/male and only 3 per cent were female/female. Of these 350 homicides involving members of the same sex, 95 per cent were male/male and only 5 per cent female/female. Thus, in as many as 200, or 36 per cent, of the homicides did an offender slay a person of the opposite sex: 16 per cent of the total 550 cases were male/female and 20 per cent were female/male slayings.

The ratio of intra-racial to interracial homicides is 15.2 to 1. The ratio of homicides involving members of the same sex (intra-sex) to homicides involving members of the opposite sex (inter-sex) is only 1.8 to 1. Therefore, a considerable error results from the use of mortality statistics to describe or infer the sex distribution of offenders, or from the use of criminal statistics to describe or infer the sex distribution of victims. The very personal nature of homicide accounts for its racially in-group character, since the quasi-caste barrier apparently prohibits the kinds of personal contacts between the races that ordinarily lead to homicide, and hence operates to reduce interracial homicides. However, intimate and personal contacts, often with high emotional content, do take place between the sexes within each race, so that a higher proportion of homicides involve victims and offenders of opposite sex.

The distribution of victims and offenders by specified race and sex groups reveals even more precisely the various patterns of personal interrelationships. Of 318 Negro male victims, 73 per cent were killed by Negro males, 24 per cent by Negro females, 3 per cent by white males, and in only 2 cases by white females. Of 103 white male victims, 75 per cent were killed by white males, 15 per cent by Negro males, 9 per cent by white females, and 2 per cent by Negro females. Of 92 Negro female victims, 84 per cent were killed by Negro males, 13 per cent by Negro females, in 3 cases by white males. Of 37 white female victims, 29 were killed by white males, 5 by white females, 3 by Negro males. In no case did a female agent cross the race line when killing a female.

Among the 550 identified relationships, 326, or 59 per cent, were of the same race *and* sex; 190, or 35 per cent, were of the same race but opposite sex; 24, or 4 per cent, were of a different race but the same sex; and 10, or 2 per cent, were of a different race and sex.

When the victim and offender are members of the same race, they are also *significantly* of the same sex nearly six times more frequently if they are male than if they are female. Of all male victims, 73 per cent were slain by persons of the same race and sex; but of all female victims, only 13 per cent were slain by persons of their same race and sex.

An interesting pattern of frequency distributions occurs for three specified race and sex groups. Each group (except white males) is slain by the following types of offenders in the same rank order of frequency:

(1) males of the same race;
(2) females of the same race;
(3) males of a different race;
(4) females of a different race.

The only exception is among white males, for whom offender-groups (2) and (3) are reversed. It may be asserted that all victims, regardless of race or sex, are homicidally assaulted most frequently by males of their own race and least frequently by females of another race.

These various data regarding race and sex of each victim and offender may provide some clue to patterns of social interaction in general. Perhaps the pattern of homicide by which victims are killed in the rank order of frequency outlined above is a reflection of the pattern of intra- and inter-race and sex relations in the general population. It may be that the majority of people do most frequently interact with males of their own race, followed in frequency by females of their own race, males of a different race, and finally females of a different race. That is to say, of the number of individuals with whom one has daily interaction in our culture, rank order of race and sex contacts follows this pattern. Such a statement at present has the status of an *a priori*, untested assumption. Research is required before broad generalizations about such a pattern can be safely asserted. In the meantime, homicide that occurs within the same race and sex group, and particularly homicide that crosses race and sex lines, may tell us something about general social patterns of interaction. Homicide may be an index to the relative amounts of such interpersonal relations in the broader culture that surrounds the players in the homicide drama. But in addition to the number of interactions, there are certain qualitative factors not readily measurable, such as intensity, duration, personal and social meaning of the relationship. For these factors too, homicide may provide some index of measurement. But it is primarily the number of interactions by race and sex that is here conjectured as most useful for such analysis.

In order to show more clearly the types of homicides these race and sex interrelationships involve, several typical cases taken from police files are sketched below. These cases of intra-racial homicide approach ideal types (in the Max Weber sense). Only slight variations appear in other cases found in the groups these summaries represent.

(1) *Negro Male/Negro Male*. In a dice game, the victim and offender had a $2 bet which the victim refused to pay. After both left the game, the offender fired three shots from his car, fatally wounding the victim as he walked along the street.

The victim struck the wife of the offender and threatened to kill her. The incensed husband bought a switch-blade knife, attempted to attack the victim, but was restrained by relatives and friends. Eluding them, he crawled out a second-story window, slid down a drainpipe, found the victim, and stabbed him in the chest.

Two inmates of a flophouse shared a bottle of wine together in a dormitory. The offender became enraged when the victim did not offer him a drink, and struck him three times across the eyes with a broomstick, causing his death.

(2) *Negro Male/Negro Female*. As a result of heavy drinking at a New Year's Eve party, a man and his common-law wife

engaged in an argument during which the husband (victim) struck his wife. She left the party, went to their home, and locked the door. The husband followed and pounded on the door, with the result that the offender took a gun from under the mattress and fired three shots through the door, fatally wounding her husband.

The offender was severely beaten and kicked by her common-law husband. In retaliation, she ran to the kitchen, obtained a butcher knife, and stabbed the victim, who was intoxicated at the time.

(3) *White Male/White Male.* Two friends became involved in an argument in a taproom over the nationality of the offender, an Italian, with uncomplimentary remarks being made by the victim about "dagos." This led to the accusation by the victim that the offender had stolen money from him. After they left the taproom, the victim threatened the offender with a broken beer bottle, whereupon the offender broke a piece of wood from a nearby fruit stand and beat the victim severely about the head.

A fist fight occurred as the result of two strangers wanting to use the same parking space. The victim was beaten to death.

(4) *White Male/White Female.* A husband and wife, married for sixteen years, engaged in an argument over household expenses. As the husband attempted to strangle his wife, she stabbed him with a kitchen knife. The husband, a heavy drinker, was under the influence of alcohol at the time of the crime.

On several occasions, the victim made advances to his eighteen-year-old sister-in-law. On the occasion of the crime he had kept her out all night, trying to force her to have sexual relations with him. Upon their return home at 6:00 A.M., his wife, assuming that her husband had raped her sister, shot him.

After beating his wife, to whom he had been married for only fourteen months, the victim handed her a loaded 45 automatic and dared her to shoot him. When he struck her again, she followed his suggestion.

(5) *Negro Female/Negro Male.* A couple had been lovers for about six years, and met frequently at a room they rented for intimate relations. The victim had been going there less frequently than usual and was accused by the slayer of being

227

interested in another man. During the argument which followed she was shot three times.

During a marital quarrel, the wife threw several beer bottles at her husband. Enraged, he armed himself with a knife and stabbed her five times.

(6) *Negro Female/Negro Female.* The victim broke into the home of the offender, a complete stranger, angry because the man she had been living with intermittently for fifteen years was there. In the altercation which ensued, the victim was stabbed in the back with a paring knife with which the offender had been preparing dinner.

The victim, intoxicated, entered a lunchroom where the offender was working and complained loudly about the food and the service. Later when the two met on the street the victim called the offender abusive names and struck her. The offender fatally wounded the victim in the neck with a piece of broken glass picked up from the street.

(7) *White Female/White Male.* A couple who had lived together for five years, but were not doing so at the time of the crime, met and drank together all evening, visiting several taprooms. An argument arose on the way home and the victim was stabbed twice. The offender, after taking some money from her pocketbook, fled.

A husband, irritated by his wife's feigned heart condition, beat her savagely about the head with an iron pipe while she lay asleep.

(8) *White Female/White Female.* Acquaintances drinking together in a bar began to argue over the attentions of the offender to the husband of the victim. As a result, the victim was shot in the stomach.

Interracial Homicides

Because of their rarity and interest to sociology, the 34 interracial homicides require special and more detailed analysis.[1]

[1] These are, of course, *criminal* homicides as recorded in police reports. If justifiable homicides (14 in the five years under review) were included, this particular interracial group would be larger, for 12 persons slain by white officers were Negro males, while 2 were whites. Four additional police officers were present during these justifiable slayings and would add to the interrelationships.

Whether the focus of analysis is in terms of rates per unit of population or of proportionate distribution within a homicide group is an important distinction, as we have previously indicated, and one that results in differential racial "chances" of becoming a victim or an offender in an interracial criminal slaying. Of the 34 homicides, 14 were Negroes killed by whites and 20 were whites killed by Negroes. In terms of criminal homicide rates per 100,000 population, Negro offenders (1.00) crossed the race line about six times more frequently than did whites (.16); and Negroes were victims (.74) approximately three times more frequently than whites (.24).

In terms of the proportionate distribution within each homicide race group, Negroes killed by whites comprise 3 per cent of all Negro victims; whereas, whites killed by Negroes comprise 14 per cent of all white victims. Negroes in interracial homicides make up 5 per cent of all Negro offenders; and whites in interracial homicides make up 11 per cent of all white offenders. Thus, of those persons criminally slain, whites were proportionately three times more frequently killed by Negroes than Negroes by whites. Of those who committed criminal homicide, whites killed Negroes proportionately twice as often as Negroes killed whites.

Within the five years examined, there appears to be no regular annual pattern of these interracial homicides. There were 9 in 1948, 6 in 1949, 4 in 1950, 5 in 1951, and 10 in 1952. Six of the 9 victims in 1948 were white, whereas 7 of the 10 victims in 1952 were Negro. While it is true that of these interracial slayings Negroes were convicted of more serious offenses than whites, and consequently were given more severe penalties, a charge of court bias on these grounds and with respect to these interracial slayings does not appear to be justified. None of the 14 whites committed homicide during another felony, which would be classified as first degree murder; whereas, 13 Negro males committed felony murder—3 during rape or attempted rape, and 10 during robbery. Of these 13 cases, 12 Negro males were convicted of first degree murder. Thus, the interracial homicides committed by Negroes were, in fact and by statute, more serious crimes than those committed by whites.

Negro Male/White Male. Among the 9 cases in which Negro males were killed by white males, one was a stabbing, 5 were shootings, 2 were beatings, and one involved the use of fire. The last case was one of negligence on the part of two white proprietors of an auto repair shop. They were acquitted of involuntary manslaughter in the deaths of their employees. The one stabbing was the result of homosexual partners arguing about the immorality of their sexual relations despite the fact that they had been homosexually associated for five years. Both had previous records; the offender for aggravated assault. Age difference is interesting in this case, for the victim was 78 years old while the offender was only 48. The slayer in this case was found guilty of second degree murder and sentenced to 6 to 18 years in the Eastern State Penitentiary.

In the one beating case, the victim was a complete stranger to his slayer. The victim was drunk and attacked the offender for no apparent reason. The white male struck back, killed the Negro, and was later acquitted of a charge of voluntary manslaughter. The Negro was 45 years old and the white 39. The victim had no previous record, the offender a record of aggravated assault. The other beating was the result of a drunken altercation that began in a taproom and ended with an exchange of vile names. The Negro victim was 62 years of age, the white offender, 46. The former had no previous record; the latter, a record for minor offenses. The slayer was convicted of second degree murder, but was given a relatively light sentence of 11 to 23 months in the county prison.

The 5 shootings resulted from different motives. They involved: a quarrel between two friends; an irate husband, jealous of the Negro male who was living with the former's wife; an accidental shot fired by an intoxicated slayer; a white male who happened upon a scene where the Negro victim was about to attack the former's mother; and a motor bandit police officer who shot his Negro victim for resisting arrest and refusing to show identification. In this last case, the officer was the only policeman not exonerated by a coroner's inquest and who was tried in court. He was acquitted of involuntary manslaughter. All told, 4 of these victims had previous records, as did 2 of the offenders. Three of the slayers were convicted, 2 for voluntary manslaughter, sentenced to 6 to 23 months in the county prison, and one was placed on probation for 11 months.

White Male/Negro Male. Robbery was the predominant motive in 10 of the 15 interracial homicides involving white male victims and Negro male offenders. All of the offenders in these 10 cases were under 25 years of age. Seven of the 10 were shootings, 2 were beatings, and one was a stabbing. It is interesting to note that the victims of shootings were all younger men and under 40 years of age; while the 2 beatings were assaults on men 64 and 65 years of age; and the one stabbing was of a 54-year-old victim. Here again is some evidence that the younger the victim is, the more likely he will defend himself if the offender has no weapon—beyond that of his fists—that could produce a decided disadvantage. Nine of the 10 Negro offenders were convicted of first degree murder, 2 of whom received the death penalty, and 7 were sentenced to life imprisonment. Because of extenuating circumstances, one was convicted of second degree murder and given a 10-to-20-year sentence. Five of the 10 offenders, but none of the victims, had a previous arrest record. One victim was a police officer.

The remaining five white male/Negro male homicides involved motives other than robbery: an inexplicable and unprovoked attack on a police officer; altercation over money in a dice game; an argument over "dirty meat" dispensed by a white grocer; an argument concerning the Negro's attention to and sex play with the victim's wife, during which altercation an innocent six-year-old bystander was killed; and a Negro who interrupted a white's physical attack on several Negro children. Two of these 5 cases were shootings, 2 were beatings, and one was a stabbing. All 5 of the offenders had previous arrest records as did 3 of the victims. The Negro who stabbed the police officer without provocation was committed to Farview, the Pennsylvania institution for the criminally insane; one case was demurred for lack of evidence; 2 slayers were acquitted; and the one who killed the white grocer was convicted of first degree murder and sentenced to life imprisonment.

White Female/Negro Male. In these 3 cases, sex played an important role. In one case, the offender raped his victim *after* he had killed her. She was a prostitute and he became incensed when she asked for $3 in addition to the wining and dining that preceded their intimate physical relationship. The other 2 cases included a rape and an attempted rape. All 3 offenders were convicted of first degree murder: one was sentenced to death, and the other 2 to life imprisonment. All 3 victims were in their forties (43, 45, 47), while the offenders were considerably younger (18, 23, 29). Two of the victims were prostitutes and had long criminal records. The 3 offenders had arrest records of offenses against the person; 2 were previously arrested for aggravated assault. One of the offenders was reported by a psychiatrist as having "little moral sense. Badly in need of institutional training and should be committed to White Hill." All 3 women were strangers to their slayers until the day of the crime. All 3 were violent homicides by stabbing, beating, and strangulation, respectively.

Negro Female/White Male. In 2 of the 3 cases, motives are unknown. The ages of the victims were 32, 36, and 49, while those of the offenders were 43, 47, and 41 respectively. Beating was the method employed in one, and stabbing in the other 2. Only one of the offenders and none of the victims had a previous arrest record. In one case the offender, enraged upon finding his common-law wife in bed with another man, killed her. One offender was sent to a mental hospital and has had no trial; one is awaiting trial; and the third received a two-year county prison sentence for voluntary manslaughter.

White Male/Negro Female. Stabbing was the method used in the 2 white male/Negro female homicides. The victims' ages were 21 and 35, while those of the offenders were 43 and 53. All four persons had previous police records, three having been arrested for offenses against the person. One victim was a patron to a Negro female prostitute who killed him during an argument over the amount of money to be paid for her services. The other male was killed during an argument with his mistress, with whom he had been living for two years prior to the crime. The prostitute was convicted of second degree murder and received an indefinite sentence to Muncy. The mistress was convicted of voluntary manslaughter and received a recommended two-year sentence to Muncy.

Negro Male/White Female. These 2 homicides involved a prostitute and a white French girl who had married an American soldier stationed in her country during the Second World War. Save for the French girl, all persons had previous arrest records of aggravated assault. In the case where the white female prostitute was the offender, an argument over money incited the homicidal assault. She accused her patron-victim of stealing $37 from her. The case involving interracial marriage was a family quarrel that apparently had been common in their marriage. Both cases were stabbings. The victims' ages were 33 and 50; those of the offenders, 27 and 46 respectively. The prostitute was convicted of second degree murder and sentenced indefinitely to Muncy; the French wife was held for the French authorities and later deported.

Race and Sex Relationships Noted in Other Studies

Most studies affirm the racially endogenous nature of homicide. Summarizing other research, Sutherland noted that "in crimes of personal violence the victims and the offenders are generally of the same social group, and have residences not far apart. Negroes murder Negroes, Italians murder Italians, and Chinese murder Chinese."[1] As a witness before the Royal Commission on Capital Punishment, Sellin pointed out that "we know that murder in particular is an intra-group crime, generally Negroes kill Negroes, whites kill whites. . . . In other words the very nature of the offence is one which causes it to occur in groups where there is a relationship between the victim and the offender."[2]

But there is not always agreement regarding the amount of interracial homicide, nor who more often crosses the race line, Negro or white offenders. Speaking primarily about the South, Porterfield says that "whites kill many more non-white men than vice versa; probably five times as many. A Negro does not dare to kill a white man as a rule. The consequences are too painful; but probably four-fifths of Negro homicide victims are struck down by members of their own race."[3] Brearley refers to the fact that mortality data give no information regarding interracial slayings: "If, obviously, the Negro is more often slain by whites than he, himself, slays a white victim, his homicide death rate is not an accurate index of his tendency to commit deeds of violence. Little evidence upon this point is available, for the death certificates upon which all homicide rates are based give information concerning the slain only."[4] In New York City during 1925, 68 Negroes were feloniously killed, 20 of whom were not slain by Negroes. In South Carolina, of a total of 89 interracial homicides, 32 whites were killed by Negroes and 57 Negroes were slain by white persons, although the last figure includes 30 deaths of Negroes at the hands of police officers.[5]

In Memphis, Tennessee, during 1923, Hoffman[6] found 7 Negroes killed by whites, but only 2 whites slain by Negroes.

---

[1] Sutherland, *Principles of Criminology*, p. 25.
[2] Sellin, *Minutes of Evidence Taken Before the Royal Commission on Capital Punishment, op. cit.*, p. 678.
[3] A. L. Porterfield, R. H. Talbert, H. R. Mundhenke, *Crime, Suicide, and Social Well-Being*, p. 102.
[4] Brearley, *Homicide in the United States*, p. 100.
[5] *Ibid.*, p. 101.
[6] F. L. Hoffman, *The Homicide Problem*, p. 81.

Bruce and Fitzgerald,[1] referring to the same city between 1920 and 1925, said that 3 per cent of the 379 known cases were whites killed by Negroes and 13 per cent were Negroes slain by whites. The total of 16 per cent interracial slayings is nearly three times higher than the 6 per cent for Philadelphia.

In Chicago during the years 1926–1927, white males killed 14 per cent of all colored male victims, and colored males were responsible for 12 per cent of all white male victims. In this instance, the proportion of white males interracially killed is slightly lower than in Philadelphia, but the proportion of Negro victims slain by whites is about five times higher than in Philadelphia. In a summary statement of the race and sex topic in *The Illinois Crime Survey*, Lashly could be writing for Philadelphia as well as Chicago: ". . . white men killed twice as many white men as white women and . . . colored men killed three times as many colored men as colored women. On the other hand white women killed 1 1/3 times as many white men as white women and colored women killed four times as many colored men as colored women."[2]

In a review of murder and manslaughter indictments in seven major judicial areas of the South, E. P. Allredge,[3] claimed that of 862 such indictments, 83 per cent involved Negroes who had killed Negroes, 3 per cent involved Negroes who had killed whites; 13 per cent included whites killing whites, and less than one per cent were whites who had killed Negroes. Compared to Philadelphia, the percentage of white-victim/Negro-offender homicides was slightly lower in these southern districts, for such interracial slayings there accounted for 3 per cent of the total, and in Philadelphia, 4 per cent. The percentage of Negro-victim/white-offender homicides in the southern areas (.8 per cent) was also less than that in Philadelphia (2 per cent). (None of these statistics include justifiable homicides.)

Several comments about the data used in the Allredge survey seem necessary. The judicial areas of Atlanta,

[1] Computed from figures given by A. A. Bruce, T. S. Fitzgerald, cited by Hans von Hentig, *The Criminal and His Victim*, p. 394.
[2] *The Illinois Crime Survey*, p. 625.
[3] Allredge, *op. cit.*, p. 132.

Nashville, Memphis, Birmingham, and Houston covered in the review included indictments in each area for a single year (October, 1940–October, 1941). These five areas had a total of 312 indictments and only 3 involved whites killed by Negroes. To these reports were added statistics from Guy B. Johnson's article in the September, 1941 issue of *The Annals*, entitled "The Negro and Crime," wherein the author analyzed 220 indictments in the Richmond judicial area, and 330 indictments from five North Carolina centers—in both areas for the years 1930–1939.[1] There were, in Richmond and North Carolina, 24 indictments of Negroes who had killed whites. Thus, 24 of the total 27 indictments charging Negroes who killed whites, came from two areas covering two ten-year spans, while only 3 such indictments came from five areas, each covering one year. Excluding Johnson's study of Richmond and North Carolina, the proportion of Negroes who killed whites (1.0 per cent) is comparable to the proportion of whites who killed Negroes (.8 per cent). For Richmond and North Carolina alone, however, homicides involving Negroes who killed whites amount to 4 per cent, a proportion identical to that in Philadelphia. Allredge fails to give any indication of the population universe from which the indictments came, provides no standardization analysis by race, and combines a ten-year span which included the last great depression (1930–1939) with a one-year period prior to the last war (1940–1941), during which the nation was beginning economic recovery. These facts cast much doubt on the validity of his contentions that his reported "fact-finding survey" presents "conclusive data covering the main aspects of the abnormal record of murder and manslaughter in the South."

Harlan found that, of the 500 consecutive criminal homicides committed in Birmingham during the period from January, 1937, to December, 1944, less than 3 per cent crossed race lines.[2] This is considerably less than the 6 per cent in Philadelphia for the 550 known interpersonal relationships.

[1] Guy B. Johnson, "The Negro and Crime," *The Annals of the American Academy of Political and Social Science*, (September, 1941), 217: 93–104.
[2] Harlan, *op. cit.*, p. 745.

Harlan's percentage is based upon cases in which the agent of homicide was unknown. Using from his data a universe that includes only identified relationships between victim and offender so that his final proportion of interracial homicides is comparable to the Philadelphia data, little difference occurs in the results, for the 5 white victims and the 9 Negro victims combined still constituted less than 3 per cent of the 478 known relationships. As in Philadelphia, so in Birmingham, female offenders never crossed race lines when killing females. Furthermore, in the southern city all interracial offenses were among males, but in Philadelphia females, both as victims and offenders, were involved in interracial homicides with males.

Garfinkel[1] studied 821 cases of homicide which occurred in ten North Carolina counties from 1930 to 1940 and found that 9 per cent of the homicides were interracial, of which 6 per cent were Negro victims and 3 per cent white victims. In Meyers' report[2] on 212 criminal homicides in St. Louis (1949–1951), only 6, or less than 3 per cent, were interracial, a proportion less than half that of Philadelphia. In St. Louis too, female offenders did not cross race lines.

In summary, previous research has discovered—as we have in Philadelphia—that homicide is predominantly an intraracial offense; that most males kill and are killed by males; and that most females also kill and are killed by males. Inconsistency of reports appears prominently with respect to the amount of interracial homicides and the proportion of whites killed by Negroes compared to the proportion of Negroes killed by whites. Although real differences in rates may exist, differential treatment of Negroes at the time of arrest or in court, differential interpretation of excusable or justifiable homicide (particularly for cases in which a white slays a Negro) and differential sources of data partially explain the prevailing inconsistency of reports on interracial homicides.

[1] Harold Garfinkel, "Research Note on Inter- and Intra-Racial Homicides," *Social Forces* (May, 1949), 27: 369–381.
[2] Meyers, Jr., *op. cit.*, p. 24.

13

HOMICIDE DURING COMMISSION
OF ANOTHER FELONY

The Felony-Murder Rule

BOTH common law and contemporary legal statutes consider homicide that occurs during the commission of certain types of felonies as murder. An historical and legal analysis of the "felony-murder rule" is not included in the present study, but one of the best legal statements on this subject is found in Wechsler and Michael's *A Rationale of the Law of Homicide.*[1] Equally enlightening and concise is Rollin M. Perkins's "The Law of Homicide."[2] The following remarks by the latter author concerning felony-murder provide an appropriate setting for analysis of the Philadelphia cases:

> The "felony-murder rule" is often couched in some such form as this: "Homicide committed while perpetrating or attempting a felony is murder." This suggests mere coincidence as sufficient for the result; but the actual requirement is causation. It is necessary to show that "death ensued in consequence of the felony." It is not necessary, however, to show that the killing was intended or even that the act resulting in death was intended. It may have been quite unexpected. If the victim of a robbery attempts to disarm his assailant, and is killed by an accidental discharge of the weapon during a struggle for its possession, the robber is guilty of murder. Emphasis upon causation rather than coincidence is important also for quite a different reason. If the killing resulted from the perpetration of the felonious design it falls within the rule even if the felony itself had been completed before the fatal blow was struck. It is homicide resulting from robbery, for

[1] Herbert Wechsler and Jerome Michael, *A Rationale of the Law of Homicide,* reprinted from *Columbia Law Review* (May and December, 1937), 37: 712–717.

[2] Rollin Perkins, "The Law of Homicide," *Journal of Criminal Law and Criminology* (March–April, 1946), 36: 401–408.

example, although the robber had taken the money from his victim and was running away with it when the killing occurred. And a killing has been committed during the perpetration or attempted perpetration of rape, if the fatal blow was struck either to render the victim helpless before the attack or while it was taking place, or to still her outcries after the act was completed, as an incident of the rape and at the scene thereof.[1]

That the felony must be distinctly different from, and independent of, the homicide is made abundantly clear in the following passage:

> It would be futile to recognize the sudden heat of passion, engendered by great provocation, as sufficiently mitigating to reduce a voluntary homicide to manslaughter, if in the next breath it was added that manslaughter is a dangerous felony and hence any homicide resulting from such an attempt must be murder. The distinction between murder and manslaughter, felonies both, makes it necessary to qualify any rule as to homicide resulting from felony by limiting it to felonies other than felonious homicide itself. This has usually been taken for granted, but at times has been forced upon the attention of the court. In such cases it has been held essential, in order to bring the case within the "felony-murder rule," that the slayer was engaged in some *other felony*, so distinct "as not to be an ingredient of the homicide" itself.[2]

For most jurisdictions in this country the "felony-murder rule" may probably be stated as:

> Homicide is murder if the death ensues in consequence of the perpetration or attempted perpetration of some other felony unless such other felony was not dangerous of itself and the method of its perpetration or attempt did not appear to involve any appreciable human risk. To this may be added the explanation, previously suggested, that the danger here referred to may fall considerably short of a plain and strong likelihood that death or great bodily injury will result, but must not be so remote that no reasonable man would have taken it into consideration.[3]

[1] *Ibid.*, p. 404.
[2] *Ibid.*, pp. 404–405.
[3] *Ibid.*, p. 405.

The Pennsylvania Penal Code includes, within a definition of first degree murder, any homicide "which shall be committed in the perpetration of, or attempting to perpetrate any arson, rape, robbery, burglary, or kidnapping."[1] Illustrative court decisions from this Commonwealth point out that

A homicide committed while fleeing from a burglary is first degree murder. Com. v. Tauza, 300 Pa. Supreme Ct. 375 (1930).[2]

When a murder occurs in the perpetration of a robbery by two persons acting in concert, both are guilty of the murder, though the killing was the act of one only. Com. v. DeLeo, 242 Pa. Supreme Ct. 510 (1914).

All participants in an attempted robbery are guilty of murder in the first degree if some one is killed in the course of the perpetration of the first named crime. Com. v. Carelli, 281 Pa. Supreme Ct. 602 (1925).

Where a homicide is committed in an attempt to perpetrate a robbery, the defense of an accidental killing is without avail. Where it is shown that the gun which fired the fatal shot was in defendant's possession for the criminal purpose of robbery, it is immaterial that the discharge was unintentionally caused while struggling with the victim, or with a third party who came to the latter's assistance. It is the fact of killing in the perpetration of or attempt to perpetrate the crime which brings the case within the statute—not the intent to kill. Com. v. Lessner, 274 Pa. Supreme Ct. 108 (1922).[3]

The Philadelphia Data

In 32 cases a felony, in addition to the killing, was being perpetrated at the time of the slaying. These cases involved 63 victim-offender relationships,[4] and of these, 57 offenders and 6 victims were engaged in felonies during which homicide occurred.[5]

---

[1] William F. Hoffman, *Pennsylvania Criminal Law and Criminal Procedure*, Article VII, Section 701, p. 121.

[2] *Ibid.*, p. 124.

[3] *Ibid.*, pp. 124–125.

[4] Including relationships between victims and multiple defendants beyond the first or principal defendant.

[5] It should be clear that not all felony-homicide is felony-murder in Pennsylvania. As the penal code declares, *only* perpetration or attempted perpetration of robbery, burglary, arson, rape, and kidnapping during which a homicide occurs constitute felony-murder.

240

Among the 57 offenders who killed during the commission of another felony, 32 were principal offenders or defendants and 25 were multiple defendants.[1] The proportion of multiple defendants among these offenders in felony-homicide is four times greater than that among offenders in all types of homicide. Only 71, or 11 per cent, were multiple defendants in addition to the first or principal defendant among the total 621 offenders; but 44 per cent were multiple defendants among offenders in felony-homicide. Among the regular cases (single defendants) of felony-homicide, 13 Negro males had committed robbery during which homicide occurred; 3 had committed rape; one was charged with resisting arrest and assault with intent to kill one person during which assault he killed another; and one, with rioting and riotous destruction of property. In 9 regular cases, white male offenders had perpetrated robberies during which victims were killed, two resisted arrest and were driving a stolen automobile, and another was involved in a burglary during which he killed two night watchmen. Fifteen additional Negro males and 10 white males were multiple defendants in homicides occurring during robberies. No Negro victims were slain by white offenders during felony-homicides, but among regular cases, 3 involved robbery in which the victim was a white male and the offender a Negro male, and one involved a white female victim raped by a Negro male. Among multiple defendants, there were 8 cases in which the victims were white males and the offenders were Negro males perpetrating robbery. White males killed only white males in all of these felony-homicides except in one case which involved a white female. In no case was a female of either race an offender in this type of homicide.

Relative to homicides in general, white males have a high representation in felony-homicides. Moreover, since all offenders in felony-homicide were male, this sex was clearly overrepresented compared to the male proportion in all

[1] The term "multiple defendants" refers to the fact that more than one person was involved in a single slaying. In more legalistic terms, the principal offender is a principal in the first degree, and multiple offenders are principals in the second degree.

homicides (82 per cent). Of the total 621 offenders, 22 per cent were white males; of the 521 male offenders, 27 per cent were white; but of 57 offenders in felony-homicide, 42 per cent were white males.

Among the 57 felony-homicide offenders, 17 were in the age group between 15 and 19 years; 21 were 20–24; 9 were 25–29; 2 were 30–34; 4 were 35–39; 3 were 40–44; and one was over fifty years of age. These offenders were considerably younger than total male offenders in all homicides with whom they may be compared. Among male offenders in all types of homicide, only two-fifths were under 25 years of age; but 38, or two-thirds, of those who killed during the commission of a felony were under 25.

Two-thirds of felony-homicide offenders have a previous arrest record. Because only males are offenders in this type of slaying, comparison is best made with male offenders in homicide in general; and for all male offenders the proportion with an arrest record is also two-thirds. Since the primary motive in all but a few of these felony-homicides was robbery, it might be expected that the offenders would be *more* likely to have a prior police record than offenders involved in non-felony-homicides. It might even be expected that those who commit homicide while engaged in a felony might be habitual offenders. Examination of the records shows the offender in felony-homicide is no more a recidivist than offenders in homicide generally. However, the greater youth of slayers in felony-homicide in part accounts for the similar proportion with a police record. Since two-thirds of these offenders were under 25 years of age compared to two-fifths of all male offenders in general, and since fewer younger persons logically would be expected to have a prior record, the similar proportion of the two types of offenders with a record takes on meaning. The implication is, then, that if age were held constant, the offender in felony-homicide is more likely to have a previous record than is the offender in non-felony-homicide. Unfortunately, the number of cases of felony-homicide in the present study is too small for holding age constant in a test of this hypothesis, but future research should seek to do so.

Shooting and beating were the two most common methods by which the 32 victims in these cases met death: 14 were shot, 13 beaten to death, 2 stabbed, and 3 were killed in miscellaneous ways. Because of the predominant number of robberies and the usual desire of the defendant to remain unknown to his victim, the overwhelming number of victims in felony-homicides were complete strangers to their slayers. Of total homicides, victims were strangers in only one-eighth of the cases, but of felony-homicides, 42, or over three-fourths, were strangers. In 8 relationships the victim was merely an acquaintance; in 2, a police officer; and in one each, a close friend, a known enemy, and a prostitute.

Eight of the 57 offenders were acquitted by the court; one case was demurred for lack of evidence; two mentally diseased offenders were committed to Farview before trial, one of whom escaped and was later fatally shot by the police for resisting arrest in another city. Forty-six were found guilty, of whom 31 were convicted of murder in the first degree, 13 of murder in the second degree, and 2 of voluntary manslaughter. Of first degree convictions, 6 were sentenced to death, 24 to life imprisonment, and one was sent to Farview.

Although it may be justifiable to kill a felon under certain circumstances, there are some situations where enough doubt exists so that a coroner's inquest is unable to determine legal justification sufficient to exonerate the defendant. Moreover, several persons may be in the process of committing a robbery, during which a police officer kills one of the perpetrators. As a result of such a justifiable homicide,[1] the other principals in the crime are held criminally responsible for the death. In 6 cases during the five years, a *victim* of criminal homicide had been committing a felony at the time of his death. In 3 cases, Negro male victims were involved in robbery, and in 2 of these the responsible offenders were also Negro males. In the third case, the victim was shot by a police officer in the line of duty, but an accomplice of the

---

[1] Justifiable homicides, or homicides performed as a police function, of which there were 14 during the five years, are not included in the present study.

victim was indicted for murder in the first degree. In one case, a Negro male criminally and sexually assaulted a Negro female, who in turn killed him; and in 2 other cases, Negro males were involved in burglary and auto theft respectively. All told, there were 6 cases in which a victim was perpetrating a felony during which he was killed, and for whose death the slayer, or another person who was held legally responsible, had to stand trial.

14

VICTIM-PRECIPITATED
CRIMINAL HOMICIDE

The Theoretical and Legal Basis for Analysis

IN many crimes, especially in criminal homicide, the victim is often·a major contributor to the criminal act. Except in cases in which the victim is an innocent bystander and is killed in lieu of an intended victim, or in cases in which a pure accident is involved, the victim may be one of the major precipitating causes of his own demise.

Although various theories of social interaction, particularly in social psychology, could help establish the framework for the present discussion, probably von Hentig, in *The Criminal and His Victim*, has provided the most useful theoretical basis for the present analysis of the victim-offender relationship. In Chapter XII, entitled "The Contribution of the Victim to the Genesis of Crime," the author refers to the "duet frame of crime" and says:

> Here are two human beings. As soon as they draw near to one another, male or female, young or old, rich or poor, ugly or attractive—a wide range of interactions, repulsions as well as attractions, is set in motion. What the law does is to watch the one who acts and the one who is acted upon. By this external criterion a subject and object, a perpetrator and a victim are distinguished. In sociological and psychological quality the situation may be completely different. It may happen that the two distinct categories merge. There are cases in which they are reversed and in the long chain of causative forces the victim assumes the role of a determinant.
>
> . . . I maintain that many criminal deeds are more indicative of a subject-object relation than of the perpetrator alone. There is a definite mutuality of some sort. . . . In the long

245

process leading gradually to the unlawful result, credit and debit are not infrequently indistinguishable. . . .

In a sense the victim shapes and moulds the criminal. . . . Although it looks one-sided as far as the final outcome goes, it is not a totally unilateral form of relationship. They work upon each other profoundly and continually, even before the moment of disaster. To know one we must be acquainted with the complementary partner.

Often victims seem to be born. Often they are society-made. Sometimes the most valuable qualities render us easy victims.[1]

In this passage, the author refers to various types of crime, but by using many illustrations of homicide, he suggests that this crime is particularly amenable to an analysis of the victim's contribution. The author classifies these victims by psychological type,[2] suggesting the importance of the victim's behavior patterns as provocative of crime. Von Hentig then extends this approach to the community, claiming that, by maintaining certain criminogenic situations, the community practically guarantees its own victimization and suffering through criminal depredations, though the individual victim of crime is perhaps to be looked upon as the "activating sufferer." Such an integrated approach assumes the essential interdependence of personality and culture, and the interrelationship of the individual and his society.[3]

In *Penal Philosophy*, Tarde frequently attacks the "legislative mistake" of concentrating too much on premeditation and paying too little attention to motives, which indicate an important interrelationship between victim and offender. That this French jurist was aware of the victim's contribution to the genesis of homicide is indicated by the following remarks: "For example, it often happens that an outraged husband premeditates killing his wife's lover should he meet

[1] Von Hentig, *The Criminal and His Victim*, pp. 383–385.

[2] Von Hentig's psychological types are not used in the present study, but they are: (1) the depressive, (2) the greedy for gain, (3) the wanton, (4) the tormentor. He claims that "there are certainly some murder cases in which the victim seemed to encourage the slayer to have the slain dispatched." ("Remarks on the Interaction of Perpetrator and Victim," *Journal of Criminal Law and Criminology* [1940–1941], 31: 304.)

[3] For a critical review of the book, see Irving A. Lanzer, *The Journal of Criminal Law and Criminology* (March–April, 1950), 40: 784–785.

him in his own house, or that a man is resolved to kill his enemy the first time the latter shall take the liberty of saying the slightest thing to offend him. Here the premeditation is conditional; if the condition is fulfilled *through some act of the victim's,* will one say that there has been murder or assassination?"[1]

In one of his satirical essays, "On Murder Considered as One of the Fine Arts," Thomas DeQuincey shows cognizance of the idea that sometimes the victim is a would-be murderer: "I could mention some people (I name no names) who have been murdered by other people in a dark lane; and so far all seemed correct enough; but, on looking further into the matter, the public have become aware that the murdered party was himself, at the moment, planning to rob his murderer, at the least, and possibly to murder him, if he had been strong enough."[2] In such cases, chance, accident, or other peculiar and unforeseen circumstances reverse the victim-offender roles.

Garofalo, too, noted that the victim may provoke another individual into attack, and though the provocation be slight, if perceived by an egoistic attacker it may be sufficient to result in homicide. This pioneer criminologist typically refers to the "perversity or utter lack of the altruistic sentiments" when he claims also that there are some murders "where the victim has done nothing to deserve the hatred or arouse the anger of the murderer, or where on account of ties of blood or benefits received, what the murderer regarded as provocation would not have been provocation for a normal man."[3] This last point by Garofalo has often been raised in criminal court.

Besides these theoretical concepts, the law of homicide has long recognized provocation by the victim as a possible reason for mitigation of the offense from murder to manslaughter, or from criminal to excusable homicide. The

---

[1] Tarde, *op. cit.,* p. 466. Emphasis is that of the present author.
[2] Thomas DeQuincey, "On Murder Considered as One of the Fine Arts," *The Arts of Cheating, Swindling, and Murder,* Edward Bulwer-Lytton, and Douglas Jerrold, and Thomas DeQuincey, New York: The Arnold Co., 1925, p. 153.
[3] Garofalo, *op. cit.,* p. 373.

immediate concern in this analysis is only with that rule of provocation that reduces murder to manslaughter. In order that such a reduction occur, there are four prerequisites.[1]

(1) There must have been adequate provocation. Adequate provocation is sometimes difficult to objectify, but, as Wechsler and Michael point out, "it must be estimated by the probability that such circumstances would affect most men in like fashion; although the passions stirred up in the actor were violent, the provocation can be said to be great only if the provocative circumstances would have aroused in most men similar desires of comparable intensity."[2] Thus Garofalo's emphasis on "provocation for the normal man" is recognized in criminal law, for the provocation must ordinarily be excessive in nature.[3] While it is probably true that most men, on even the gravest provocation, will not kill, some men will kill on relatively slight provocation. Although not every technical battery, for example, is sufficient to constitute adequate provocation by law, a hard blow inflicting considerable pain or injury is usually sufficient.[4]

(2) The killing must have been in the heat of passion.

(3) The killing must have followed the provocation before there had been a reasonable opportunity for the passion to cool. If the homicidal act does not follow closely upon the provocative circumstances, the lapse of

---

[1] For an excellent discussion of the rule of provocation, from which these four requirements are taken, see: Rollin M. Perkins, "The Law of Homicide," *Journal of Criminal Law and Criminology* (March–April, 1946), 36: 412–427; and Herbert Wechsler and Jerome Michael, *A Rationale of the Law of Homicide*, pp. 1280–1282. A general review of the rule of provocation, both in this country and abroad, may be found in *The Royal Commission on Capital Punishment, 1949–1953 Report*, Appendix 11, pp. 453–458.

[2] Wechsler and Michael, *op. cit.*, p. 1281.

[3] See Perkins, *op. cit.*, p. 413, who says: "The problem of provocation in the homicide cases cannot be considered effectively without keeping constantly in mind the relation of the retaliatory act to the provocative one. The foundation principle is that where the former is not unreasonably excessive and out of proportion to the latter, the basis of mitigation is established (if the latter was not altogether inadequate); but where it is unreasonably excessive and out of proportion no mitigation will be recognized."

[4] Perkins, *op. cit.*, p. 413, says: "Knocking a person down with a heavy stick, or hitting him over the head with a revolver, are rather obvious instances of such force; but a weapon is not indispensable for this purpose. Thus even a blow with the fist may be sufficient to reduce an intentional killing to manslaughter, particularly if it is a blow in the face or a 'staggering' blow."

time may intensify or diminish the agent's passion. "For example," say Wechsler and Michael, "if a substantial interval of time or an apology intervened between insult and retaliation therefore, these would have to be considered in determining the extent of the provocation."[1] This means that a distinction must be sharply drawn between defensive and revengeful force by the actor.[2] In general, the greater the provocation, the longer will be the cooling time permitted by judicial interpretations of the rule. Furthermore, neither a mutual quarrel or combat *per se*,[3] a mere challenge to a fist fight,[4] gestures, nor simple trespassing is generally adequate to constitute provocation.

[1] Wechsler and Michael, *op. cit.*, p. 1282.

[2] See Perkins, *op. cit.*, p. 414, who says: "If the one assailed has killed his assailant within the legal privilege of self-defense he is guilty of no crime at all. This is not the present problem. For the moment we are concerned with a killing caused, not in self-defense, but in the heat of passion engendered by an attack that failed and after the immediate danger had passed. In one case, for example, deceased shot at the defendant and missed him. This so angered the defendant that he shot the other in the back while he was running away, thus causing his death. This was clearly not within the privilege of self-defense, but this provocation was held sufficient to reduce the grade of homicide to manslaughter.

"An unsuccessful attempt to commit a battery is seldom likely to arouse the same degree of passion in a reasonable man as will be engendered by the actual blow intended. Hence the fact that the assailant did not actually hit the defendant is one of the important circumstances in the particular case. Such an attack is less likely to be regarded as adequate provocation than one that succeeds. But just as not every actual blow will be sufficient for this purpose, so not every failure will leave it insufficient. The unsuccessful attack may be so vicious in extreme cases as to constitute adequate provocation."

[3] See *ibid.*, p. 415, who points out: "A wordy altercation will not of itself be sufficient to mitigate to manslaughter a killing that is otherwise murder. On the other hand a mutual encounter which goes beyond words to actual blows or to a manifestation of intent to use immediate and violent force may constitute adequate provocation; and in determining the adequacy of the provocation in such a case the entire quarrel, including the words, will be taken into consideration."

[4] See *ibid.*, p. 416: "Suppose, for example, two men were engaged in a tussle on a vacant lot and one caused the death of the other. If it was a friendly encounter—a mere test of strength without anger and without intent to cause serious harm, it was not unlawful. And if death resulted quite unexpectedly from such a struggle it is no crime at all, but excusable homicide. If the facts were the same except that the two were mutually engaged in an angry fight—but without intent to cause death or great bodily injury—and death should result quite unexpectedly to one, the other would be guilty of manslaughter. This is not because of the rule of provocation but because the death resulted from an unlawful, although apparently not dangerous, battery. Such an accidental killing is not excused by the common law because it resulted from unlawful conduct characterized as *malum in se*." Also, *ibid.*, p. 418: "The same must be said of a threat to slap, made in the course of a verbal dispute, and the further step of removing the coat in preparation for fisticuffs."

Firmly established in common law is the rule that provocative words are not recognized as adequate provocation to reduce a willful killing to manslaughter, "however abusive, aggravating, contemptuous, false, grievous, indecent, insulting, opprobrious, provoking, or scurrilous they may be."[1] The use of insulting words by the victim may be considered, however, in determining the degree of murder, or in assessing the severity of punishment for murder when the law provides more than one possible penalty. There are some other acts which do not involve actual physical contact between victim and offender prior to the homicide, which are recognized in some jurisdictions, either by statute of by local mores, as adequate provocation. Such, for example, are: adultery, seduction of the offender's juvenile daughter, rape of the offender's wife or close relative.

Finally, (4), a causal connection must exist between provocation, the heat of passion, and the homicidal act. Perkins claims that "the adequate provocation must have engendered the heat of passion, and the heat of passion must have been the cause of the act which resulted in death."[2]

Of particular importance to the present study are the court interpretations of the rule of provocation in Pennsylvania. The following is a brief summary of some of these judicial interpretations taken from William Hoffman's *Pennsylvania Criminal Law and Criminal Procedure:*[3]

[1] *Ibid.*, p. 419.
[2] *Ibid.*, p. 425. The term "cause" is here used in a legal and not a psychological sense.
[3] William Hoffman, *op. cit.*, pp. 123–125. Most of these judicial pronouncements were written by Judge Agnew in 1868. In that year, a man named Drum was charged with murder in Westmoreland Co., Pa. Because the president judge of that county was related to the defendant, the Supreme Court assigned Judge Agnew, one of the justices of the Supreme Court, to preside at the trial in the Court of Oyer and Terminer of Westmoreland County. Although not carried to the Supreme Court, the case was considered by that body to have been so ably tried, and Judge Agnew's charge to the jury so enlightening on the subject of murder in general, that the entire procedure was reprinted in the Supreme Court Reports, Vol. 58, p. 9. The case is still used as a model of procedure in murder trials in this Commonwealth, and Judge Agnew's charge to the jury forms the basis of many contemporary charges in homicide. (*Ibid.*, p. 139.)

To reduce an intentional blow, stroke, or wounding, resulting in death, to manslaughter there must be sufficient cause of provocation, and a state of rage or passion without time to cool, placing the person beyond the control of his reason and suddenly impelling him to the deed.

If there be provocation without passion, or passion without sufficient cause of provocation; or there be time to cool and reason has resumed its sway, the killing will be murder.

Insulting or scandalous words, or actual indignities of a light or trivial kind, to the person are not sufficient cause of provocation.

To excuse homicide by a plea of self-defense, it must appear that the slayer had no other possible or at least probable means of escaping, and that his act was one of necessity.

If the object of the assailant appears to be to commit only an ordinary assault and battery, it will not excuse a man of equal or nearly equal strength in taking his assailant's life with a deadly weapon. The act of the slayer must not be entirely disproportioned to the attack upon him.

When it comes to a question whether one man shall flee or another shall live, the law decides that the former shall rather flee than that the latter shall die.

The burden is upon the slayer to prove that there was an actual necessity for taking life or a seeming one so reasonably apparent and convincing to him as to lead him to believe he could defend himself only in that way.

Homicide committed under apprehension one's life is in danger is manslaughter unless such homicide was committed with malice.

Where one is killed by a wound in a vital part, administered through a deadly weapon, no words of profanity, reproach, abuse, or slight assault are provocations sufficient to free the party killing from the guilt of murder. The law imposes upon every one the duty of keeping his passions under reasonable restraint, and, therefore, if one lashes himself into a passion at some slight provocation, and without reasonable excuse, he cannot defend against murder because of such passion; nor can he, at the recollection of some past injury or insult or blackhand demand for money, work himself into a heat over it, and so excuse himself; the act, to reduce the killing from murder to manslaughter, must be upon sufficient and sudden provocation. To warrant taking life in self-defense there must be a reasonable ground for belief, upon the part of the slayer, that he is in imminent danger of loss of his own life or suffering serious bodily harm at the hands of the person killed, and the same rule applies to persons acting in defense of others.

Definition and Illustration

The term *victim-precipitated* is applied to those criminal homicides in which the victim is a direct, positive precipitator in the crime. The role of the victim is characterized by his having been the first in the homicide drama to use physical force directed against his subsequent slayer. The victim-precipitated cases are those in which the victim was the first to show and use a deadly weapon, to strike a blow in an altercation—in short, the first to commence the interplay of resort to physical violence.

In seeking to identify the victim-precipitated cases recorded in police files it has not been possible always to determine whether the homicides strictly parallel legal interpretations. In general, there appears to be much similarity. In a few cases included under the present definition, the nature of the provocation is such that it would not legally serve to mitigate the offender's responsibility. In these cases the victim was threatened in a robbery, and either attempted to prevent the robbery, failed to take the robber seriously, or in some other fashion irritated, frightened, or alarmed the felon by physical force so that the robber, either by accident or compulsion, killed the victim. Infidelity of a mate or lover, failure to pay a debt, use of vile names by the victim, obviously means that he played an important role in inciting the offender to overt action in order to seek revenge, to win an argument, or to defend himself. However, these mutual quarrels and wordy altercations do not constitute sufficient provocation under law, nor are they included in the present interpretation of victim-precipitated homicide.

Below are sketched several typical cases to illustrate the pattern of these homicides. Primary demonstration of physical force by the victim, supplemented by scurrilous language,

252

characterizes the most common victim-precipitated homicides. All of these slayings were listed by the police as criminal homicides, none of the assailants was exonerated by a coroner's inquest, and all the assailants were tried in criminal court.

A husband accused his wife of giving money to another man, and while she was making breakfast, he attacked her with a milk bottle, then a brick, and finally a piece of concrete block. Having had a butcher knife in hand, she stabbed him during the fight.

A husband threatened to kill his wife on several occasions. In this instance, he attacked her with a pair of scissors, dropped them, and grabbed a butcher knife from the kitchen. In the ensuing struggle that ended on their bed, he fell on the knife.

In an argument over a business transaction, the victim first fired several shots at his adversary, who in turn fatally returned the fire.

The victim was the aggressor in a fight, having struck his enemy several times. Friends tried to interfere, but the victim persisted. Finally, the offender retaliated with blows, causing the victim to fall and hit his head on the sidewalk, as a result of which he died.

A husband had beaten his wife on several previous occasions. In the present instance, she insisted that he take her to the hospital. He refused, and a violent quarrel followed, during which he slapped her several times, and she concluded by stabbing him.

During a lovers' quarrel, the male (victim) hit his mistress and threw a can of kerosene at her. She retaliated by throwing the liquid on him, and then tossed a lighted match in his direction. He died from the burns.

A drunken husband, beating his wife in their kitchen, gave her a butcher knife and dared her to use it on him. She claimed that if he should strike her once more she would use the knife, whereupon he slapped her in the face and she fatally stabbed him.

A victim became incensed when his eventual slayer asked for money which the victim owed him. The victim grabbed a hatchet and started in the direction of his creditor, who pulled out a knife and stabbed him.

A victim attempted to commit sodomy with his girl friend, who refused his overtures. He struck her several times on the side of her head with his fists before she grabbed a butcher knife and cut him fatally.

A drunken victim with knife in hand approached his slayer during a quarrel. The slayer showed a gun, and the victim dared him to shoot. He did.

During an argument in which a male called a female many vile names, she tried to telephone the police. He grabbed the phone from her hands, knocked her down, kicked her, and hit her with a tire gauge. She ran to the kitchen, grabbed a butcher knife, and stabbed him in the stomach.

The Philadelphia Data

The 588 criminal homicides in this study provide sufficient background information to establish much about the nature of the victim-offender relationship. Of these cases, 150, or 26 per cent, have been designated, on the basis of the previously stated definition, as VP cases.[1] The remaining 438, therefore, have been designated as non-VP cases. Thorough study of police files, theoretical discussions of the victim's contribution, and previous analysis of criminal homicide suggest that there may be important differences between VP and non-VP homicides. Whenever the number of VP cases is sufficiently large to permit detailed analysis, comparison is made between VP and non-VP cases. The discussion that follows (with respect to race, sex, age, etc.) reveals some interesting differences and similarities between the two.[2] (Table 28.)

[1] In order to facilitate reading of the following sections, the *victim-precipitated* cases are referred to simply as VP cases or VP homicides. Those homicides in which the victim was not a direct precipitator are referred to as non-VP cases.

[2] The present analysis of the complex interrelationship of victim and offender is not entirely foreign to the conceptual schemes of personal interplay found in *Theory of Games and Economic Behavior*, by von Neumann and Morgenstern. The present study makes no attempt to analyze the homicide drama in terms of "the theory of strategy," or "statistical decision functions which minimize the maximum risk," but an experimental design that could test these ideas might be fruitful. See, for example, John von Neumann and Oskar Morgenstern, *Theory of Games and Economic Behavior*, Princeton: Princeton University Press, 1944; Abraham Wald, "Statistical Decision Functions Which Minimize Risk," *Annals of Mathematics* (April, 1945), 46: 265–280; John MacDonald, "The Theory of Strategy," *Fortune* (June, 1949), pp. 100–110; Leonid Hurwicz, "Game Theory and Decisions," *Scientific American* (February, 1955), 192: 78–83.

Race. Because Negroes and males have been shown by their high rates of homicide, assaults against the person, etc., to be more criminally aggressive than whites and females, it may be inferred that there are more Negroes and males among VP victims than among non-VP victims. The data confirm this inference. Nearly 80 per cent of VP cases compared to 70 per cent of non-VP cases involve Negroes, a proportional difference that results in a *significant* association between race and VP homicide.

Sex. As victims, males comprise 94 per cent of VP homicides, but only 70 per cent of non-VP homicides, showing a *significant* association between sex of the victim and VP homicide.

Since females have been shown by their low rates of homicide, assaults against the person, etc., to be less criminally aggressive than males, and since females are less likely to precipitate their own victimization than males, we should expect more female *offenders* among VP homicides than among non-VP homicides. Such is the case, for the comparative data reveal that females are twice as frequently offenders in VP slayings (29 per cent) as they are in non-VP slayings (14 per cent)—a proportional difference which is also highly *significant*.

The number of white female offenders (16) in this study is too small to permit statistical analysis, but the tendency among both Negro and white females as separate groups is toward a much higher proportion among VP than among non-VP offenders. As noted above, analysis of Negro and white females as a combined group does result in the finding of a *significant* association between female offenders and VP homicide.

Age. The age distributions of victims and offenders in VP and non-VP homicides are strikingly similar. Study of the data suggests that age has no apparent effect on VP homicide. The median age of VP victims is 33.3 years, while that of non-VP victims is 31.2 years.

Methods. In general, there is a *significant* association

TABLE 28
VICTIM-PRECIPITATED AND NON-VICTIM-PRECIPITATED CRIMINAL HOMICIDE BY SELECTED VARIABLES, PHILADELPHIA, 1948–1952

Race and Sex of Victim	Total Victims		Victim-Precipitated		Non-Victim-Precipitated	
	Number	Per Cent of Total	Number	Per Cent of Total	Number	Per Cent of Total
Both Races	588	100.0	150	100.0	438	100.0
Male	449	76.4	141	94.0	308	70.3
Female	139	23.6	9	6.0	130	29.7
Negro	427	72.6	119	79.3	308	70.3
Male	331	56.3	111	74.0	220	50.2
Female	96	16.3	8	5.3	88	20.1
White	161	27.4	31	20.7	130	29.7
Male	118	20.1	30	20.0	88	20.1
Female	43	7.3	1	.7	42	9.6
Age of Victim						
Under 15	28	4.8	—	—	28	6.4
15–19	25	4.3	7	4.7	18	4.1
20–24	59	10.0	18	12.0	41	9.4
25–29	93	15.8	17	11.3	76	17.3
30–34	88	15.0	20	13.3	68	15.5
35–39	75	12.8	25	16.7	50	11.4
40–44	57	9.7	23	15.3	34	7.8
45–49	43	7.3	13	8.7	30	6.8
50–54	48	8.2	11	7.3	37	8.5
55–59	26	4.4	6	4.0	20	4.6
60–64	18	3.1	7	4.7	11	2.5
65 and over	28	4.7	3	2.0	25	5.7
Total	588	100.0	150	100.0	438	100·0
Method						
Stabbing	228	38.8	81	54.0	147	33.6
Shooting	194	33.0	39	26.0	155	35.4
Beating	128	21.8	26	17.3	102	23.3
Other	38	6.4	4	2.7	34	7.7
Total	588	100.0	150	100.0	438	100.0
Place						
Home	301	51.2	80	53.3	221	50.5
Not Home	287	48.8	70	46.7	217	49.5
Total	588	100.0	150	100.0	438	100.0
Interpersonal Relationship						
Relatively close friend	155	28.2	46	30.7	109	27.3
Family relationship	136	24.7	38	25.3	98	24.5
(Spouse)	(100)	(73.5)	(33)	(86.8)	(67)	(68.4)
(Other)	(36)	(26.5)	(5)	(13.2)	(31)	(31.6)

256

TABLE 28 (continued)

	Total Victims		Victim-Precipitated		Non-Victim-Precipitated	
	Number	Per Cent of Total	Number	Per Cent of Total	Number	Per Cent of Total
Acquaintance	74	13.5	20	13.3	54	13.5
Stranger	67	12.2	16	10.7	51	12.8
Paramour, Mistress, Prostitute	54	9.8	15	10.0	39	9.8
Sex rival	22	4.0	6	4.0	16	4.0
Enemy	16	2.9	6	4.0	10	2.5
Paramour of offender's mate	11	2.0	1	.7	10	2.5
Felon or police officer	6	1.1	1	.7	5	1.3
Innocent bystander	6	1.1	—	—	6	1.5
Homosexual partner	3	.6	1	.7	2	.5
Total	550	100.0	150	100.0	400	100.0
Presence of alcohol during offense						
Present	374	63.6	111	74.0	263	60.0
Not Present	214	36.4	39	26.0	175	40.0
Total	588	100.0	150	100.0	438	100.0
Presence of alcohol in the victim						
Present	310	52.7	104	69.3	206	47.0
Not Present	278	47.3	46	30.7	232	53.0
Total	588	100.0	150	100.0	438	100.0
Previous arrest record of victim						
Previous arrest record	277	47.1	93	62.0	184	42.0
Offenses against the person	150	25.5 (54.2)	56	37.3 (60.2)	94	21.5 (50.1)
Other offenses only	127	21.6 (45.8)	37	24.7 (39.8)	90	20.5 (49.9)
No previous arrest record	311	52.9	57	38.0	254	58.0
Total	588	100.0	150	100.0	438	100.0
Previous arrest record of offender						
Previous arrest record	400	64.4	81	54.0	319	67.7
Offenses against the person	264	42.5 (66.0)	49	32.7 (60.5)	215	45.6 (67.4)
Other offenses only	136	21.9 (34.0)	32	21.3 (39.5)	104	22.1 (32.6)
No previous arrest record	221	35.6	69	46.0	152	32.3
Total	621	100.0	150	100.0	471	100.0

257

between method used to inflict death and VP homicide. Because Negroes and females comprise a larger proportion of offenders in VP cases, and because previous analysis has shown that stabbings occurred more often than any of the other methods of inflicting death,[1] it is inferred that the frequency of homicides by stabbing is greater among VP than among non-VP cases. The data support such an inference and reveal that homicides by stabbing account for 54 per cent of the VP cases but only 34 per cent of non-VP cases, a difference which is *significant*. The distribution of shootings, beatings, and "other" methods of inflicting death among the VP and non-VP cases show no significant differences. The high frequency of stabbings among VP homicides appears to result from an almost equal reduction in each of the remaining methods; yet the lower proportions in each of these three other categories among VP cases are not separately very different from the proportions among non-VP cases.

Place and Motive. There is no important difference between VP and non-VP homicides with respect to the home/not-home dichotomy, nor with respect to motives listed by the police. Slightly over half of both VP and non-VP slayings occurred in the home. General altercations (43 per cent) and domestic quarrels (20 per cent) rank highest among VP cases, as they do among non-VP cases (32 and 12 per cent), although with lower frequency. Combined, these two motives account for a slightly larger share of the VP cases (3 out of 5) than of the non-VP cases (2 out of 5).

Victim-Offender Relationships. The 150 VP homicides constitute a universe too small to subdivide into the 16 possible specified race and sex categories, but several gross classifications are sufficiently large to permit valid comparisons with non-VP cases. Intra-racial slayings predominate in both groups, but interracial homicides comprise a larger share of VP cases (8 per cent) than they do of non-VP cases (5 per cent). Although VP cases make up one-fourth of all criminal

[1] See Chapter 5.

258

homicides, they account for over one-third (35 per cent) of all interracial slayings. Thus it appears that a homicide which crosses race lines is often likely to be one in which the slayer was provoked to assault by the victim. The association between interracial slayings and VP homicides, however, is not statistically significant.

Homicides involving victims and offenders of opposite sex (regardless of which sex is the victim or which is the offender) occur with about the same frequency among VP cases (34 per cent) as among non-VP cases (37 per cent). But a *significant* difference between VP and non-VP cases does emerge when determination of the sex of the victim, relative to the sex of his specific slayer, is taken into account. Of all criminal homicides for which the sex of both victim and offender is known, 88 involve a male victim and a female offender; and of these 88 cases, 43 are VP homicides. Thus, it may be said that 43, or 29 per cent, of the 150 VP homicides, compared to 45, or only 11 per cent, of the 400 non-VP homicides, are males slain by females.

It seems highly desirable, in view of these findings, that the police thoroughly investigate every possibility of strong provocation by the male victim when he is slain by a female—and particularly, as noted below, if the female is his wife, which is also a strong possibility. It is, of course, the further responsibility of defense counsel, prosecuting attorney, and subsequently the court, to determine whether such provocation was sufficient either to reduce or to eliminate culpability altogether.

The proportion that Negro male/Negro male and white male/white male homicides constitute among VP cases (45 and 13 per cent) is similar to the proportion these same relationships constitute among non-VP cases (41 and 14 per cent). The important contribution of the Negro male as a victim-precipitator is indicated by the fact that Negro male/Negro female homicides are proportionately nearly three times as frequent among VP cases (25 per cent) as they are among non-VP cases (9 per cent). It is apparent, therefore, that Negroes and males not only are the groups most likely to make positive and direct contributions to the genesis of their own victimization, but that, in particular, Negro males more frequently provoke females of their own race to slay them than they do males of their own race.

For both VP and non-VP groups, close friends, relatives, and acquaintances are the major types of specific relationships between victims and offenders. Combined, these three relationships constitute 69 per cent of the VP homicides and 65 per cent of the non-VP cases. Victims are relatives of their slayers in one-fourth of both types of homicide. But of 38 family slayings among VP cases, 33 are husband-wife killings; while of 98 family slayings among non-VP cases, only 67 are husband-wife killings. This proportional difference results in a *significant* association between mate slayings and VP homicide.

Finally, of VP mate slayings, 28 victims are husbands and only 5 are wives; but of non-VP mate slayings, only 19 victims are husbands while 48 are wives. Thus there is a *significant* association between husbands who are victims in mate slayings and VP homicide. This fact—namely, that *significantly* more husbands than wives are victims in VP mate slayings—means that (1) husbands actually may provoke their wives more often than wives provoke their husbands to assault; or (2) assuming that provocation by wives is as intense and equally as frequent, or even more frequent, than provocation by husbands, then husbands may not receive and define provocation stimuli with as great or as violent a reaction as do wives; or, (3) husbands may have a greater felt sense of guilt in a marital conflict for one reason or another, and receive verbal insults and overt physical assaults without retaliation as a form of compensatory punishment; or (4) husbands may withdraw more often than wives from the scene of marital conflict, and thus eliminate, for the time being, a violent overt reaction to their wives' provocation. Clearly, this is only a suggestive, not an exhaustive, list of probable explanations. In any case, we are left with the undeniable fact that husbands more often than wives are major precipitating factors in their own homicide deaths.

Alcohol. The previous discovery of an association between the presence of alcohol in the homicide situation and Negro male offenders, combined with knowledge of the important contribution Negro males make to their own victimization, suggests an association (by transitivity) between VP homicide and the presence of alcohol. Moreover, whether alcohol is present in the victim or offender, lowered inhibitions due to ingestion of alcohol may cause an individual to give vent more freely to pent-up frustrations, tensions, and emotional conflicts that have either built up over a prolonged period of time or that arise within an immediate emotional crisis. The data do in fact confirm the suggested hypothesis above and reveal a *significant* association between VP homicide and alcohol in the homicide situation. Comparison of VP to non-VP cases with respect to the presence of alcohol in the homicide situation (alcohol present in either the victim, offender, or both), reveals that alcohol was present in 74 per cent of the VP cases and in 60 per cent of the non-VP cases. The proportional difference results in a *significant* association between alsohol and VP homicide. Again it should be noted that the association is not necessarily a causal one, or that a causal relationship is not proved by the association.

Because the present analysis is concerned primarily with the contribution of the victim to the homicide, it is necessary to determine whether an association exists between VP homicide and presence of alcohol in the victim. No association was found to exist between VP homicide and alcohol in the offender. But victims had been drinking immediately prior to their death in more VP cases (69 per cent) than in non-VP cases (47 per cent). A positive and *significant* relationship is, therefore, clearly established between victims who had been drinking and who precipitated their own death. In many of these cases the victim was intoxicated, or nearly so, and lost control of his own defensive powers. He frequently was a victim with no intent to harm anyone maliciously. Nonetheless, he struck the friend, acquaintance, or wife, who later became his assailant. Impulsive, aggressive,

261

and often dangerously violent, the victim was the first to slap, punch, stab, or in some other manner commit an assault. Perhaps the presence of alcohol in this kind of homicide victim played no small part in his taking the first and major physical step toward victimization. Perhaps if he had not been drinking he would have been less violent, less ready to plunge into an assaultive stage of interaction. Or, if the presence of alcohol had no causal relation to his being the aggressor, perhaps it reduced his ability to defend himself from retaliatory assault, and contributed in this way to his death.

Previous Arrest Record. The victim-precipitator is the first actor in the homicide drama to display and to use a deadly weapon; and the description of him thus far infers that he is in some respects an offender in reverse. Because he is the first to assume an aggressive role, he probably has engaged previously in similar but less serious physical assaults. On the basis of these assumptions several meaningful hypotheses were established and tested. Each hypothesis is supported by empirical data, which in some cases reach the level of statistical significance accepted by this study; and in other cases indicate strong associations in directions suggested by the hypotheses. A summary of each hypothesis with its collated data follows:

(1) In VP cases, the victim is more likely than the offender to have a previous arrest, or police, record. The data show that 62 per cent of the victims and 54 per cent of the offenders in VP cases have a previous record.

(2) A higher proportion of VP victims than non-VP victims have a previous police record. Comparison reveals that 62 per cent of VP victims but only 42 per cent of non-VP victims have a previous record. The association between VP victims and previous arrest record is a *significant* one.

(3) With respect to the percentage having a previous arrest record, VP victims are more similar to non-VP offenders than to non-VP victims. Examination of the data reveals no significant difference between VP victims and non-VP

offenders with a previous record. This lack of a significant difference is very meaningful and confirms the validity of the proposition above. While 62 per cent of VP victims have a police record, 68 per cent of non-VP offenders have such a record, and we have already noted in (2) above that only 42 per cent of non-VP victims have a record. Thus, the existence of a statistically *significant* difference between VP victims and non-VP victims and the *lack* of a statistically significant difference between VP victims and non-VP offenders indicate that the victim of VP homicide is quite similar to the offender in non-VP homicide—and that the VP victim more closely resembles the non-VP offender than the non-VP victim.

(4) A higher proportion of VP victims than of non-VP victims have a record of offenses against the person. The data show a *significant* association between VP victims and a previous record of offenses against the person, for 37 per cent of VP victims and only 21 per cent of non-VP victims have a record of such offenses.

(5) Also with respect to the percentage having a previous arrest record of offenses against the person, VP victims are more similar to non-VP offenders than non-VP victims. Analysis of the data indicate support for this assumption, for we have observed that the difference between VP victims (37 per cent) and non-VP victims (21 per cent) is *significant*; this difference is almost twice as great as the difference between VP victims (37 per cent) and non-VP offenders (46 per cent), and this latter difference is not significant. The general tendency again is for victims in VP homicides to resemble offenders in non-VP homicides.

(6) A lower proportion of VP offenders have a previous arrest record than do non-VP offenders. The data also tend to support this hypothesis, for 54 per cent of offenders in VP cases, compared to 68 per cent of offenders in non-VP cases, have a previous police record.

In general, the rank order of recidivism—defined in terms of having a previous arrest record and of having a previous record of assaults—for victims and offenders involved in the two types of homicide is as follows:

	Per Cent with Previous Arrest Record	Per Cent with Previous Record of Assault
(1) Offenders in non-VP Homicide	68	46
(2) Victims in VP Homicide	62	37
(3) Offenders in VP Homicide	54	33
(4) Victims in non-VP Homicide	42	21

Because he is the initial aggressor and has provoked his subsequent slayer into killing him, this particular type of victim (VP) is likely to have engaged previously in physical assaults which were either less provoking than the present situation, or which afforded him greater opportunity to defer attacks made upon him. It is known officially that over one-third of them had assaulted others previously. It is not known how many had formerly provoked others to assault them. In any case, the circumstances leading up to the present crime in which he plays the role of victim are probably not foreign to him since he has, in many cases, participated in similar encounters before this, his last episode.

Summary. Criminal homicide usually involves intense personal interaction in which the victim's behavior is often an important factor. As Porterfield has recently pointed out, "the intensity of interaction between the murderer and his victim may vary from complete non-participation on the part of the victim to almost perfect co-operation with the killer in the process of getting killed. . . . It is amazing to note the large number of would-be murderers who become the victim."[1] By defining a VP homicide in terms of the victim's direct, immediate, and positive contribution to his own death, manifested by his being the first to make a physical assault, it has been possible to identify 150 VP cases.

Comparison of this VP group with non-VP cases reveals *significantly* higher proportions of the following characteristics among VP homicides:

(1) Negro victims;
(2) Negro offenders;

[1] Porterfield and Talbert, *Mid-Century Crime in Our Culture*, pp. 47–48.

264

(3) male victims;

(4) female offenders;

(5) stabbings;

(6) victim-offender relationships involving male victims of female offenders;

(7) mate slayings;

(8) husbands who are victims in mate slayings;

(9) alcohol in the homicide situation;

(10) alcohol in the victim;

(11) victims with a previous arrest record;

(12) victims with a previous arrest record of assault.

In addition, VP homicides have slightly higher proportions than non-VP homicides of altercations and domestic quarrels; interracial slayings; victims who are close friends, relatives, or acquaintances of their slayers.

Empirical evidence analyzed in the present study lends support to, and measurement of, von Hentig's theoretical contention that "there are cases in which they [victim and offender] are reversed and in the long chain of causative forces the victim assumes the role of a determinant."[1]

In many cases the victim has most of the major characteristics of an offender; in some cases two potential offenders come together in a homicide situation and it is probably only chance which results in one becoming a victim and the other an offender. At any rate, connotations of a victim as a weak and passive individual, seeking to withdraw from an assaultive situation, and of an offender as a brutal, strong, and overly aggressive person seeking out his victim, are not always correct. Societal attitudes are generally positive toward the victim and negative toward the offender, who is often feared as a violent and dangerous threat to others. However, data in the present study—especially that of previous arrest record—mitigate, destroy, or reverse these connotations of victim-offender roles in one out of every four criminal homicides.

[1] Von Hentig, *The Criminal and His Victim*, p. 383.

265

IV

THE OFFENDER AFTER THE CRIME

15

HOMICIDE-SUICIDE

THIS chapter is concerned only with those persons who first commit homicide, and then inflict death upon themselves. There is, unfortunately, a paucity of information about this group, in both homicide and suicide literature. Guerry, Lacassagne, Tarde, Durkheim, Morselli, Ferri, and Verkko have laid the foundations for analysis of homicide and suicide as separate phenomena, but have not analyzed homicide slayers who kill themselves.

There appears to be some scientific dispute regarding relationships between the rates and causes of homicide, on the one hand, and of suicide, on the other. Although some parallelisms have been noted, generally suicide and homicide have been found changing inversely with one another. Commenting on this inverse relationship, Durkheim said:

> But this antagonism, once granted, may be explained in either of two ways. Either homicide and suicide form two opposite currents, so opposed that one can gain only through the other's loss, or they are two different channels of a single stream, fed by a single source, which consequently cannot move in one direction without receding to an equal extent in the other. Italian criminologists adopted the second of these explanations. In suicide and homicide they see two manifestations of the same state, two effects of the same cause, expressing itself at times in one form, at times in another, but unable to assume both simultaneously.[1]

Durkheim, himself, said that "it is even a general rule that where homicide is very common it confers a sort of immunity against suicide."[2] But Verkko claimed that the "assertion

[1] Durkheim, *op. cit.*, p. 340.
[2] *Ibid.*, p. 351.

that suicides and crimes against life are supplementary phenomena, i.e., that in a country where crimes against life are
frequent there cannot be many suicides and vice versa, has
been confuted by this review. In Finland, Estonia, and Latvia,
both homicides and suicides are frequent; in Iceland, Ireland,
and Norway, infrequent. The asserted antagonism is no
longer perceptible except in South Europe."[1] In a recent
article on homicide in England, Max Grünhut commented
on the "misleading oversimplification" involved in comparing these two phenomena, but says that "a comparison
between the curves for murder and suicide seems to confirm
the classical doctrine that murder and suicide are mutual
substitutes; the year 1942, with an exceptionally high number
of 159 murder cases, had the lowest figure for suicides among
males for the last fifty years—2,477."[2] Porterfield, comparing
the ratios and indices of deaths from suicide and homicide in
86 cities, concluded that these death causes are "opposite
types of adjustment."[3] Elsewhere, the same author concluded
from his national analysis that "the secular, especially
upper-class, society is more given to suicide, and the depressed
folk society resorts more to crime, both when studied by
states and by cities."[4]

There is a plethora of psychological and psychoanalytical
analyses of suicide, a review of which goes beyond even the
periphery of the present study. Suffice it to say that Alice
Raven,[5] for example, speaks of both murder and suicide as
marks of an abnormal mind. Philip Lehrman,[6] Karl Men-

---

[1] Verkko, *Homicides and Suicides in Finland and Their Dependence on
National Character*, p. 157.

[2] Max Grünhut, "Murder and the Death Penalty in England," *The Annals
of the American Academy of Political and Social Science*, (*Murder and the
Penalty of Death*) (November, 1952), 284: 160.

[3] Austin Porterfield, Robert Talbert, and Herbert R. Mundhenke, *Crime,
Suicide, and Social Well-Being*, p. 95.

[4] Austin Porterfield, "Suicide and Crime in Folk and in Secular Society,"
The American Journal of Sociology (June, 1952), 57: 338. The author here
uses Ogburn and Nimkoff's "folk-secular continuum" instead of the "ideal
polar types" of sacred and secular described by Becker and contrasted by
Redfield and by MacIver.

[5] Alice Raven, "Murder and Suicide as Marks of an Abnormal Mind,"
The American Sociological Review (1929), 21: 315–333.

[6] Philip R. Lehrman, "Some Unconscious Determinants of Homicide,"
Psychiatric Quarterly (1939), 13: 605.

ninger,[1] Paul Schilder,[2] G. Zilboorg,[3] and Walter Bromberg,[4] are a few authors who have described the similar underlying, and often unconscious, motivations of suicide and homicide. Bromberg, for example, believes that "the victim often represents the murderer in the latter's unconscious," and that "analytic interpretation of suicide and murder leads to the 'paradoxical formulation' that in terms of the unconscious system 'murder is suicide and suicide is murder.' "[5] Sometimes "murder is seen as bizarre forms of attempted suicide,"[6] and in other cases "suicide is murder; desire to kill turned on self."[7]

Without detailed comparative analysis, it is interesting to note that Calvin Schmid,[8] in his study of suicide in Minneapolis, found that the incidence of suicide for males was highest on Tuesday and lowest on Saturday. In Philadelphia, as previously noted, the incidence of homicide among males was highest on Friday and Saturday, and lowest Monday and Tuesday—the opposite of male suicides in Minneapolis. Furthermore, Schmid observed that the maximum number of male suicides occurred in January and February, the two months of lowest frequency of homicide in Philadelphia. Of course there are many variables that would have to be examined before significant statements could be made about these two phenomena in two different cities, but the general inverse temporal pattern is nonetheless striking.

The major focus of attention at present is with those persons who commit suicide after having killed another person. Among others, Porterfield has remarked on the need

[1] Karl Menninger, "Psychoanalytic Aspects of Suicide," *The International Journal of Psycho-Analysis* (1933), 14: 387.
[2] Paul Schilder, "The Attitude of Murderers Towards Death," *Journal of Abnormal and Social Psychology* (1936), 13: 3.
[3] G. Zilboorg, "Some Sidelights on the Psychology of Murder," *Journal of Nervous and Mental Disease* (1935), 81: 442.
[4] Walter Bromberg, "A Psychological Study of Murder," *The International Journal of Psycho-Analysis* (1951), 32: 1–2.
[5] *Ibid.*
[6] "Murder Is Seen as Bizarre Form of Attempted Suicide," *Science News Letter* (December, 1939), 36: 377.
[7] "Suicide Is Murder; Desire to Kill Turned on Self," *Science News Letter* (May, 1945), 47: 295.
[8] Calvin F. Schmid, "Suicide in Minneapolis, Minnesota," *The American Journal of Sociology* (July, 1953), 39: 42.

for such analysis: ". . . of special importance would be a study of the extent to which persons who commit homicide kill themselves immediately after the homicidal act. This suicide-murder combination is apparently more common in the South than elsewhere."[1] The following analysis of such cases in Philadelphia includes those who killed themselves immediately after the homicidal act or at some later time during the period covered by this study. The total number is not sufficiently large to permit many generalizations, nor to make many comparisons with those who did not commit suicide.

Among the 621 persons who were charged with having committed criminal homicide, only 24, or less than 4 per cent, later killed themselves. Of these, 11 are Negro males, 11 are white males, one is a Negro female and one a white female. Although whites are one-fourth of all offenders, they *significantly* make up half of the homicide-suicides.

It may be true of homicide-suicide as well as of the two phenomena separately, that a higher-status group commits suicide with greater frequency than a lower-status group.

It is probably safe to assert that whites in Philadelphia have a more rigid class structure than Negroes and violate less frequently the prevailing mores and laws. These assumptions, combined with the observed race differentials in homicide-suicide, coincide with the conclusion of Jacqueline and Murray Straus that "the suicide rate will vary *directly* . . . with the degree to which a society is closely structured."[2] These statements recall a theoretical affinity to the writings of Durkheim, Cavan, Schmid, *et al.*, who agree that one of the major factors in the differential incidences of suicide among people of varying ethnic and other types of groups is to be found in the degree of their "group solidarity," "anomie," or "psycho-social isolation." Finally, in terms of Porterfield's "folk-secular continuum," if the Negroes in Philadelphia correspond closely to the "depressed folk society" and whites to the "secular society," then the author's

---

[1] Austin Porterfield, "Indices of Suicide and Homicide by States and Cities: Some Southern-Non-Southern Contrasts with Implications for Research," *The American Sociological Review* (August, 1949), 14: 490.

[2] Jacqueline and Murray Straus, *op. cit.*, p. 469.

contention that the former is more likely to find justification in his mores for crimes such as homicide is of theoretical value in understanding race differentials in homicide-suicide.[1]

In Philadelphia, males comprise 83 per cent of all homicide offenders, but make up 22 of the 24 homicide-suicides. This *significantly* higher proportion of males in homicide-suicide is probably best interpreted by reference once more to Durkheim's comment that "woman kills herself less, and she kills others less, not because of physiological differences from man but because she does not participate in collective life in the same way."[2]

The proportion of homicide-suicide cases among total homicide offenders appears to be universally low in this country. In Philadelphia only about four out of every one hundred who commit criminal homicide kill themselves. Dublin and Bunzel[3] found that in 611 cases of homicide, 9 per cent of the slayers committed suicide. Of 763 persons implicated in 739 homicides occurring in Atlanta, Birmingham, Memphis, and New Orleans during 1921–1922, 2 per cent of the offenders committed suicide.[4] This proportion disagrees with Porterfield's belief that such cases are more frequent in the South than in the North. Of the 760 homicides in Cook County during 1926–1927, 4 per cent of the assailants killed themselves—a percentage similar to that in Philadelphia. Also like Philadelphia, most were white suicides, for only 6 were non-white and 25 were white out of the 31.[5] In Minneapolis, Schmid[6] noted that only 3 out of 375 persons who committed suicide between 1928 and 1932 did so after homicide. Among the 318 persons who received original death sentences in Pennsylvania between 1918 and 1939, only 2 committed suicide.[7]

---

[1] Austin Porterfield, "Suicide and Crime in Folk and in Secular Society," *op. cit.*, p. 334.

[2] Durkheim, *op. cit.*, p. 341.

[3] Dublin and Bunzel, *op. cit.*, p. 130.

[4] J. J. Durrett and W. G. Stromquist, "Preventing Violent Death," *Survey*, (July, 1925), 59: 437.

[5] *The Illinois Crime Survey*, p. 612.

[6] Calvin Schmid, "Suicide in Minneapolis, Minnesota," *op. cit.*, p. 47.

[7] John M. Gregory, "Report on the Death Penalty in Pennsylvania for the Years 1918–1939 Inclusive," (unpublished report in the author's files).

In contrast to the United States, homicide-suicide cases in England comprise a much larger proportion of offenders.[1] From 1900 through 1949 in England and Wales, there were 7,454 murders known to the police. Suspects of these murders who committed suicide numbered 1,674, or 22 per cent. Excluding those cases involving victims less than one year of age, 31 per cent of the murder suspects committed suicide. There were 2,834 persons arrested for murder during this period, and the ratio of persons arrested to those suspects who committed suicide was only 1.7 to 1.[2] In Philadelphia, during the 1948–1952 period, the ratio of persons arrested for criminal homicide to those suspects who killed themselves was 25 to 1. In 1950 the police reported 122 persons, aged one year and over, murdered in England and Wales. While in 3 of these cases nobody could be detected as the possible perpetrator, the police suspected 109 persons responsible for the 119 murder cases. Of these, 35 per cent committed suicide.[3] For the same year (1950) the police reported 117 criminal homicides in Philadelphia. In 11 of these, the perpetrators escaped detection and apprehension, and 7 persons were multiple defendants in addition to the first defendant. All told, the police suspected 113 persons, of whom only 3 committed suicide. The higher proportion of homicide-suicides in England is obvious.

Although there were 24 offenders in Philadelphia who committed suicide, they killed 26 persons. The difference is accounted for by two double homicides[4] in 1949. In most

[1] See, for example, E. Roy Calvert, "Murder and the Death Penalty," *Nation* (October 16, 1929), 129: 405–407; W. N. East, *Medical Aspects of Crime*, London: J. and A. Churchill, 1936, p. 369; W. N. East, *Society and the Criminal*, Springfield, Illinois: Charles C. Thomas, 1951, p. 355; Viscount Templewood, *The Shadow of the Gallows*, London: Victor Gollancz, Ltd., 1951, p. 159; *Royal Commission on Capital Punishment, 1949–1953 Report*, pp. 298–302. For an exceptionally interesting and comprehensive discussion of suicide pacts, *cf.*, *Royal Commission on Capital Punishment* pp. 164–176.
[2] Based on *Royal Commission on Capital Punishment, 1949–1953 Report*, Appendix 3, Table 1, pp. 298–301.
[3] *Criminal Statistics for England and Wales, 1950*, London, 1951, p. xxvi, cited by Max Grünhut, "Murder and the Death Penalty in England," *op. cit.*, p. 158.
[4] A double homicide is one in which two persons are killed by the same slayer either at the same time and place or within a very short period of time elapsing between the two slayings.

cases the offender killed himself shortly after having slain his victim. Whether he committed suicide out of remorse, fear of punishment, or some other motive is difficult to determine. Probably Ruth Cavan's belief is correct, that in the majority of cases the murder and suicide seem part of the same act. She points out that "the person interprets his difficulty as sufficient to prohibit adjustment; he has, he believes, reached the end of the way, and suicide is a means of solution for him. But his happiness has been ruined or is prevented by some person. Before he kills himself he kills that person, in anger and revenge, or in jealousy and to prevent another from succeeding where he has failed."[1] If the suicide occurs at a later period than the homicide, remorse or fear has probably been the reason. If the suicide occurs immediately after the homicide, or within a relatively short period of time thereafter, either both deaths were impulsive or both premeditated.

Probably the suicide that immediately follows homicide is motivationally closely allied with the criminal slaying; but when two events are separated in time a secondary motive intervenes. In 18 cases out of 24 the offender killed himself immediately after the homicide; in 6 cases he committed suicide after a considerable lapse of time, 3 in the county prison, and 3 elsewhere.

Motives for killing the 26 victims have been recorded as family quarrel (10), jealousy (6), revenge (3), accidental (1), altercation (1), ill health (1), unknown (4). Methods by which these victims of homicide met death were: shooting (15), stabbing (6), asphyxiation by gas (2), strangulation (1), beating (1), poisoning (1). The offender killed himself by shooting (10), jumping from a bridge (3), asphyxiation by gas (3), stabbing (2), slashing of throat or wrists (2), hanging (2), and poisoning (2).

According to the definition of violence used in this study, it is interesting to note that 20 of these 26 victims were killed violently, 3 by two acts, 6 by three to five acts, 10 by more

[1] Ruth Cavan, *Suicide*, Chicago: University of Chicago Press, 1928, p. 262.

than five acts, and 1 by severe beating. All 6 of the non-violently killed were whites. Homicide-suicide cases, therefore, are *significantly* more violent than homicides in general. Of all homicides, half the victims were killed violently; whereas among homicide-suicide cases three-quarters met death violently, and half were killed with extraordinary violence (more than five acts). So intensely did the offender feel about the events and persons involved in the circumstances surrounding the slaying that he apparently responded in equally intense proportions by violently assaulting the object whom he defined as obstructing satisfaction of his goals. In most of these cases, as mentioned below, the relationship between the homicide-suicide offender and his victim was intimate, characterized by strong emotional attachment, and maintained over a long period of time. The frustration-aggression thesis seems most appropriate as a partial explanation for these cases which result in higher frequency of violent and very violent slayings. It may be contended further that so strongly felt was the offender's frustration that a single assaultive act—or even a series of assaultive acts—against another person was not sufficient to alleviate his aggressive impulse or reactions; and when the external object contributing to frustration (the victim) was eliminated, he turned inward—to self—as the only additional outlet for his remaining aggression. Such an explanation assumes a certain amount of reserve aggression energy, which, upon finding an outlet, seeks to expend itself entirely at one time, and if all such energy is not released by killing another, the bearer of such energy—namely, self—is eliminated. If, however, all aggression energy is vented on the victim, we must posit a feeling of remorse, guilt, or fear after the slaying to account for newly created frustration and aggression energy that results in self-destruction.

The guilt hypothesis suggests that following his killing of another person, the individual may suffer such a threat to his self-esteem that he feels the only way to demonstrate the hatred society should inflict upon him is to kill himself. Suicide thus becomes a means of showing his agreement

276

with the social norms which he has long ago internalized. Moreover, in acting suicidally this individual not only turns against himself a violent reaction to continued frustration, but also may attempt, consciously or unconsciously, to control his environment by stimulating sympathy and even guilt in other people.

Also contrary to general criminal homicide is the relatively smaller number of homicide-suicide cases with alcohol present. Alcohol was present in the homicide situation in as many as 6 to 7 out of 10 homicides in general, but in only 3 out of 10 homicides followed by suicide. Partially because all homicides involving whites have a low frequency of alcohol present, the lower frequency of alcohol in the homicide-suicide situation is a reflection of the relatively high proportion of whites among homicide-suicide offenders. Furthermore, 12 of the 17 cases with no alcohol present have been designated unofficially as first degree murder cases. Perhaps the lower incidence of alcohol in homicide-suicide situations indicates a greater likelihood of premeditation by the offender. At any rate, the acts of homicide and suicide combined—if not premeditated, rational behavior—were committed, more often than homicide alone, without benefit of lowered inhibitions due to alcohol.

Because most homicide-suicides involve a close personal relationship between victim and offender (as detailed below), it is inferred that a higher proportion of these cases than of all homicides take place in the home—hence, not in the street, in a taproom, or elsewhere. The data confirm this inference and reveal that while just slightly over half of all homicides occurred in the home, 20 of the homicide-suicides occurred there. Of these 20, 11 were in the home of both, 7 in the home of the victim, and 2 in the home of the offender. Frequency of cases was highest in the bedroom (8) and living room (8), followed by kitchen (4), highway (4), taproom (1), and drugstore (1).

Suicide that follows homicide is often suggested as being caused, in part, by feelings of guilt and remorse. If the suicide immediately followed the homicide and both acts

277

were premeditated, perhaps guilt or remorse feelings were also anticipated. If the two acts occurred in close temporal sequence and both were impulsive acts, perhaps those same feelings arose immediately after the homicide and were too oppressive to bear. Whatever the circumstances, if there were feelings of guilt and/or remorse, we should expect homicide-suicide offenders to have lived normally within the framework of the general culture value-system. Extreme guilt or remorse feelings at the horror of having killed another human being (particularly a loved one), therefore, would not be unexpected. From these assumptions, we may infer that homicide-suicide offenders, being ordinarily law-abiding individuals normally regulated by prevailing mores, experience arrest for law violation less frequently than homicide offenders in general. The data do in fact show that one-third of homicide-suicide offenders have a previous arrest record compared to nearly two-thirds of all offenders. Five of the 8 with police records were arrested for offenses against the person—all for aggravated assault. Only one victim has an arrest record, and that was for a relatively minor offense.

The median age of those who committed suicide (38.3 years) is about 7 years *older* than that for all offenders (31.9 years), while the median age of victims of the homicide-suicide group (30.1 years) is about 5 years *younger* than that for all victims (35.1 years). None of the offenders is under 25 years of age, but 6 of the victims are under this age.

The most common type of homicide-suicide is that which involves an intimate relation of adults of the opposite sex. Cavan[1] has similarly noted that close relations between victim and offender in such cases were maintained for some time prior to the killings. In many cases the "if-I-can't-have-you-no-one-else-can" attitude is manifested by the offender. Not only is the slayer frustrated because of a thwarted love-object or goal, but he is often spurned, rejected, made to feel inferior, a failure, or undesired. An injured pride or attacked conception of self is added to his frustration. Henry and

[1] *Ibid.*, p. 258.

Short have suggested the following explanation, which remains to be tested:

> The psychological basis of legitimization of other-oriented aggression may also be helpful in accounting for the empirical fact that suicide and homicide often are committed by the same person. . . . If the aggression operates to destroy the flow of nurturance, we would expect—as in the case of divorce—a resultant inhibition of aggression and internalization of the values of the source of frustration. These processes would serve to deny legitimacy to outward expression of aggression consequent to future frustration and the result would be an increased tendency to express aggression inwardly against the self. Murder destroys the source of frustration in the external world. The internalization consequent to the loss of nurturance re-established the source of frustration within the self. And the self becomes the legitimate target for aggression.[1]
>
> The hypothesis that persons who follow murder with suicide are persons who deprive themselves through the murder of a primary source of nurturance (as well as a primary source of frustration) may be tested by comparing the degree of positive attachment of murderer and victim prior to the homicide among those who later commit suicide and among those who do not commit suicide.[2]

The "degree of positive attachment" which these authors suggest as the chief criterion for differentiation between those homicides followed by, and those not followed by suicide would be difficult to quantify and measure. Perhaps some light is shed on the problem by pointing out that in 18 of the 26 victim-offender relationships, the victim was a relative of the offender, and in another 7, the victim was the offender's paramour. These combined intimate "primary sources of nurturance" comprise all but one of the relationships among homicide-suicide cases. Of total homicides, however, relatives and paramours comprise only one-third of the victim-offender relationships. These empirical facts, showing a *significantly* high proportion of close personal attachments between offenders who commit suicide and their victims,

---

[1] Henry and Short, *op. cit.*, pp. 116–117.
[2] *Ibid.*, pp. 126–127.

provide a crude test of the hypothesis suggested but not confirmed by Henry and Short.[1]

That the typical interpersonal relationship between victim and offender in homicide-suicide cases is a personal and intimate one prior to the slaying, is abundantly clear in the following examples summarized from police files:

A female victim and male offender were next-door neighbors and lovers. Together with another couple they had been making the rounds of taprooms, after which the four went to his apartment. The other couple were in the kitchen making sandwiches when they heard a shot, rushed to the living room, found the woman shot in the head. The offender went to his bedroom and shot himself, while his friend tried unsuccessfully to wrest the gun from him.

A husband claimed his wife constantly nagged him because he could not satisfy her sexually. One evening, during a particularly boisterous argument, he went to the cellar, got a pistol, and fired four shots at his wife, two of which wounded her. He then grabbed a hatchet and struck her several times on the head. Four days later, in the county prison, he stabbed himself in the heart.

A husband accused his wife of extra-marital relations. She was in the process of leaving him to take a separate apartment for herself and two daughters when he shot her in their bedroom, immediately after which he shot himself. The argument began while they were both drinking heavily in the kitchen.

Both a father and his daughter, living together alone, were in poor health. One evening he telephoned his son and informed him that he had just poisoned his daughter and was about to commit suicide. Both the father and daughter were dead on arrival of the police.

A husband and wife had been separated for eighteen months.

---

[1] It may, perhaps, be contended that identifying a relationship in terms of family member or paramour still does not measure the degree of "primary source of nurturance," and that a close friend or homosexual partner, in some cases, may satisfy more adequately a need for nurturance. However, the homosexual partners in the Philadelphia cases were not the only homosexual relations the offenders enjoyed. Moreover, all but one of the homicide-suicide cases involved intense, frequent, and very intimate association between victim and offender prior to their deaths. We are assuming that such associations are more characteristic of husbands and their wives, parents and their children, and sweethearts than of other types of relationships.

He had left their home, but he retained and managed their small store. According to the note left by the husband, he had been cheated out of his property rights by his wife, son, and daughter, and was once beaten severely by his son. One evening he entered the store while his wife was attending it, shot her, and then himself. Both were dead when the police arrived.

An unmarried couple had been going together for the past six years. One day the young girl wrote him that she was leaving him for another man. Jealous and seeking revenge, he sought her out, found her walking along the street one evening, shot her four times, and then turned the pistol toward his own head.

In a case where no motive was discovered, a husband returned home from work and discovered his wife and son lying on the kitchen floor beside the gas range. All burners were turned on and the oven door was open. The woman was 48 years old and the son 3. Both were dead when the man found them. There was no apparent reason for the occurrence, as both mother and son were in good health, and the wife was presumably in good spirits when her husband left for work in the morning.

A wife accused her husband of repeatedly staying out all night and of having extra-marital sexual relations. One morning at 11:50, after one of his all-night escapades, she queried him again. Unable to restrain his temper, he located his gun, shot her nine times in the presence of their fourteen-year-old daughter, then shot himself in the chest.

A man and woman had been having extra-marital relations for six months. Both were married to other mates, although she was separated from her husband. While drinking, the couple began arguing about their relationships, particularly the woman's inept care of her eleven-year-old daughter. The man had a revolver in his possession, fired five shots at his paramour, went home, told his wife what he had been doing and what he had just done. After his confession, he drank poison in his wife's presence, left the house, and boarded a train for New York City, where he was found dead on a dark street.

An estranged husband waited for his wife to return home from work in order to induce her to return and live with him. She refused, she claimed, because he had constantly beaten her. With this rejection he became enraged, pulled out a gun he was prepared to use in case of rejection, shot her five times, and ran from the scene. Four days later his body was discovered in the Delaware River.

Homicide-suicide is a phenomenon that primarily involved persons of the opposite sex. The ratio of opposite-sex to same-sex relationships among all homicides is 0.6 to 1, but among homicide-suicides, nearly 9 to 1. There were 26 victim-offender relationships, among which were 11 Negro female/Negro male; 10 white female/white male; 2 white male/white male; and one each of Negro male/Negro male, Negro male/Negro female, and white male/white female. Among these homicide-suicide cases none were interracial, and there were no cases involving females alone. There were only three cases of homicide-suicide among males, but in two of these a female was involved either as a victim in double homicide, or as a seriously wounded bystander who was an intended homicide victim. In 18 cases family members were victims of homicide. In 10, the victims were wives killed by their husbands; in 2, sons killed by their fathers. In one each, a daughter was killed by her father, a son by his mother, a mother by her son, a husband by his wife, a grand-niece by her grand-uncle, and a brother-in-law by his wife's brother. A female was the victim in 6 of the 7 cases involving paramours.

It is interesting to note that in only one of the 47 cases in which a wife killed her husband did she later commit suicide; but that in 10 of the 53 cases in which a husband killed his wife did he commit suicide. Examination of mate slayings ending in suicide infers that the differential is due to greater feelings of guilt and remorse on the part of husbands. We know from previous analysis that of victim-precipitated mate slayings, 28 husbands and only 5 wives were victims who contributed to their own death by making the first assault. The wife who killed her husband after he had slapped or beaten her is less likely to feel remorse or guilt than if she had not been so provoked. Husbands killed their wives *significantly* more often without provocation, and this fact implies that husbands had greater guilt and remorse feelings

—hence, they more frequently committed suicide after slaying their mates.

Finally, analysis of these homicide-suicide cases leads to the conclusion that more persons who commit murder in the first degree inflict death upon themselves as punishment for their crimes than are legally executed by the state. Evaluation by three Criminal Investigation Division Officers of the Homicide Squad and by the author led to the conclusion that 12 of the 24 homicide-suicide slayers had committed felonious, malicious, and premeditated murder for which (had they survived) they would have been indicted and probably convicted. It is, of course, difficult to predict what sentence they would have received, but out of 621 offenders in criminal homicide, 77 were convicted of first degree murder, only 7 of whom were sentenced to death. It is obvious, therefore, even with the relatively low proportion of suicide after homicide in this country, that more offenders inflict death upon themselves than are put to death by collective society. This generalization is probably applicable on the national level also, but homicide-suicides throughout the country have been neither enumerated nor analyzed in detail.

16

UNSOLVED HOMICIDES

The Problem of Definition

THERE is little doubt among students in the field of criminology that some criminal homicides are never reported, or, if reported or discovered by the police, some are never "cleared by arrest." The state pathologist of a New England state recently expressed the belief that only one out of every 10 murders in that state ever is discovered, that it is "easy to get away with murder in the state," and that it is "a simple matter to dispose of a body."[1] These may be slight exaggerations of the real situation, but of deaths reported as suicides, accidents, or deaths due to natural causes, there are probably *some* criminal homicides. The absence of coroners or medical examiners in the state referred to means that the above estimate is probably not applicable to Philadelphia, which has a capable medical examiner.

In a chapter called "Popular Fallacies in Homicide Investigation," Le Moyne Snyder refers to the Chaucerian myth that "murder will out." He says: "If this were true there would be no purpose in writing this book. While feature writers stress the theme that the perfect murder has never been committed, the fact is that *the number of unsolved homicides is enormous.* Based on the number of murders discovered after the victim has been dead for years, it is only too apparent that many victims are buried and a homicide never suspected in connection with their deaths."[2] In an article entitled "Crime Does Pay," Max Huhner[3] points out that in New York State alone there were over 1,000 unsolved mur-

---

[1] *The New York Times*, July 8, 1952.
[2] Snyder, *op. cit.*, p. 335.
[3] Max Huhner, "Crime Does Pay," *Journal of Criminal Law and Criminology* (November–December, 1939), 30: 492.

ders in a single year, and that in many cases the victims could not even be identified.

In view of these estimates regarding the number of criminal deaths which either are never detected, or for whom perpetrators are never discovered, it seems desirable for various reasons to analyze the available data on unsolved homicides. As a means of maintaining valid police statistics and as an index of efficient police administration, the number of unsolved cases is important. A high proportion of unsolved homicides *may* indicate ineptitude of the police. On the other hand, a police force may be well organized, free of corruption, unusually efficient, and well trained; yet because of its being understaffed, fail to have sufficient time to investigate adequately all cases. To these factors that affect the proportion of unsolved homicides should be added: size and density of a community; prevailing mores regarding respect for law and authority; the extent to which the culture pattern ennobles the dignity and worth of individual human life; the degree to which members of the community have internalized prevailing culture values; the amount of internal and external pressure to confess. Despite diligent police efforts to discover the perpetrator, sometimes no one may be found, and a homicide may be carried in the records as unsolved. If the homicide occurs in a large metropolitan community that permits escape into the relative anonymity of secondary relationships, the offender may elude the police for years. If disrespect for law and the police is common, friends and acquaintances of the offender may harbor him and aid in his eluding punishment. On the contrary, when a law-abiding citizen, with an adequately socialized personality, kills in the heat of passion, and if the culture norms emphasize respect for human life, he is most likely to aid the police by freely confessing his role in the slaying. Desire to ease his conscience, to repent publicly, or even to seek expiation by means of the legally imposed sanctions, could function to the benefit of the police and result in a solved rather than an unsolved criminal statistic.

Although the term "unsolved" is used often in homicide

literature, few attempts have been made to present a precise definition of the term.[1] There are several different possible definitions, and a final choice must necessarily be arbitrary and subject to qualifications. At the outset, justifiable and excusable homicides must be excluded from consideration. Beyond this exclusion, an unsolved criminal or felonious homicide may differentially be interpreted as one in which:

(1) a suspect has been arrested, brought to trial, but not convicted;

(2) a suspect has been arrested, but has not been brought to trial;

(3) a suspect is known to the police but has escaped arrest;

(4) no suspect has been identified by the police.

During the years covered in the present study, determination that a homicide was justifiable or excusable rested with the coroner's inquest, and all slayers exonerated by that body were excluded from our analysis of criminal homicide in Philadelphia. On the basis of this fact, the following definition of unsolved homicide has been formulated for use in the present study:

An unsolved homicide is one in which a coroner's inquest deems that a perpetrator (or perpetrators), unknown, is responsible for a death not declared justifiable or excusable, and for which the police are unable to detect a person sufficiently suspect[2] that his arrest should be caused, if located.

This definition may not cover all extraneous circumstances that could occur in an individual killing, but for all practical purposes, it is sufficiently precise. No dogmatic definition can cover all possible events, but another qualification may be made with respect to time intervals. For example:

[1] For some insight into this problem, see Max Stern, "A Study of Unsolved Murders in Wisconsin from 1924–1928," *Journal of Criminal Law and Criminology* (February, 1931), 21: 513–536.

[2] The phrase "sufficiently suspect" implies that a *prima facie* case can be presented at a preliminary hearing before the minor judiciary; that there is apparently sufficient evidence to justify conviction, or, at least, evidence so strong and convincing as to require contradictory evidence to nullify it.

(*a*) Is a criminal homicide unsolved from the moment an offense is known to the police until a suspect sufficiently subject to arrest has been discovered? Or (*b*) is the homicide unsolved only after the coroner's inquest has declared an unknown perpetrator responsible for criminal death? If the latter question is answered affirmatively rather than the former, then a homicide may remain in an anomalous status for several weeks until the inquest is held—neither solved nor unsolved. To eliminate this difficulty, the first question must be answered affirmatively. Since an unknown assailant is never exonerated, it may be possible to delimit the definition of unsolved to those cases of homicide in which no suspect, sufficiently subject to arrest if located, is known to the police.[1]

The *Uniform Crime Reports* use the term "cleared by arrest" to indicate that one or more persons has been apprehended for the perpetration of an offense known to the police and is available for prosecution. Our definition of unsolved does not entirely coincide with those cases not cleared by arrest. A suspect may be known to the police, may have been held responsible by the inquest, even indicted by the grand jury and yet, remain a fugitive. In such a case, the offense is not cleared by arrest, but so far as the police are concerned, the case is solved. If a suspect has been arrested, held responsible by an inquest, but not indicted by a grand jury (a rarity), and if the police are satisfied that he is responsible for the crime, the case is considered solved, although further attempts are occasionally made to seek another possible suspect. If a suspect is arrested and indicted, but not convicted in court, the police carry the case as solved even though the death has not been declared justifiable or excusable by any legal body.

In his article on unsolved murders in Wisconsin, Max Stern designated as unsolved "a killing responsibility for which has not been attached to any person, within at least a year of the commission of the killing, to the satisfaction of

[1] This definition is, to all intents and purposes, the one used by the Philadelphia Homicide Squad.

a court or jury with the exception of killings construed by the courts as justifiable or excusable homicides."[1] This definition is neither better nor worse than that employed in the present research. But Stern's definition fails to account for a case in which the offender is acquitted in criminal courts, although there remains little or no doubt in the minds of the police or prosecutor that he is the actual perpetrator. The court may have acquitted him because the evidence presented was not convincing beyond a "reasonable doubt" and not because his act was considered legally excusable. In such a case as this, the Philadelphia police make little additional effort to locate another suspect, because none is believed to exist. They therefore classify the case as solved.

The use of a time interval of one year suggested by Stern is similarly arbitrary; yet if a court adjudication is part of the definition, some such time limit is necessary. However, in the sense used in this study, the offense is unsolved from the moment the police are informed until they acquire sufficient evidence to charge a suspect with homicide. All of the unsolved criminal homicides included in the present research have maintained the status of unsolved for two or more years duration. Obviously, however, 1948 homicides are more firmly fixed as unsolved than 1952 cases because the former have endured over a longer time period. For research purposes, the line of demarcation between solved and unsolved must be drawn at some point in time, and two years is probably a reasonable time for the 1952 unsolved cases to mature.

In his analysis of homicides in *The Illinois Crime Survey*, Lashly adopted the following definition: "Unsolved or uncleared murder is murder in which no charge has been filed and no arrest made after a finding by the coroner that a murder has been committed."[2] However, in many cases in Cook County, the coroner's jury named the slayer and ordered his arrest and presentment to the grand jury, but because no arrest was made and no one presented, the case

---

[1] Stern, *op. cit.*, p. 521.
[2] *The Illinois Crime Survey*, p. 619.

was listed as unsolved. In Philadelphia these are listed as solved but fugitive cases, of which there were 13.

In his definition, Lashly was not concerned whether an individual once arrested ever stood trial, or, if prosecution was started, whether a conviction resulted. Thus, the author is of the opinion that once a person is arrested in connection with a particular homicide, that killing may be considered as solved so far as the police are concerned. The responsibility for the case from that point on, "is upon the process of prosecution and judicial administration, and not upon the police."[1] This is the same attitude that prevails in the Homicide Squad in Philadelphia and was the one incorporated into the present definition.

The Philadelphia Data

Extent. Of the 588 criminal homicides between 1948 and 1952, 38, or slightly more than 6 per cent, are classified as unsolved.

Comparisons with other communities must necessarily be crude, and in the absence of universally accepted operational definitions, reference to unsolved cases in homicide literature must be cautiously interpreted. During the period 1924–1928, in Wisconsin, Stern counted 173 felonious homicides, of which 23 per cent were classified as unsolved.[2] Of the 760 criminal homicides in Cook County during 1926–1927, Lashly reported 37 per cent as unsolved.[3] In their study of homicide in Memphis, Bruce and Fitzgerald recorded 411 victims, 8 per cent of whom were killed by unknown perpetrators.[4] Of 500 criminal homicides in Birmingham between 1937 and 1944, Harlan reported that slightly over 4 per cent were committed by unknown agents.[5] Of 212 murders and non-negligent manslaughters in St. Louis, 1949–1951, Meyers lists only 3 per cent as having been committed by unknown perpetrators.[6]

[1] *Ibid.*, p. 621.
[2] Stern, *op. cit.*, p. 528.
[3] *The Illinois Crime Survey*, p. 620.
[4] Cited by von Hentig, *The Criminal and His Victim*, p. 394.
[5] Harlan, *op. cit.*, p. 745.
[6] Meyers, Jr., *op. cit.*, p. 26.

In order to arrive at a valid cleared-by-arrest rate, it is necessary to add the 13 fugitive to the 38 unsolved cases, which results in 51 cases, or close to 9 per cent not cleared by arrest. Reversed, 91 per cent were cleared by arrest, and it is this proportion that can be compared to national police data. The *Uniform Crime Reports* consistently show that murder and non-negligent manslaughter are cleared by arrest in slightly over 90 per cent of such offenses known to the police. For the calendar year 1950, 1,601 cities covering a population of 54,690,179 reported that 94 per cent of these offenses were cleared.[1] More meaningful, however, is the comparison of Philadelphia to other large metropolitan areas of comparable or near-comparable size. (Table 29.) Philadelphia ranks eleventh among 18 cities of 250,000 population or over, when the cleared-by-arrest rates in these cities for the same period, 1948–1952, are compared.[2] The range is from a high of nearly 99 per cent cleared by arrest in Buffalo, to a low of 84 per cent in Seattle. These figures are admittedly crude because of the many uncontrolled variables previously mentioned, but in the absence of more adequate data, they are useful. All told, there were 6,435 criminal homicides in the 18 cities during the five years, and the police were able to make arrests in 90 per cent of the cases. Hence, one perpetrator out of every 10 who committed criminal homicide known to the police was able to escape apprehension.[3]

Compared with Solved Cases. Comparison of the unsolved with solved criminal homicides in Philadelphia reveals some interesting differences.

A larger proportion of the victims of unsolved than of

[1] *Uniform Crime Reports* (1951), 22: 41.
[2] Data collected from the police in these cities in response to a communication from the author.
[3] Perhaps it would be more precise to say that one perpetrator of felonious homicide out of 10 was able to escape apprehension by the police *at least for a year*. Data on homicides cleared by arrest were submitted by the police from these cities during 1954. The last year included in the tabulations was 1952. Thus, the minimal time between commission of the crime and recording of the crime as unsolved should be used when discussing the number of offenders not yet arrested. Some offenses listed as unsolved from 1948 to 1951, for example, may have been cleared by arrest in 1952 so that an offender may have escaped arrest for four or five years, but was eventually arrested. Offenses occurring in 1952 may be cleared in 1955, but, recorded in 1954, are listed as not cleared.

TABLE 29

CRIMINAL HOMICIDES CLEARED BY ARREST, FOR
18 CITIES OVER 250,000 POPULATION, 1948–1952

City	Number of Criminal Homicides	Per Cent Cleared by Arrest
Buffalo	84	98.8
Cincinnati	193	98.5
Washington, D.C.	473	97.0
Dallas	298	96.3
Columbus	81	96.3
Milwaukee	73	95.9
Baltimore	433	94.7
St. Paul	37	94.6
Akron	43	93.0
Kansas City, Mo.	229	92.6
Philadelphia	588	91.3
Pittsburgh (a)	126	91.3
Los Angeles	398	90.0
Boston	211	88.6
Chicago	1,415	87.6
Miami	188	86.2
New York	1,467	84.9
Seattle	69	84.1
All Cities	6,435	90.1

Source: Police reports submitted to the author in response to a questionnaire.
(a) The report from Pittsburgh is an exception since it covers the period 1949–1953.

solved homicides are white; but even more interesting is the fact that whites are numerically in the majority among unsolved cases. (Table 30.) White victims comprise one-fourth of all solved homicides, but over one-half of the unsolved cases. On the assumption that these, like the solved cases, are mostly intra-racial killings, the analyst is left with the *a posteriori* dilemma of explaining such a race differential. Are Negro witnesses more likely than whites to admit knowledge of a homicide? Are Negro offenders more likely to confess a slaying? Are white homicides more likely to be committed under the shield of privacy where no witnesses are available to inform the police? Are white offenders more astute at the art of premeditated murder or of escaping detection than Negro slayers? In any case, the police are no less diligent in their search for white than for Negro offenders.

Approximately one-fourth of the victims of both solved and unsolved homicides are female, but *white* females are twice as frequently victims of unsolved slayings (16 per cent)

291

TABLE 30
UNSOLVED AND SOLVED CRIMINAL HOMICIDES,
BY RACE AND SEX OF VICTIM, PHILADELPHIA,
1948–1952

	UNSOLVED		SOLVED	
	Number	Per Cent of Total	Number	Per Cent of Total
Negro				
Male	13	34.2	318	57.8
Female	4	10.5	92	16.7
Total	17	44.7	410	74.5
White				
Male	15	39.5	103	18.7
Female	6	15.8	37	6.8
Total	21	55.3	140	25.5
Both Races				
Male	28	73.7	421	76.5
Female	10	26.3	129	23.5
Total	38	100.0	550	100.0

than of solved ones (7 per cent). Similarly, white males are twice the proportion among the unsolved (40 per cent) than they are among the solved (19 per cent).

Police authorities can only speculate about the motives involved in an unsolved homicide, but in some cases there are sufficient clues, leaving little doubt that robbery was a motive. In 16 of the 38 cases it is believed that robbery was the original motivating factor that resulted in homicide. If these observations are correct, robbery was the predominant motive among unsolved slayings. The incidence of robbery among unsolved cases (42 per cent) is 7 times the proportion this motive comprises among the solved cases (6 per cent). Because homicide during robbery is a felony-murder, 2 out of every 5 of the unsolved cases may be classified a murder in the first degree. In 11 of the unsolved homicides no motive was established by the police, in 6 altercation was listed; and in one each, it was suspected, jealousy, revenge, desire to eliminate a bastard child, and rape was the motive. One case was listed as a sniper-killing. Because robbery constituted such a high proportion of the unsolved cases, it is probably safe to assume that most of the victims were strangers to their slayers.

Victims of unsolved homicides have a median age of 40.8 years compared to 35.1 years for all victims, but the most striking difference concerns the victims 65 years of age and older. The 7 victims in this age group among the unsolved (18 per cent) are proportionately four to five times greater than the number of victims in this age group among the solved cases (4 per cent). Homicides involving robbery and burglary are apt to be cases in which witnesses are not present. In some of these cases victims were watchmen in used-car lots, factories, and stores—an occupation common for older men who have retired from their previous and more strenuous life occupations. Furthermore, some of these victims were older persons walking the street at night—victims who were vulnerable and physically unable to protect themselves against assaults by younger persons.

Two-fifths of the victims of unsolved homicides were beaten to death compared to only one-fifth of the victims of solved cases. Contrariwise, only one-fourth of unsolved cases were stabbings compared to two-fifths of the solved cases. The predominant intra-racial nature of homicide, the higher proportion of whites and females among the unsolved, and the knowledge that white females are most frequently beaten by white males—all lead us to deduce that most of the unknown assailants were white males.

Because 60 per cent of all victims of robbery-homicide were killed violently, and because robbery was the motive in two-fifths of the unsolved cases, it is not unexpected that 60 per cent of all victims of unsolved slayings were killed violently.

It is interesting and unexpected that the incidence of victims with a previous arrest record is nearly as high for unsolved cases (42 per cent) as for solved cases (48 per cent).

Although both the unsolved and solved cases have distributions showing highest frequencies on the same days of the week and during the same six-hour period, a slightly higher proportion of unsolved killings (71 per cent) took place during the week-end from Friday to Sunday than was true of the solved homicides (65 per cent), and more of the unsolved (66 per cent) than of the solved (49 per cent) occurred between 8:00 P.M. and 2:00 A.M. Probably this difference is explained by the greater proportion of robberies among the unsolved and the fact that robberies occur more often over the week-end and under the protective cloak of the night hours. The fact that most victims of robbery-homicide are strangers to their assailants probably accounts for the additional fact that twice as many unsolved (58 per cent) as solved (28 per cent) homicides occur on the public street or highway, and, therefore, more frequently outside the home (68 per cent of the unsolved compared to 48 per cent of the solved cases).

In summary, there is no uniform definition of an unsolved criminal homicide. An operational definition is necessary for analysis but is arbitrary and unlikely to include all possible extenuating circumstances. The concept of "cleared by arrest" used in uniform police reporting is only an approximation. Thirty-eight of the 588 criminal homicides have been classified as unsolved, and comparison of this group with the solved homicides reveals that the unsolved cases have higher proportions of:

(1) white male and white female victims;
(2) victims 65 years of age or over;
(3) robbery motives;
(4) victims who were strangers to their assailants;[1]
(5) beatings;
(6) week-end slayings;
(7) deaths occurring outside the home, and in the street.

One thing is certain: by any definition an unsolved homicide is different from a solved homicide. A universally accepted definition of an unsolved crime—particularly homicide—would aid considerably in future research that seeks to compare and contrast these cases with solved ones. More abundant and precise research in this area may demonstrate relatively consistent patterns among unsolved cases, and, hence, could be of valuable assistance in police investigation.

[1] Strongly suggested, but, of course, not confirmed by the available data.

17

ADJUDICATION

The Tempo of Legal Procedure (Table 31)

TWO-THIRDS of the offenders in criminal homicide[1] who were taken into custody by the police were arrested on the same day they committed the crime.[2] In 88 per cent of the cases they were arrested within the first week after the crime, and in only 7 per cent did more than a month elapse before arrest was made. Regardless of sex, about two-thirds of white offenders were apprehended on the same day of the crime. Among Negroes, however, sex differences are noticeable. While three-fifths of Negro male offenders were arrested on the same day of the homicide, over four-fifths of Negro females were arrested during this same period. Probably the higher proportion of Negro females who killed their husbands due to extreme provocation account for this sex differential among Negroes. Most male offenders killed their victims outside the home (in the street, in a taproom, etc.), and ran immediately from the scene of the brawl. The wife who stabbed her husband in a kitchen with a butcher knife had no place to run. Furthermore, she was more likely

[1] N = 607 offenders; 14 of the 621 offenders known to the police were fugitives at the time of the study, and were involved in 13 cases.

[2] Because of difficulties of ascertaining for each case the exact hour of arrest, "time of arrest" was tabulated in terms of days. Hence, if an offender committed his crime at 11:00 P.M. and was arrested two hours later, or at 1:00 A.M. the following day, a "second day" classification was given. In the few cases where such a situation occurred, the resultant statistic, of course, tends to be biased against rapid apprehension by the police. Should an hourly basis be employed, therefore, the police record of quick arrest would appear slightly better than the distribution reported above. The same comment applies to the other data related to the time element in legal procedure from arrest to grand jury indictment and appearance before the trial jury.

Finally, homicide does not exist until the victim has died, so that the assault may have occurred on one day and the death several days or weeks later. The "time of arrest" is here interpreted as the time between death of the victim and arrest. In most cases, the assault and death occur on the same day. See *supra.*, pp. 113–115.

TABLE 31

**TIME INTERVAL BETWEEN DEATH OF VICTIM AND SUBSEQUENT
LEGAL PROCESSES, BY RACE AND SEX OF OFFENDER,
CRIMINAL HOMICIDE, PHILADELPHIA, 1948–1952**

(In per cent)

Legal Process and Time Interval from Death of Victim	Both Races			Negro			White		
	Total	Male	Female	Total	Male	Female	Total	Male	Female (e)
Arrest (a)									
Less than 1 day	64.8	61.3	80.5	64.5	59.8	82.6	65.6	65.2	—
1 day	12.9	14.2	6.5	13.0	15.0	5.4	12.3	12.3	—
2–7 days	10.2	11.0	6.5	9.0	9.7	6.5	13.6	14.5	—
8–14 days	1.8	2.2	—	2.0	2.5	—	1.3	1.5	—
15–30 days	3.4	3.4	3.7	4.0	4.2	3.3	2.0	1.5	—
More than 30 days	6.9	7.8	2.8	7.5	8.8	2.2	5.2	5.0	—
Total	100.0	100.0	100.0	100.0	100.0	100.0	100.0	100.0	100.0
	(607)	(499)	(108)	(453)	(361)	(92)	(154)	(138)	(16)
Coroner's Inquest (b)									
Less than 3 weeks	1.3	1.1	2.3	1.0	1.0	1.3	2.2	1.6	—
3–4 weeks	31.0	30.9	31.8	31.2	30.8	32.9	30.6	31.2	—
5–6 weeks	38.3	38.2	38.6	38.6	37.8	42.1	37.3	39.3	—
7–8 weeks	16.5	17.5	11.4	17.3	18.3	13.2	14.2	15.6	—
9–12 weeks	8.6	8.8	8.0	8.5	9.3	5.3	9.0	7.4	—
13–16 weeks	2.3	2.1	3.4	.8	1.0	—	6.7	4.9	—
More than 16 weeks	1.9	1.4	4.5	2.6	1.9	5.3	—	—	—
Total	100.0	100.0	100.0	100.0	100.0	100.0	100.0	100.0	100.0
	(522)	(434)	(88)	(388)	(312)	(76)	(134)	(122)	(12)
Presentment Before Grand Jury (c)									
4 weeks	19.8	19.0	23.8	17.7	16.1	24.1	26.7	27.4	—
5–6 weeks	29.5	28.3	34.6	30.1	29.2	33.3	27.5	25.6	—
7–8 weeks	25.7	26.1	23.8	26.8	26.6	27.5	22.1	24.8	—
9–12 weeks	15.2	16.1	10.9	14.9	16.1	10.4	16.0	16.2	—
13–16 weeks	4.8	5.2	3.0	4.4	5.3	1.2	6.1	5.1	—
More than 16 weeks	5.0	5.2	3.9	6.1	6.7	3.5	1.5	.9	—
Total	100.0	100.0	100.0	100.0	100.0	100.0	100.0	100.0	100.0
	(560)	(459)	(101)	(429)	(342)	(87)	(131)	(117)	(14)
Court Trial (d)									
1–3 months	11.0	10.6	12.5	11.7	11.5	12.4	8.5	7.9	—
4–6 months	43.9	43.1	47.1	43.6	42.9	46.1	45.0	43.9	—
7–9 months	17.8	18.8	13.5	18.3	18.9	15.7	16.3	18.4	—
10–12 months	14.6	14.4	15.4	14.5	14.2	15.7	14.7	14.9	—
More than 12 months	10.6	11.3	7.7	10.3	11.2	6.7	11.6	11.4	—
Pending	2.1	1.8	3.8	1.6	1.2	3.4	3.9	3.5	—
Total	100.0	100.0	100.0	100.0	100.0	100.0	100.0	100.0	100.0
	(556)	(452)	(104)	(427)	(338)	(89)	(129)	(114)	(1)

(a) The 607 offenders include only those who were in police custody. Thus 14 fugitive (including one multiple defendant after the first principal) are not included.

(b) A coroner's inquest is, of course, held for each death so that each of the 621 offenders fugitive or not, was held responsible for a homicide. However, for 99 offenders th date of the coroner's inquest was not reported in police files.

(c) Of the 621 offenders, the date of presentment before a grand jury was not reporte or was not applicable for 61 offenders.

(d) Of the 607 offenders in police custody, the date of court trial was not reported o was not applicable for 51 offenders.

(e) Category too small for breakdown by percentage distribution.

to call the police for assistance to transport her victim to the hospital than was the male slayer of a male. After notification, the police usually arrived on the scene of the crime within two or three minutes. In more than a few cases eye-witnesses were available; in others, the offender made a ready confession; and in others, he often went home to await the arrival of police authorities. The distribution of offenders according to the duration of time between commission of the homicide and arrest by the police, reveals that few criminal homicides long remain a mystery. Within a month after the crime, over 90 per cent of the perpetrators were in custody.

The unwritten rule that a suspect should have a preliminary hearing before the minor judiciary within three days after arrest was generally adhered to among the cases examined. (Table 32.) Nineteen per cent of the offenders[1] had a hearing the same day they were arrested; another 61 per cent had a hearing the first day after arrest, 9 per cent on the second day, and 3 per cent on the third day. All told, 92 per cent of the offenders appeared before a magistrate within three days after arrest. Although 80 per cent had a hearing by the end of the first day after arrest, 95 per cent of the Negro females appeared before the magistrate by that time, a higher proportion that is probably best accounted for by the higher proportion of Negro females arrested on the day of the crime, thus making more of them available for a preliminary hearing the next day.

A coroner's inquest was held to determine the nature of, and responsibility for, the death within a relatively short time after the crime in most cases. Before a month after the death of the victim, one-third of the cases had appeared before an inquest. Within 6 weeks, 70 per cent of the cases had appeared, and by the end of the second month after the crime, 87 per cent.[2] Only 2 per cent required more than 4 months to reach the inquest stage of legal process. There were no important race or sex differences with respect to

[1] N = 557; 50 of 607 offenders were not reported or did not apply here.
[2] N = 522; most of the 1948 dates were not supplied, so that 99 of the 607 were not reported or did not apply here.

TABLE 32

TIME INTERVAL BETWEEN ARREST AND PRELIMINARY HEARING,
BY RACE AND SEX OF OFFENDER, CRIMINAL HOMICIDE,
PHILADELPHIA, 1948–1952

(In per cent)

Arrest and Hearing	Both Races			Negro			White		
	Total	Male	Female	Total	Male	Female	Total	Male	Fema (a)
Time Interval									
Less than 1 day	19.2	19.5	17.8	17.1	17.3	16.1	25.9	25.6	—
1 day	61.0	57.9	75.2	61.4	56.7	79.3	60.0	61.2	—
2 days	8.8	9.9	4.0	11.1	13.1	3.4	1.5	.8	—
3 days	2.7	3.1	1.0	1.7	2.1	—	5.9	5.8	—
4 days	1.3	1.3	1.0	1.0	1.2	—	2.2	1.7	—
5 days	1.2	1.3	—	1.4	1.8˙	—	—	—	—
6 days or more	5.9	7.0	1.0	6.4	7.8	1.2	4.4	5.0	—
Total Reported	100.0 (557)	100.0 (456)	100.0 (101)	100.0 (422)	100.0 (335)	100.0 (87)	100.0 (135)	100.0 (121)	100.0 (14

(a) Category too small for breakdown by percentage distribution.

the time that elapsed between the crime and the inquest, and the earlier lead which Negro females enjoyed appears to have been absorbed in the time between the hearing and the inquest.

The amount of time elapsing between death of the victim and presentment of the case before the grand jury is some index to the speed of legal procedure. Within a month after the death pronouncement, 20 per cent of the suspects were indicted. During the second month, another 55 per cent were indicted, and during the third month, another 15 per cent.[1] Thus the offender appeared before a grand jury in 9 out of 10 cases within 3 months after a victim died as the result of a homicidal attack. No important differences appear according to race or sex, except, perhaps, that the Negro female again passed through this legal procedure somewhat more quickly than the total group. Within two months, the Negro female offender appeared before the grand jury in nearly 85 per cent of the cases, contrasted to 75 per cent of the total group.

[1] N = 560; 61 of the 621 offenders were not reported or did not apply here.

298

A speedy trial is assumed to be desirable. It prevents an innocent person, charged with criminal homicide, from languishing in the county prison; it assures the guilty the early certainty of their fate; it saves the county taxpayer from continued expenditure of keeping the untried defendant in the local prison; and, together with the certainty of justice, a speedy trial may operate as a deterrent. In 11 per cent of the cases for which a trial date was reported,[1] the defendant appeared in criminal court in less than 3 months after the death of the victim, or, to all intents and purposes, after the act of criminal assault. An additional 44 per cent were tried between the fourth and sixth months, which means that over half (55 per cent) of the defendants who had committed criminal homicide were tried within 6 months after the crime took place. Nine months after the crime nearly three-quarters had been tried (73 per cent), and by the end of the year, 88 per cent of the cases had been adjudicated. Only 12 per cent of the cases required more than one year from the commission of the crime to pass through the court trial. At the time of examination of the records, only 2 per cent of the cases were pending final adjudication.

Court Disposition

In the legal procedures from arrest to conviction there are several statistical levels available for analysis of the offenders in any type of crime. For purposes of the present study of offenders in criminal homicide, analysis has been made on each of the following levels:

(1) the number of suspects taken into custody by the police (N = 607);

(2) the number of suspects taken into custody by the police and made available for prosecution (N = 563);

(3) the number of persons who actually experienced a court trial (N = 526);

---

[1] N = 556; 51 of the 607 offenders were not reported or did not apply. If a defendant had more than one trial, the first was used as a means of determining time between crime and trial, and the last trial was used to determine court disposition.

(4) the number of persons for whom data were reported relative to the degree of criminal homicide designated by a court of record (N = 509);

(5) the number of persons convicted and sentenced by a court of record (N = 387).

Two-thirds of the 607 offenders who were taken into custody by the police were found guilty of criminal homicide. One-fifth were acquitted, 4 per cent were not tried because of lack of sufficient evidence (*nolle prosequi*), 2 per cent were pending at the time data were collected, and 8 per cent were disposed of in other ways (natural death, institutionalized because of insanity, etc.). (Table 33.)

Of special interest are the 526 defendants who actually experienced a court trial. The distribution by race and sex relative to disposition of this group is as follows:

| | Total | | Negro | | White | | Male | | Female | |
	No.	%	No.	%	No.	%	No.	%	No.	%
Guilty	404	76.8	331	80.9	73	62.4	337	78.6	67	69.1
Not Guilty	122	23.2	78	19.1	44	37.6	92	21.4	30	30.9
Total	526	100.0	409	100.0	117	100.0	429	100.0	97	100.0

The race distribution shows a *significant* association between Negroes and convictions, for 81 per cent of these 409 Negroes who were tried were found guilty, compared to only 62 per cent guilty of the 117 whites tried. There is no significant association by sex, for 79 per cent of the males and 69 per cent of the females were guilty.

A *significantly* smaller proportion of offenders in victim-precipitated homicide (62 per cent) than in non-VP homicide (82 per cent) were found guilty.[1] Among the VP offenders, there is also a *significant* association between race and conviction, for 77, or 67 per cent, of the 115 Negroes who experienced a court trial were found guilty, compared to only 11, or 41 per cent, of the 27 whites.

Of several variables suspected of being related to court disposition, the police-recorded motive of homicide shows

---

[1] Of the 142 VP offenders tried, 88 were guilty; and of the 384 non-VP offenders tried, 316 were guilty.

TABLE 33
DISPOSITION OF OFFENDER IN CRIMINAL HOMICIDE, AMONG
PERSONS MADE AVAILABLE FOR PROSECUTION, BY RACE
AND SEX, PHILADELPHIA, 1948–1952

(In per cent)

position	Both Races			Negro			White		
	Total	Male	Female	Total	Male	Female	Total	Male	Female (a)
ilty	66.6	67.6	62.0	73.1	74.8	66.3	47.4	48.6	—
t Guilty	20.1	18.4	27.8	17.2	14.7	27.1	28.6	28.3	—
lle Prosequi	3.5	2.8	6.5	2.4	2.2	3.3	6.5	4.3	—
nding	1.9	1.8	2.8	1.8	1.4	3.3	2.6	2.9	—
her	7.9	9.4	.9	5.5	6.9	—	14.9	15.9	—
Total	100.0	100.0	100.0	100.0	100.0	100.0	100.0	100.0	100.0
	(607)	(499)	(108)	(453)	(361)	(92)	(154)	(138)	(16)

(a) Category too small for breakdown by percentage distribution.

some interesting differences between those declared guilty
and those not guilty. (Table 34.) As might be expected, the
highest frequency of guilty verdicts was found among those
offenders who had committed robbery at the time of the
slaying (43 guilty; 3 not guilty). After robbery, the rank order
of guilty verdicts according to motive was: revenge (23

TABLE 34
DISPOSITION ACCORDING TO MOTIVE, CRIMINAL
HOMICIDE, PHILADELPHIA, 1948–1952

(In per cent)

Motive	Total	Guilty	Not Guilty	Other
Altercation of relatively trivial origin, insult, curse, jostling, etc.	36.4	35.2	49.2	23.5
Domestic quarrel	13.7	13.1	12.3	18.5
Jealousy	10.9	12.6	4.9	11.1
Altercation over money	10.2	12.4	6.6	4.9
Robbery	8.1	10.6	2.5	3.7
Revenge	4.9	5.7	1.6	6.2
Accidental	4.6	4.2	8.2	1.2
Self-defense	1.3	—	6.6	—
Halting felon	1.2	1.0	2.5	—
Escaping arrest	1.0	.7	1.6	1.2
Concealing birth	.8	.5	.8	2.5
Other motives	4.1	3.2	1.6	12.3
Unknown	2.8	.7	1.6	14.8
Total	100.0	100.0	100.0	100.0
	(607)	(404)	(122)	(81)

guilty; 2 not guilty), altercation over money (50; 8), jealousy (51; 6), domestic quarrel (53; 15), altercation (142; 60). Combined, these six major motives involved in criminal homicide accounted for nine-tenths of all guilty verdicts. Moreover, four-fifths of the offenders whose motives were among these six were found guilty. None of the 8 defendants whom the police listed as having killed in self-defense were convicted of criminal homicide, but 17 of the 27 defendants who contended the slaying was accidental were declared guilty.

In general, it may be said that among those suspects arrested for criminal homicide and available for prosecution,[1] two-thirds were convicted and sentenced. Approximately 14 per cent were convicted and sentenced for murder in the first degree, 20 per cent for murder in the second degree, 25 per cent for voluntary manslaughter, and 11 per cent for involuntary manslaughter. The remaining 30 per cent were acquitted or otherwise disposed. Of the 509 persons for whom data were reported relative to the degree of criminal homicide designated by a court of record, 76 per cent were convicted and sentenced, while the remainder were acquitted or otherwise disposed.

Of the 387 offenders convicted and sentenced, and for whom information was available, 20 per cent were guilty of first degree murder, 29 per cent of second degree murder, 36 per cent of voluntary manslaughter, and 15 per cent of involuntary manslaughter. (Table 35.) Although there is a *significant* association between race and conviction, with a larger proportion of Negroes found guilty than of whites, no association is found between race and the degree of criminal homicide. On the other hand, while no association is found between sex and conviction, there is a *significant* association between sex and the degree of homicide. The primary contribution to this association is the fact that males comprised

---

[1] Excluding those who committed suicide, who died, were declared insane, etc., 563 were made available for prosecution. Relative to convictions for all types of offenses prosecuted in Philadelphia, 1948–1952, the District Attorney's office reported the following: 1948, not reported; 1949, 70 per cent guilty; 1950, 73 per cent guilty; 1951, "we could find no report;" 1952, 80 per cent guilty (*Annual Report 1952*, District Attorney's Office of Philadelphia, p. 44).

TABLE 35

DEGREE OF CRIMINAL HOMICIDE DESIGNATED BY A COURT OF
RECORD, BY RACE AND SEX OF THREE CLASSIFICATIONS OF
OFFENDERS, PHILADELPHIA, 1948–1952

(In per cent)

	Both Races			Negro			White		
(1) Offenders Available for Prosecution and for whom Degree of Homicide was Reported	Total	Male	Female	Total	Male	Female	Total	Male	Female (a)
Degree of Homicide									
First degree murder	15.7	18.7	3.1	16.1	20.0	1.2	14.5	14.7	—
Second degree murder	27.7	28.2	25.8	28.8	29.7	25.6	23.9	23.5	—
Voluntary manslaughter	41.9	39.1	53.6	42.9	39.4	56.1	38.5	38.3	—
Invol. manslaughter	14.7	14.0	17.5	12.2	10.9	17.1	23.1	23.5	—
Total	100.0	100.0	100.0	100.0	100.0	100.0	100.0	100.0	100.0
	(509)	(412)	(97)	(392)	(310)	(82)	(117)	(102)	(15)
(2) Offenders Sentenced									
Degree of Homicide									
First degree murder	19.9	23.2	3.2	19.6	23.5	1.7	21.6	21.7	—
Second degree murder	29.2	29.6	27.0	29.2	29.5	27.6	29.2	30.0	—
Voluntary manslaughter	35.7	32.7	50.8	37.6	34.1	53.4	26.2	26.7	—
Invol. manslaughter	15.2	14.5	19.0	13.6	12.9	17.2	23.0	21.7	—
Total	100.0	100.0	100.0	100.0	100.0	100.0	100.0	100.0	100.0
	(387)	(324)	(63)	(322)	(264)	(58)	(65)	(60)	(5)
(3) Offenders Sentenced who had a Previous Arrest Record									
Degree of Homicide									
First degree murder	20.6	23.2	2.8	20.5	23.4	3.1	20.8	22.5	—
Second degree murder	32.1	32.8	27.8	32.1	32.8	28.1	32.1	32.6	—
Voluntary manslaughter	33.6	30.3	55.4	36.2	32.3	59.4	22.6	22.5	—
Invol. manslaughter	13.7	13.7	13.9	11.2	11.5	9.4	24.5	22.5	—
Total	100.0	100.0	100.0	100.0	100.0	100.0	100.0	100.0	100.0
	(277)	(241)	(36)	(224)	(192)	(32)	(53)	(49)	(4)

(a) Category too small for breakdown by percentage distribution.

324, or 84 per cent, of the 387 offenders convicted and sentenced, but accounted for 75, or 97 per cent, of the 77 defendants convicted of murder in the first degree.

Although the difference may not be statistically significant, it is interesting to note that approximately three-fourths of those persons convicted for murder in either the first or second degree had a previous arrest record, compared to two-thirds of those convicted of manslaughter. Of those convicted, a larger proportion of whites than of Negroes had an arrest record. Of 264 Negro males convicted and sentenced, 192, or 73 per cent, had a previous record; of 60 white males convicted, 49, or 82 per cent, had a record. Similarly, 32 of the 55 Negro females convicted had an arrest record, as did 4 of the 5 white females.

The incidence of those convicted of criminal homicide in general, and of murder in particular, who had a previous arrest record, contradicts statements previously made by many authors. It will be recalled that these authors claimed that the murderer, especially, is usually a first offender. The Philadelphia data show exactly the reverse: that the murderer, particularly and more frequently than the homicide offender in general, has a previous record of contact with the law.

No significant differences emerge in the distribution of offenders according to age and degree of homicide. There is, however, a slight tendency for the younger age groups under 30 years to have a higher proportion of offenders convicted of first degree murder. (Appendix I, Tables 28, 29.)

Among those not sentenced to death or to life imprisonment, half were given minimum sentences of imprisonment for 4 years or more. (Table 36.) Only one was sentenced to a minimum of 20 years, one to a minimum of 15 years, 24 to 10 years minimum, 80 to minimum sentences ranging from 5 to 9 years, and 135 to minimum sentences that were less than 5 years. The same proportion (18 per cent) were sentenced to serve a minimum of less than 2 years as were sentenced to life imprisonment. Fourteen per cent, most of whom were women, were given indefinite sentences; and 4 per cent were placed on probation, most of whom were convicted of involuntary manslaughter.

Court Disposition Noted in Other Studies[1]

Comparison of court dispositions cannot be made with

[1] Unlike previous reviews, these are presented without much detailed analysis or comparison because of the incomparability of most reports. Original source material was not available. Moreover, no review of sentences for convicted offenders is offered. The more refined the reports become after general presentation of disposition and designation of degree, the more incomparable the data are. Rather than engage in unwarranted comparisons, they have been omitted.

TABLE 36

MINIMUM SENTENCE, BY DEGREE OF CRIMINAL HOMICIDE, AND BY RACE AND SEX OF OFFENDER, PHILADELPHIA, 1948–1952

Degree of Homicide Race and Sex	Total	Per Cent	Per Cent of Total	(1)	(2)	(3)	(4)	(5)	(6)	(7)	(8)	(9)	(10)	(11)
First degree murder														
Both races	77	100.0	(19.9)	7	70									
Male	75	97.4		7	68									
Female	2	2.6			2									
Negro	63	81.8		6	57									
Male	62	80.5		6	56									
Female	1	1.3			1									
White	14	18.2		1	13									
Male	13	16.9		1	12									
Female	1	1.3			1									
Second degree murder														
Both races	113	100.0	(29.2)			2	24	15	23	15	13	4	17	
Male	96	84.9				1	23	14	23	15	12	4	4	
Female	17	15.1				1	1	1	—	—	1	—	13	
Negro	94	83.2				2	20	13	20	12	11	—	16	
Male	78	69.0				1	19	12	20	12	10	—	4	
Female	16	14.2				—	1	1	—	—	1	—	12	
White	19	16.8				—	4	2	3	3	2	4	1	
Male	18	15.9				—	4	2	3	3	2	4	—	
Female	1	.9				—	—	—	—	—	—	—	1	

TABLE 36 (continued).

Degree of Homicide Race and Sex	Total	Per Cent	Per Cent of Total	(1)	(2)	(3)	(4)	(5)	(6)	(7)	(8)	(9)	(10)	(11)
Voluntary manslaughter			(35.6)											
Both races	138	100.0						1	16	23	29	36	28	5
Male	106	76.8						1	15	22	26	33	7	2
Female	32	23.2						—	1	1	3	3	21	3
Negro	121	87.7						1	14	21	22	31	27	5
Male	90	65.2						1	13	20	19	28	7	2
Female	31	22.5						—	1	1	3	3	20	3
White	17	12.3						—	2	2	7	5	1	—
Male	16	11.6						—	2	2	7	5	—	—
Female	1	.7						—	—	—	—	—	1	—
Involuntary manslaughter			(15.3)											
Both races	59	100.0								1	8	31	9	10
Male	47	79.7								1	7	27	5	7
Female	12	20.3								—	1	4	4	3
Negro	44	74.6								1	7	24	9	3
Male	34	57.6								1	6	20	5	2
Female	10	17.0								—	1	4	4	1
White	15	25.4								—	1	7	—	7
Male	13	22.0								—	1	7	—	5
Female	2	3.4								—	—	—	—	2
Total	387			7	70	2	24	16	39	39	50	71	54	15
Per Cent of Total	(100.0)			(1.8)	(18.1)	(0.5)	(6.2)	(4.1)	(10.1)	(10.1)	(12.9)	(18.4)	(13.9)	(3.9)

Reference Data for Table 36 (Columns 1–11):

(1) Death. (2) Life Imprisonment. (3) More than 10 years but less than life imprisonment. (4) 10 years. (5) 8–9 years. (6) 6–7 years. (7) 4–5 years. (8) 2–3 years. (9) Less than 2 years. (10) Indefinite. (11) Probation.

the detail and precision that has generally been possible for previously analyzed factors, for such comparison requires a thorough examination of court records. However, several observations that a sample review of homicide literature reveals may be noted.

The proportion of persons arrested and available for prosecution and who were later convicted on charges of criminal homicide appears to be less in other studies than is the case in Philadelphia. The same may be said regarding those who actually were tried; that is, the proportion convicted is less in other studies. For example, Brearley[1] found in South Carolina (1920–1926), that 52 per cent of those tried were convicted, a proportion considerably less than the 77 per cent noted in Philadelphia. In South Carolina, those who were Negroes were found guilty in 64 per cent of the verdicts, while white persons accused were convicted in only 32 per cent of the cases. We have noted that Negroes were found guilty in a *significantly* higher proportion than whites in Philadelphia as well, but it is interesting to point out that nearly as many whites in Philadelphia were guilty (62 per cent) as were Negroes in South Carolina (64 per cent).

Guy B. Johnson,[2] in his analysis of the Negro and homicide in selected areas of Virginia, North Carolina, and Georgia during the 1930's, reported guilty verdicts in 74 per cent, 79 per cent, and 76 per cent of total indictments in each of the respective areas. Differences in the proportions of those convicted in the Negro/Negro and white/white groups were not consistent, but convictions of Negroes who had killed whites were consistently higher than any of the in-group homicide convictions.

Examination of the disposition of homicide cases in Massachusetts between 1925 and 1941 revealed that 64 per cent of all cases resulted in a verdict of guilty in Middlesex County, and 54 per cent in Suffolk County.[3]

---

[1] Brearley, *Homicide in the United States*, p. 110.
[2] Johnson, *op. cit.*, p. 99.
[3] Herbert B. Ehrmann, "The Death Penalty and the Administration of Justice," *The Annals of the American Academy of Political and Social Science* (November, 1952), 284: 78.

The 206 cities, each with a population of 250,000 and over, reporting to the F.B.I. in 1950, showed that 63 per cent of persons charged with murder and non-negligent manslaughter were found guilty.[1] This is a proportion remarkably close to the 66 per cent we have noted for a comparable group in Philadelphia.

In their analysis of 611 homicides (1922–1924), Dublin and Bunzel found that only 43 per cent of the 458 who should have been prosecuted were declared guilty. However, of the 258 who actually were brought to trial, three-fourths were guilty,[2] which is a proportion almost identical to that for Philadelphia defendants who actually were brought to trial.

An exceptionally low proportion of convictions was noted by Lashly in *The Illinois Crime Survey*. Of all persons charged with murder in Cook County, only 24 per cent were found guilty in 1926, and 19 per cent in 1927. A slightly higher proportion of colored males (31 per cent) than of white males (23 per cent) were guilty in 1926, as was true in 1927 (28 and 17 per cent).[3]

Frankel[4] observed that of the 505 individuals who were before a court on murder charges during the period 1931–1935, 42 per cent were disposed of without conviction and 58 per cent were found guilty.

The Allredge study[5] of Negro-white differentials in criminal homicide in seven sections of the South, 1940–1941, reported that, like Philadelphia, two-thirds of all persons indicted were convicted. The conviction percentages varied, however, according to the intra- or interracial nature of the homicide. When Negroes killed whites, 89 per cent were convicted; when Negroes killed Negroes, only 67 per cent were convicted; when whites killed whites, 64 per cent were convicted; and when whites killed Negroes, only 43 per cent were convicted. On the contrary, acquittals were more frequent

[1] *Uniform Crime Reports* (1951), 22: 52.
[2] Dublin and Bunzel, *op. cit.*, p. 130.
[3] *The Illinois Crime Survey*, p. 628.
[4] Frankel, *op. cit.*, p. 678.
[5] Allredge, *op. cit.*, p. 133; Garfinkel (*op. cit.*, p. 374) notes a similar intra- and interracial distribution, but with acquittals higher for whites who killed whites.

for whites: whites who killed Negroes, 29 per cent; whites who killed whites, 28 per cent; Negroes who killed Negroes, 21 per cent; and Negroes who killed whites, 7 per cent. We have previously observed that, in Philadelphia, Negroes who killed whites were more severely dealt with by the courts, but that such treatment was justifiable on the grounds that Negroes had committed more felony-murders than whites. It is not easy to evaluate race differentials of conviction without some knowledge of the circumstances involved in the whole homicide situation. When race comparisons, or inter-racial comparisons, are noted, more standardization than is now usually applied should be provided. For example, Negro felony-murderers should be compared with white felony-murderers.

Perhaps one selected comparison from abroad might add to the perspective of Philadelphia. Between 1900 and 1949 in England and Wales, 3,130 persons appeared for trial at assizes. During this same period, 658 were acquitted or not tried, 428 were insane on arraignment, 798 were guilty but insane, and 2,154 were convicted.[1] Thus the proportion of convictions, not including the guilty-but-insane class of defendants, was 69 per cent, or slightly lower than the 77 per cent in Philadelphia among those who actually were tried. By adding the guilty-but-insane group to those convicted, however, 95 per cent of those held for trial at assizes in England were guilty. Because the British statistics refer to murder, it is necessary to make comparisons on the basis of Philadelphia convictions for murder in the first and second degrees. Thus, there were reported in Philadelphia police files, 221 persons charged with first or second degree murder. Of these, 190, or 86 per cent, were found guilty and sentenced. The British proportion of convictions is still higher, even on this more comparable basis, but the wide differential that exists between an incorrect comparison of homicide convictions in Philadelphia with murders in England is considerably diminished.

[1] *Royal Commission on Capital Punishment, 1949–1953 Report*, pp. 300–301.

Most reported distributions of convicted offenders according to the degree of homicide is more like than unlike the distribution in Philadelphia. A selected but fairly representative group of studies makes clear this generalization. The comparisons are necessarily crude because of variations in the periods of time covered, the existence of differential penalties for homicide, and so forth. In an examination of 162 selected cases in the records of the District Attorney's office in Philadelphia, during a period ranging from 1927 to 1932, it was observed that of the indicted cases of criminal homicide, 12 per cent were first degree murder, 28 per cent were second degree murder, only 16 per cent voluntary manslaughter, and 9 per cent involuntary manslaughter.[1] These proportions are considerably divergent from those in the present study, particularly for voluntary manslaughter. However, the earlier study was designed to test the deterrent effect of capital punishment sixty days following the dates of executions, and for this reason probably includes a total group too selective for adequate comparison.

DePorte and Parkhurst[2] reported that 21 per cent of the 388 persons convicted in 37 counties in New York State were found guilty of first degree murder, a proportion like the 20 per cent in the present study. Brearley[3] noted the distributions in several areas for varying time periods:

(1) of 172 verdicts of guilty in Rhode Island during the years 1896–1927, 23 were for first degree murder, 43 for second degree murder, 104 for manslaughter, and 2 for assault with a deadly weapon;

(2) in Manhattan Borough of New York City there were, from 1922 through 1928, a total of 1,551 homicides, and for these offenses only 22 persons were convicted of first degree murder, one for every 71 homicides.

From 1909 to 1928, North Carolina reported 4,043 indictments for the three major types of criminal homicide, of which 10 per cent were for first degree murder, 66 per cent for

---

[1] Robert H. Dann, *The Deterrent Effect of Capital Punishment*, Friends Social Service Series, Bulletin No. 29, Third Month, 1935, p. 7.
[2] DePorte and Parkhurst, *op. cit.*, p. 66.
[3] Brearley, *op. cit.*, pp. 121–122, 127.

second degree murder, and 25 per cent for manslaughter. The 152 sentences for first degree murder represented 38 per cent of the 395 indictments for this offense. Of these 152 cases, 70 per cent were committed by Negroes.[1] Comparatively, a higher proportion of Negroes (81 per cent) in Philadelphia comprised those persons convicted of first degree murder. However, this is exactly the same proportion Negroes share among those convicted of homicide, regardless of degree.

In Middlesex and Suffolk Counties, Massachusetts, during the period 1925–1941, first degree murder accounted for 17 per cent of all capital cases in the former county, and only 4 per cent in the latter. Second degree murder accounted for one-fifth in both counties, and manslaughter, 26–30 per cent.[2] In Rhode Island, 1896–1927, there were 211 persons indicted for murder, of whom 26 were convicted of murder in the first degree, 39 were convicted of murder in the second degree, and 66 were convicted of manslaughter. In Massachusetts, 1896–1916, 405 persons were indicted for murder of whom 23 and 150 were convicted of first and second degree murder, respectively, and 81, of manslaughter.[3] Commenting on the proportionate differences between these two states with respect to convictions for first degree murder, Sellin pointed out that convictions for first degree murder in Massachusetts were less probably because of the average jury's unwillingness to convict at a time when the death penalty was mandatory in that state.[4]

Finally, this brief review of several studies relating murders to manslaughters cannot fail to mention at least one of

[1] *Capital Punishment in North Carolina.* Special Bulletin No. 10, The North Carolina State Board of Charities and Public Welfare, Raleigh, North Carolina: 1929, p. 173.

[2] Ehrmann, *op. cit.*, p. 78.

[3] H. A. Phelps, "Effectiveness of Life Imprisonment as a Repressive Measure Against Murder in Rhode Island," *Journal of the American Statistical Association* (March Supplement, 1928), 23: 174–181.

[4] Thorsten Sellin, *Minutes of Proceedings and Evidence*, No. 17, June 1–2, 1954, p. 699. (Joint Committee of the Senate and the House of Commons on Capital and Corporal Punishment and Lotteries, Ottawa, 1954.) See also Sellin's comments as a witness in London before the Royal Commission on Capital Punishment, *op. cit.*, for data comparing the ratio of murder to manslaughter.

Verkko's interesting observations in Finland and Europe. Resembling somewhat his previous "laws" regarding the fluctuations of homicides by sex, he claims that murders fluctuate in number less than do other crimes against life, and says that "the greater the number of crimes against life the more limited among them is the percentage of premeditated crimes, murders; and vice versa, with crimes against life declining, the percentage of murders grows."[1] An historical survey of criminal homicide in Philadelphia, based upon data similar to those used in the present study, would make an interesting comparison to Verkko's European data with respect to this generalization.

Insanity

Insanity will not reduce the degree of murder, as insanity is a complete defense, exonerating the accused, or it is no defense at all. Com. v. Wireback, 190 Pa. Supreme Ct. 155 (1899).

Insanity, to be a valid defense, must actually exist in the defendant at the time of the act. Com. v. Washington, 202 Pa. Supreme Ct. 148 (1902).

It is for the jury to decide whether or not the defendant was legally insane at the time the murder was committed. Com. v. Preston, 188 Pa. Supreme Ct. 429 (1898); Com. v. Kilpatrick, 204 Pa. Supreme Ct. 218 (1903).[2]

The proportion of offenders in criminal homicide who were declared insane by the courts was relatively small. Only 17 offenders of the 621 were so identified, although 3 additional offenders who committed suicide after homicide were considered insane as well. Because there were 2 double homicides, there were 19 different victim-offender interrelationships. The race and sex distribution was: 3 Negro male/Negro male cases; 2 Negro male/Negro female; 7 white male/white male; 1 white male/Negro male; 2 Negro female/Negro male; 1 Negro female/Negro female; and 3 white female/white male.[3] There were, therefore, 17 offenders

[1] Verkko, *Homicides and Suicides in Finland*, p. 79.

[2] William F. Hoffman, *Pennsylvania Criminal Law and Criminal Procedure*, p. 126.

[3] The diagonal line again represents "killed by." Thus Negro male/Negro male reads, Negro male killed by Negro male.

312

responsible for 19 deaths, and all relationships but one were intra-racial. Ten victims were family relations (6 wives, 2 husbands, 1 mother, 1 daughter), 2 were close friends, 2 were acquaintances, and 2 were strangers. Obviously then, persons victimized by offenders later declared insane were, like victims in general, intimately associated with their slayers.

Motives recorded by the police for these offenders include altercations, domestic quarrels, jealousy, robbery, and unknown. These homicides were more violent in nature than homicides in general, for while 50 per cent of all victims were killed violently, 13 of the 19 victims of insane offenders were violently slain. Eight of the victims died by shooting, 7 by stabbing, 3 by beating, and 1 by asphyxiation. Three of the homicides occurred in a mental institution (Byberry), 8 took place in the home, and 8 outside the home. Of those that took place in the home, 6 were in kitchens and 2 in living rooms. Alcohol was absent from the homicide situation in 13 of the cases, present in both the victim and offender in 2 cases, present in the victim only in 2, and in the offender only in 3 cases. The relatively high proportion of offenders who had not been drinking indicates the lack of association between alcohol and the type of homicide which is committed by persons later declared insane.

The number of cases is too small for generalization. Perhaps the only important fact that can be drawn from these data *is* the number. Relative to other reports noted below—particularly from England—these 17 offenders (2.7 per cent) constitute an exceptionally small proportion of total offenders.

This cursory examination of several other studies is no attempt at comprehensiveness,[1] but is intended to show the typically low proportion of insane offenders in criminal homicide reported in this country compared to England.

[1] For a concise historical and legal review of insanity with reference to homicide, see Edwin R. Keedy, "Irresistible Impulse as a Defense in the Criminal Law," *University of Pennsylvania Law Review* (May, 1952), 100: 956–993; also, the Isaac Ray Award book by John Biggs, Jr., *The Guilty Mind: Psychiatry and the Law of Homicide*, New York: Harcourt, Brace and Co., 1955.

The studies and reports included in this section are selected as representative of the general patterns found throughout the literature.

Phelps[1] reported that of 330 persons charged in the courts with illegal killing in Rhode Island during the years 1896–1927, only 12, or slightly less than 4 per cent, were declared legally insane. In their analysis of a select group of 611 cases of homicide, Dublin and Bunzel[2] discovered only 8 insane, which was less than 2 per cent of the "458 assailants answerable to the law," and 3 per cent of the 258 who were actually brought to trial. Only 4 of the 153 murderers tried in Cook County during 1926 and 1927, or less than 3 per cent, were declared insane.[3] In his personality study of 200 murderers, Cassidy[4] found only 2 per cent insane and committed to institutions.

Thus, consistently it is reported that approximately 2 to 4 per cent of homicide offenders are insane. If the universe from which the insane proportion is taken refers to all those arrested for criminal homicide, the proportion is usually 2 per cent or less; if the universe is those brought to trial, or those available for trial, typically 3 or 4 per cent are reported insane.

In England, however, about one-third or more of all offenders are declared insane during some stage of legal procedure, either before or after trial. Occasionally, the proportion rises even above this level and may reach, in some years, near the 50 per cent mark. Taking the "guilty but insane" and the "insane and unfit to plead" together, as a percentage of murders known to the police (which is the largest universe used), it was observed that in 1920 the insane represented 33 per cent, and in 1935, 49 per cent.[5] This means that in 1935, about half of all the murders known to have been committed were perpetrated by persons declared insane!

[1] H. A. Phelps, "Rhode Island's Threat Against Murder," *Journal of Criminal Law and Criminology* (February, 1925), 15: 552–567.
[2] Dublin and Bunzel, *op. cit.*, p. 130.
[3] *Illinois Crime Survey*, p. 628.
[4] Cassidy, *op. cit.*, pp. 296–297.
[5] *Guilty But Insane, the Murder Trend*, p. 6. *Annual Report*, 1937–1938, National Council for the Abolition of the Death Penalty.

As the National Council for the Abolition of the Death Penalty has pointed out: "The importance of these statistics lies in their demonstration that murder in England and Wales is to a great extent a crime of insane people. It is legitimate to assume from the circumstances of nearly all the cases in which murder is followed by the suicide of the perpetrator that the state of his mind was so abnormal as to amount to mental derangement. While it is not always possible to produce exact proof of insanity in such cases, it is reasonable to class them with the others in which insanity has been proved."[1]

Figures supplied by the Royal Commission on Capital Punishment indicate that the fifty-year period from 1900 through 1949 contained 4,173 persons arrested for murder, of whom 1,226, or 29 per cent, were declared insane. Moreover, of 3,130 persons who appeared for trial at assizes, 428 were insane on arraignment and 798 were declared "guilty but insane." Combining these two insane groups, 39 per cent of all persons brought for trial at assizes were declared insane.[2]

The much higher proportion of legal insanity in England may partially be accounted for by the mandatory death penalty for murder in England, a fact which probably affects the decision of juries when determining a verdict. The high incidence of the "guilty but insane" classification in England may be

(1) a method of escape from an abhorrent duty,

(2) an index of increasing awareness and recognition of serious mental and emotional disturbances in offenders, or

(3) the result of more detailed psychiatric examination of the homicide offender than is the case in this country.

[1] *Ibid.*, p. 323. If, for the Philadelphia offenders in homicide, it is also assumed that those persons who committed suicide following homicide were sufficiently deranged mentally so as to be declared insane, the 24 offenders who killed themselves could be added to the 17 who were pronounced insane. This total of 41 still constitutes less than 7 per cent of all offenders, a proportion five to seven times less than that in England.

[2] Computed from *Royal Commission on Capital Punishment, 1949–1953 Report*, pp. 300–301.

Abrahamsen, for example, does not believe that the number of reported insane offenders in this country is valid, since most murderers are not given a psychiatric analysis.[1] It seems doubtful, however, that even eliminating these possible explanations for the differentials between the two countries, the proportion in the United States would be very much closer to the British figure. Diagnosis of legal insanity is somewhat subjective, but suicide is an objective fact. There is no doubt that many more offenders commit suicide in England, and since the two phenomena are somewhat related, the proportionate difference between the homicide-suicide rate in this country and in England is probably a good index of the insane differentials.

Perhaps there are important characteristic differences between homicide committed by the insane offender and the sane one, but the literature throws little light on them, and the number of insane cases in Philadelphia is too small for such comparisons. However, East noted that murder by sane offenders occurred most frequently in the age group 21 to 30 years, being 45 per cent of 250 cases. Among 325 insane murders 32 per cent occurred in the age group 21 to 30, and 31 per cent in the age group 31 to 40.[2] For England, at least, the same author observed a further distinction in a comparison of insane murderers admitted to Broadmoor, with 200 sane offenders in a series he investigated. Strangers were in danger more than twice as much from normal offenders as from the insane. Wives and other relatives appeared to be menaced to a greater degree, for these combined family relationships were victims in 32 per cent of the homicides committed by sane offenders and in 56 per cent of the homicides committed by insane offenders.[3]

Perhaps the same type of intimate, personal victim is indicated in a recent study by Albert Kurland, director of medical research at Spring Grove State Hospital in Maryland, and his associates. In this analysis of 52 psychotic murderers, 12 were men who had killed their wives, 8 were

[1] Abrahamsen, *op. cit.*, p. 158.
[2] East, *Society and the Criminal*, p. 376.
[3] East, *Medical Aspects of Crime*, p. 369.

men who had murdered their children, and 2 were women who had slain their husbands. A persecution complex and unconscious homosexuality were found prevalent among these male offenders.[1]

Adequate follow-up studies of offenders in criminal homicide to determine the number who commit suicide or who become insane in prison have not been made. It would be interesting to know how generally valid is Lawes' statement made from Sing Sing, that "of those who have become insane after entering prison (since 1890), 23 per cent had been committed for murder."[2]

[1] Albert A. Kurland, Jacob Morgenstern, and Carolyn Sheets, "A Comparative Study of Wife Murderers Admitted to a State Psychiatric Hospital," *The Journal of Social Therapy* (January, 1955), 1: 7–15.
[2] Lawes, *Life and Death in Sing Sing*, p. 41.

18

SUMMARY

THIS study has attempted to discover and to analyze patterns in criminal homicide from among 588 cases that occurred in Philadelphia, Pennsylvania, between January 1, 1948, and December 31, 1952. The primary source of data was the files of the Homicide Squad, Philadelphia Police Department. Answers were sought to a series of questions regarding 588 victims and 621 offenders involved in criminal homicide with respect to the following: race, sex, and age differences; methods and weapons used to inflict death; seasonal and other temporal patterns; spatial patterns; the relationship between the presence of alcohol and homicide; the degree of violence in homicide; motives; the interpersonal relationship between victim and offender; homicide during the commission of another felony; victim-precipitated homicide; homicide-suicide; unsolved homicide; the tempo of legal procedure; court disposition; and insanity. Suggested associations of numerous attributes of victims and offenders were tested primarily by the chi-square test of significance. A review of the most important reports and studies on criminal homicide in this country has been presented to provide perspective to the local patterns in Philadelphia.

No previous study known to the author has analyzed criminal homicide with the detail and precision of the present research. Moreover, several areas described in this study are either novel to homicide research or are more comprehensively treated than previously. We have shown that much confusion of terminology pervades the literature, that data about victims are often confused with data about offenders; rates per population unit are sometimes confused with reports about proportionate distributions or relative fre-

318

quencies within the universe examined. The general concept of homicide, which includes both criminal and non-criminal homicide, is sometimes reported as just criminal homicide; and criminal homicide, which includes all degrees of murder and manslaughter, is sometimes referred to as murder alone. Furthermore, this study has constantly emphasized the invalidity of inferring characteristics about victims from criminal statistics, some of which supply data only for offenders; or of inferring characteristics about offenders from mortality statistics, which supply data only for victims.

Most previous research has examined *either* the victim *or* the offender. In the present work, analysis has been made of *both* victims and offenders, separately, as distinct units, but also as mutually interacting participants. A societal perspective is interested both in the active, "to kill," and in the passive, "to be killed." It is one type of analysis to consider victims as a social group and offenders as another social group; it is quite a different and more refined type of analysis to consider specific victim-offender relationships, and to find race, sex, age, and other patterns among them.

It has been demonstrated that, although criminal homicide is largely an unplanned act, nonetheless there are in the act discernible, empirical uniformities of specific social phenomena. We have found that there is a *significant* association between criminal homicide and the race and sex of both victims and offenders. Negroes and males involved in homicide far exceed their proportions in the general population, and have rates in homicide many times greater than whites and females. The race-sex specific rate per 100,000 for both victims and offenders reveals the following rank order of magnitude: Negro males, Negro females, white males, white females. Although Negroes of either sex, and males of either race, are positively related to criminal slayings, the association between race and homicide is statistically more *significant* than that between sex and homicide. The relationship of Negroes and males to criminal homicide in Philadelphia confirms reports and studies made elsewhere in this country, although the proportion of female offenders is reportedly much higher in England than in the United States. One of the striking differences between victims and offenders is the fact that white females are nearly three times more likely to be victims than offenders in criminal homicide.

A *significant* association exists between age and criminal homicide, with the age group 20–24 years having the highest rate among offenders, and age groups 25–29 and 30–34 having the highest rate among victims. Offenders, in general, are younger than victims, and Pollak's comments on female "delay" in crime appear to be supported by the fact that females as offenders are older, but as victims are younger than males. The importance of the race factor among offenders is particularly striking in view of the fact that the lowest five-year age-specific rates for Negro males and females are similar to, or higher than the highest of such rates for white males and females, respectively. Although males of both races more frequently commit criminal homicide during their twenties than during any other period of life, Negro males in their early sixties kill as frequently as white males in their early twenties.

Significant associations exist between methods of inflicting death and the race and sex of both victims and offenders. Other studies report higher proportionate use of firearms than is the case in Philadelphia, but we have shown that the hypothesis of a causal relationship between the homicide rate and the proportionate use of firearms should be rejected. We have seen that 39 per cent of all 588 criminal homicides were due to stabbings, 33 per cent to shootings, 22 per cent to beatings, and 6 per cent to other and miscellaneous methods. However, there appears to be a cultural preference by race and sex for particular types of methods and weapons used to inflict death. Males, if Negro, usually stab and are stabbed to death; and if white, beat and are beaten to death. Females generally stab their victims with a kitchen knife, but are very often beaten to death. It is suggested that lack of physical strength relative to the male means that the female must, in most cases of violent encounter with a male, resort to weapons that remove this disadvantage. We have also noted a general and crude relationship between age of the offender and predilection for certain types of weapons, with the incident use of firearms highest among offenders under 20 and those over 50 years of age. It may be that these age groups (as do women who slay men) require some weapon to maintain distance between themselves and their victims, and to offset their limited physical power when involved in an episode of violence.

Although criminal homicides tend to increase during the hot summer months, there is no significant association either by seasons or by months of the year. Other studies report inconsistent conclusions. But homicide is *significantly* related to days of the week and hours of the day. The week-end in general, and Saturday night in particular, are *significantly* associated with criminal homicide, as are the hours between 8:00 P.M. and 2:00 A.M. Between 8:00 P.M. Friday and midnight Sunday there were, during the five years under review, 380 criminal homicides; but from the beginning of Monday morning to 8:00 P.M. Friday, there were only 208. Thus, on the average, 65 per cent of all homicides occurred during the shorter time span of 52 hours, while only 35 per cent occurred during the longer time span of 116 hours. These findings, in general, agree with previous studies of temporal patterns in criminal homicide.

The time between assault and death of the victim varies according to the method employed by the offender. Relatively quick death (within ten minutes after assault) occurred for half of the victims in a shooting, for less than three-tenths in a stabbing, and for only one-sixteenth in a beating. About a third of the victims were dead within ten minutes after assault, slightly less than three-fifths before the first hour had passed, and four-fifths within a day. Only 5 per cent lived more than ten days after being assaulted. Probably fewer persons today die from aggravated assault wounds than was true a generation ago. The data suggest that improved communication with the police, more rapid transportation to a hospital, and advanced medical technology have contributed to the decreasing homicide rates in this country during the last twenty-five years.

321

There is a *significant* association between place where the crime occurred and the race and sex of both victims and offenders. In terms of total cases, the most dangerous single place is the highway (public street, alley, or field), although more slayings occur in the home than oustide the home. Men kill and are killed most frequently in the street, while women kill most often in the kitchen but are killed in the bedroom. For victims and offenders of each race and sex group *significant* differences have been noted with respect to the particular method used to inflict death in a specific place. Most cases of Negro males who kill Negro males involve a stabbing in a public street; most cases of white males who kill white males involve a beating in a public street. However, the high proportion of females who kill with a butcher knife in a kitchen, and of those who are killed in a bedroom by being beaten is associated with the fact that 84 per cent of all female offenders slay males and 87 per cent of all female victims are slain by males. In general, there is a slight tendency for homicides to occur outside the home more frequently during the summer months when collective life is more frequent outdoors than during the winter months, but no association is found between the home/not-home dichotomy and days of the week or hours of the day.

Either or both the victim and the offender had been drinking immediately prior to the slaying in nearly two-thirds of the cases. The presence of alcohol in the homicide situation appears to be *significantly* associated with Negroes—either as victims or offenders—and, separately, with Negro male and female victims. Particular caution must be exercised in evaluating the presence of alcohol in these homicides, since drinking—particularly on Saturday night, the time of highest incidence of homicide—is an integral part of the mores of most groups involved in this crime. A *significantly* higher proportion of week-end homicides than of homicides occurring during the remainder of the week had alcohol present (in either the victim, the offender, or both). An association between alcohol, week-end slayings, and the payment of wages on Friday was indicated and crudely confirmed by the available data. We have, therefore, suggested that when the socio-economic group most likely to commit homicide almost simultaneously receives its weekly wages, purchases alcohol, and socially interacts, it is not unlikely that the incidence of homicide should also rise. Most other studies which examine the relationship between alcohol and homicide analyze the victim *or* the offender, but not the victim and the offender together. This is a failing which has been corrected in the present study, although more precise measurement of the amount of alcohol in the organism at the time of the slaying is called for in future research. Furthermore, gross rates of alcoholism in a city, or other given population unit, on the one hand, compared with gross rates of homicide on the other, are inadequate tools for measuring the relationship between alcohol and homicide, and produce imperfect links between objective fact and theory. The important question is whether alcohol was present in the victim, the offender, or both, at the time of assault. Only by answering this question is it possible to determine whether a relationship exists between alcohol and homicide.

Alcohol is a factor also strongly related to the violence with which an offender kills his victim. Homicides committed by men are *significantly* more violent (as violence is defined in this study) than those committed by women; but there is no association of violence with race or age of the offender. It is clear, however, that slayings with excessive degrees of violence predominate in the home, and are most likely to involve a husband-wife relationship in which the wife is the victim of her husband's brutal beating.

Contrary to many past impressions, analysis of offenders in criminal homicide reveals a relatively high proportion who have a previous police or arrest record. Of total offenders, nearly two-thirds have a previous arrest record, and of total victims, almost half have such a record. Having a previous record is *significantly* associated with males both among victims and offenders, and is obvious from the fact that more male *victims* have such a record than do female *offenders*.

323

The data have further confirmed the hypotheses which state that (1) when an offender has a previous record, he is more likely to have a record of offenses against the person than against property; and that (2) when he has a record of offenses against the person he is more likely than not to have a record of having committed a serious assault offense, such as aggravated assault or assault with intent to kill. Furthermore, analysis of separate race-sex groups reveals that a greater proportion of Negro male and female victims have a previous arrest record than white male and female offenders, respectively. It is of interest to future attempts at prevention and control of potential offenders in criminal homicide, that a larger proportion of offenders with an arrest record have a record of aggravated assault than of all types of property offenses combined. A *significant* relationship is noted also between presence of alcohol in the offender and the offender with a previous arrest record.

Criminal homicide usually results from a vaguely defined altercation, domestic quarrel, jealousy, argument over money, and robbery. These five police-recorded motives are involved in 8 out of every 10 cases. Homicide appears, however, to be more personalized when directed against or by women. There are a few important differences according to motive and the race of either victim or offender.

Most of the 550 identified victim-offender relationships may be classified as primary group relations. Close friends and relatives accounted for over half of the contacts. We have hypothesized, on the basis of previous knowledge, that a higher proportion of primary group relationships characterize victim-offender contacts when females are victims than when males are victims. Observation confirms the hypothesis, for the combined categories which involve primary group contacts constitute 59 per cent of all victim-offender relationships among males, but *significantly* as much as 84 per cent among females. Because white males were killed more frequently than Negro males during the commission of a robbery, the former were also more frequently strangers to their slayers than the latter. Finally, comparison was made of the age of each victim with that of the offender responsible for his death. It was found that 11 victims were infants under one year of age, 26 victims were the same age as their slayers, and of the remaining relationships for which an age difference occurred, about 6 out of 10 offenders were younger than their respective victims. If the victim-offender age differential was 25 years or less, offenders were younger or older than their victims in almost equal proportions; but if the age differential was over 25 years, offenders were younger than their victims in over three-fourths of the relationships.

Mate slayings have been given special attention. Of the 100 husband-wife homicides, 53 victims were wives and 47 were husbands. *Significantly*, the number of wives killed by their husbands constitutes 41 per cent of all women killed, whereas husbands slain by their wives make up only 11 per cent of all men killed. Thus, when a woman committed homicide, she was more likely than a man to kill her mate; and when a man was killed by a woman, he was most likely to be killed by his wife. Husbands were often killed by their wives in the kitchen with a butcher knife, but nearly half of the wives were slain in the bedroom. More male than female offenders in these spouse slayings were found guilty, were convicted of more serious degrees of homicide, and committed suicide.

In 94 per cent of the cases, the victim and the offender were members of the same race, but in only 64 per cent were they of the same sex. Thus, the ratio of intra- to interracial homicide is 15.2 to 1; but the ratio of intra- to inter-sex homicide is only 1.8 to 1. In general, it may be said that victims were homicidally assaulted most frequently by males of their own race, and least frequently by females of another race. Rates per 100,000 population indicate that Negro offenders crossed the race line about six times more frequently than white offenders; but also, that Negroes were victims about three times more frequently than whites in these interracial homicides.

In 32 cases of criminal homicide involving 57 offenders and 6 victims, a felony, in addition to the killing, was perpetrated at the time of the slaying. In most cases, the other

325

felony was robbery, and white males accounted for a larger proportion of these felony-homicides than they did among all homicides in general.

The term *victim-precipitated* homicide has been introduced to refer to those cases in which the victim is a direct, positive precipitator in the crime—the first to use physical force in the homicide drama. After establishing a theoretical and legal basis for analysis, the Philadelphia data reveal several factors *significantly* associated with the 150 victim-precipitated homicides, which is 26 per cent of all the homicides. These factors are: Negro victims and offenders; male victims; female offenders; stabbings; victim-offender relationships involving male victims and female offenders; mate slayings; husbands who were victims in mate slayings; alcohol in the homicide situation; alcohol in the victim; and victims with a previous arrest record, particularly an arrest record of assault. Thus, in most of these cases, the roles and characteristics of the victim and offender are reversed, and the victim assumes the role of determinant. This study has been one of the first to provide significant empirical data to support von Hentig's assertions about the contribution of the victim to the genesis of his own victimization.

Of all offenders arrested for criminal homicide, 4 per cent —half of whom were whites—committed suicide after the crime. In these cases, victims and offenders of the opposite sex outnumbered those of the same sex by a ratio of 9 to 1. Of the 24 homicide-suicides, 22 were males, nearly half of whom were men who had killed their wives. In only one of the 47 cases in which a wife killed her husband did she later commit suicide; but in 10 of the 53 cases in which a husband killed his wife he committed suicide. Analysis and evaluation of these homicide-suicides indicate that half of the homicides would have been classified as first degree murder had the offender experienced a court trial. As a result, even with the low amount of suicide after homicide in this country, more offenders inflict death upon themselves than are put to death by the social sanction of legal execution. Twelve persons who committed suicide appear to have committed first degree

326

murder. Thus the number of self-inflicted "executions" is greater than the 7 offenders who were sentenced to death by a court of record. Finally, suicide following homicide is 5 to 6 times more frequent in England than in the United States.

Of the 588 homicides, 38 have been classified as unsolved. It has been necessary to explore possible definitions of an unsolved case, and suggest an operationally useful definition. Comparisons of the unsolved with solved cases reveal that the former have higher proportions of: white male and female victims; victims 65 years of age and over; robbery as a prelude to the slaying; victims who were strangers to their assailants; beatings; week-end slayings; and assaults that occurred in the public street.

Finally, analysis has been made of the tempo of legal procedures, of court disposition, designation of the degree of homicide, insanity, and sentences imposed by the court. Two-thirds of the offenders were arrested on the same day the crime was committed, and over half appeared in court for trial within six months after the crime. Two-thirds of those taken into police custody, and over three-quarters of those who experienced a court trial were declared guilty. Proportionately, Negroes and males were convicted more frequently than whites and females; but previous analysis of the nature of these cases reveals that Negroes and males had in fact committed more serious offenses, and that a charge of unjust race and sex discrimination in court would not be necessarily correct. Of the 387 offenders convicted and sentenced, 20 per cent were guilty of murder in the first degree, 29 per cent, of murder in the second degree, 36 per cent, of voluntary manslaughter, and 15 per cent, of involuntary manslaughter. Less than 3 per cent of the offenders were declared insane by the courts, which is a proportion similar to that reported in other studies in this country, but considerably smaller than the 30 per cent or more reported insane in England.

19

IMPLICATIONS AND SUGGESTIONS
FOR RESEARCH

THE patterns of criminal homicide described and analyzed in the present study probably pose as many problems as they provide answers to questions raised in the first chapter. Whichever approach a theory of causation of homicide and other assault crimes may take—biological, psychological, or sociological—it certainly must encompass the observations of empirical regularities which emerged from the foregoing analysis. Theories of social action should not be in a vacuum, but must begin with observed facts, produce paradigms of reality, hypothesize new associations of facts, test them, and restate confirmed interpretations until prediction and control become possible.

The data and significant associations of variables that depict major patterns of the elements involved in criminal homicide suggest that there may exist a sub-culture of violence within the larger community culture that surrounds it, and that the conduct norms of the former are in conflict with those of the latter. Sellin has observed: "Conduct norms are, therefore, found wherever social groups are found, i.e., universally. They are not the creation of any one normative group; they are not confined within political boundaries; they are not necessarily embodied in law. . . . Significant is the presence or absence in that violator of the criminal law norm as applying to the life situation involved, the manner in which this norm was incorporated in personality, the place it has in the violator's configuration of personality elements and scale of values, and its strength. Ultimately science must be able to state that if a person with certain personality elements in a certain configuration happens to be placed in a certain typical life situation, he will probably react in a certain manner, whether the law punishes this response as a crime or tolerates it as unimportant."[1]

Our analysis implies that there may be a sub-culture of violence which does not define personal assaults as wrong or antisocial; in which quick resort to physical aggression is a socially approved and expected concomitant of certain stimuli; and in which violence has become a familiar but often deadly partner in life's struggles. Attacks against the person are made without compunction, despite the middle-class value-system which views such acts as the most heinous of crimes. A conflict or inconsistency of social norms is most apparent, and the value-system of the reference group with which the individual differentially associates and identifies, determines whether assaultive behavior is necessary, expected, or desirable in specific social situations. When an insult or argument is defined as trivial and petty by the prevailing culture norms, but as signals for physical attack by a sub-cultural tradition, culture conflict exists. When a blow of the fist is casually accepted as normal response to certain stimuli, when knives are commonly carried for personal defense, and a homicidal stabbing is as frequent as Saturday night, then social control against violence is weak. Under such circumstances there appears to be a sub-culture where the collective id dominates social consciousness—i.e., where the basic urges, drives, and impulses of the group members are less harmonized with each other or external reality; where basic desires are less inhibited, restricted, or restrained; where reduction of tension and satisfaction of needs are characterized by immediacy and directness; and where the social regulators of conduct are weak and less omnipresent than in the larger culture of which this collectivity is a part. Thus, altercations that lead to homicide become symptoms of unconscious destructive impulses laid bare in a sub-culture where toleration—if not encouragement—of violence is part of the normative structure.

[1] Thorsten Sellin, *Culture Conflict and Crime*, New York: Social Science Research Council, 1938, pp. 30, 44-45.

329

Additional implications and suggestions for further research follow.

(1) The high incidence of homicide among Negroes requires combined research by students of race and crime to fathom all the ramifications this consistent finding implies. Future research should provide for more precise standardization of race and sex than has been the case in past research. Negroes and whites should be compared on the basis of several controlled variables, including socio-economic status, education, occupation, etc. A crude attempt in the present study to determine whether the high Negro homicide rate is attributable to the fact that the greatest proportion of Negroes are in the lower end of the occupational hierarchy failed to produce any significant difference in the white and Negro male rate among offenders. A biological explanation of the significant race differential is certainly not an implication of this study, although the door to future research in this area should not be closed any more than to other avenues of objective research. However, more fruitful research seems at present to lie in analysis of the socio-psychological position of whites and Negroes. Our data suggest that a sub-culture of violence exists among a certain portion of the lower socio-economic group—especially comprised of males and Negroes. The social controls of the larger community are weakened in this sub-cultural milieu; and aggression, manifested in terms of homicidal assaults, is heightened. But why in terms of homicidal assaults? Homicide and other assaultive acts combined constitute only one index of aggression. Why should a quantitatively unknown but presumed greater amount of frustration in the environment of the Negro, so largely a convergent result of discrimination, restricted mobility, and conflicting moral norms, find aggressive outlet specifically in a high incidence of homicide? The Henry and Short[1] thesis of other-oriented aggression manifested by lower-status groups and self-oriented aggression manifested by higher-status groups may be a partial answer.

[1] Henry and Short, *op. cit.*

Finally, with respect to race, a general impression which emerged out of the raw data in police files suggests that many homicides were committed by recent Negro migrants from the South. A study of migration patterns, and of the impact of urbanization on the homicide rate might prove of some value.

(2) The invalidity and unreliability of information available on occupation in the police files made impossible a detailed analysis of homicide according to this variable, although thorough reading of each homicide case left little doubt that at least 9 out of 10 offenders were in the skilled, semiskilled, service, unskilled, and unemployed categories. Even with additional research that is able to determine with greater accuracy whether a significant association exists between occupation and homicide, we shall still be confronted with difficult questions about such a relationship should it exist. Surely it is not the mere fact of occupation which explains why a laborer commits homicide more frequently than a clerk. Intelligence, resourcefulness, education, frustration related to occupation, work attitudes, job opportunities, personality types in different occupations, primary group relationships arising out of occupation contacts, etc., must be explored more fully.

(3) In addition to more studies regarding indices of social disorganization and crimes against the person, such as homicide, we need more precise research regarding the relationship between density of population and homicide. Perhaps the theoretical statements of early sociologists such as Durkheim and Tarde, combined with contemporary empirical demographic data would be suggestive of meaningful questions to ask about density and homicide. Are personal animosities, leading to violent outbursts and assaults, increased in those ecological areas where collective life is immersed in the density of population and where there is proportionately a greater number of personal contacts? More precise measurements of the degree of social integration (particularly in primary groups) suggested by Durkheim in his explanation of differential rates of suicide, combined

with a study of the density of varied population groups may add something of value to a neglected area of interdisciplinary research. The recent study of suicide in London by Peter Sainsbury[1] provides an excellent example for a similar study of homicide.

(4) Although we have rejected the idea that homicide rates are higher in the United States than in England because of easier access to firearms, it cannot be denied that a culture habit of carrying some deadly weapon is conducive to usage, and, hence, homicide. A lower-class culture tradition, particularly among Negro males, of carrying switchblade and other types of knives classified as deadly weapons, is undoubtedly related to the high number of stabbings recorded in the present study. A 1952 ordinance in Philadelphia and a 1956 state law prohibit the sale and possession of such knives. It would be of some interest to know how effectively these laws are enforced, and the extent to which they play some part in reducing criminal homicide. However, so long as butcher knives are used in the kitchen and wives feel sufficiently justified by reason or by passion to kill their husbands, the rate of female offenders in criminal homicide will not be appreciably reduced by legislation of any sort. Veli Verkko's comments[2] regarding greater fluctuations in the male homicide rate and the relative stability of the female homicide rate seem most appropriate at this point, and should be subjected to further research.

(5) An hypothesis has been suggested that the lower rate of homicide in general, and of criminal homicide in particular, compared to a generation ago, are partially due to better communication with the police, more rapid transportation to a hospital, and advances in medical technology. Empirical research is suggested which would test this hypothesis to determine, first, its validity, and second, the degree to which these three factors combined contribute to the observed lower rates of criminal slayings today. As official statistics record an increase of offenses against the person—particu-

[1] Peter Sainsbury, *Suicide in London*, London: The Institute of Psychiatry, 1955.
[2] Verkko, *Homicides and Suicides in Finland*, pp. 55–56.

larly of aggravated assault and of assault with intent to kill—while simultaneously recording a decrease in homicide, we cannot blithely accept the latter as an index of lessened hostility, less destructive aggression outlet, high standard of living, or any of the other socio-psychological explanations without consideration of the three factors mentioned above. In short, if the means of communication, transportation, and medical therapy were today the same as twenty-five years ago, would the amount of potential homicidal assaults be similar? Examination of hospital records of assault victims admitted for emergency care, the types of assaults suffered, and the kinds of treatment administered, may aid analysis. Expert medical evaluation of individual admissions of assault victims who died during an earlier period, but could have survived under present medical treatment, would be an important part of such analysis. Here is an obvious, but promising line of research suggested by the present study. These three factors—communication, transportation, and medical technology—are more or less "surface" and pedestrian explanations of the continued decrease of homicide rates. They lack the sophistication of the more complex sociological and psychoanalytical interpretations. Yet we may discover that these three factors contribute more fully than do any other factors to this decrease.

(6) Police authorities and the pathologist should make every effort to collect data on the amount of alcohol in the blood stream, urine, liver, or brain of the victim, and the amount of alcohol in the offender. The works of Gettler and Tiber, Dubowski and Shupe, and others should be consulted for standardizing the practice of more precise measurement of the presence of alcohol in the organism.[1] Research into the relationship between alcohol and homicide (and other assault crimes) should relate each individual victim to his specific offender, and thus go beyond most present studies which fail to account for the dynamic interplay of these two persons in a single homicide situation. Furthermore, additional research on the association between homicide, alcohol,

[1] See Chapter 8, p. 135, note 1.

and simultaneous payment of wages to semiskilled laborers and unskilled laborers may confirm the hypothesis reported in the present study. Perhaps city-wide staggering of the days when most wage earners are paid would reduce the concentrated consumption of alcohol. Because alcohol has been shown to be related to homicide, scattered pay days might either (*a*) reduce the homicide rate, or (*b*) merely distribute homicides more evenly throughout the week or, (*c*) have no effect whatever. At least, social experimentation may be worth while.

(7) There is not, at present, an adequate explanation for the much higher proportions of suicides after homicide and of legal insanity in England compared to the United States. Race, sex, and age standardizations apparently do not supply satisfactory answers to the obvious questions that might be raised. Does the answer lie in differential rates of conviction? In the relatively greater certainty of prolonged punishment in England? In an assumed higher value put on human life in that country, and, hence, in a greater sense of guilt and need for punishment because of having committed homicide? Or in deeper national character differentials than any of these factors suggest? Research should attempt to answer how homicide-suicide fits into general theories of each type of violent death separately and combined. However, paucity of empirical facts about homicide-suicide at present prevents statistical confirmation of many sociologic and psychoanalytic hypotheses. The most pressing need in this area of research is for data.

(8) Additional studies of a larger number of unsolved homicides compared to solved cases should be made, and may provide new insights of benefit to police investigation.

(9) Comparison of coroners' records with police files could demonstrate more precisely the differences involved in the use of either as source material for generalizations about homicide.

(10) Historical and anthropological analyses of homicide focused on both victims and offenders would make useful comparisons to our present understanding of the phenomenon.

The difficulties involved in such analyses are as great as those involved in an international comparison of homicide statistics. This last type of comparison is also needed for fuller understanding of differential variables associated with the almost universally condemned act of private killing. The work done by Sellin[1] and Verkko[2] in international comparison, and the study of the law of primitive man by Hoebel[3] provide a beginning for these types of research.

(11) If criminal homicide were committed by persons who had not previously been arrested, identification of potential offenders would probably be impossible. Students of criminology who speculate that the typical slayer is a first offender who has never given society reason to suspect his subsequent behavior, generally speak of the unpredictability of homicide. Typical is the following statement by two psychiatrists:

> It is our opinion that the discipline of psychiatry has not yet developed valid criteria of sufficient degree of predictive reliability to justify hard and fast distinction *before* the act between the individual who is likely to commit a crime of violence, such as rape or homicide, and the one who will not ever translate his emotional conflicts into aggressive, destructive behavior.[4]

Frankel observes: "To completely fathom the secret processes of the mind of a man which impels him to kill another human being has not yet been vouchsafed to even the most profound student of the mainsprings of human action."[5] East, too, contends that because murder is an intensely emotional situation in which a man "who has always behaved in a perfectly normal manner except for the few seconds in his life when the murder is committed,"[6] we can hardly predict his outburst. The present study implies that these

[1] Sellin, "Is Murder Increasing in Europe?" *op. cit.*
[2] Verkko, "Survey of Current Practices in Criminal Statistics," Part I and Part III, *op. cit.*
[3] Hoebel, *The Law of Primitive Man.*
[4] Bernard A. Cruvant, and Francis N. Waldrop, "The Murderer in the Mental Institution," *The Annals of the American Academy of Political and Social Science* (November, 1952), 284: 36.
[5] Frankel, *op. cit.*, p. 686.
[6] East, *Society and the Criminal*, p. 383.

335

statements are not applicable to most Philadelphia offenders, nor to offenders in criminal homicide generally.

Joseph Catton, Clinical Professor of Medicine at Stanford University, believes that "out of each one hundred persons who are the killers of tomorrow, there are sixty who will slay regardless of what is done concerning them or the society in which they live."[1] The author found about 40 per cent of offenders who had observable emotional or behavioral traits that were other than normal or who were previously in conflict with the law. Nevertheless, early recognition and positive treatment of this group may save the lives of a few by preventing some potential homicide offenders from committing their major crimes. At least, Catton believes the effort is worth while.

Abrahamsen speaks optimistically of this effort and says that "if we know that certain inner conflicts and frustrations cause lifelong suffering which may culminate in a crime such as homicide, there is a great chance to detect and prevent potential crimes. A way to find those potential murderers would be to establish clinics in which all antisocial persons would be examined and receive treatment."[2]

Sir John Macdonell's statement that homicide is generally the last of a series of acts of violence sounds plausible in view of the findings in this study. The Philadelphia data have shown that 64 per cent of offenders have a previous arrest record, that of these 66 per cent have a record of offenses against the person, and that of these 73 per cent have a record of aggravated assault. Many of the persons previously arrested were convicted but given relatively light sentences and probably little constructive attention. The facts suggest that homicide is the apex crime—a crescendo built upon previous assault crimes. Wechsler and Michael[3] also referred to this phenomenon and suggested that society should make attempts—feeble though they may be at first—to recognize early and to treat more carefully the potential homicide

[1] Joseph Catton, *Behind the Scenes of Murder*, New York: W. W. Norton and Co., Inc., 1940, p. 291.
[2] Abrahamsen, *op. cit.*, p. 175.
[3] Wechsler and Michael, *op. cit.*, pp. 757–761.

offenders. The implication, then, is that if sufficient attention, supervision, and follow-up by appropriate authorities were applied to the person who commits aggravated assault, assault with intent to kill, or a series of less serious personal assaults, society would be able to exercise some control over the offense of homicide, and the number of killings accordingly might decrease.

(12) Future research should make clear when mortality statistics (victim data only) and when criminal statistics (usually offender data only) are used, and should devote more attention to study of the victim. We have noted the importance of victim-offender relationships and the fact that the victim, as well as the offender, often has a previous record of contact with the law. The 150 victim-precipitated cases have demonstrated that some persons are almost "homicide prone." Perhaps the psychological studies of "accident-prone" persons could be applied also to homicide.

(13) In view of many of the findings and implications in this study, and particularly in view of the fact that a large proportion of both victims and offenders have a previous record, it may be contended that crime is a social institution, that the structure and functions of this institution can be compared to other universally acknowledged institutions. Perhaps the modes of procedure are less structuralized and less formalized than those of the more positive institutions, but needs and interests may be satisfied and functions served by behavior that contravenes the law as well as by behavior that conforms to the law. In some cases the victim of homicide is an offender in reverse, and in some, the victim and offender are both previous criminal offenders who have made repeated attacks against the social order. In such cases, the death of one and the penal segregation of the other may not be totally undesirable. Homicide may seem to be an extreme means of eliminating an element of society that has been consistently deviant and dangerous, but the institution of which homicide may be a part functions on a more violent level of social interaction than other and more constructive institutions. The relation between associations, institutions,

and interests described by MacIver[1] could provide a useful conceptual scheme for analysis of the sort suggested by these comments.

(14) Erroneous statements are often made about the annual number of first degree murders. The number of criminal homicides reported by the F.B.I. in *Uniform Crime Reports* is frequently and incorrectly published in the press or reported by public officials as the number of murders, or even as the number of first degree murders committed. Actually, there are no accurate data available regarding the number of first degree murders annually committed in this country. Court or prison statistics are not valid as indexes of the amount of such murders. It would be, therefore, of considerable value to the researcher, to the police, and to other authorities, if there were available some valid measurement of the amount of first degree murder known to have been committed. Valid information could tell us about the volume and trend of first degree murders for different periods of time, both in total and for different segments of the population and geographical areas. It could further provide a basis for the evaluation of existing preventive and remedial programs and for action by legislative bodies. Finally, it could give us some idea of the ratio of first degree murders to the total amount of criminal homicide known to the police.

It might be possible to have a panel of judges (not in the legal sense, necessarily) evaluate the legal designation of all cases of criminal homicide found in the police files of a given community. Probably determination of cases according to all the refined degrees of criminal homicide would be too difficult a task, but relatively accurate determination of at least first degree murders would be of sufficient value and as much as could be expected from this method. Homicide cases that do not appear or are not legally designated in court would be included in the total number evaluated. These are the homicide-suicide, fugitive, unsolved, nol-prossed, and other

[1] R. M. MacIver, *Society: A Textbook of Sociology*, New York: Rinehart and Co., Inc., 1937, pp. 11–16.

338

types of cases. There would be some probable error of estimation of the number of first degree murders for various and obvious reasons, but the true amount of such offenses could be safely asserted to lie somewhere between a conservative estimated minimum and a liberal estimated maximum. Several factors could aid in establishing a minimum number of cases as capital ones. These factors are: confessions of premeditation, felony-murders, cases that fit precisely into the legal interpretation of first degree murder, and judicial precedence. Beyond this minimum number, expert evaluation of criminal homicides listed and described by the police could establish an upper limit. This minimum-maximum range could provide the most valid index available of the amount of first degree murders. Replication of such a procedure from one community to another, from one state or region to another, could provide useful comparative statistics, and could make possible a more accurate measurement of the deterrent value of capital punishment than is now possible by using crude homicide rates.

(15) Follow-up studies of murderers and other offenders in criminal homicide could examine the post-offense adjustment of these persons. Prison records are usually more comprehensive than any other source material for criminological research, despite the fact that they are wholly inadequate as a valid index of the amount and type of crime in a community. Research might examine the status and role of the inmate sentenced for having committed criminal homicide; how he fits into the social hierarchy of the prison community as described by Clemmer,[1] Hayner and Ash,[2] McCorkle and Korn,[3] and others; how he adjusts or fails to adjust to institutional and post-institutional experience. By means of

[1] Donald Clemmer, *The Prison Community*, Boston: Christopher Publishing House, 1940.
[2] Norman S. Hayner and Ellis Ash, "The Prisoner Community as a Social Group," *American Sociological Review* (June, 1939), 4: 362–369.
[3] Lloyd W. McCorkle and Richard R. Korn, "Resocialization Within Walls," *The Annals of the American Academy of Political and Social Science* (May, 1954), 293: 88–98. For a useful list of previous studies of the prison community, see Morris G. Caldwell, "Group Dynamics in the Prison Community," *Journal of Criminal Law, Criminology and Police Science* (January–February, 1956), 46: 648–657.

an open-end interview, the researcher might seek to uncover attitudes of these offenders toward the offense they have committed, the victim, society at large, and their arrest, court, and prison experience. Analysis of tendencies toward suicide, feelings of remorse or guilt, desire for expiation through punishment, and other such reactions—all related to the pre-offense characteristics of the offender and the type of homicide he committed—could prove of value to both prison and parole authorities.

There can be little debate with Frankel's statement that "much scientific work remains to be done and systematic inquiries will have to be made to give us more accurate knowledge of the inherent characteristics of the individual murderer, the social and economic environment out of which he grows and the motives which impel him to such a grave act."[1] The study of criminal homicide is part of the larger study of human behavior, of unusual deviance from conduct norms that govern the lives even of many who kill. From such a study we should hope to learn more about the relationship between the individual and his social group, to contribute substantially to the increasing empiricism of the social sciences, and to link more firmly theory to fact.

[1] Frankel, *op. cit.*, p. 688.

BIBLIOGRAPHY

Books

Abrahamsen, David. *Crime and the Human Mind.* New York: Columbia University Press, 1944.

Ahearn, Danny. *How to Commit a Murder.* New York: Ives Washburn, 1930.

Alexander, Franz, and Healy, W. *Roots of Crime.* New York: Alfred A. Knopf, 1935.

Arkin, H., and Colton, R. R. *An Outline of Statistical Methods,* 4th ed. New York: Barnes and Noble, Inc., 1939.

Aschaffenburg, Gustav. *Crime and its Repression.* Boston: Little, Brown and Co., 1913.

Biggs, John, Jr. *The Guilty Mind: Psychiatry and the Law of Homicide.* New York: Harcourt, Brace and Co., 1955.

Bjerre, Andreas. *The Psychology of Murder.* London: Longmans, Green, 1927.

Bonger, W. A. *Criminality and Economic Conditions.* Boston: Little, Brown, and Co., 1916.

Bossard, J. H. S. *The Sociology of Child Development.* New York: Harper and Brothers, 1948.

Bossard, James H. S., and Boll, Eleanor. *Family Ritual.* Philadelphia: University of Pennsylvania Press, 1950.

Brearley, H. C. *Homicide in the United States.* Chapel Hill: The University of North Carolina Press, 1932.

Brownlee, K. A. *Industrial Experimentation,* 4th ed. New York: Chemical Publishing Co., Inc., 1953.

Bye, Raymond T. *Capital Punishment in the United States.* Philadelphia: The Committee on Philanthropic Labor of Philadelphia, 1918.

Calvert, E. Roy. *Capital Punishment in the Twentieth Century.* London and New York: G. P. Putnam's Sons, 1927.

Casey, Robert S., and Perry, James W. (editors). *Punched Cards, Their Applications to Science and Industry.* New York: Reinhold Publishing Corporation, 1951.

Catton, Joseph. *Behind the Scenes of Murder.* New York: W. W. Norton and Co., Inc., 1940.

Cavan, Ruth. *Suicide*. Chicago: University of Chicago Press, 1928.

Cleckley, Hervey. *The Mask of Sanity*. St. Louis: C. V. Mosby Co., 1941.

Clemmer, Donald. *The Prison Community*. Boston: Christopher Publishing House, 1940.

Cohen, Louis H. *Murder, Madness and the Law*. New York: The World Publishing Co., 1952.

DeQuincey, Thomas, Bulwer-Lytton, Edward, and Jerrold, Douglas. *The Arts of Cheating, Swindling, and Murder*. New York: The Arnold Co., 1925.

DeQuiros, Bernaldo. *Modern Theories of Criminality*. Boston: Little, Brown, and Co., 1911.

Dexter, Edwin. *Weather Influences: An Empirical Study of the Mental and Psychological Effects of Definite Meteorological Conditions*. New York: Macmillan and Co., 1904.

Dollard, John, Miller, Neal E., Doob, Leonard, Mowrer, O. H., and Sears, Robert R. *Frustration and Aggression*. New Haven: Yale University Press, The Institute of Human Relations, 1939.

Durkheim, Emile. *Suicide: A Study in Sociology*. Translated by John A. Spaulding and George Simpson. Glencoe, Illinois: The Free Press, 1951.

East, W. N. *Medical Aspects of Crime*. London: J. and A. Churchill, 1936.

East, W. N. *Society and the Criminal*. Springfield, Illinois: Charles C. Thomas Co., 1951.

Elliott, Mabel. *Crime in Modern Society*. New York: Harper and Brothers, 1952.

Elwin, Verrier. *Maria Murder and Suicide*. London: Oxford University Press, 1943.

Ferri, Enrico. *Criminal Sociology*. Boston: Little, Brown, and Co., 1917.

Fink, Arthur. *Causes of Crime*. Philadelphia: University of Pennsylvania Press, 1938.

Fisher, R. A. *Statistical Methods for Research Workers*, 6th ed. London: Oliver and Boyd, 1936.

Freud, Anna. *The Ego and the Mechanism of Defense*. Translated by Cecil Baines. New York: International Universities Press, Inc., 1946.

Fry, Margery. *Arms of the Law*. London: Victor Gollancz, Ltd., 1951.

Garofalo, Baron Raffaele. *Criminology*. Boston: Little, Brown, and Co., 1914.

Gillin, J. L. *The Wisconsin Prisoner*. Madison: University of Wisconsin Press, 1946.

Glueck, Sheldon, and Glueck, Eleanor. *After-Conduct of Discharged Offenders*. London: Macmillan and Co., Ltd., 1946.

Glueck, Sheldon, and Glueck, Eleanor. 500 *Criminal Careers*. New York: Alfred A. Knopf, 1930.

Hagood, M. J. *Statistics for Sociologists*. New York: Henry Holt and Co., 1941.

Handbook of Correctional Psychology. Edited by Robert M. Lindner and Robert V. Seliger. New York: Philosophical Library, 1947.

Henry, Andrew F., and Short, James F., Jr. *Suicide and Homicide*. Glencoe, Illinois: The Free Press, 1954.

Hoebel, E. Adamson. *The Law of Primitive Man*. Cambridge, Massachusetts: Harvard University Press, 1954.

Hoffman, Frederick L. *The Homicide Problem*. Newark, New Jersey: The Prudential Press, 1925.

Hoffman, William F. *Pennsylvania Criminal Law and Criminal Procedure*, 4th ed. Wynnewood, Pa.: William F. Hoffman, 1952.

Holbrook, Steward H. *Murder Out Yonder*. New York: Macmillan and Co., 1941.

Hooton, Earnest Albert. *The American Criminal, An Anthropological Study*, Vol. 1. Cambridge, Massachusetts: Harvard University Press, 1939.

Hurwitz, Stephan. *Criminology*. Copenhagen: G. E. C. Gads Forlag, 1952.

Hynd, Alan. *Murder! Great True Crime Cases*. New York: Penguin Books, Inc., 1947.

The Illinois Crime Survey. Chicago: Illinois Association for Criminal Justice and the Chicago Crime Commission, 1929.

Jackson, Joseph Henry (editor). *San Francisco Murders*. New York: Bantam Books, Duell, Sloan and Pearce, 1947.

Jesse, F. Tennyson. *Murder and Its Motives*. New York: Alfred A. Knopf, 1924.

Kenny, C. S. *Outlines of Criminal Law*, 10th ed. Cambridge, England: The University Press, 1920.

Lawes, Lewis E. *Life and Death in Sing Sing*. Garden City, New York: Garden Publishing Co., 1928.

Lawes, Lewis E. *Meet the Murderer.* New York: Harper and Brothers, 1940.

Lindner, Robert M. *Rebel without a Cause.* New York: Greene and Stratton, 1944.

Lombroso, Cesare. *Crime, Its Causes and Remedies.* Boston: Little, Brown, and Co., 1911.

MacIver, R. M. *Society: A Textbook of Sociology.* New York: Rinehart and Co., Inc., 1937.

Mayo-Smith, Richard. *Statistics and Sociology.* New York: Macmillan and Co., 1907.

The Medicolegal Necropsy. Edited by Thomas B. Magath. (Symposium held at 12th Annual Convention of the American Society of Clinical Pathologists, Milwaukee, Wisconsin, June 9, 1933.) Baltimore: The Williams and Wilkins Co., 1934.

The Missouri Crime Survey. New York: The Macmillan Co., 1926.

The Modern Approach to Criminal Law. Preface by P. H. Winfield. Collected essays by Davies, Jackson, *et al.* London: Macmillan and Co., Ltd., 1945.

Moroney, M. J. *Facts from Figures.* Harmondsworth, England: Penguin Books, 1951.

Morris, Albert. *Homicide: An Approach to the Problem of Crime.* Boston: Boston University Press, 1955.

Parmelee, Maurice. *Criminology.* New York: Macmillan and Co., 1918.

Pollak, Otto. *The Criminality of Women.* Philadelphia: University of Pennsylvania Press, 1950.

Porterfield, Austin L. *Youth in Trouble.* Fort Worth: Leo Potishman Foundation, 1946.

Porterfield, Austin L., Talbert, Robert H. and Mundhenke, H. R. *Crime, Suicide, and Social Well-Being.* Fort Worth: Leo Potishman Foundation, 1948.

Porterfield, Austin L., and Talbert, Robert H. *Mid-Century Crime in Our Culture: Personality and Crime in the Cultural Patterns of American States.* Fort Worth: Leo Potishman Foundation, 1954.

Pound, Roscoe. *Criminal Justice in America.* New York: Henry Holt and Co., 1930.

Radzinowicz, Leon. *A History of English Criminal Law and Its Administration from 1750—The Movement for Reform, 1750–1833.* New York: Macmillan and Co., 1948.

Radzinowicz, Leon. *The Modern Approach to Criminal Law.* London: Macmillan and Co., Ltd., 1945.

Riasonovsky, V. A. *Customary Law of the Nomadic Tribes of Siberia.* Tienstin, 1938.

Sacks, Jerome Gerald. *Troublemaking in Prison.* Washington, D.C.: The Catholic University of America, 1942.

Sainsbury, Peter. *Suicide in London.* London: The Institute of Psychiatry, 1955.

Schlapp, Max, and Smith, Edward H. *The New Criminology.* New York: Boni and Liveright, 1928.

Sellin, Thorsten. *Culture Conflict and Crime.* New York: Social Science Research Council, 1938.

Sellin, Thorsten. *Crime and the Depression.* New York: Social Science Research Council Memorandum, 1937.

Sellin, Thorsten. *The Criminality of Youth.* Philadelphia: The American Law Institute, 1940.

Semmes, Raphael. *Crime and Punishment in Early Maryland.* Baltimore: The Johns Hopkins Press, 1938.

Sethna, M. J. *Society and the Criminal.* Bombay: Leaders' Press Ltd., 1952.

Sleeman, Colonel James L. *Thug, or a Million Murders.* London: Sampson Low, Marston and Co., Ltd., 1933.

Snyder, Le Moyne. *Homicide Investigation.* Springfield, Illinois: Charles C. Thomas, 1950.

Stanley, Leo L. *Men at Their Worst.* New York: D. Appleton-Century, 1940.

Stephen, J. F. *A History of the Criminal Law,* 3 vols. London: Macmillan and Co., Ltd., 1883.

Sutherland, E. H. *Principles of Criminology.* New York: Lippincott, 1947.

Taft, Donald. *Criminology.* New York: Macmillan and Co., 1952.

Tallack, William. *Penological and Preventive Principles,* 2nd ed. London: Wertheimer, Lea, and Co., 1896.

Tarde, Gabriel. *Penal Philosophy.* Boston: Little, Brown and Co., 1912.

Templewood, Viscount. *The Shadow of the Gallows.* London: Victor Gollancz, Ltd., 1951.

Thomas, Franklin. *The Environmental Basis of Society.* New York: D. Appleton-Century, 1925.

Tulchin, Simon H. *Intelligence and Crime.* Chicago: University of Chicago Press, 1939.

Turkus, Burt, and Fedor, Sid. *Murder, Inc.* Garden City, New York: Doubleday and Co., Inc., Permabook Ed., 1952.

Uniform Crime Reporting. A Complete Manual for Police, Revised. New York: Committee on Uniform Crime Records, International Association of Chiefs of Police, 1929.

Verkko, Veli. *Homicides and Suicides in Finland and Their Dependence on National Character.* Copenhagen: G. E. C. Gads Forlag, 1951.

Vollmer, August. *The Police and Modern Society.* Berkeley, California: University of California Press, 1936.

Von Hentig, Hans. *Crime: Causes and Conditions.* New York: McGraw-Hill Book Co., Inc., 1947.

Von Hentig, Hans. *The Criminal and His Victim.* New Haven: Yale University Press, 1948.

Wertham, Frederic. *Dark Legend: A Study in Murder.* New York: Duell, Sloan and Pearce, 1941.

Wertham, Frederic. *The Show of Violence.* New York: Doubleday and Co., 1949.

Wilson, E. Bright. *An Introduction to Scientific Research.* New York: McGraw-Hill Book Co., 1952.

Yule, G. U., and Kendall, M. G. *An Introduction to the Theory of Statistics*, 14th ed. New York: Hafner Publishing Co., 1950.

Public Documents

Canada. *Minutes of Proceedings and Evidence.* Witness: Prof. Thorsten Sellin. Ottawa: Joint Committee of the Senate and the House of Commons on Capital and Corporal Punishment and Lotteries, 1954.

Commonwealth of Pennsylvania. *Store Sales Analyses, Calendar Year, 1953, Special Summaries.* Harrisburg, Pa.: Liquor Control Board, Bureau of Accounting and Service, Statistics Division, 1953.

Federal Bureau of Investigation, U.S. Department of Justice. *Uniform Crime Reports.* Vol. 19, No. 2. Washington: Government Printing Office, 1948.

Federal Bureau of Investigation, U.S. Department of Justice. *Uniform Crime Reports.* Vol. 21, No. 2. Washington: Government Printing Office, 1950.

Federal Bureau of Investigation, U.S. Department of Justice. *Uniform Crime Reports.* Vol. 22, No. 1. Washington: Government Printing Office, 1951.

Federal Bureau of Prisons. *National Prisoner Statistics, Prisoners in State and Federal Institutions, 1950.* Washington: Government Printing Office, 1954.

Great Britain. *Minutes of Evidence Taken Before the Royal Commission on Capital Punishment.* Witness: Prof. Thorsten Sellin. London: H.M. Stationery Office, 1951.

Great Britain. *Royal Commission on Capital Punishment, 1949–1953 Report.* London: H.M. Stationery Office, 1953.

National Office of Vital Statistics, United States Public Health Service, Federal Security Agency. *Special Report—Deaths and Crude Death Rates for Each Cause, by Race and Sex: United States, 1950.* Washington: Government Printing Office, 1953.

National Office of Vital Statistics, United States Public Health Service, Federal Security Agency. *Special Report—Deaths from Homicide, 1920–1937.* Washington: Government Printing Office, 1939.

National Office of Vital Statistics, United States Public Health Service, Federal Security Agency. *Special Report—Mortality Summary for United States Registration States: Homicide.* Washington: Government Printing Office, 1942.

National Office of Vital Statistics, United States Public Health Service, Federal Security Agency. *Special Report—Number of Deaths from Homicide and Death Rates per 100,000 Estimated Population, 1920–1935.* Washington: Government Printing Office, 1937.

National Office of Vital Statistics, United States Public Health Service, Federal Security Agency. *Vital Statistics Rates in the United States, 1900–1940.* Washington: Government Printing Office, 1947.

The North Carolina State Board of Charities and Public Welfare. *Capital Punishment in North Carolina.* Special Bulletin No. 10, Raleigh, North Carolina, 1929.

The Philadelphia Area Census Commission and The Philadelphia City Planning Commission. *Census Tract Index to Philadelphia Streets and House Numbers,* 2nd ed. Philadelphia: Health and Welfare Council, Inc., 1952.

United Nations. Verkko, Veli. "Survey of Current Practices in Criminal Statistics," Part I, Part III. *International Group of Experts on the Prevention of Crime and the Treatment of Offenders,* 1950.

U.S. Bureau of the Census, U.S. Department of Commerce. *Mortality Statistics.* Washington: Government Printing Office.

U.S. Bureau of the Census. *U.S. Census of Population: 1950.* Vol. III, *Census Tract Statistics*, Chap. 42. Washington: Government Printing Office, 1952.

U.S. Bureau of the Census. *U.S. Census of Population: 1950.* Vol. IV, *Special Reports*, Part 2, Chap. C, Institutional Population. Washington: Government Printing Office, 1953.

U.S. Bureau of the Census. *U.S. Census of Population.* Vol. IV, *Special Reports*, Part 3, Chap. B, Nonwhite Population by *Race.* Washington: Government Printing Office, 1953.

U.S. Bureau of the Census. *U.S. Census of Population:* 1950, Vol. III, *Census Tract Statistics*, Chap. 42, Washington: Government Printing Office, 1952.

Reports

Annual Police Reports. (1948–1952)
Akron, Ohio
Baltimore, Maryland
Boston, Massachusetts
Buffalo, New York
Chicago, Illinois
Cincinnati, Ohio
Columbus, Ohio
Dallas, Texas
Kansas City, Missouri
Los Angeles, California
Miami, Florida
Milwaukee, Wisconsin
New York, New York
Philadelphia, Pennsylvania
Pittsburgh, Pennsylvania
St. Paul, Minnesota
Seattle, Washington
Washington, D.C.

Annual Report. District Attorney's Office of Philadelphia, 1952.

Annual Report. (1937–1938). National Council for the Abolition of the Death Penalty. (*Guilty But Insane, the Murder Trend.*)

Basutoland Medicine Murder. A Report on the Recent Outbreak of "Diretlo" Murders in Basutoland. London: H.M. Stationery Office, 1951.

Growdon, C. H. *A Group Study of Juvenile Homicide*. Columbus, Ohio: State Bureau of Juvenile Research, Department of Public Welfare, 1950.

Harris, Alfred. *A Study of First and Second Degree Murder Discharges in Eight States*. A Report to the Annual Congress of the American Prison Association, 1939.

Health and Welfare Council, Inc. *Philadelphia Public Health Survey*. A Report to the Philadelphia City Planning Commission. Philadelphia: Health and Welfare Council, Inc., 1949.

Institute of Public Administration. *Crime Records in Police Management, New York City*. A Report Prepared for the Mayor's Committee on Management Survey. New York: Institute of Public Administration, 1952.

Institute of Public Administration. *The New York Police Survey*. A Report for the Mayor's Committee on Management Survey. New York: Institute of Public Administration, 1952.

The Metropolitan Life Insurance Co. *Statistical Bulletin*. "Effect of the War upon Suicide and Homicide Rates." (June, 1920), pp. 2–4.

The Metropolitan Life Insurance Co. *Statistical Bulletin*. "Homicide and the Law." (August, 1924).

The Metropolitan Life Insurance Co. *Statistical Bulletin*. "The Homicide Death Rate Changes Little." (October, 1932), pp. 5–8.

The Metropolitan Life Insurance Co. *Statistical Bulletin*. "Homicide Death Rates in the Industrial Population of American States and Canadian Provinces." (December, 1926), pp. 1–4.

The Metropolitan Life Insurance Co. *Statistical Bulletin*. "Punishment for Murder." (February, 1952), pp. 4–6.

Ralston, Robert. *The Delay in the Execution of Murderers*. A Report to the 17th Annual Convention of the Pennsylvania Bar Association, Bedford Springs, Pa., 1911.

Articles

Alexander, Franz. "The Need for Punishment and the Death-Instinct," *International Journal of Psycho-Analysis*, (1929), 10: 256–269.

Allredge, E. P. "Why the South Leads the Nation in Murder and Manslaughter," *The Quarterly Review*, Nashville, Tennessee, (April, May, June, 1942), 2: 123–134.

Alpert, H. "Suicides and Homicides," *The American Sociological Review*, (October, 1950), 15: 673–675.

Arado, C. C. "Homicides Committed in Drunken Brawls," *Journal of Criminal Law and Criminology*, (September, 1932), 23: 473–478.

Baker, N. F. "Reversible Error in Homicide Cases," *Journal of Criminal Law and Criminology*, (May, 1932), 23: 28–50.

Banay, Ralph. "Alcoholism and Crime," *Quarterly Journal of Studies on Alcohol*, (March, 1942), pp. 686–716.

Banay, Ralph. "Homicide Among Children," *Federal Probation*, (1947), 11: 11–19.

Banay, Ralph. "Study in Murder," (*Murder and the Penalty of Death*), *The Annals of the American Academy of Political and Social Science*, (November, 1952), 284: 26–34.

Banay, Ralph. "A Study of 22 Men Convicted of Murder in the First Degree," *Journal of Criminal Law and Criminology*, (July, 1943), 34: 106–111.

Barnhart, K. E. "Negro Homicides in the United States," *Social Science*, (April, 1932), 7: 141–159.

Barnhart, K. E. "A Study in Homicide in the United States," *Social Science*, (April, 1932), 7: 141–159.

Bender, L. "Psychiatric Mechanisms in Child Murderers," *Journal of Nervous and Mental Disease*, (1934), 80: 32–47.

Bendiner, Robert. "The Man Who Reads Corpses," *Harper's Magazine*, (February, 1955), 210: 62–67.

Berg, I. A., and Fox, Vernon. "Factors in Homicides Committed by 200 Males," *Journal of Social Psychology*, (August, 1947), 26: 109–119.

Blinn, Keith W. "First Degree Murder—a Workable Definition," *Journal of Criminal Law and Criminology*, (1950), 40: 729–735.

Bossard, James H. S. "The Law of Family Interaction," *American Journal of Sociology*, (January, 1945), 50: 292–295.

Bowers, Warner F., Marchant, Frederick T., Judy, Kenneth H. "The Present Story on Battle Casualties from Korea," *Surgery, Gynecology, and Obstetrics*, (November, 1951), 93: 529–542.

Brearley, H. C. "Homicide in South Carolina: a Regional Study," *Social Forces*, (December, 1929), 8: 218–221.

Brearley, H. C. "The Negro and Homicide," *Social Forces*, (1930), 9: 247–253.

Bromberg, Walter. "A Psychological Study of Murder," *The International Journal of Psycho-Analysis*, (1951), 32: 1–2.

Bullock, Henry Allen. "Urban Homicide in Theory and Fact," *Journal of Criminal Law, Criminology, and Police Science*, (January–February, 1955), 45: 565–575.

Caldwell, Morris G. "Group Dynamics in the Prison Community," *Journal of Criminal Law, Criminology, and Police Science*, (January-February, 1956), 46: 648–657.

Calvert, E. Roy. "Murder and the Death Penalty," *The Nation*, (October 16, 1929), 129: 405–407.

Carpenter, Niles, and Haenszel, William M. "Migratoriness and Criminality in Buffalo," *Social Forces*, 9: 254–255.

Cassidy, J. "Personality Study of 200 Murderers," *Journal of Criminal Psychopathology*, (1941), 2: 296–304.

Catlin, George. "Alcoholism," *Encyclopedia of the Social Sciences*, Edited by Edwin R. A. Seligman. Vol. I, 1949.

"Chicago's Inferiority in Homicide," *Christian Century*, (March 26, 1930), 47: 389.

Cohen, Joseph. "The Geography of Crime," *The Annals of the American Academy of Political and Social Science*, (September, 1941), 217: 33–34.

Cohen, L. H., and Coffin, T. E. "The Pattern of Murder in Insanity: a Criterion of the Murderer's Abnormality," *Journal of Criminal Law and Criminology*, (November, 1946), 37: 262–287.

Coleman, S. "Intoxication in Mitigation of Murder," *Journal of Criminal Law and Criminology*, (May, 1940), 31: 72–77.

Cooper, C. R. "Divorce by Murder," *American Mercury*, (September, 1939), 48: 42–49.

Curran and Schilder. "A Constructive Approach to the Problems of Childhood and Adolescence," *Journal of Criminal Psychopathology*, (1940), 2: 125–142.

Dann, Robert H. "The Deterrent Effect of Capital Punishment," *Friends Social Service Series*, Bulletin No. 29, Third Month, 1935.

Dawson, J. M. "Crime in Texas Shows Increase: New All-Time Record for Homicides," *Christian Century*, (August 15, 1934), 51: 1052.

351

"Defining the Crime of Murder," *Journal of Criminal Law and Criminology*, 12: 121.

De Porte, J. V., and Parkhurst, E. "Homicide in New York State. A Statistical Study of the Victims and Criminals in 37 Counties in 1921–30," *Human Biology*, (1935), 7: 47–73.

"Domestic Quarrels Deadlier than Gangster Slayings," *Science News Letter*, (March 11, 1939), 35: 152.

Doyle, Frederick T. "Marshalling of Proofs in Homicide Cases," *Journal of Criminal Law and Criminology*, (March–April, 1946), 36: 473–484.

Dublin, L. I., and Bunzel, Bessie. "Thou Shalt Not Kill: A Study of Homicide in the United States," *Survey Graphic*, (March, 1935), 24: 127–131.

Dubowski, K. M., and Shupe, L. M. "Improved Semimicro Distillation Apparatus," *American Journal of Clinical Pathology*, (1952), 22: 147–149.

Durrett, J. J., and Stromquist, W. G. "Preventing Violent Death," *Survey*, (July 15, 1925), 54: 435–438.

East, W. Norwood. "The Problem of Alcohol in Relation to Crime," *The British Journal of Inebriety*, (1939), 37: 55 ff.

Ehrmann, Herbert B. "The Death Penalty and the Administration of Justice," *The Annals of the Academy of Political and Social Science*, (November, 1952), 284: 73–84.

Elliott, Mabel. "Crime and the Frontier Mores," *American Sociological Review*, (April, 1944), 9: 185–192.

Fenichel, O. "The Clinical Aspect of the Need for Punishment," *International Journal of Psycho-Analysis*, (1928), 9: 47–70.

Fisher, R. S. "Alcohol, Accidents and Crime," *Current Medical Digest*, (1952), 19: 37–41.

Ford, Richard. "Critical Times in Murder Investigation (Time of Assault, Incapacitation, and Death)," *Journal of Criminal Law, Criminology, and Police Science*, (January–February, 1953), 43: 672–678.

Frankel, Emil. "One Thousand Murderers," *Journal of Criminal Law and Criminology*, (January, 1939), 29: 672–688.

Frenkel, Helene. "The Murderer Who Is Not Motivated by Personal Gain," *Social Science Abstracts*, (1930), 2: 947.

Garfinkel, Harold. "Research Note on Inter- and Intra-Racial Homicides," *Social Forces*, (May, 1949), 27: 369–381.

"Geography of Homicide," *The American Journal of Public Health*, (April, 1932), 22: 414–415.

Gettler, A. O., and Tiber, S. "Quantitative Determination of Ethyl Alcohol in Human Tissues," *Archives of Pathology*, (January, 1927), 3: 78–83.

Gillin, J. L. "Social Backgrounds of Sex Offenders and Murderers," *Social Forces*, (December, 1935), 14: 232–239.

Gillin, J. L. "Wisconsin Murderer," *Social Forces*, (May, 1934), 12: 550–556.

Glazer, Daniel. "Criminality Theories and Behavioral Images," *The American Journal of Sociology*, (March, 1956), 61: 433–444.

Gray, M. A., and Moore, Merrill. "Incidence and Significance of Alcoholism in the History of Criminals," *Journal of Criminal Psychopathology*, (October, 1941), 3: 316.

Greene, James E. "Motivations of a Murderer," *Journal of Abnormal Social Psychology*, (1948), 43: 526–531.

Grünhut, Max. "Murder and the Death Penalty in England," *The Annals of the American Academy of Political and Social Science*, (*Murder and the Penalty of Death*), (November, 1952), 284: 158–166.

Grünhut, Max. "Statistics in Criminology," *The Journal of the Royal Statistical Society*, Series A (General), (1951), 114: 139–162.

Harlan, Howard. "Five Hundred Homicides," *Journal of Criminal Law and Criminology*, (1950), 40: 736–752.

Harlan, Howard, and Wherry, Jack. "Delinquency and Housing," *Social Forces*, (1948), 27: 58–61.

Harno, Albert J. "Some Significant Developments in Criminal Law and Procedure in the Last Century," *Journal of Criminal Law, Criminology, and Police Science*, (November–December, 1951), 42: 427–467.

Hayner, Norman, and Ash, Ellis. "The Prisoner Community as a Social Group," *American Sociological Review*, (June, 1939), 4: 362–369.

Helpern, Milton. "The Post Mortem Examination in Cases of Suspected Homicide," *Journal of Criminal Law and Criminology*, (March, 1946), 36: 485–522.

Hobbs, A. H. "Criminality in Philadelphia, 1790–1810, Compared with 1937," *The American Sociological Review*, (April, 1943), 8: 198–202.

Hobbs, A. H. "Relationship Between Criminality and Economic Conditions," *Journal of Criminal Law and Criminology*, (May–June, 1943), 34: 5–10.

Hoffman, Frederick L. "The Homicide Record for 1929," *Spectator*, (March 22, 1930).

Hoffman, Frederick L. "The Homicide Record for 1931," *Spectator*, (March, 1932).

Hoffman, Frederick L. "The Increase in Murder," *The Annals of the American Academy of Political and Social Science*, (1926), 125: 20–29.

"Homicide Committed in Drunken Brawls," *Journal of Criminal Law and Criminology*, (1934), 23: 473.

Howard, George Elliott. "Alcohol and Crime: A study in Social Causation," *The American Journal of Sociology*, (July, 1918), 24: 61–80.

Johnson, Guy B. "The Negro and Crime," *The Annals of the American Academy of Political and Social Science*, (September, 1941), 217: 93–104.

Karpman, B. "Criminality, the Super-Ego and the Sense of Guilt," *Psychological Review*, (1930), 17: 280–296.

Keedy, Edwin R. "Criminal Attempts at Common Law," *The University of Pennsylvania Law Review*, (1954), 102: 464–489.

Keedy, Edwin R. "History of the Pennsylvania Statute Creating Degrees of Murder," *The University of Pennsylvania Law Review*, (1949), 97: 759 ff.

Keedy, Edwin R. "Irresistible Impulse as a Defense in the Criminal Law," *The University of Pennsylvania Law Review*, (May, 1952), 100: 956–993.

Keedy, Edwin R. "A Problem of First Degree Murder: Fisher vs. the United States," *The University of Pennsylvania Law Review*, (1950), 99: 267–292.

Kephart, William M. "A Quantitative Analysis of Intragroup Relationships," *American Journal of Sociology*, (May, 1950), 55: 544–549.

Kephart, William M., and Monahan, Thomas P. "Desertion and Divorce in Philadelphia," *American Sociological Review*, (December, 1952), 17: 719–727.

Kilmer, T. W. "Alcoholism, Its Relation to Police Work and Jurisprudence," *Correction*, (1933), 3: 11–12.

Kilpatrick, J. J. "Murder in the Deep South," *Survey Graphic*, (October, 1943), 32: 395–397.

Kurland, Albert A., Morgenstern, Jacob, and Sheets, Carolyn. "A Comparative Study of Wife Murderers Admitted to a State Psychiatric Hospital," *The Journal of Social Therapy*, (January, 1955), 1: 7–15.

Lehrman, Philip R. "Some Unconscious Determinants of Homicide," *Psychiatric Quarterly*, (1939), 13: 605.

Lobinger, C. S. "Homicide Concept: A Study in Comparative Criminal Law," *Journal of Criminal Law and Criminology*, (November, 1918), 9: 373–377.

Lottier, S. "Distribution of Criminal Offenses in Metropolitan Regions," *Journal of Criminal Law and Criminology*, (1938), 29: 37–50.

Lunden, W. A. "The Murder Cycle and the Business Cycle," *Federator*, (July, 1940), 15: 152–159.

MacDonald, A. "Death Penalty and Homicide," *The American Journal of Sociology*, (1911), 16: 88–116.

Matheson, J. C. M. "Alcohol and Female Homicides," *The British Journal of Inebriety*, (1939), 37: 87 ff.

Maynard, L. M. "Murder in the Making," *American Mercury*, (June, 1929), 17: 129–135.

McCorkle, L. W., and Korn, R. R. "Resocialization Within Walls," *The Annals of the American Academy of Political and Social Science*, (May, 1954), 293: 88–98.

Menninger, Karl. "Psychoanalytic Aspects of Suicide," *International Journal of Psycho-Analysis*, (1933), 14: 387.

Merz, Charles. "Bigger and Better Murders," *Harper's Magazine*, (August, 1927), 155: 338–343.

Meyers, Alvin F., and others. "Men Who Kill Women," Part 1, *Journal of Clinical Psychopathology*, (1945–1946), 7: 441–472. Part 2, *Journal of Clinical Psychopathology*, (1946–1947), 8: 481–517.

"Mind of the Murderer," *Spectator*, (August 16, 1924), 133: 221–222.

Miner, John R. "Church Membership and the Homicide Rate," *Human Biology*, (1929), 1: 562–564.

"More Murders," *Literary Digest*, (April 5, 1930), 105: 13.

Moses, Earl R. "Differentials in Crime Rates Between Negroes and Whites, Based on Comparisons of Four Socio-economically Equated Areas," *American Sociological Review*, (August, 1947), 12: 411–420.

"Motives for Murder," *Journal of Criminal Law and Criminology*, (May, 1931), 22: 923.

"Murder in France," *Literary Digest*, (April 16, 1931), 109: 16.

"Murder Is Seen as Bizarre Form of Attempted Suicide," *Science News Letter*, (December, 1939), 36: 377.

"Murder Records," *Journal of Criminal Law and Criminology*, (May, 1931), 22: 922.

"Murderous America," *Literary Digest*, (July 21, 1928), 98 : 17.

Murphy, Fred J., Shirley, Mary M., and Witmer, Helen L. "The Incidence of Hidden Delinquency," *American Journal of Ortho-Psychiatry*, (October, 1946), 16: 686–696.

Nunberg, H. "The Sense of Guilt and the Need for Punishment," *International Journal of Psycho-Analysis*, (1926), 7: 420–433.

"Our 12,000 Killings in 1926," *Literary Digest*, (July 2, 1927), 94: 12–13.

Park, R. E. "Murder and the Case Study Method," *The American Journal of Sociology*, (November, 1930), 36: 447–454.

Patterson, R. M. "Psychiatric Study of Juveniles Involved in Homicide," *American Journal of Ortho-Psychiatry*, (1943), 13: 125–130.

Perkins, R. M. "The Law of Homicide," *Journal of Criminal Law and Criminology*, (March, 1946), 36: 391–454.

Phelps, H. A. "Effectiveness of Life Imprisonment as a Repressive Measure Against Murder in Rhode Island," *Journal of the American Statistical Association*, (March Supplement, 1928), 23: 174–181.

Phelps, H. A. "Rhode Island's Threat Against Murder," *Journal of Criminal Law and Criminology*, (February, 1925), 15: 552–567.

Porterfield, Austin L. "Indices of Suicide and Homicide by States and Cities: Some Southern-Non-Southern Contrasts with Implications for Research," *The American Sociological Review*, (August, 1949), 14: 481–490.

Porterfield, Austin L. "Suicide and Crime in Folk and in Secular Society," *The American Journal of Sociology*, (January, 1952), 57: 331–338.

"Psychology of Murder, a Study in Criminal Psychology," *Journal of Criminal Law and Criminology*, (1927), 18: 443.

Rabin, A. E. "Homicide and Attempted Suicide: A Rorschach Study," *American Journal of Ortho-Psychiatry*, (1946), 16: 516–524.

Raven, A. "Murder and Suicide as Marks of an Abnormal Mind," *The American Sociological Review*, (1929), 21: 315–333.

Raven, A. "A Theory of Murder," *The American Sociological Review*, (April, 1930), 22: 108–118.

"Recent Criminal Cases," *Journal of Criminal Law and Criminology*, (May, 1940), 31: 72–74.

"Relative to Punishment for Murder in the Second Degree," *Journal of Criminal Law and Criminology*, (May, 1914), 5: 95.

Rosenzweig, S., and others. "The Psychodynamics of an Uxoricide," *American Journal of Ortho-Psychiatry*," (1942), 12: 283–294.

Rotman, D. B. "Alcoholism and Crime," *Federal Probation*, (July–September, 1947), pp. 31–35.

Schilder, Paul. "The Attitude of Murderers Towards Death," *Journal of Abnormal and Social Psychology*, (1936), 13: 3.

Schmid, Calvin F. "Suicide in Minneapolis, Minnesota," *The American Journal of Sociology*, (July, 1953), 39: 42.

Schmid, Calvin F. "Study of Homicides in Seattle," *Social Forces*, (June, 1926), 4: 745–756.

Seagle, William. "Homicide,"·*Encyclopedia of the Social Sciences*. Edited by Edwin R. A. Seligman. Vol. VII, 1949.

Sellin, Thorsten. "The Basis of a Crime Index," *Journal of Criminal Law and Criminology*, (September, 1931), 22: 335–356.

Sellin, Thorsten. "Is Murder Increasing in Europe?" *The Annals of the American Academy of Political and Social Science*, (1926), 125: 29–37.

Sellin, Thorsten. "Status and Prospects of Criminal Statistics in the United States," *Festskrift tillagnad Karl Schlyter den 21 december 1949*, (Dedicated publication in honor of Karl Schlyter, December 21, 1949), Stockholm: 1949.

Sellin, Thorsten. "The Measurement of Criminality in Geographic Areas," *Proceedings of The American Philosophical Society*, (April, 1953), 97: 163–167.

Shupe, L. M. "Alcohol and Crime. A Study of The Urine Alcohol Concentration Found in 882 Persons Arrested During or Immediately After the Commission of a Felony," *Journal of Criminal Law, Criminology, and Police Science*, (January–February, 1954), 44: 661–664.

Shupe, L. M., and Dubowski, K. M. "Ethyl Alcohol in Blood and Urine," *American Journal of Clinical Pathology*, (1952), 22: 901–910.

Spain, D. M., Bradess, V. A., and Eggston, A. A. "Alcohol and Violent Death. A One-Year Study of Consecutive Cases in a Representative Community," *Journal of the American Medical Association*, (1951), 146: 334–335.

Stearns, Albert Warren. "Homicide in Massachusetts," *The American Journal of Psychiatry*, (July, 1924–April, 1925), 4: 725–749.

Stern, Max. "A Study of Unsolved Murders in Wisconsin from 1924–1928," *Journal of Criminal Law and Criminology*, (February, 1931), 21: 4: 513–536.

Straus, Jacqueline, and Straus, Murray. "Suicide, Homicide, and Social Structure in Ceylon," *The American Journal of Sociology*, (March, 1953), 58: 461–469.

"Suicide is Murder; Desire to Kill Turned on Self," *Science News Letter*, (May, 1945), 47: 295.

"Suicide and Homicide in Illinois," *Journal of Criminal Law and Criminology*, (April, 1932–March, 1933), 23: 863.

Sutherland, E. H. "Murder and the Death Penalty," *Journal of Criminal Law and Criminology*, (May, 1924–February, 1925), 15: 522–529.

"Terrific Homicide Rate in U.S. Falls," *Literary Digest*, (December 12, 1936), 122: 12–13.

Tersiev, N. "The Evaluation of Their Deeds on the Part of Condemned Murderers," *Social Science Abstracts*, (October, 1930), 2: 1661–1662.

Thomas, W. I. "The Persistence of Primary-Group Norms in Present-Day Society and Their Influence in Our Educational System," in Herbert S. Jennings and others, *Suggestions of Modern Science Concerning Education*. New York: Macmillan and Co., 1917.

Topping, C. W. "The Death Penalty in Canada," *The Annals of the American Academy of Political and Social Science*, (November, 1952), (*Murder and the Penalty of Death*), 284: 147–157.

Train, A. "Why Do Men Kill?" *Collier's*, (January 27, 1912), 48: 13–14.

Vance, R. B., and Wynne, W., Jr. "Folk Rationalizations in the Un-Written Law," *The American Journal of Sociology*, (January, 1934), 39: 483–492.

Venn, F. E. "Murder," *Independent*, (November 8, 1924), 113: 361–362.

Vold, George. "Extent and Trend of Capital Crimes in the United States," *The Annals of the American Academy of Political and Social Science* (*Murder and the Penalty of Death*), (November, 1952), 284: 1–7.

Von Hentig, Hans. "The Criminality of the Negro," *Journal of Criminal Law and Criminology*, (January–February, 1940), 30: 662–680.

Von Hentig, Hans. "Remarks on the Interaction of Perpetrator and Victim," *Journal of Criminal Law and Criminology*, (1940–1941), 31: 303–309.

Von Hentig, Hans. "Some Problems Regarding Murder Detection," *Journal of Criminal Law and Criminology*, (May, 1938), 29: 108–118.

Von Moschzisker, Michael. "Capital Punishment in the Pennsylvania Courts," *Pennsylvania Bar Association Quarterly*, (January, 1949), pp. 1–16.

Wade, J. W. "Acquisition of Property by Wilfully Killing Another—A Statutory Solution," *Harvard Law Review*, (March, 1936), 49: 715–755.

Waldrop, Francis N., and Cruvant, Bernard A. "The Murderer in the Mental Institution," *The Annals of the American Academy of Political and Social Science*, (November, 1952), 284: 35–44.

Wallerstein, James S., and Wyle, Clement J. "Our Law Abiding Law Breakers," Reprint from *Probation*, (April, 1947).

Wechsler, Herbert, and Michael, Jerome. "A Rationale of the Law of Homicide," Reprint from *Columbia Law Review*, (May, December, 1937), 37: 701–761.

Wilentz, W. C. "The Alcohol Factor in Violent Deaths," *American Practitioner and Digest of Treatment*, (1953), 4: 21–24.

Wilner, I. "Unintentional Homicide in the Commission of an Unlawful Act," *University of Pennsylvania Law Review*, (May, 1939), 87: 811–836.

Wolfgang, Marvin E. "Political Crimes and Punishments in Renaissance Florence," *Journal of Criminal Law, Criminology, and Police Science*, (January–February, 1954), 44: 555–581.

Work, M. N. "Crime Among Negroes in Chicago," *The American Journal of Sociology*, (1901), 6: 204–223.

Yen, Ching-Yueh. "A Study of Crime in Peiping." Edited by Maxwell S. Stewart. Peiping, China: Yenching University, Department of Sociology and Social Work, Series C, No. 20, December, 1929.

Zilboorg, Gregory. "Some Sidelights on Psychology of Murder," *Journal of Nervous and Mental Disease*, (April, 1935), 81: 442.

Unpublished Material

Carter, Sam. "The History of the Habitual Offender Law in Kansas." Unpublished Master's thesis, University of Kansas, Lawrence, Kansas, 1935. Pp. 84.

Gregory, John M. "Association of the Homicide Rate with Fluctuation in Business Cycles." Unpublished seminar paper, University of Pennsylvania, 1951. Pp. 17.

Gregory, John M. "Report on the Death Penalty in Pennsylvania for the Years 1918–1939 Inclusive," Unpublished seminar paper, University of Pennsylvania, 1950. Pp. 2.

Meyers, Arthur C., Jr. "Murder and Non-Negligent Manslaughter: A Statistical Study." Unpublished manuscript, St. Louis University. Pp. 26.

On the Job Training Memorandum. Homicide Squad. Philadelphia, 1954. (Mimeographed).

Surveillance Training Memorandum. Homicide Squad. Philadelphia, 1954. (Mimeographed.)

TABLE 1

CRIMINAL HOMICIDE, VICTIMS AND OFENDERS, BY RACE,
SEX, AND AGE, PHILADELPHIA, 1948–1952

Victims	Both Races			Negro			White		
	Total	Male	Female	Total	Male	Female	Total	Male	Female
Under 15	28	20	8	14	11	3	14	9	5
15–19	25	19	6	20	17	3	5	2	3
20–24	59	48	11	45	36	9	14	12	2
25–29	93	61	32	77	48	29	16	13	3
30–34	88	61	27	67	48	19	21	13	8
35–39	75	62	13	64	53	11	11	9	2
40–44	57	44	13	41	33	8	16	11	5
45–49	43	34	9	34	29	5	9	5	4
50–54	48	41	7	32	29	3	16	12	4
55–59	26	22	4	14	11	3	12	11	1
60–64	18	17	1	10	9	1	8	8	—
65 and over	28	20	8	9	7	2	19	13	6
All ages	588	449	139	427	331	96	161	118	43
Offenders (a)									
Under 15	5	4	1	2	1	1	3	3	—
15–19	61	58	3	48	46	2	13	12	1
20–24	102	87	15	72	61	11	30	26	4
25–29	107	82	25	89	66	23	18	16	2
30–34	94	74	20	75	57	18	19	17	2
35–39	81	69	12	59	50	9	22	19	3
40–44	58	46	12	43	32	11	15	14	1
45–49	54	40	14	40	28	12	14	12	2
50–54	20	19	1	17	16	1	3	3	—
55–59	18	15	3	14	11	3	4	4	—
60–64	9	7	2	3	2	1	6	5	1
65 and over	11	10	1	5	4	1	6	6	—
All ages	620	511	109	467	374	93	153	137	16

(a) The age of one offender is unknown. Throughout the age tables relative to offenders the total universe is 620 instead of 621.

TABLE 2

DISTRIBUTION OF PHILADELPHIA POPULATION, 1950; BY RACE, SEX, AND AGE

Age	Both Races			Negro			White		
	Total	Male	Female	Total	Male	Female	Total	Male	Female
Under 15	465,996	236,230	229,766	100,721	50,066	50,655	365,275	186,164	179,111
15–19	130,116	63,531	66,585	25,295	11,612	13,683	104,821	51,919	52,902
20–24	161,511	76,601	84,910	30,873	13,189	17,684	130,638	63,412	67,226
25–29	179,643	86,638	93,005	37,563	16,970	20,593	142,080	69,668	72,412
30–34	170,054	80,615	89,439	33,844	15,174	18,670	136,210	65,441	70,769
35–39	166,695	79,092	87,603	33,647	15,274	18,373	133,048	63,818	69,230
40–44	152,834	73,681	79,153	28,669	13,608	15,061	124,165	60,073	64,092
45–49	137,886	66,849	71,037	25,959	12,734	13,225	111,927	54,115	57,812
50–54	132,171	64,740	67,431	21,324	10,888	10,436	110,847	53,852	56,995
55–59	112,353	55,051	57,302	14,215	7,175	7,040	98,138	47,876	50,262
60–64	91,104	44,200	46,904	10,103	5,058	5,045	81,001	39,142	41,859
65 and over	171,242	74,634	96,608	16,755	7,647	9,108	154,487	66,987	87,500
All ages	2,071,605	1,001,862	1,069,743	378,968	179,395	199,573	1,692,637	822,467	870,170

Source:

U.S. Bureau of the Census, *U.S. Census of Population:* 1950, Vol. III, *Census Tract Statistics,* Chapter 42, U.S. Government Printing Office, Washington, D.C., 1952, p. 57.

TABLE 3

METHOD AND WEAPON OF CRIMINAL HOMICIDE, BY RACE
AND SEX OF VICTIM AND OFFENDER, PHILADELPHIA, 1948–1952

	VICTIM								
	Both Races			Negro			White		
	Total	Male	Female	Total	Male	Female	Total	Male	Female
Method									
Stabbing	228	181	47	200	160	40	28	21	7
Shooting	194	152	42	145	117	28	49	35	14
Beating	128	96	32	60	41	19	68	55	13
Other	38	20	18	22	13	9	16	7	9
Total	588	449	139	427	331	96	161	118	43
Weapon									
Penknife, switch-blade knife	123	103	20	110	92	18	13	11	2
Kitchen knife, ice pick	96	72	24	83	63	20	13	9	4
Pistol, revolver	164	129	35	121	98	23	43	31	12
Rifle, shotgun	30	23	7	24	19	5	6	4	2
Fists, feet	88	62	26	37	23	14	51	39	12
Blunt instrument	47	36	11	28	20	8	19	16	3
Other	40	24	16	24	16	8	16	8	8
Total	588	449	139	427	331	96	161	118	43
	OFFENDER								
Method									
Stabbing	233	163	70	206	141	65	27	22	5
Shooting	204	182	22	159	143	16	45	39	6
Beating	146	143	3	81	79	2	65	64	1
Other	38	24	14	21	11	10	17	13	4
Total	621	512	109	467	374	93	154	138	16
Weapon									
Penknife, switch-blade knife	126	104	22	118	97	21	8	7	1
Kitchen knife, ice pick	98	52	46	83	41	42	15	11	4
Pistol, revolver	169	147	22	131	115	16	38	32	6
Rifle, shotgun	35	30	5	28	23	5	7	7	—
Fists, feet	100	97	3	47	46	1	53	51	2
Blunt instrument	55	54	1	41	40	1	14	14	—
Other	38	28	10	19	12	7	19	16	3
Total	621	512	109	467	374	93	154	138	16

363

TABLE 4

WEAPON EMPLOYED BY OFFENDER IN CRIMINAL HOMICIDE, BY AGE, PHILADELPHIA, 1948–1952

Weapon	AGE						
	Under 20	20–29	30–39	40–49	50–59	60 and over	Total
Penknife, switchblade knife	16	46	34	22	6	2	126
Kitchen knife, ice pick	5	33	29	21	7	3	98
Pistol, revolver	24	49	50	27	14	4	168
Rifle, shotgun	4	13	13	1	2	2	35
Fists, feet	8	38	28	19	4	3	100
Blunt instrument	6	24	10	9	4	2	55
Other	3	6	11	13	1	4	38
Total	66	209	175	112	38	20	620

TABLE 5

MONTH, DAY, AND HOURS AT PLACE OF OCCURRENCE OF CRIMINAL HOMICIDE, BY RACE AND SEX OF VICTIM, PHILADELPHIA, 1948–1952

Month and Place	Both Races			Negro			White		
	Total	Male	Female	Total	Male	Female	Total	Male	Female
January	37	27	10	25	19	6	12	8	4
Home	18	12	6	14	10	4	4	2	2
Not Home	19	15	4	11	9	2	8	6	2
February	34	24	10	26	20	6	8	4	4
Home	24	15	9	18	13	5	6	2	4
Not Home	10	9	1	8	7	1	2	2	—
March	48	38	10	34	25	9	14	13	1
Home	22	12	10	19	10	9	3	2	1
Not Home	26	26	—	15	15	—	11	11	—
April	50	38	12	39	30	9	11	8	3
Home	27	18	9	22	15	7	5	3	2
Not Home	23	20	3	17	15	2	6	5	1
May	62	48	14	40	31	9	22	17	5
Home	27	20	7	20	17	3	7	3	4
Not Home	35	28	7	20	14	6	15	14	1
June	50	41	9	40	33	7	10	8	2
Home	27	21	6	22	18	4	5	3	2
Not Home	23	20	3	18	15	3	5	5	—
July	43	34	9	35	28	7	8	6	2
Home	19	12	7	17	11	6	2	1	1
Not Home	24	22	2	18	17	1	6	5	1
August	58	39	19	40	28	12	18	11	7
Home	26	15	11	16	10	6	10	5	5
Not Home	32	24	8	24	18	6	8	6	2
September	61	47	14	49	40	9	12	7	5
Home	29	22	7	24	20	4	5	2	3
Not Home	32	25	7	25	20	5	7	5	2

TABLE 5 (continued)

Month and Place	Both Races			Negro			White		
	Total	Male	Female	Total	Male	Female	Total	Male	Female
October	49	39	10	33	26	7	16	13	3
Home	24	18	6	17	13	4	7	5	2
Not Home	25	21	4	16	13	3	9	8	1
November	47	36	11	33	26	7	14	10	4
Home	27	19	8	19	15	4	8	4	4
Not Home	20	17	3	14	11	3	6	6	—
December	49	38	11	33	25	8	16	13	3
Home	31	22	9	26	19	7	5	3	2
Not Home	18	16	2	7	6	1	11	10	1
Day & Place									
Monday	58	37	21	38	25	13	20	12	8
Home	30	14	16	21	10	11	9	4	5
Not Home	28	23	5	17	15	2	11	8	3
Tuesday	41	31	10	26	19	7	15	12	3
Home	9	6	3	7	4	3	2	2	—
Not Home	32	25	7	19	15	4	13	10	3
Wednesday	55	38	17	39	26	13	16	12	4
Home	26	15	11	20	13	7	6	2	4
Not Home	29	23	6	19	13	6	10	10	—
Thursday	48	23	25	25	12	13	23	11	12
Home	35	12	23	16	5	11	19	7	12
Not Home	13	11	2	9	7	2	4	4	—
Friday	100	79	21	72	56	16	28	23	5
Home	52	37	15	40	29	11	12	8	4
Not Home	48	42	6	32	27	5	16	15	1
Saturday	187	158	29	152	128	24	35	30	5
Home	87	71	16	79	67	12	8	4	4
Not Home	100	87	13	73	61	12	27	26	1
Sunday	99	83	16	75	65	10	24	18	6
Home	62	51	11	51	43	8	11	8	3
Not Home	37	32	5	24	22	2	13	10	3
Hours & Place									
8:00 P.M.–1:59 A.M.	292	227	65	229	177	52	63	50	13
Home	143	100	43	119	86	33	24	14	10
Not Home	149	127	22	110	91	19	39	36	3
2:00 A.M.–7:59 A.M.	97	73	24	64	50	14	33	23	10
Home	60	42	18	46	36	10	14	6	8
Not Home	37	31	6	18	14	4	19	17	2
8:00 A.M.–1:59 P.M.	54	34	20	34	22	12	20	12	8
Home	28	13	15	19	10	9	9	3	6
Not Home	26	21	5	15	12	3	11	9	2
2:00 P.M.–7:59 P.M.	145	115	30	100	82	18	45	33	12
Home	70	51	19	50	39	11	20	12	8
Not Home	75	64	11	50	43	7	25	21	4

TABLE 6

DISTRIBUTION OF TOTAL VICTIMS WHO DIED WITHIN VARIOUS
PERIODS OF TIME BETWEEN ASSAULT AND DEATH,
ACCORDING TO METHOD BY WHICH VICTIM MET
DEATH, PHILADELPHIA, 1948–1952

Time Period	Total	Method			
		Stabbing	Shooting	Beating	Other
Less than 10 minutes	181	65	93	8	15
10 minutes to 1 hour	151	90	44	10	7
Less than 1 hour	332	155	137	18	22
1 hour to 1 day	126	41	34	42	9
Less than 1 day	458	196	171	60	31
More than 1 day	99	18	22	54	5
Uncertain	31	14	1	14	2

TABLE 7

PLACE OF OCCURRENCE AND METHOD OF CRIMINAL HOMICIDE,
BY RACE AND SEX OF VICTIM, PHILADELPHIA, 1948–1952

Place and Method	Both Races			Negro			White		
	Total	Male	Female	Total	Male	Female	Total	Male	Female
In the Home	301	206	95	234	171	63	67	35	32
Stabbing	123	94	29	110	86	24	13	8	5
Shooting	99	71	28	77	60	17	22	11	11
Beating	54	27	27	28	13	15	26	14	12
Other	25	14	11	19	12	7	6	2	4
In the Home of Both	123	71	52	94	61	33	29	10	19
Stabbing	56	41	15	51	39	12	5	2	3
Shooting	32	16	16	20	11	9	12	5	7
Beating	18	4	14	11	2	9	7	2	5
Other	17	10	7	12	9	3	5	1	4
In the Home of Victim	81	55	26	58	38	20	23	17	6
Stabbing	27	19	8	24	17	7	3	2	1
Shooting	25	19	6	21	16	5	4	3	1
Beating	24	15	9	9	4	5	15	11	4
Other	5	2	3	4	1	3	1	1	—
In the Home of Offender	51	44	7	43	38	5	8	6	2
Stabbing	17	14	3	14	11	3	3	3	—
Shooting	26	24	2	23	22	1	3	2	1
Beating	6	5	1	4	4	—	2	1	1
Other	2	1	1	2	1	1	—	—	—
In the Home of Another	46	36	10	39	34	5	7	2	5
Stabbing	23	20	3	21	19	2	2	1	1
Shooting	16	12	4	13	11	2	3	1	2
Beating	6	3	3	4	3	1	2	—	2
Other	1	1	—	1	1	—	—	—	—

366

TABLE 7 (continued)

Place and Method	Both Races			Negro			White		
	Total	Male	Female	Total	Male	Female	Total	Male	Female
Bedroom	112	64	48	81	50	31	31	14	17
Stabbing	32	20	12	27	18	9	5	2	3
Shooting	32	23	9	25	19	6	7	4	3
Beating	33	14	19	16	6	10	17	8	9
Other	15	7	8	13	7	6	2	—	2
Kitchen	71	50	21	56	41	15	15	9	6
Stabbing	47	36	11	43	33	10	4	3	1
Shooting	16	10	6	10	7	3	6	3	3
Beating	4	2	2	1	—	1	3	2	1
Other	4	2	2	2	1	1	2	1	1
Living Room	71	55	16	55	47	8	16	8	8
Stabbing	22	19	3	20	18	2	2	1	1
Shooting	38	29	9	29	25	4	9	4	5
Beating	9	6	3	5	3	2	4	3	1
Other	2	1	1	1	1	—	1	—	1
Stairway	40	31	9	37	29	8	3	2	1
Stabbing	21	18	3	20	17	3	1	1	—
Shooting	13	8	5	13	8	5	—	—	—
Beating	5	4	1	3	3	—	2	1	1
Other	1	1	—	1	1	—	—	—	—
Outside the Home	287	243	44	193	160	33	94	83	11
Stabbing	105	87	18	90	74	16	15	13	2
Shooting	95	81	14	68	57	11	27	24	3
Beating	74	69	5	32	28	4	42	41	1
Other	13	6	7	3	1	2	10	5	5
Highway	177	149	28	134	112	22	43	37	6
Stabbing	69	57	12	65	54	11	4	3	1
Shooting	57	49	8	46	39	7	11	10	1
Beating	46	42	4	22	19	3	24	23	1
Other	5	1	4	1	—	1	4	1	3
Taproom	48	43	5	32	29	3	16	14	2
Stabbing	20	16	4	16	13	3	4	3	1
Shooting	13	12	1	10	10	—	3	2	1
Beating	15	15	—	6	6	—	9	9	—
Other	—	—	—	—	—	—	—	—	—
Other Commercial Place	47	38	9	21	14	7	26	24	2
Stabbing	12	10	2	7	5	2	5	5	—
Shooting	24	20	4	11	8	3	13	12	1
Beating	6	5	1	2	1	1	4	4	—
Other	5	3	2	1	—	1	4	3	1
Other	22	19	3	11	9	2	11	10	1
Stabbing	5	5	—	2	2	—	3	3	—
Shooting	1	1	—	1	1	—	—	—	—
Beating	10	8	2	5	3	2	5	5	—
Other	6	5	1	3	3	—	3	2	1

TABLE 8

PLACE OF OCCURRENCE OF CRIMINAL HOMICIDE, BY RACE AND SEX OF OFFENDER, PHILADELPHIA, 1948–1952

PLACE	Total	RACE		SEX	
		Negro	White	Male	Female
Bedroom	110	84	26	82	28
Kitchen	69	54	15	37	32
Living Room	78	61	17	68	10
Stairway	43	36	7	33	10
Highway	195	155	40	181	14
Taproom	50	33	17	46	4
Other Commercial Place	54	35	19	46	8
Other	22	9	13	19	3
Total	621	467	154	512	109
In the Home of:					
Both	126	94	32	74	52
Victim	88	67	21	77	11
Offender	55	45	10	37	18
Another	47	43	4	41	6
In the Home	316	249	67	229	87
Not in the Home	305	218	87	283	22

TABLE 9

CRIMINAL HOMICIDE AND THE PRESENCE OF ALCOHOL, BY RACE AND SEX OF VICTIM, PHILADELPHIA, 1948–1952

Alcohol	Both Races			Negro			White		
	Total	Male	Female	Total	Male	Female	Total	Male	Female
Alcohol Present in Both Victim and Offender	256	202	54	206	164	42	50	38	12
Alcohol Present in the Victim Only	54	50	4	40	37	3	14	13	1
Alcohol Present in the Offender Only	64	39	25	50	31	19	14	8	6
Total: Alcohol Present in the Homicide Situation	374	291	83	296	232	64	78	59	19
Total: Alcohol Absent from the Homicide Situation	214	158	56	131	99	32	83	59	24
Grand Total	588	449	139	427	331	96	161	118	43

368

TABLE 10

PRESENCE OF ALCOHOL DURING CRIMINAL HOMICIDE BY METHOD,
BY PLACE, AND BY RACE AND SEX OF VICTIM,
PHILADELPHIA, 1948–1952

Method and Place	Both Races			Negro			White		
	Total	Male	Female	Total	Male	Female	Total	Male	Female
Alcohol Present in Both Victim and Offender	256	202	54	206	164	42	50	38	12
Stabbing	113	87	26	102	79	23	11	8	3
Home	60	44	16	55	41	14	5	3	2
Not Home	53	43	10	47	38	9	6	5	1
Shooting	65	54	11	56	49	7	9	5	4
Home	37	29	8	32	27	5	5	2	3
Not Home	28	25	3	24	22	2	4	3	1
Beating	66	52	14	38	28	10	28	24	4
Home	30	17	13	20	11	9	10	6	4
Not Home	36	35	1	18	17	1	18	18	—
Other	12	9	3	10	8	2	2	1	1
Home	9	8	1	9	8	1	—	—	—
Not Home	3	1	2	1	—	1	2	1	1
Alcohol Present in the Victim Only	54	50	4	40	37	3	14	13	1
Stabbing	26	24	2	24	22	2	2	2	—
Home	16	15	1	14	14	—	1	1	—
Not Home	10	9	1	10	8	2	1	1	—
Shooting	16	15	1	12	11	1	4	4	—
Home	9	9	—	7	7	—	2	2	—
Not Home	7	6	1	5	4	1	2	2	—
Beating	12	11	1	4	4	—	8	7	1
Home	1	—	1	—	—	—	1	—	1
Not Home	11	11	—	4	4	—	7	7	—
Other	—	—	—	—	—	—	—	—	—
Alcohol Present in the Offender Only	64	39	25	50	31	19	14	8	6
Stabbing	24	17	7	22	16	6	2	1	1
Home	15	10	5	13	9	4	2	1	1
Not Home	9	7	2	9	7	2	—	—	—
Shooting	26	16	10	21	13	8	5	3	2
Home	13	5	8	10	4	6	3	1	2
Not Home	13	11	2	11	9	2	2	2	—
Beating	9	4	5	4	1	3	5	3	2
Home	7	3	4	2	—	2	5	3	2
Not Home	2	1	1	2	1	1	—	—	—
Other	5	2	3	3	1	2	2	1	1
Home	4	1	3	3	1	2	1	—	1
Not Home	1	1	—	—	—	—	1	1	—

TABLE 11

TOTAL PRESENCE OF ALCOHOL DURING CRIMINAL HOMICIDE, BY METHOD, BY PLACE, AND BY RACE AND SEX OF VICTIM, PHILADELPHIA, 1948–1952

	Both Races			Negro			White		
	Total	Male	Female	Total	Male	Female	Total	Male	Femal
Presence of Alcohol, In the Home									
Stabbing	90	69	21	82	64	18	8	5	3
Shooting	59	43	16	49	38	11	10	5	5
Beating	38	20	18	22	11	11	16	9	7
Other	13	9	4	12	9	3	1	—	1
Total	200	141	59	165	122	43	35	19	16
Presence of Alcohol, Outside the Home									
Stabbing	73	59	14	66	53	13	7	6	1
Shooting	48	42	6	40	35	5	8	7	1
Beating	49	47	2	24	22	2	25	25	—
Other	4	2	2	1	—	1	3	2	1
Total	174	150	24	131	110	21	43	40	3
No Alcohol, In the Home									
Stabbing	33	25	8	28	22	6	5	3	2
Shooting	40	28	12	28	22	6	12	6	6
Beating	16	7	9	6	2	4	10	5	5
Other	12	5	7	7	3	4	5	2	3
Total	101	65	36	69	49	20	32	16	16
No Alcohol, Outside the Home									
Stabbing	32	28	4	24	21	3	8	7	1
Shooting	47	39	8	28	22	6	19	17	2
Beating	25	22	3	8	6	2	17	16	1
Other	9	4	5	2	1	1	7	3	4
Total	113	93	20	62	50	12	51	43	8

TABLE 12

VIOLENCE IN CRIMINAL HOMICIDE, BY RACE AND SEX OF
OFFENDER, BY DEGREE OF VIOLENCE AND BY PRESENCE OF
ALCOHOL IN THE OFFENDER, PHILADELPHIA, 1948–1952

	Both Races			Negro			White		
	Total	Male	Female	Total	Male	Female	Total	Male	Female
Non-violence Alcohol	306	233	73	234	174	60	72	59	13
Present	154	122	32	125	96	29	29	26	3
No Alcohol	152	111	41	109	78	31	43	33	10
Violence Alcohol	315	279	36	233	200	33	82	79	3
Present	189	168	21	146	127	19	43	41	2
No Alcohol	126	111	15	87	73	14	39	38	1
Degree of Violence									
2 acts	61	52	9	47	39	8	14	13	1
3–5 acts	95	82	13	77	65	12	18	17	1
More than 5 acts	49	44	5	39	34	5	10	10	—
Severe Beating	93	89	4	59	55	4	34	34	—
Severe Beating prior to one stab	13	9	4	9	5	4	4	4	—
Severe Beating prior to one shot	4	3	1	2	2	—	2	1	1

TABLE 13

VIOLENCE IN CRIMINAL HOMICIDE, BY RACE AND SEX OF
VICTIM AND BY DEGREE OF VIOLENCE, BY METHOD, BY PLACE,
AND BY PRESENCE OF ALCOHOL IN THE VICTIM,
PHILADELPHIA, 1948–1952

	Both Races			Negro			White		
	Total	Male	Female	Total	Male	Female	Total	Male	Female
Non-Violence	294	242	52	211	182	29	83	60	23
Stabbing	110	97	13	99	88	11	11	9	2
Home	58	51	7	53	47	6	5	4	1
Not Home	52	46	6	46	41	5	6	5	1
Shooting	99	85	14	78	69	9	21	16	5
Home	54	46	8	44	40	4	10	6	4
Not Home	45	39	6	34	29	5	11	10	1
Beating	59	47	12	24	19	5	35	28	7
Home	17	8	9	7	4	3	10	4	6
Not Home	42	39	3	17	15	2	25	24	1
Other	26	13	13	10	6	4	16	7	9
Home	14	7	7	8	5	3	6	2	4
Not Home	12	6	6	2	1	1	10	5	5
Alcohol									
Present	154	133	21	116	102	14	38	31	7
No Alcohol	140	109	31	95	80	15	45	29	16
Violence	294	207	87	216	149	67	78	58	20
Stabbing	118	84	34	101	72	29	17	12	5
Home	65	43	22	57	39	18	8	4	4
Not Home	53	41	12	44	33	11	9	8	1
Shooting	95	67	28	67	48	19	28	19	9
Home	45	25	20	33	20	13	12	5	7
Not Home	50	42	8	34	28	6	16	14	2
Beating	69	49	20	36	22	14	33	27	6
Home	37	19	18	21	9	12	16	10	6
Not Home	32	30	2	15	13	2	17	17	—
Other	12	7	5	12	7	5	—	—	—
Home	11	7	4	11	7	4	—	—	—
Not Home	1	—	1	1	—	1	—	—	—
Alcohol									
Present	156	119	37	130	99	31	26	20	6
No Alcohol	138	88	50	86	50	36	52	38	14
Degree of Violence									
2 acts	65	51	14	52	43	9	13	8	5
3–5 acts	87	63	24	67	50	17	20	13	7
More than 5 acts	52	32	20	43	25	18	9	7	2
Severe Beating	72	47	25	41	22	19	31	25	6
Severe Beating prior to one stab	13	9	4	9	5	4	4	4	—
Severe Beating prior to one shot	5	5	—	4	4	—	1	1	—

TABLE 14

PRESENCE OF ALCOHOL IN THE VICTIM IN VIOLENT
AND NON-VIOLENT CRIMINAL HOMICIDE, BY RACE AND SEX OF
VICTIM, PHILADELPHIA, 1948–1952

(In Per Cent)

	Both Races			Negro			White		
	Total	Male	Female	Total	Male	Female	Total	Male	Female (a)
Violence									
Alcohol									
Present	46.9	57.5	42.5	60.2	66.4	46.3	33.3	34.5	—
No Alcohol	53.1	42.5	57.5	39.8	33.6	53.7	66.7	65.5	—
Total	100.0	100.0	100.0	100.0	100.0	100.0	100.0	100.0	100.0
	(294)	(207)	(87)	(216)	(149)	(67)	(78)	(58)	(20)
Non-Violence									
Alcohol									
Present	52.4	55.0	40.4	55.0	56.0	48.3	45.8	51.7	—
No Alcohol	47.6	45.0	59.6	45.0	44.0	51.7	54.2	48.3	—
Total	100.0	100.0	100.0	100.0	100.0	100.0	100.0	100.0	100.0
	(294)	(242)	(52)	(211)	(182)	(29)	(83)	(60)	(23)

(a) Category too small for breakdown by percentage distribution.

TABLE 15

TYPE OF PREVIOUS ARREST RECORD, BY RACE AND SEX
OF VICTIM AND OFFENDER IN CRIMINAL HOMICIDE,
PHILADELPHIA, 1948–1952

	Both Races			Negro			White		
VICTIMS	Total	Male	Female	Total	Male	Female	Total	Male	Female
No Previous Arrest Record	311	207	104	195	128	67	116	79	37
Previous Arrest Record	277	242	35	232	203	29	45	39	6
Offenses Against the Person	150	133	17	122	110	12	28	23	5
Aggravated Assault	101	96	5	87	83	4	14	13	1
Offenses Other Than Those Against the Person	127	109	18	110	93	17	17	16	1
Offenses Against Property	40	36	4	35	31	4	5	5	—
OFFENDERS									
No Previous Arrest Record	221	164	57	149	104	45	72	60	12
Previous Arrest Record	400	348	52	318	270	48	82	78	4
Offenses Against the Person	264	238	26	211	186	25	53	52	1
Aggravated Assault	192	171	21	161	141	20	31	30	1
Offenses Other Than Those Against the Person	136	110	26	107	84	23	29	26	3
Offenses Against Property	57	38	19	50	32	18	7	6	1

Note:

"Offenses Against the Person" includes aggravated assaults.

"Offenses Other Than Those Against the Person" includes offenses against property. "Offenses Against Property" means that the individual has a record of property offense *only* and has no record of any other type of offense.

TABLE 16

NUMBER OF OFFENSES FOR WHICH OFFENDER HAD BEEN
ARRESTED PRIOR TO INSTANT OFFENSE OF CRIMINAL
HOMICIDE, BY RACE AND SEX, PHILADELPHIA, 1948–1952

mber of revious ffenses	Both Races			Negro			White		
	Total	Male	Female	Total	Male	Female	Total	Male	Female
e	106	88	18	86	71	15	20	17	3
o	87	71	16	72	56	16	15	15	—
ee	40	37	3	32	29	3	8	8	—
ır	44	40	4	30	26	4	14	14	—
e	37	33	4	28	25	3	9	8	1
to Ten	56	51	5	48	43	5	8	8	—
re than Ten	30	28	2	22	20	2	8	8	—
Total	400	348	52	318	270	48	82	78	4

Table 17

MOTIVE IN CRIMINAL HOMICIDE, BY RACE AND SEX OF
VICTIM AND OF OFFENDER, PHILADELPHIA, 1948–1952

Victim	Both Races			Negro			White		
	Total	Male	Female	Total	Male	Female	Total	Male	Fema
Altercation of relatively trivial origin; insult, curse, jostling, etc.	206	183	23	153	134	19	53	49	4
Domestic quarrel	83	47	36	66	40	26	17	7	10
Jealousy	68	40	28	60	38	22	8	2	6
Altercation over money	62	54	8	56	50	6	6	4	2
Robbery	40	36	4	10	8	2	30	28	2
Revenge	31	23	8	23	18	5	8	5	3
Accidental	23	16	7	17	12	5	6	4	2
Self-defense	8	7	1	8	7	1	—	—	—
Halting of felon	7	7	—	7	7	—	—	—	—
Escaping arrest	6	5	1	2	2	—	4	3	1
Concealing birth	6	2	4	3	2	1	3	—	3
Other	20	11	9	6	3	3	14	8	6
Unknown	28	18	10	16	10	6	12	8	4
Total	588	449	139	427	331	96	161	118	43
Offender									
Altercation of relatively trivial origin; insult, curse, jostling, etc.	227	197	30	165	136	29	62	61	1
Domestic quarrel	83	46	37	64	34	30	19	12	7
Jealousy	69	52	17	60	45	15	9	7	2
Altercation over money	64	55	9	59	51	8	5	4	1
Robbery	49	49	—	31	31	—	18	18	—
Revenge	30	27	3	23	20	3	7	7	—
Accidental	28	24	4	20	16	4	8	8	—
Self-defense	8	6	2	8	6	2	—	—	—
Halting of felon	7	7	—	6	6	—	1	1	—
Escaping arrest	6	6	—	2	2	—	4	4	—
Concealing birth	5	—	5	2	—	2	3	—	3
Other	26	25	1	17	17	—	9	8	1
Unknown	19	18	1	10	10	—	9	8	1
Total	621	512	109	467	374	93	154	138	16

TABLE 18

MOTIVE IN CRIMINAL HOMICIDE BY AGE OF OFFENDER,
PHILADELPHIA, 1948–1952

MOTIVE	Total	AGE					
		10–19	20–29	30–39	40–49	50–59	60 and Over
tercation of relatively trivial origin; insult, curse, jostling, etc.	227	26	74	61	40	18	8
mestic quarrel	83	2	21	31	18	4	7
lousy	69	2	27	22	13	5	—
tercation over money	64	4	19	22	12	6	1
bbery	49	15	27	5	1	1	—
venge	30	—	12	10	7	—	1
cidental	28	7	8	7	6	—	—
f-defense	8	—	2	2	4	—	—
lting felon	6	—	1	3	1	1	—
caping arrest	6	3	1	—	1	—	1
ncealing birth	5	—	4	1	—	—	—
her	26	6	12	6	1	—	1
known	19	1	1	5	8	3	1
Total	620	66	209	175	112	38	20

TABLE 19

MOTIVE IN CRIMINAL HOMICIDE BY AGE OF OFFENDER,
PHILADELPHIA, 1948–1952

(In Per Cent)

MOTIVE	Total	AGE					
		10–19	20–29	30–39	40–49	50–59	60 and Over (a)
ercation of relatively rivial origin; insult, urse, jostling, etc.	36.6	39.4	35.4	34.9	35.7	47.4	—
mestic quarrel	13.4	3.0	10.1	17.7	16.1	10.5	—
lousy	11.1	3.0	12.9	12.6	11.6	13.2	—
ercation over money	10.3	6.1	9.1	12.6	10.7	15.8	—
bbery	7.9	22.7	12.9	2.8	.9	2.6	—
venge	4.8	—	5.7	5.7	6.2	—	—
cidental	4.5	10.6	3.8	4.0	5.4	—	—
f-defense	1.3	—	1.0	1.1	3.6	—	—
lting felon	1.0	—	.5	1.7	.9	2.6	—
aping arrest	1.0	4.6	.5	—	.9	—	—
ncealing birth	.8	—	1.9	.6	—	—	—
er	4.2	9.1	5.7	3.4	.9	—	—
known	3.1	1.5	.5	2.9	7.1	7.9	—
Total	100.0 (620)	100.0 (66)	100.0 (209)	100.0 (175)	100.0 (112)	100.0 (38)	100.0 (20)

(a) Category too small for breakdown by percentage distribution.

377

TABLE 20

TYPE OF INTERPERSONAL RELATIONSHIP BETWEEN VICTIM AND PRINCIPAL OFFENDER,
BY RACE AND SEX OF VICTIM, BY PLACE, AND VIOLENCE,
CRIMINAL HOMICIDE, PHILADELPHIA, 1948–1952

Race and Sex	Total	Close Friend	Family Relation- ship	Acquaint- ance	Stranger	Paramour, Mistress, Prostitute	Sex Rival	Enemy	Paramour of Offender's Mate	Felon or Police Officer	Innocent Bystander	Homo- sexual Partner
Both Races	550	155	136	74	67	54	22	16	11	6	6	3
Male	421	143	69	66	60	27	20	15	9	6	3	3
Female	129	12	67	8	7	27	2	1	2	—	3	—
Negro	410	126	98	59	32	43	20	12	11	2	5	2
Male	318	114	55	51	29	24	19	11	9	2	2	2
Female	92	12	43	8	3	19	1	1	2	—	3	—
White	140	29	38	15	35	11	2	4	—	4	1	1
Male	103	29	14	15	31	3	1	4	—	4	1	1
Female	37	—	24	—	4	8	1	—	—	—	—	—
Place												
Home	289	74	112	30	12	38	11	3	6	—	2	1
Not Home	261	81	24	44	55	16	11	13	5	6	4	2
Non-violence	279	89	57	36	37	30	11	4	7	3	4	1
Violence	271	66	79	38	30	24	11	12	4	3	2	2

Note:

Because there are 38 criminal homicides for which no known perpetrators have been identified, only 550 interpersonal relationships are known.

TABLE 21

AGE RELATIONSHIP BETWEEN VICTIM AND OFFENDER, BY DIFFERENTIAL NUMBER OF YEARS

Age Differential	Total	Offender older than victim	Offender younger than victim
1– 5 years	214	103	111
6–10 years	113	44	69
11–15 years	73	30	43
16–20 years	53	25	28
21–25 years	44	19	25
26–30 years	36	12	24
31–35 years	14	4	10
36–40 years	15	—	15
41–45 years	13	2	11
46–50 years	5	1	4
er 50 years	3	1	2
Total	583	241	342
ctim an infant	11		
ctim same age	26		
Total	620		

TABLE 22

RACE AND SEX OF VICTIM BY RACE AND SEX OF OFFENDER, CRIMINAL HOMICIDE, PHILADELPHIA, 1948–1952

VICTIM	OFFENDER								
	Both Races			Negro			White		
	Total	Male	Female	Total	Male	Female	Total	Male	Female
th Races	550	445	105	416	327	89	134	118	16
Male	421	333	88	324	247	77	97	86	11
Female	129	112	17	92	80	12	37	32	5
gro	410	321	89	396	309	87	14	12	2
Male	318	241	77	307	232	75	11	9	2
Female	92	80	12	89	77	12	3	3	—
hite	140	124	16	20	18	2	120	106	14
Male	103	92	11	17	15	2	86	77	9
Female	37	32	5	3	3	—	34	29	5

TABLE 23
TIME INTERVAL BETWEEN DEATH OF VICTIM AND SUBSEQUENT LEGAL PROCESSES, BY RACE AND SEX OF OFFENDER, CRIMINAL HOMICIDE, PHILADELPHIA, 1948–1952

Legal Process and Time Interval from Death of Victim	Both Races			Negro			White		
	Total	Male	Female	Total	Male	Female	Total	Male	Fem
Arrest									
Less than 1 day	393	306	87	292	216	76	101	90	1
1 day	78	71	7	59	54	5	19	17	
2–7 days	62	55	7	41	35	6	21	20	
8–14 days	11	11	—	9	9	—	2	2	—
15–30 days	21	17	4	18	15	3	3	2	
More than 30 days	42	39	3	34	32	2	8	7	
Total	607	499	108	453	361	92	154	138	1
Coroner's Inquest									
Less than 3 weeks	7	5	2	4	3	1	3	2	
3–4 weeks	162	134	28	121	96	25	41	38	
5–6 weeks	200	166	34	150	118	32	50	48	
7–8 weeks	86	76	10	67	57	10	19	19	—
9–12 weeks	45	38	7	33	29	4	12	9	3
13–16 weeks	12	9	3	3	3	—	9	6	3
More than 16 weeks	10	6	4	10	6	4	—	—	
Not Reported	99	78	21	79	62	17	20	16	4
Total	621	512	109	467	374	93	154	138	1
Presentment Before Grand Jury									
4 weeks	111	87	24	76	55	21	35	32	
5–6 weeks	165	130	35	129	100	29	36	30	6
7–8 weeks	144	120	24	115	91	24	29	29	—
9–12 weeks	85	74	11	64	55	9	21	19	
13–16 weeks	27	24	3	19	18	1	8	6	
More than 16 weeks	28	24	4	26	23	3	2	1	1
Not Reported or Applicable	61	53	8	38	32	6	23	21	
Total	621	512	109	467	374	93	154	138	1
Court Trial									
1–3 months	61	48	13	50	39	11	11	9	
4–6 months	244	195	49	186	145	41	58	50	8
7–9 months	99	85	14	78	64	14	21	21	—
10–12 months	81	65	16	62	48	14	19	17	
More than 12 months	59	51	8	44	38	6	15	13	
Pending	12	8	4	7	4	3	5	4	1
Not Reported or Applicable	51	47	4	26	23	3	25	24	1
Total	607	499	108	453	361	92	154	138	1

Note:

The 607 offenders include only those who were in police custody. Thus, 14 fugiti (including one multiple defendant after the first principal) are not included. coroner's inquest is, of course, held for each death so that each of the 621 offende fugitives or not, was held responsible for a homicide. Similarly, a universe of was used for time interval between crime and grand jury.

TABLE 24

TIME INTERVAL BETWEEN ARREST AND PRELIMINARY
HEARING, BY RACE AND SEX OF OFFENDER, CRIMINAL
HOMICIDE, PHILADELPHIA, 1948–1952

rrest and Hearing	Both Races			Negro			White		
	Total	Male	Female	Total	Male	Female	Total	Male	Female
ime Interval									
Less than 1									
day	107	89	18	72	58	14	35	31	4
1 day	340	264	76	259	190	69	81	74	7
2 days	49	45	4	47	44	3	2	1	1
3 days	15	14	1	7	7	—	8	7	1
4 days	7	6	1	4	4	—	3	2	1
5 days	6	6	—	6	6	—	—	—	—
6 days or more	33	32	1	27	26	1	6	6	—
Not reported or not applicable	50	43	7	31	26	5	19	17	2
Total	607	499	108	453	361	92	154	138	16

TABLE 25

DISPOSITION OF OFFENDER IN CRIMINAL HOMICIDE,
BY RACE AND SEX, PHILADELPHIA, 1948–1952

ace and Sex		DISPOSITION				
	Total	Guilty	Not Guilty	*Nolle Prosequi*	Pending	Other
oth Races	607	404	122	21	12	48
Male	499	337	92	14	9	47
Female	108	67	30	7	3	1
legro	453	331	78	11	8	25
Male	361	270	53	8	5	25
Female	92	61	25	3	3	—
/hite	154	73	44	10	4	23
Male	138	67	39	6	4	22
Female	16	6	5	4	—	1

381

TABLE 26
DISPOSITION, BY MOTIVE OF OFFENDER IN CRIMINAL HOMICIDE, PHILADELPHIA, 1948–1952

Motive	Total	Guilty	Not Guilty	Other
Altercation of relatively trivial origin; insult, curse, jostling, etc.	221	142	60	19
Domestic quarrel	83	53	15	15
Jealousy	66	51	6	9
Altercation over money	62	50	8	4
Robbery	49	43	3	3
Revenge	30	23	2	5
Accidental	28	17	10	1
Self-defense	8	—	8	—
Halting felon	7	4	3	—
Escaping arrest	6	3	2	1
Concealing birth	5	2	1	2
Other motives	25	13	2	10
Unknown	17	3	2	12
Total	607	404	122	81

TABLE 27
DEGREE OF CRIMINAL HOMICIDE DESIGNATED BY A COURT OF RECORD, BY RACE AND SEX OF THREE CLASSIFICATIONS OF OFFENDERS, PHILADELPHIA, 1948–1952

Offenders Available for Prosecution and for whom Degree of Homicide was Reported	Both Races			Negro			White		
	Total	Male	Female	Total	Male	Female	Total	Male	Fem
Degree of Homicide									
First degree murder	80	77	3	63	62	1	17	15	2
Second degree murder	141	116	25	113	92	21	28	24	4
Vol. manslaughter	213	161	52	168	122	46	45	39	6
Invol. manslaughter	75	58	17	48	34	14	27	24	3
Total	509	412	97	392	310	82	117	102	1
Offenders Sentenced *Degree of Homicide*									
First degree murder	77	75	2	63	62	1	14	13	1
Second degree murder	113	96	17	94	78	16	19	18	1
Vol. manslaughter	138	106	32	121	90	31	17	16	1
Invol. manslaughter	59	47	12	44	34	10	15	13	2
Total	387	324	63	322	264	58	65	60	5
Offenders Sentenced, who had a Previous Arrest Record *Degree of Homicide*									
First degree murder	57	56	1	46	45	1	11	11	—
Second degree murder	89	79	10	72	63	9	17	16	
Vol. manslaughter	93	73	20	81	62	19	12	11	
Invol. manslaughter	38	33	5	25	22	3	13	11	
Total	277	241	36	224	192	32	53	49	

382

TABLE 28

DEGREE OF CRIMINAL HOMICIDE DESIGNATED BY A COURT
OF RECORD, BY AGE OF OFFENDER AVAILABLE FOR
PROSECUTION, PHILADELPHIA, 1948–1952

Age	Total	First Degree Murder	Second Degree Murder	Voluntary Manslaughter	Involuntary Manslaughter
10–19	54	16	12	18	8
20–29	182	31	53	69	29
30–39	138	17	39	63	19
40–49	97	12	27	44	14
50–59	27	4	6	13	4
60 and over	10	—	4	6	—
Total	508	80	141	213	74

TABLE 29

DEGREE OF CRIMINAL HOMICIDE DESIGNATED BY A COURT
OF RECORD, BY AGE OF OFFENDER AVAILABLE FOR
PROSECUTION, PHILADELPHIA, 1948–1952

(In Per Cent)

Degree	AGE						
	Total	10–19	20–29	30–39	40–49	50–59	60+ (a)
First Degree Murder	15.7	29.6	17.0	12.3	12.4	14.8	—
Second Degree Murder	27.8	22.2	29.1	28.3	27.8	22.2	—
Voluntary Manslaughter	41.9	33.3	37.9	45.7	45.3	48.1	—
Involuntary Manslaughter	14.6	14.8	15.9	13.8	14.4	14.8	—
Total	100.0 (508)	100.0 (54)	100.0 (182)	100.0 (138)	100.0 (97)	100.0 (27)	100.0 (10)

(a) Category too small for breakdown by percentage distribution

APPENDIX II

NUMBER OF CRIMINAL HOMICIDES BY POLICE DISTRICT,
PHILADELPHIA, 1948–1952

Police District	Number of Homicides
2	4
5	11
6	47
9	22
14	13
15	7
16	38
17	52
19	55
23	100
24	6
26	14
27	5
29	36
30	6
31	88
32	19
33	35
35	4
37	10
38	5
39	7
41	2
Fairmount Park	2
Total	588

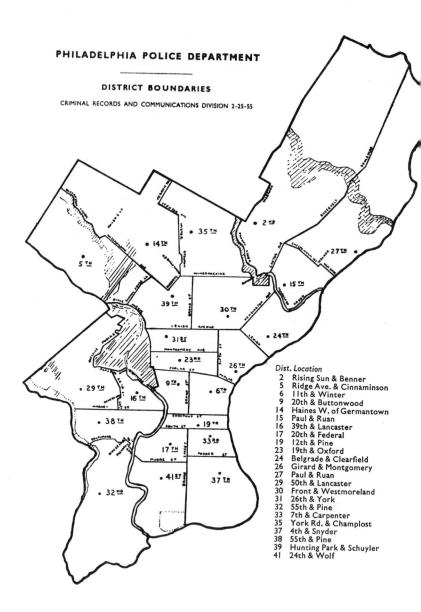

PHILADELPHIA POLICE DEPARTMENT

DISTRICT BOUNDARIES

CRIMINAL RECORDS AND COMMUNICATIONS DIVISION 2-25-55

Dist. Location
2   Rising Sun & Benner
5   Ridge Ave. & Cinnaminson
6   11th & Winter
9   20th & Buttonwood
14 Haines W. of Germantown
15 Paul & Ruan
16 39th & Lancaster
17 20th & Federal
19 12th & Pine
23 19th & Oxford
24 Belgrade & Clearfield
26 Girard & Montgomery
27 Paul & Ruan
29 50th & Lancaster
30 Front & Westmoreland
31 26th & York
32 55th & Pine
33 7th & Carpenter
35 York Rd. & Champlost
37 4th & Snyder
38 55th & Pine
39 Hunting Park & Schuyler
41 24th & Wolf

Philadelphia Police Department District Boundaries

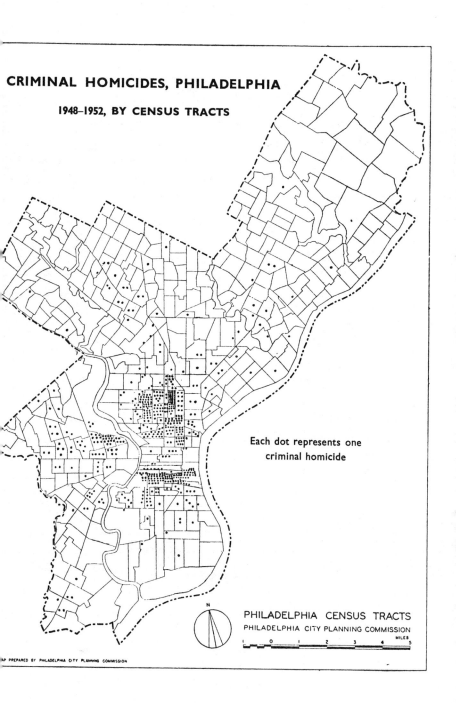

CRIMINAL HOMICIDES, PHILADELPHIA

1948–1952, BY CENSUS TRACTS

Each dot represents one
criminal homicide

PHILADELPHIA CENSUS TRACTS
PHILADELPHIA CITY PLANNING COMMISSION
MILES
0   1   2   3   4   5

MAP PREPARED BY PHILADELPHIA CITY PLANNING COMMISSION

Philadelphia Census Tracts

POLICE DEPARTMENT
PHILADELPHIA

Division No._____ Case No._____ Date_____

Name of Deceased _____

Report of Death by Detective_____Div. No._____Badge No._____

Date and Time Uniform Police Arrived at Scene_____

First on Scene_____Badge No._____District_____

_____Badge No._____District_____

_____Badge No._____District_____

Statement by Deceased (if any)_____

_____

_____

By Whom Reported to Police_____Address_____

By Whom Found_____Address_____

Body - Where Found and Position

Identifying Marks on Body_____

How Long a Resident of United States_____of Philadelphia_____

Occupation_____Civil Condition_____

Body Photographed by_____Badge No._____

Body Finger-printed by _____Badge No._____

Criminal Record (Yes, No)_____Photo. No._____

Body Searched by_____Badge No._____

Property Found on Body

Disposition of Property_____Date_____

Body Removed to_____ By Order of_____

MOTIVE (describe briefly)

Résumé of Homicide Case

WITNESS SHEET

DEFENDANT (describe fully and include Criminal Record)

Date and time of occurrence _____

Place of occurrence _____

Hospital_____ Doctor_____ Time of death_____

Day, date and time reported to Homicide Division_____

Weapon_____ Where recovered & by whom_____

Disposition of weapon _____

Weather _____

IDENTIFICATION WITNESSES

CIVILIAN WITNESSES

NAME	ADDRESS	STATEMENT (yes, no)	OBSERVATIONS OF WITNESS-answer yes or no on Police Record & attach same.

Witness Sheet

POLICE DEPARTMENT

REPORT OF INVESTIGATING OFFICER

Name_____ Address_____

Age___ Sex___ Color___ Weight___ Height___ Nationality_____

Date of Death_____ Date and Location of Autopsy_____

_____ Coroner's Physician_____

History of Case:_____

_____

_____

_____

_____

Ex. Exam.:_____

_____

_____

_____

_____

Autopsy:_____

_____

_____

_____

_____

Remarks:_____

_____

_____

_____

_____

Diagnosis and Cause of Death:_____

_____

_____

_____

Date:_____ Signed:_____

Report of Investigating Officer

REQUEST FOR FIREARM EXAMINATION

POLICE DEPARTMENT
PHILADELPHIA, PA.

Prepare in duplicate. One set for each Firearm. Submit set and exhibit to Ballistic Laboratory. Laboratory retains original, duplicate to be receipted and returned to official file as evidence.

DATE

TO: **POLICE BALLISTIC LABORATORY**	FROM *(Dist.)*	**STAMP**

WEAPON MAKE		CALIBER	SERIAL #
MODEL		BARREL LGTH.	COLOR

GRIPS & OTHER IDENTIFYING PARTS

CONTENTS OF WEAPON (*Describe number of cartridges and fired casings*)

ANY EXTRA AMMUNITION FOUND ☐ NO ☐ YES	NUMBER	TYPE

SPENT PROJECTILES AND FIRED CASINGS (*Where found, when, by whom*)

PERSONS ARRESTED (*In connection with submission*)

NAME	AGE	COLOR	ADDRESS	CHARGES PLACED

LOCATION OF ARRESTS (*Also date and time*)

ARRESTING OFFICERS (*Names, Nos, District*)

REMARKS (*Describe in detail arrest or confiscation. Note requests for specific examinations or comparisons by Ballistic. Report reason on weapons submitted for safekeeping.*)

DISPOSITION (*Status of violators or defendants; if held for hearing or court; is weapon required as evidence*)

SIGNATURE (*Confiscating Officer*)	APPROVED (*Commanding Officer*)

No weapon will be turned over to any officer except upon presentation of official receipt, nor will any weapon be returned to officers for any purpose other than presentation as evidence in Court, without written request to and approval by the Police Commissioner.

EXTREME CARE SHALL BE EXERCISED BY SUBMITTING OFFICER, TO PROTECT AND PRESERVE THE ORIGINAL CONDITION OF SUBMITTED SPECIMENS. EACH SPECIMEN SHALL BE INDIVIDUALLY WRAPPED IN PAPER.

The arresting and/or confiscating officer shall personally submit exhibits IMMEDIATELY FOLLOWING MAGISTRATE'S HEARING, WHERE AN ARREST IS MADE; IN OTHER CASES SUBMISSION SHALL BE MADE UPON COMPLETING NECESSARY PRELIMINARY INVESTIGATION.

When additional evidence is submitted in the same case, such as a fatal bullet or fired casings found subsequent to the submission of a weapon, the date of original submission shall be noted in REMARKS.

Owners requesting return of confiscated weapons shall be notified that all requests must be IN WRITING to the Police Commissioner.

Request for Firearm Examination

INDEX

Abrahamsen, David, 21, 91, 151, 157, 185, 186, 316, 336

Accidental homicide, 189, 191, 230, 231, 275, 301, 302; *see also* Motives in criminal homicide

Acquaintance relationship, 204, 205, 206, 207, 208, 209, 210, 218, 228, 230, 243, 260, 265, 313; *see also* Victim-offender relationships

Adjudication; *see* Court designation and disposition; Insanity; Legal procedure, tempo of; *Significant* associations

Adjustment, post-offense, 339

Age, criminal homicide by; *see also Significant* associations
court disposition of, 304
felony-homicide in, 242
homicide-suicide in, 278
husband-wife, 210, 233
methods and weapons used in, 6, 88–89, 320–321
motives in, 6, 195
in other studies, 70–78
previous record related to, 8, 180–181
and race, 6, 65–70, 320
rates and distributions in Philadelphia of, 65–70
and sex, 6, 65–70, 320
in unsolved cases, 293, 294, 327
victim-offender relationships in, 6, 8, 210–212, 230–233, 320, 325; *see also* Interpersonal relationships
victim-precipitated cases of, 255, 256
violence in, 161, 323

Aggravated assault, 80, 101, 116, 117, 118, 119, 174, 176, 177, 178–180, 182, 230, 232, 233, 321, 324, 333, 337; *see also* Previous record

Agnew, Judge, 250

Akron, Ohio, 25, 90, 291

Alabama; *see* Birmingham; Jefferson County

Alcohol in criminal homicide; *see also* Conduct norms; Medical technology; *Significant* associations
classification of terms, 135–137
homicide-suicide and, 277, 280–281
among husband-wife cases, 132, 227, 253, 280, 281
insanity related to, 313
legal ramifications of, 153–156
methods and weapons related to, 141, 144
motives related to, 151
noted in other studies, 143–156
by previous record, 151, 180–181, 324
by race, 8, 136–141
research suggestions for, 335
by sex, 8, 136–141
spatial patterns related to, 121–124, 129, 132
temporal patterns related to, 101, 109, 132, 141–143, 146, 151–152, 322–323, 334
tests for the presence of, 134–135, 147–149, 153, 333
victim-offender relationships and, 227, 228, 230
victim-precipitated cases by, 140, 257, 261–262, 265, 326
violence and, 134, 165–167, 323

Alcoholism, 144, 145, 146, 147, 150, 153

Alexander, Franz, 186

Allredge, E. P., 41, 43, 235, 308
Altercation (general), 188, 189, 191, 192, 194, 195, 196, 197, 199, 213, 226, 227, 228, 230, 231, 232; *see also* Motives in criminal homicide
Altercation over money, 191, 194, 195, 198, 226, 231, 232, 233, 275, 301, 302, 324; *see also* Motives in criminal homicide
Arado, C. C., 154
Arkin, H., 18
Arrest record; *see* Previous record
Arson; *see* Felony-homicide
Aschaffenburg, Gustav, 97, 145
Ash, Ellis, 339
Atlanta, Georgia, 41, 235, 273
Austria, 56

Baines, Cecil, 185
Baltimore, Maryland, 25, 90, 291
Banay, Ralph, 76, 94, 144–145, 171–172, 187
Barnes, Harry Elmer, 74, 97
Basutoland, 186
Beatings; *see* Methods and weapons of inflicting death
Becker, Howard, 270
Belgrade Institute of Legal Medicine, 153
Bender, L., 21
Benoit-Smullyan, Emile, 74
Berg, I. A., 21, 157–158, 162, 165, 183
Biggs, John, Jr., 313
Birmingham, Alabama, 41, 42, 43, 44, 50, 52, 75, 76, 93, 94, 110, 133, 146, 236–237, 273, 289
Bjerre, Andreas, 21
Blinn, Keith W., 20
Boll, Eleanor, 87
Bonger, W. A., 145–146

Bossard, J. H. S., 87, 120, 193
Boston, Massachusetts, 25, 291
Bowers, Warner F., 119
Bradess, V. A., 135
Brearley, H. C., 12, 21, 45, 53–54, 59, 61, 71, 82, 92, 97, 102, 103–104, 105, 106, 171, 234, 307, 310
Broadmoor, England, 316
Bromberg, Walter, 270
Brownlee, K. A., 18
Bruce, A. A., 235, 289
Buffalo, New York, 25, 90, 290, 291
Bulgaria, 62
Bullock, Henry Allen, 120
Bulwer-Lytton, Edward, 247
Bunzel, Bessie, 40, 43, 51, 76, 92, 101, 169–170, 273, 308, 314
Burglary; *see* Felony-homicide
Byberry, Pennsylvania, 313
Bye, Raymond T., 5
Bystander, innocent, 204, 205, 206, 207, 209, 231; *see also* Victim-offender relationships

Caldwell, Morris G., 339
California; *see* Los Angeles
Calvert, E. Roy, 5, 59, 274
Canada, 79, 171
Capital punishment, 5, 26, 111, 112, 231, 232, 283, 304, 310, 311, 315, 326–327, 339
Carter, Sam, 183
Casey, Robert S., 16
Cassidy, J. H., 21, 51, 76, 147, 170, 196, 314
Catlin, George, 150
Catton, Joseph, 336
Causation of criminal homicide, 4, 6, 21, 133, 139, 150–151, 187, 261, 262, 328; *see also* Hypotheses, criminal homicide
Cavan, Ruth, 272, 275, 278

394

Census tracts, 120
Ceylon, 57
Chamber of Commerce, Philadelphia, 142
Chicago, Illinois, 25, 45, 196, 219, 235, 291; *see also* Illinois Crime Survey
Chile, 62
China, 57–58
Chi-square test, 17–18, 318; *see also* Statistical technique
Cincinnati, Ohio, 25, 291
Cleared by arrest, 180, 284, 287, 290, 294; *see also* Unsolved criminal homicide
Cleckley, Hervey, 186
Clemmer, Donald, 339
Close friend relationship, 204, 205, 206, 207, 208, 209, 210, 218, 227, 243, 260, 265, 280, 313, 324; *see also* Victim-offender relationships
Cohen, Joseph, 103
Colorado; *see* Denver
Colton, R. R., 18
Columbus, Ohio, 25, 90, 149, 150, 291
Concealing birth, 190, 191, 292, 301; *see also* Motives in criminal homicide
Conduct norms, 7, 328–329; *see also* Sub-cultural patterns
  deviance from, 340
  of drinking, 104, 109, 129, 132, 139–140, 141, 142, 143, 144–145, 146, 322
  and homicide-suicide, 276–277, 278
  internalization of, 285, 328
  leisure and week-end, 108–109, 112, 125, 132, 142–143
  methods of criminal homicide relative to, 80, 81, 83, 86, 127–128, 144, 332

motives of criminal homicide relative to, 129, 131, 132, 141, 142, 143, 146
national differences of, 64, 334
of personal violence, 117, 159, 160, 161, 188–189, 329
race and, 44, 81, 83, 86, 128, 129, 139–140, 146, 188–189, 193–194, 212, 225–226, 328–329, 332
sex differences and, 188–189, 192–193, 204, 225–226
social class and, 81, 83, 86, 142, 143, 146, 189, 330, 332, 340
spatial patterns of criminal homicide relative to, 87, 121–122, 125–130, 131, 133
temporal patterns of criminal homicide relative to, 129, 131, 132, 141, 142, 143, 146
Control of criminal homicide; *see* Hypotheses, criminal homicide; Prediction of criminal homicide; Prevention of criminal homicide
Cook County, Illinois; *see* Illinois Crime Survey
Copenhagen, Denmark, 145
Coroner, 10, 11, 12, 15, 146, 284, 286–288, 296, 297, 334
County prison, 230, 231, 233, 280, 299
Court designation and disposition, 299–315; *see also* Legal procedure, tempo of; Manslaughter; Murder; *Significant* associations
  by age, 304
  classifications of offenders and, 299–300, 303
  in felony-homicide, 232, 243–244
  of husband-wife homicides, 216–217, 233, 325
  insanity and, 312–317, 327

Court designation and disposition
  legal ramifications of alcohol relative to, 153–156
  by motives, 301–302
  noted in other studies, 304, 307–317, 327
  by previous record, 11, 303–304
  by race, 10, 11, 13, 229, 230–233, 243–244, 300–304, 307–312, 327
  by sex, 10, 13, 229–233, 243–244, 300–304, 308, 327
  by type of sentence, 230–233, 243, 304–306
  of victim-precipitated homicide, 217, 300
Court records, 13, 16, 41, 173, 174, 288, 338; see also Court designation and disposition
Crimes against the person, 7, 22, 96–97, 101, 112, 144–146, 149, 165, 174, 176, 177, 178–182, 263, 278, 324, 337; see also Aggravated assault; Previous record
Crimes against property, 96–97, 101, 176, 178–180, 324; see also Previous record
Criminal record; see Previous record
Criminal statistics; see Court designation and disposition; Court records; Police
Cruvant, Bernard A., 335
Culture conflict; see Conduct norms; Sub-cultural patterns
Curran, 21

Dallas, Texas, 25, 291
Dann, Robert H., 310
Davies, D. S., 20
Days of occurrence; see Temporal patterns

Death certificates; see Mortality statistics
Death penalty; see Capital punishment
Degrees of homicide, 9, 13, 22–24, 72, 153–156, 157, 190, 230–233, 238–240, 247–252, 283, 300–304, 305–306, 309–310, 319, 326–327, 338–339; see also Law of homicide; Manslaughter; Murder
Denmark, 62, 145
Density of population, 74, 331–332
Denver, Colorado, 98
De Porte, J. V., 45, 52, 77, 94, 103, 171, 310
De Quincey, Thomas, 247
De Quiros, Bernaldo, 96, 97, 168
Dexter, Edwin, 98
Disposition; see Court designation and disposition
District Attorney's Office, Philadelphia, 302, 310
Dollard, John, 185
Domestic quarrel, 87, 191, 192, 195, 196, 199, 213, 227, 228, 233, 253, 265, 275, 301, 302, 313, 324; see also Husband-wife homicides; Motives in criminal homicide
Doob, Leonard W., 185
Double homicide, 274
Doyle, Frederick T., 14
Dublin, Louis I., 40, 43, 51, 76, 92, 101, 169–170, 273, 308, 314
Dubowski, K. M., 135, 333
Durkheim, Emile, 47, 72–73, 74, 105, 192, 193, 204, 269, 272, 273, 331
Durrett, J. J., 273

East, W. N., 150, 153, 274, 316, 335

Eastern State Penitentiary, Pennsylvania, 230

Ecology, 120, 331–332
see also Spatial patterns in criminal homicide

Eggston, A. A., 135

Ehrmann, Herbert B., 307, 311

Elliott, Mabel, 47, 48, 49, 73–74, 91

Elwin, Verrier, 58–59, 104, 186

Enemy relationship, 204, 205, 206, 207, 209, 243, 247; see also Victim-offender relationships

England, 56, 59, 60–61, 62, 63, 77, 91, 92, 97, 111, 113, 150, 198–199, 219–220, 270, 274, 309, 312, 314–316, 320, 327, 332, 334; see also Great Britain; Royal Commission on Capital Punishment

Estonia, 270

Excusable homicide, 13, 16, 20, 22, 23, 24, 286, 287, 288; see also Degrees of homicide; Law of homicide

Family relationship, 7, 204, 205–210, 212–217, 219, 227, 228, 231, 253, 260, 265, 279, 313, 316, 324; see also Husband-wife homicides

Farview, Pennsylvania, 232, 243

Federal Bureau of Investigation; see Uniform Crime Reports

Federal Bureau of Prisons; see Prison statistics

Fedor, Sid, 196

Felon relationship, 204, 206, 207, 209, 240–244; see also Felony-homicide

Felony-homicide, 9, 22, 130, 170, 190, 229, 230, 231, 232, 292, 339
in Philadelphia, 240–244, 325–326

rule of, 238–240

Fenichel, O., 186

Ferri, Enrico, 21, 97, 269

Fink, Arthur, 134

Finland, 61, 62, 80, 112, 113, 151–152, 270, 312

Firearms; see Methods and weapons of inflicting death

First offender, 11, 168–172, 184, 335

Fisher, R. A., 17

Fisher, R. S., 135

Fitzgerald, T. S., 235, 289

Florence, Italy, 187

Florida, 92; see also Miami

Ford, Richard, 114

Foreign-born, 52, 76

Fox, Vernon, 21, 157–158, 162, 165, 183

France, 59, 70, 95, 96, 97, 105, 198

Frankel, Emil, 21, 40, 75, 76, 95, 218–219, 308, 335, 340

Frenkel, Helene, 186, 221

Freud, Anna, 185

Frustration-aggression, 75, 185, 276–277, 278, 330, 331, 336

Fry, Margery, 198

Fugitive, 13, 16, 287, 288, 289, 295, 338

Gang killings, 196

Garfinkel, Harold, 237, 308

Garofalo, Baron Raffaele, 21, 143–144, 156–157, 185, 247, 248

Georgia, 42, 307; see also Atlanta

Germany, 56, 59, 60, 92, 97, 197–198, 220

Gettler, A. O., 135, 148, 333

Gillin, J. L., 77, 94–95, 147, 183, 197

Glazer, Daniel, 3

Glueck, Eleanor, 174

Glueck, Sheldon, 174

Grand jury, 10, 15, 287, 288, 296, 298

Gray, M. A., 146

Great Britain, 145, 153; *see also* England

Greene, James E., 186

Gregory, John M., 273

Growdon, C. H., 46, 53, 95, 197, 219

Grünhut, Max, 12, 270, 274

Guerry, A. M., 96, 269

Hagood, M. J., 18

Halting of felon, 191, 301

Harlan, Harold, 42, 43, 44, 50, 52, 75, 93, 110, 133, 146, 197, 236–237, 289

Harno, A. J., 20

Harvard Medical School, 144

Hayner, Norman, 339

Healy, William, 186

Henry, Andrew F., 54–56, 75, 146–147, 185, 278–279, 280, 330

Hobbs, A. H., 5

Hoebel, E. Adamson, 58, 335

Hoffman, Frederick L., 5, 12, 40, 52, 71, 76, 91, 94, 102, 116, 234

Hoffman, William F., 22, 113, 154, 180, 240, 250, 312

Holloway Prison, England, 150

Home/not-home differences
  homicide-suicide and, 277
  by motives, 194–195
  noted in other studies, 133
  by race and sex, 7, 123–124, 130–133, 164–165, 194–195
  by temporal patterns, 131–133, 322
  victim-precipitated homicide and, 256, 258
  by violence, 164–165

Homicide, definition of, 16, 20–27, 72, 113, 252–254, 326; *see also* Law of homicide

Homicide Squad, Philadelphia, 5, 13–15, 24, 80, 85, 108, 113, 135, 187, 193, 283, 287, 299, 318; *see also* Police

Homicide-Suicide; *see also Significant* associations
  by age, 278
  alcohol related to, 277, 280–281
  amount of, 16, 272–274, 282–283, 326, 338
  as first degree murder, 283, 326–327
  husband-wife, 216, 217, 280–283, 325, 326
  insanity related to, 312, 315–317, 334
  methods and weapons in, 275, 280–282
  motives in, 275–277, 280–281
  noted in other studies, 273–274, 278–280, 327
  previous arrest record and, 278
  psychological factors underlying, 269–271, 275, 276–278, 340
  by race, 10, 272–273, 276, 282, 326
  research suggestions for, 317, 340
  by sex, 10, 272, 280–283, 326
  spatial patterns of, 277, 280–282
  victim-offender relationships in, 276, 278–283
  victim-precipitated, 282–283
  violence in, 275–276, 280–282

Homosexual partner, 204, 206, 207, 209, 230, 280: *see also* Victim-offender relationships

Hooton, Ernest A., 21

Hours of occurrence; *see* Temporal patterns in criminal homicide

398

Houston, Texas, 41, 236
Howard, George E., 145
Huhner, Max, 284
Hurwicz, Leonid, 254
Husband-wife homicides; *see also*
Significant associations
age and, 210, 233
alcohol related to, 132, 227,
253, 280, 281
amount of, 212–217, 325
court designation and disposition of, 216–217, 233, 325
and homicide-suicide, 216, 217,
280–283, 325, 326
insanity related to, 313, 316–
317
investigation of, 212
by methods and weapons, 213–
216, 227, 228, 233, 253, 280,
281, 323, 325
by motives, 213, 215, 227, 228,
233, 253, 280, 281
noted in other studies, 199, 208,
218–221, 316–317
by race, 212–214
sex differences in, 212–221, 325
spatial patterns in, 87, 132, 213,
215–216, 253, 280, 281, 323,
325
temporal patterns in, 48–49, 87,
126–127, 132
victim-precipitated, 217, 253,
256, 260, 265, 282–283
violence in, 165, 213, 214, 323
Hypotheses, criminal homicide,
relative to; *see also* Research
suggestions; *Significant* associations
alcohol, 139–140, 142–143, 146–
147, 322–323
density of population, 74, 331–
332
frequency of personal contacts,
225

guilt and remorse in homicide-
suicide, 276–280, 282–283; *see
also* Frustration-aggression
medical technology, 116–119,
321, 332–333
migration, 331
murder as a proportion of the
homicide rate, 312
previous arrest record, 174,
176–177, 180–182, 324
primary group relationships,
204, 206–210
sex ratio and the homicide rate,
61–64, 95
status, 54–56, 75
time between assault and death,
116–119, 321
time of occurrence, 96–98, 142–
143
victim-precipitated homicide,
258–265, 326
violence, 208
weapons, type of, 82, 86
working with the Philadelphia
data, 6–11

Iceland, 270
Illinois; *see* Chicago; Illinois
Crime Survey
Illinois Crime Survey, 12, 45, 50,
78, 93, 104, 196, 219, 235,
273, 288, 289, 308, 314
Imprisonment; *see* Eastern State
Penitentiary; Farview; Mun-
cy; Sentence, years of
India, 58–59, 104, 186
Infant slaying, 57, 210, 211, 324
Insanity, 11, 13, 97, 232, 300, 302,
312–317, 327, 334
Interpersonal relationships; *see
also Significant* associations;
Victim-offender relation-
ships; Victim-precipitated
criminal homicide

Interpersonal relationships
  acquaintance, 204, 205, 206, 207, 208, 209, 210, 218, 228, 230, 243, 260, 265, 313
  close friend, 204, 205, 206, 207, 208, 209, 210, 218, 227, 243, 260, 265, 280, 313, 324
  enemy, 204, 205, 206, 207, 209, 243, 247
  family relationship, 7, 204, 205–210, 212–217, 219, 227, 228, 231, 253, 260, 265, 279, 313, 316, 324; *see also* Husband-wife homicides
  felon, 204, 206, 207, 209, 240–244; *see also* Felony-homicide
  homosexual partner, 204, 206, 207, 209, 230, 280
  innocent bystander, 204, 205, 206, 207, 209, 231
  mistress, 199, 204, 207, 209, 219, 233
  paramour, 199, 204, 205, 206, 207, 208, 209, 210, 227, 253, 279, 280
  paramour of offender's mate, 186, 204, 205, 206, 207, 209
  police officer, 204, 205, 206, 207, 209, 231, 232, 243
  prostitute, 204, 207, 209, 232, 233, 243
  sex rival, 204, 205, 206, 207, 209, 219
  stranger, 204, 205, 206, 207, 208, 209, 212, 219, 221, 227, 228, 230, 293, 294, 313, 316, 324, 327
Investigation of homicide; *see* Police
Ireland, 145, 270
Italy, 56, 62, 97, 145, 187

Jealousy, 126, 157, 185, 188, 189–190, 191, 192, 193, 195, 196, 198, 213, 228, 230, 275, 292, 301, 302, 313; *see also* Motives in criminal homicide
Jefferson County, Alabama, 52, 94
Jellinek, E. M., 146
Jennings, Herbert S., 188
Jerrold, Douglas, 247
Jersey City, New Jersey, 90
Jesse, F. Tennyson, 185
Johnson, Guy B., 41, 236, 307
Joliet Penitentiary, Illinois, 170
Judy, Kenneth H., 119
Justifiable homicide, 13, 16, 20, 22, 23, 24, 228, 243, 286, 287, 288; *see also* Degrees of homicide; Law of homicide
Juvenile homicide, 46, 53, 66–67, 95, 197, 219

Kansas, 183
Kansas City, Missouri, 25, 90, 291
Kansas State Penitentiary, 183
Karpman, Ben, 186
Keedy, Edwin R., 22, 313
Kendall, M. G., 18
Kenny, C. S., 20
Kephart, William M., 193
Kilmer, Theron W., 144
Kilpatrick, J. J., 76, 170–171
Knives; *see* Methods and weapons of inflicting death; Subcultural patterns
Korn, Richard R., 339
Kropotkin, P., 97
Kurland, Albert A., 316–317

Lacassagne, A., 95, 269
Lanzer, Irving A., 246
Lashly, Arthur, 12, 93, 104, 105, 235, 288, 289, 308; *see also* Illinois Crime Survey
Latvia, 270
Law of homicide, 22–24, 58, 113,

153–156, 190, 238–240, 247–252, 292, 312; *see also* Degrees of homicide
Lawes, Lewis E., 144, 169, 172, 196, 317
Leffingwell, Albert, 97
Legal procedure, tempo of, 10, 295–299, 327
Lehrman, Philip R., 270
Lindner, Robert M., 186
Lobinger, C. S., 20
Lombroso, Cesare, 21, 97
London, England, 332
Lorton, Virginia, 169
Los Angeles, California, 25, 90
Louisiana; *see* New Orleans

McBee punch cards, 16
McCorkle, Lloyd W., 339
MacDonald, Arthur, 77, 111–112, 198, 219
MacDonald, John, 254
Macdonell, Sir John, 174, 180, 198, 336
MacIver, Robert M., 270, 338
Magath, Thomas B., 114
Manslaughter, 41, 101, 102, 103, 112, 231, 289
    adjudication of, 216–217, 231, 233, 235, 243, 302–306, 308–312, 327
    alcohol and, 151, 152, 153–156
    degrees of, 216–217, 243, 302–306, 338
    distinguished from other types of homicide, 20, 26, 338
    legal ramifications of, 22, 23–24, 113, 153–156, 239, 247–252
    motives in, 196
    in other countries, 105, 151, 152, 153
    as part of a criminal homicide rate, 25, 45, 71, 110, 116, 289, 290

prison commitment for, 40, 304–306
race and sex distributions of, 41, 230, 233, 235, 302–306, 308–312
terminology confusion regarding, 25–26, 105, 149, 318–319, 338
victim-offender relationships in, 216–217, 229–233
Marchant, Frederick T., 119
Maria murder, 58–59, 104, 186
Maryland; *see* Baltimore; Spring Grove
Massachusetts, 42, 45, 72, 147, 197, 307, 311; *see also* Boston; Massachusetts State Prison; Middlesex County; Suffolk County
Massachusetts State Prison, 183, 218
Mate slayings; *see* Husband-wife homicides
Matheson, J. C. M., 150
Mayo-Smith, Richard, 96–97
Medical examiner, 15, 122, 148, 156, 158, 284, 333
Medical technology, 116–119, 321, 332–333
Memphis, Tennessee, 41, 234–235, 236, 273, 289
Menninger, Karl, 270–271
Methods and weapons of inflicting death; *see also Significant* associations
    by age, 6, 88–89, 320–321
    alcohol related to, 141, 144
    classification and general discussion of, 81–83
    in felony-homicide, 243
    in homicide-suicide, 275, 280–282
    in husband-wife homicides, 213–216, 227, 228, 233, 253, 280, 281, 323, 325

401

Methods and weapons of inflicting death
insanity related to, 313
in other studies, 81–82, 90–95
by race, 6, 84–95, 320
by sex, 6, 9, 84–95, 320
spatial patterns related to, 87, 89, 122, 124, 127–129, 322
temporal patterns related to, 100, 107
time between assault and death related to, 115, 321
unsolved cases related to, 293, 294, 327
victim-offender relationships and, 226–233, 253–256, 258, 265, 295, 326
victim-precipitated cases by, 253–256, 258, 265, 326
violence by, 158–159, 162, 163–164
Metropolitan Life Insurance Company, 196
Meyers, Arthur C., Jr., 45, 51, 75–76, 94, 103, 110–111, 237, 289
Miami, Florida, 25, 291
Michael, Jerome, 20, 238, 248, 249, 336
Michigan, 72, 158, 183
Middlesex County, Massachusetts, 307, 311
Miller, Neal E., 185
Milwaukee, Wisconsin, 25, 90
Minneapolis, Minnesota, 271, 273
Minnesota; see Minneapolis; St. Paul
Missouri; see Kansas City; St. Louis
Mistress relationship, 199, 204, 207, 209, 219, 233; see also Victim-offender relationships
Monahan, Thomas P., 193

Moore, Merrill, 146
Morgenstern, Jacob, 317
Morgenstern, Oskar, 254
Moroney, M. J., 17
Morris, Albert, 3, 4
Morselli, Enrico, 269
Mortality statistics, 12, 13, 24, 26, 34–36, 49, 50, 51, 52, 53, 59, 71, 76, 82, 90, 91, 92, 94, 95, 102, 105, 116, 119, 122, 146, 158, 223, 224, 234, 318, 337
Moses, Earl R., 39
Motives in criminal homicide; see also Significant associations
(general)
by age, 6, 195
alcohol related to, 151
classification of, 185–190
court disposition by, 301–302
homicide-suicide and, 275–277, 280–281
husband-wife homicides by, 213, 215, 227, 228, 233, 253, 280, 281
insanity related to, 11, 313
noted in other studies, 195–199
by race, 6, 191, 192–195
by sex, 6, 9, 191, 192–195, 212
spatial patterns related to, 194–195
temporal patterns related to, 87, 294
among unsolved cases, 292, 293, 294, 327
victim-offender relationships by, 226–233
victim-precipitated cases by, 258
violence and, 195
(specific)
accidental, 189, 191, 230, 231, 275, 301, 302

402

altercation (of trivial origin, insult, curse, etc.), 188, 189, 191, 192, 194, 195, 196, 197, 199, 213, 226, 227, 228, 230, 231, 232

altercation (over money), 191, 194, 195, 198, 226, 231, 232, 233, 275, 301, 302, 324

concealing birth, 190, 191, 292, 301

domestic quarrel, 87, 191, 192, 195, 196, 199, 213, 227, 228, 233, 253, 265, 275, 301, 302, 313, 324; *see also* Husband-wife homicides

escaping arrest, 191, 231, 301

halting of felon, 191, 301

jealousy, 126, 157, 185, 188, 189–190, 191, 192, 193, 195, 196, 198, 213, 228, 230, 275, 292, 301, 302, 313

other, 189, 191, 195, 231, 232, 275, 292, 301

revenge, 127, 185, 186, 188, 189–190, 191, 197, 198, 199, 213, 227, 228, 232, 275, 292, 301–302

robbery, 186, 188, 191, 194, 197, 199, 208, 212, 218, 231, 238, 240–243, 252, 292, 293, 294, 301, 313, 324, 326

self-defense, 189, 191, 213, 301, 302

unknown, 189, 191, 213, 232, 275, 301, 313

Mowrer, O. H., 185

Multiple offenders, 27, 50, 51, 88, 95, 99–100, 138, 240, 241, 274

Muncy, Pennsylvania, 233

Mundhenke, H. R., 234, 270

Murder, 4, 21, 41, 80, 97, 101, 156–158, 168, 169, 270–272, 277, 279, 335

adjudication of, 216–217, 231, 232, 233, 235, 243–244, 302–306, 308, 327

alcohol and, 143, 147, 149, 150, 151, 152, 153–156

and the death penalty, 283, 304–306

degrees of, 9, 10–11, 216–217, 229–230, 232, 243–244, 277, 302–306, 308–312, 326–327, 338–339

as distinguished from other types of homicide, 20, 26, 338

felony-, 9, 22, 23, 130, 172, 229–230, 238–244, 292, 339

insanity and, 312–317

legal ramifications of, 9, 22–23, 153–156, 238–240, 247–252, 312

motives of, 185–186, 187, 188, 196, 197–199

in other countries, 59–60, 61, 72, 77, 78, 105, 112, 113, 150, 151, 152, 153, 197–199, 219, 220, 274, 309, 314–315

as part of a criminal homicide rate, 25, 45, 71, 110, 116, 289, 290

previous record and, 11, 170–172, 183, 303–304

prison commitment for, 40, 72, 304–306

race and sex distributions of, 11, 40, 41, 59, 60, 61, 74, 93, 197–198, 208, 220, 302–306, 308–312

terminology confusion regarding, 25–26, 52, 56, 59, 75, 77, 91, 149, 318–319, 338

unsolved, 284, 288, 289

Murder;
   victim-offender relationships in,
      208, 216–217, 219–220, 229–
      233
Murphy, Fred J., 173

Nashville, Tennessee, 41, 236
National Council for the Aboli-
      tion of the Death Penalty,
      314, 315
National statistics; *see* Mortality
      statistics; Uniform Crime
      Reports
Native-born, 52, 74, 76, 170
Necropsy, 114, 135, 147, 148, 153
Negroes; *see* Race
Neumann, John von, 254
New Jersey, 40, 75, 76, 90, 95, 218
New Orleans, Louisiana, 52, 76, 273
New South Wales, 145
New York, 45, 52, 94, 103, 171,
      284, 310; *see also* Buffalo;
      New York City
New York City, 25, 98, 148, 196,
      234, 310
New Zealand, 92
Nimkoff, Meyer F., 270
Nissen, Hartvig, 151
Nolle prosequi, 216, 232, 243, 300,
      301, 338
Non-violence in criminal homi-
      cide; *see* Violence in criminal
      homicide
Norms; *see* Conduct norms
North Carolina, 41, 236, 237, 307,
      310
Norway, 62, 151, 270
Nunberg, H., 186

Occupation, 36–39, 142–143, 330,
      331, 334
Offender in criminal homicide,
      definition of, 26–27
Ogburn, William F., 270

Ohio, 25, 46, 90, 149, 150, 219,
      291; *see also* Akron; Cin-
      cinnati; Columbus

Paramour, 199, 204, 205, 206, 207,
      208, 209, 210, 227, 253, 279,
      280; *see also* Victim-offender
      relationships
Paramour of offender's mate, 186,
      204, 205, 206, 207, 209; *see
      also* Victim-offender relation-
      ships
Parkhurst, E., 45, 52, 77, 94, 103,
      171, 310
Parmelee, Maurice, 96
Parole, 174
Peiping, 57
Pennsylvania; *see also* Philadelphia
   the death sentence in, 273
   felony-murder in, 9, 240
   general criminal homicide rate
      of, 24, 45
   insanity and the law in, 11, 312
   intoxication no excuse for
      crime in, 153
   the law of homicide in, 22–24
   law regarding switchblade
      knives in, 332
   offenses against the person in,
      180
   offenses against property in, 180
   provocation as a mitigating
      circumstance in, 250
Philadelphia; *see also* Homicide
      Squad, Philadelphia
   climatological data for, 99
   as a community case study, 5
   general conviction rates for all
      offenses in, 302
   general homicide rates in, 24–25
   law regarding switchblade
      knives in, 81, 332
   when wages are paid in, 142
Pittsburgh, Pennsylvania, 25

Perkins, Rollin M., 20, 238–239, 248, 249–250
Perry, J. W., 16
Phelps, H. A., 311, 314
Place of occurrence; *see* Spatial patterns in criminal homicide
Poison, 47, 56–57, 81, 90, 95
Police; *see also* Homicide Squad, Philadelphia; Previous record; Uniform Crime Reports
    communication with, 118, 321, 332
    investigation, 5, 7, 13–15, 36, 83, 114, 121, 135, 136, 149, 156, 188, 205, 212, 259, 286, 287, 288, 289, 290, 294, 295, 296, 297, 300, 302, 313, 321, 332, 333, 334
    officer, 82, 204–207, 212, 231, 232, 243
    records, 5, 10–17, 113, 120, 121, 135, 141, 156, 158, 172–173, 174–175, 176, 180, 181, 182, 196, 226, 331, 338
    reports, 25, 39, 49, 90, 199, 294
    statistics, 13, 15–17, 25–27, 34–36, 49, 59, 105, 118, 121, 135, 168, 180, 223, 224, 285, 290, 299, 318, 337, 338
Pollak, Otto, 36, 47–48, 49, 56–57, 73, 95, 218, 320
Porterfield, Austin L., 111, 146, 147, 173, 234, 264, 270, 271–273
Post-mortem examinations; *see* Necropsy
Pound, Roscoe, 20
Prediction of criminal homicide, 3, 4, 8, 176–177, 182, 324, 328–329, 335, 336–337, 338
Preliminary hearing, 297–298
Prevention of criminal homicide, 4, 8, 176–177, 182, 324, 335, 336–337, 338, 339

Previous record; *see also* First offenders; *Significant* associations
    by age, 8, 180–181
    alcohol related to, 151, 180–181, 324
    arrest, 168, 169, 172, 173–184, 323–324, 336
    court, 168, 169, 171, 172, 173, 174, 183
    court designation and disposition by, 11, 303–304
    criminal, 151, 168, 169, 170–172, 173, 183
    definition and classification of, 8, 168, 172–175, 177, 178
    felony-homicide and, 9, 242
    homicide-suicide and, 278
    by number of previous offenses, 177
    in other studies, 168–172, 183–184
    prison, 168, 169, 170–172, 173, 174, 183
    by race, 8, 170–171, 175–179, 181, 183–184, 323
    research suggestions for, 335–337
    by sex, 8, 171, 175–179, 181, 183, 184, 323
    by type of previous offense, 178–181, 324
    unsolved cases and, 293
    victim-offender relationships and, 230, 231, 232, 233
    victim-precipitated cases and, 257, 262–265, 326
Prima facie evidence, 286
Primary group relationships, 7, 8, 127, 203–207, 209, 210, 279, 324, 331; *see also* Husband-wife homicides; Interpersonal relationships; *Significant* associations

405

Prison; *see also* Sentence, years of
   community, 339–340
   records, 13, 174, 338
   statistics, 13, 40, 49–50, 58, 72,
      168–172, 338, 339
Probation, 231, 304, 305, 306
Prostitute, 204, 207, 209, 232, 233,
      243; *see also* Victim-offender
      relationships
Provocation; *see* Victim-preci-
      pitated criminal homicide
Prussia, 62
Psychology of criminal homicide,
      4, 6, 11, 20, 21, 145, 157, 158,
      162–163, 169, 177, 180, 181,
      185–188, 245–247, 260–261,
      276–280, 282–283, 315–317,
      330, 335, 336
Punishment; *see* Court designa-
      tion and disposition; Sen-
      tence, years of

Quetelet, Adolphe, 96

Race, criminal homicide by; *see
      also* Conduct norms; Eco-
      logy; Justifiable homicide;
      Regional variations; *Signi-
      ficant* associations; Sub-cul-
      tural patterns
   and age, 6, 65–70, 320
   alcohol related to, 8, 136–141
   court disposition of, 10, 11, 13,
      229, 230, 231, 232, 233, 300–
      304, 307–312, 327
   felony-homicide in, 9, 241–244,
      326
   homicide-suicide in, 10, 272–
      273, 276, 282, 326
   husband-wife, 212–214
   insanity in, 312–313
   inter- and intra-racial, 8, 9,
      34–35, 222–226, 228–233,
      258–259, 282, 293, 307, 308–
      309, 313, 325
      methods and weapons used in,
         6, 84–95, 320
      motives in, 6, 191, 192–195
      and occupation, 36–39
      in other studies, 39–46
      previous record related to, 8,
         170–171, 175–179, 181, 183–
         184, 323
      rates and distributions in Phila-
         delphia of, 31–39, 319
      research suggestions for, 330–
         331, 332
      and sex, 6, 31–36, 319–320
      spatial patterns of, 7, 122–133,
         322
      tempo of legal procedure for,
         295–299
      temporal patterns of, 99–100,
         106–109
      unsolved cases of, 291–292, 293,
         294, 327
      victim-offender relationships in,
         6, 8, 9, 206–208, 212–214,
         222–237, 258–259, 272–273,
         276, 282, 324, 325
      victim-precipitated cases of, 9,
         255–256, 259–260, 261, 264,
         326
      violence in, 160–167, 232, 323
Radzinowicz, Leon, 20, 198
Rape, 22, 101, 117, 227, 229, 232,
      239, 240, 241, 292; *see also*
      Felony-homicide
Rates, general, of criminal homi-
      cide, 24–27
Raven, Alice, 21, 186, 270
Redfield, R., 270
Recidivism; *see* Previous record
Regional variations, 40–44, 76–
      77, 80, 103, 116, 170, 234–237,
      271–272, 273, 307
Research suggestions, 5, 6, 11, 19,
      36, 64, 106, 116–119, 133,
      142–143, 177, 181, 182, 187,

226, 242, 294, 312, 317, 328–340; *see also* Hypotheses, criminal homicide

Revenge, 127, 185, 186, 188, 189–190, 191, 197, 198, 199, 213, 227, 228, 232, 275, 292, 301–302; *see also* Motives in criminal homicide

Rhode Island, 310, 311, 314

Richmond, Virginia, 41, 171, 236

Robbery, 186, 188, 191, 194, 197, 199, 208, 212, 218, 231, 238, 240–243, 252, 292, 293, 294, 301, 313, 324, 326; *see also* Motives in criminal homicide

Rotman, D. B., 145

Royal Commission on Capital Punishment, 12, 60, 77–78, 80, 174, 199, 220, 234, 248, 274 309, 311, 315

Rural homicide, 45, 92, 218

Russia, 95

St. Louis, Missouri, 45, 51, 75, 94, 103, 110–111, 237, 289

St. Paul, Minnesota, 25, 90

Sacks, Jerome G., 169

Sainsbury, Peter, 332

Salmiala, Bruno, 151, 152

Schilder, Paul, 21, 271

Schlapp, Max, 21

Schmid, Calvin F., 51, 94, 104, 105, 271, 272, 273

Sears, Robert R., 185

Seasonal variations; *see* Temporal patterns in criminal homicide

Self-defense, 189, 191, 213, 301, 302; *see also* Motives in criminal homicide

Sellin, Thorsten, 12, 80, 172, 234, 311, 328–329, 335

Sentence, years of, 230, 231, 232, 233, 304–306

Seattle, Washington, 25, 51, 90, 94, 290

Serbia, 62

Sex, criminal homicide by; *see also* Conduct norms; *Significant* associations
  and age, 6, 65–70, 320
  alcohol related to, 8, 136–141
  court disposition of, 10, 11, 13, 229, 230, 231, 232, 233, 300–304, 308, 327
  felony-homicide in, 9, 240–244, 326
  homicide-suicide in, 10, 272, 280–283, 326
  husband-wife, 212–221, 325
  insanity in, 312–313
  methods and weapons used in, 6, 9, 84–95, 320
  motives in, 6, 9, 191, 192–195, 212
  in other studies, 46–64
  previous record related to, 8, 171, 175–179, 181, 183, 184, 323
  and race, 6, 31–36, 319–320
  rates and distributions in Philadelphia of, 31–36, 319
  spatial patterns of, 7, 122–133, 322
  tempo of legal procedure for, 295–299
  temporal patterns of, 99–100, 103, 106–109
  unsolved cases of, 291–292, 293, 294, 327
  victim-offender relationships in, 6, 8, 9, 126–128, 204–209, 212–237, 259, 322, 324, 325; *see also* Interpersonal relationships
  victim-precipitated cases of, 9, 255–256, 259–260, 261, 265, 326
  violence in, 160–167, 232, 323

Sex rival, 204, 205, 206, 207, 209, 219; *see also* Victim-offender relationships

Sheets, Carolyn, 317

Shirley, Mary M., 173

Shootings; *see* Methods and weapons of inflicting death

Short, James F., Jr., 54–56, 75, 146–147, 185, 279–280, 330

Shupe, L. M., 135, 149, 333

Significant associations in criminal homicide

  age and
    race, 67, 320
    sex, 67, 320
    victim-offender relationship, 211, 212

  alcohol and
    days of occurrence, 141–142, 322
    previous arrest record, 181, 324
    race and sex, 137–139, 140, 141, 165, 167, 322
    victim-precipitated homicide, 261, 265, 326
    violence, 165–166, 167, 323

  court disposition and
    race, 300, 302, 307
    victim-precipitated homicide, 300

  days of occurrence, 106, 321
    and presence of alcohol, 141–142, 322

  degree of homicide and sex, 302

  homicide-suicide and
    primary group relationships, 279
    race, 272
    sex, 273
    violence, 276

  hours of occurrence, 106, 108, 321

  husband-wife homicides and

    sex, 213, 214, 325
    victim-precipitated cases, 260, 265, 282, 326
    violence, 214, 323

  methods of inflicting death and
    race, 83–84, 320, 322
    sex, 83–84, 320, 322
    victim-precipitated cases, 258, 265, 326

  motives and
    race, 190, 193, 194
    sex, 190

  previous arrest record and
    alcohol, 181, 324
    race, 175, 176, 324
    sex, 176, 323
    victim-precipitated cases, 262, 263, 265, 326

  primary group relationships and
    homicide-suicide, 279
    sex, 206, 324

  race and
    age, 67, 320
    alcohol and sex, 137–139, 140, 141, 165, 167, 322
    court disposition, 300, 302, 307
    general frequency distribution, 32, 46, 319
    homicide-suicide, 272
    methods of inflicting death, 83–84, 320, 322
    motives, 190, 193, 194
    previous arrest record, 175, 176, 324
    sex and victim-offender relationships, 225
    sex comparison, 32–33, 35, 319, 324
    spatial patterns, 123, 130, 322
    victim-precipitated cases, 255, 264, 300, 326
    weapons, 85–86, 320, 322

sex, and
　age, 67, 320
　alcohol and race, 137–139,
　　140, 141, 165, 167, 322
　degree of homicide, 302
　general frequency distribu-
　　tion, 32, 319, 324, 325
　homicide-suicide, 273
　husband-wife homicides, 213,
　　214, 325
　methods of inflicting death,
　　83–84, 320, 322
　motives, 190
　previous arrest record, 176,
　　323
　primary group relationships,
　　206, 324
　race and victim-offender re-
　　lationships, 225
　race comparison, 32–33, 35,
　　319, 324
　spatial patterns, 123, 125,
　　127, 130, 131, 322
　victim-offender relationships,
　　206, 324
　victim-precipitated homicide,
　　255, 259, 260, 265, 282,
　　326
　violence, 160, 162, 214, 323
　weapons, 85–86, 320, 322
spatial patterns and
　race, 123, 130, 322
　sex, 123, 125, 127, 130, 131,
　　322
temporal patterns, 106, 108, 321
　and alcohol, 141–142, 322
victim-offender relationship and
　age, 211–212
　race and sex, 225
　sex, 206, 324
victim-precipitated　homicide
　and
　alcohol, 261, 265, 326
　court disposition, 300

husband-wife homicides, 260,
　265, 282, 326
methods of inflicting death,
　258, 265, 326
previous arrest record, 262,
　263, 265, 326
race, 255, 264, 300, 326
sex, 255, 259, 265, 326
violence and
　alcohol, 165–166, 167, 323
　homicide-suicide, 276
　husband-wife homicides, 214,
　　323
　sex, 160, 162, 214, 323
weapons and
　race, 85–86, 320, 322
　sex, 85–86, 320, 322
Simpson, George, 47
Sing Sing Prison, New York, 169,
　171, 317
Sleeman, James L., 186
Smith, Edward H., 21
Synder, Le Moyne, 13, 86, 114,
　144, 188, 284
Spain, D. M., 135, 147–148
Spatial patterns in criminal homi-
　cide; see also Significant
　associations
alcohol related to, 121–124, 129,
　132
by census tracts, 120, 387
classification of terms, 121–122
conduct norms and, 87, 121,
　122, 125–130, 131, 133
ecology of, 120
homicide-suicide and, 277, 280–
　282
husband-wife homicides and,
　87, 132, 213, 215–216, 253,
　280, 281, 323, 325
insanity related to, 313
by methods and weapons, 87,
　89, 122, 124, 127–129, 322
motives related to, 194–195

Spatial patterns in criminal homicide;
noted in other studies, 133
by race, 7, 122–133, 164–165, 194–195, 322
by sex, 7, 122–133, 164–165, 194–195, 322
temporal patterns related to, 131–132
among unsolved cases, 293, 294, 327
victim-offender relationships and, 122–123, 226–233, 322
victim-precipitated cases by, 256, 258
violence related to, 162, 164–165, 323
Spaulding, John A., 47
Social class, 36–39, 44, 54–55, 81, 83, 85–86, 142–143, 146, 188–189, 193, 329, 330, 332, 340; see also Occupation; Sub-cultural patterns
Social control, 329, 330 see also Prediction of criminal homicide; Prevention of criminal homicide; Sub-cultural patterns
South Carolina, 53, 71, 103–104, 234, 307
Spring Grove State Hospital, Maryland, 316
Stabbings; see Methods and weapons of inflicting death
Stanford University, 336
Statistical technique, 17–19, 42–44, 137, 139–140, 165–167; see also Chi-square test
Stephen, J. F., 20
Stearns, Albert Warren, 45, 72, 147, 183, 197, 218
Stern, Max, 286, 287–288, 289
Stranger relationship, 204, 205, 206, 207, 208, 209, 212, 219,

221, 227, 228, 230, 293, 294, 313, 316, 324, 327; see also Victim-offender relationships
Straus, Jacqueline, 57, 272
Straus, Murray, 57, 272
Stromquist, W. G., 273
Sub-cultural patterns, 81, 158, 188–189, 193, 328–329, 330, 332; see also Conduct norms; Social class
Suicide, 54, 57, 59, 70, 75, 97, 148, 192, 271, 284; see also Homicide-suicide
Suffolk County, Massachusetts, 307, 311
Sullivan, W. C., 150
Sutherland, Edwin H., 41, 58, 70, 100–101, 116, 144, 233–234
Sweden, 61, 62
Switzerland, 62

Taft, Donald, 139
Talbert, Robert H., 111, 146, 147, 234, 264, 270
Tarde, Gabriel, 20, 80, 185, 218, 246, 269, 331
Tarnowsky, Pauline, 95
Teeters, Negley, 97
Templewood, Viscount, 5, 60, 274
Temporal patterns in criminal homicide; see also Significant associations
alcohol related to, 101, 109, 132, 141–143, 146, 151–152, 322–323, 334
by days, 7
in other studies, 110–113
in Philadelphia, 106–109, 321, 322
by hours, 7
in other studies, 110–113
in Philadelphia, 108–109, 321
husband-wife homicides and, 48–49, 87, 126–127, 132

by months and seasons, 7
  in other studies, 96–98, 100–
    106
  in Philadelphia, 98–100, 321,
    322
by methods and weapons of
  inflicting death, 100, 107, 115,
    321
motives related to, 87, 294
by race, 99–100, 106–109
by sex, 99–100, 103, 106–109
spatial patterns related, 131–132
suicide related to, 271
tempo of legal procedure, 295–
  299
time between assault and death,
  7, 113–119, 148, 321
among unsolved cases, 293–294,
  327
victim-offender relationships
  and, 109
Tennessee; see Memphis; Nashville
Terminology, confusion of, 16,
  24–27, 34–36, 41, 51, 52, 54–
  56, 58, 59, 75, 77, 91, 168–
  169, 183, 219, 318–319, 338
Tersiev, N., 151
Texas; see Dallas; Houston
Thomas, Franklin, 97
Thomas, W. I., 188
Thugs, 186
Tiber, S., 135, 148, 333
Time between assault and death,
  7, 113–119, 148, 321
Time of occurrence; see Temporal
  patterns in criminal homicide
Topping, C. W., 79, 171
Tulchin, Simon H., 21, 170
Turkus, Burt, 196
Turner, J. W. C., 20

Ukraine, 21, 151, 221
Uniform Crime Reports, 20, 25,
  27, 39, 41, 48, 49, 70, 75,
  101, 102, 105, 116, 117, 183,
  287, 290, 308, 338
United States Bureau of the
  Census, 24, 37, 170, 171
Unsolved criminal homicide; see
  also Cleared by arrest; Police
  by age, 293, 294, 327
  amount of, 13, 16, 289–290, 327
  compared with solved cases,
    290–294, 327
  definition of, 10, 27, 284–289,
    290
  methods and weapons used in,
    293, 294, 327
  motives in, 292, 293, 294, 327
  noted in other studies, 289–290
  previous arrest record of victims in, 293
  by race, 291–292, 293, 294, 327
  by sex, 291–292, 293, 294, 327
  spatial patterns related to, 293,
    294, 327
  suggestions for research in, 334,
    338
  temporal patterns related to,
    293–294, 327
  victim-offender relationships in,
    293, 294, 327
  violence in, 293

Vance, R. B., 186
Verce, Fornasari di, 145
Verkko, Veli, 5, 12, 61–64, 77,
  112, 113, 144, 152, 269–270,
  312, 332, 335
Vermont, 92
Victim-offender relationships; see
  also Husband-wife homicides;
  Interpersonal relationships;
  Significant associations
  age differences in, 6, 8, 210–
    212, 230–233, 320, 325
  alcohol related to, 227, 228, 230

Victim-offender relationships;
 definition and classification of
  terms, 203–206, 324
 in felony-homicides, 240–244
 in homicide-suicides, 276, 278–
  283
 insanity and, 11, 313, 316
 inter- and intra-racial, 8, 9,
  34–35, 222–226, 228–233,
  258–259, 282, 293, 307, 308–
  309, 313, 325
 by methods and weapons, 226–
  233, 253–256, 258, 265, 295,
  326
 by motives, 226–233
 noted in other studies, 217–221
 previous record and, 230, 231,
  232, 233,
 by race, 6, 8, 9, 206–208, 212–
  214, 222–237, 258–259, 272–
  273, 276, 282, 324, 325
 by sex, 6, 8, 9, 126–128, 204–
  209, 212–237, 259, 322, 324,
  325
 spatial patterns related to, 122–
  123, 226–233, 322
 temporal patterns related to,
  109
 in unsolved cases, 293, 294, 327
 in victim-precipitated cases,
  245–265, 282, 283, 326
 and violence, 162–163, 208–209,
  213, 214, 232, 323
Victim-precipitated criminal homicide; see also Significant
 associations
 by age, 255, 256
 alcohol related to, 140, 257,
  261–262, 265, 326
 court disposition of, 217, 300
 definition and illustration of,
  252–254
 felony-homicide in, 252
 homicide-suicide in, 282–283

in husband-wife homicides, 217,
  253, 256, 260, 265, 282–283
 by methods and weapons, 253–
  256, 258, 265, 326
 by motives, 258
 by previous arrest record, 257,
  262–265, 326
 by race, 9, 255–256, 259–260,
  261, 264, 326
 research suggestions for, 337
 by sex, 9, 255–256, 259–260,
  261, 265, 326
 spatial patterns related to, 256,
  258
 theoretical and legal basis for
  analysis of, 245–252
 victim-offender relationships in,
  256–257, 258–260, 265, 282,
  283, 326
Violence in criminal homicide;
 see also Significant associations
 by age, 161, 323
 alcohol and, 134, 165–167, 323
 definition and classification of
  terms, 8, 156–160
 homicide-suicide and, 275–276,
  280–282
 husband-wife homicides and,
  165, 213, 214, 323
 insanity related to, 313
 methods and weapons used
  with, 158–159
 motives and, 162, 163–164, 195
 noted in other studies, 165
 psychological factors underlying, 157–159, 162–163
 by race and sex, 160–167, 232, 323
 spatial patterns related to, 162,
  164–165, 323
 unsolved cases and, 293
 victim-offender relationships
  and, 162–163, 208–209, 213,
  214, 232, 323

412

Virginia, 307; *see also* Lorton; Richmond
Vital statistics; *see* Mortality statistics
Vold, George, 42, 43, 116–117
Von Hentig, Hans, 12, 48–49, 59–60, 71–72, 73, 153, 196, 197–198, 208, 220, 235, 245–246, 265, 289, 326

Wald, Abraham, 254
Waldrop, Francis N., 335
Wales; *see* England
Wallerstein, James S., 173
Washington; *see* Seattle
Washington, D.C., 25
Weapons; *see* Methods and weapons of inflicting death

Weather Bureau, Philadelphia, 99
Wechsler, Herbert, 20, 238, 248, 249, 336
Wertham, Frederick, 186
White Hill, Pennsylvania, 232
Whites, *see* Race
Wilentz, W. C., 135, 148–149
Wilson, E. B., 18
Wisconsin, 77, 147, 183, 197, 287, 289; *see also* Milwaukee
Witmer, Helen L., 173
Wolfgang, Marvin E., 187
Wyle, Clement J., 173
Wynne, W., Jr., 186

Yen, Ching-Yueh, 57–58
Yule, G. U., 18

Zilboorg, Gregory, 271

413

PATTERSON SMITH SERIES IN
CRIMINOLOGY, LAW ENFORCEMENT, AND SOCIAL PROBLEMS

1. *Lewis: *The Development of American Prisons and Prison Customs, 1776–1845*
2. Carpenter: *Reformatory Prison Discipline*
3. Brace: *The Dangerous Classes of New York*
4. *Dix: *Remarks on Prisons and Prison Discipline in the United States*
5. Bruce et al.: *The Workings of the Indeterminate-Sentence Law and the Parole System in Illinois*
6. *Wickersham Commission: *Complete Reports, Including the Mooney-Billings Report*. 14 vols.
7. Livingston: *Complete Works on Criminal Jurisprudence*. 2 vols.
8. Cleveland Foundation: *Criminal Justice in Cleveland*
9. Illinois Association for Criminal Justice: *The Illinois Crime Survey*
10. Missouri Association for Criminal Justice: *The Missouri Crime Survey*
11. Aschaffenburg: *Crime and Its Repression*
12. Garofalo: *Criminology*
13. Gross: *Criminal Psychology*
14. Lombroso: *Crime, Its Causes and Remedies*
15. Saleilles: *The Individualization of Punishment*
16. Tarde: *Penal Philosophy*
17. McKelvey: *American Prisons*
18. Sanders: *Negro Child Welfare in North Carolina*
19. Pike: *A History of Crime in England*. 2 vols.
20. Herring: *Welfare Work in Mill Villages*
21. Barnes: *The Evolution of Penology in Pennsylvania*
22. Puckett: *Folk Beliefs of the Southern Negro*
23. Fernald et al.: *A Study of Women Delinquents in New York State*
24. Wines: *The State of Prisons and of Child-Saving Institutions*
25. *Raper: *The Tragedy of Lynching*
26. Thomas: *The Unadjusted Girl*
27. Jorns: *The Quakers as Pioneers in Social Work*
28. Owings: *Women Police*
29. Woolston: *Prostitution in the United States*
30. Flexner: *Prostitution in Europe*
31. Kelso: *The History of Public Poor Relief in Massachusetts, 1820–1920*
32. Spivak: *Georgia Nigger*
33. Earle: *Curious Punishments of Bygone Days*
34. Bonger: *Race and Crime*
35. Fishman: *Crucibles of Crime*
36. Brearley: *Homicide in the United States*
37. *Graper: *American Police Administration*
38. Hichborn: *"The System"*
39. Steiner & Brown: *The North Carolina Chain Gang*
40. Cherrington: *The Evolution of Prohibition in the United States of America*
41. Colquhoun: *A Treatise on the Commerce and Police of the River Thames*
42. Colquhoun: *A Treatise on the Police of the Metropolis*
43. Abrahamsen: *Crime and the Human Mind*
44. Schneider: *The History of Public Welfare in New York State, 1609–1866*
45. Schneider & Deutsch: *The History of Public Welfare in New York State, 1867–1940*
46. Crapsey: *The Nether Side of New York*
47. Young: *Social Treatment in Probation and Delinquency*
48. Quinn: *Gambling and Gambling Devices*
49. McCord & McCord: *Origins of Crime*
50. Worthington & Topping: *Specialized Courts Dealing with Sex Delinquency*
51. Asbury: *Sucker's Progress*
52. Kneeland: *Commercialized Prostitution in New York City*

* new material added

PATTERSON SMITH SERIES IN
CRIMINOLOGY, LAW ENFORCEMENT, AND SOCIAL PROBLEMS

53. *Fosdick: *American Police Systems*
54. *Fosdick: *European Police Systems*
55. *Shay: *Judge Lynch: His First Hundred Years*
56. Barnes: *The Repression of Crime*
57. †Cable: *The Silent South*
58. Kammerer: *The Unmarried Mother*
59. Doshay: *The Boy Sex Offender and His Later Career*
60. Spaulding: *An Experimental Study of Psychopathic Delinquent Women*
61. Brockway: *Fifty Years of Prison Service*
62. Lawes: *Man's Judgment of Death*
63. Healy & Healy: *Pathological Lying, Accusation, and Swindling*
64. Smith: *The State Police*
65. Adams: *Interracial Marriage in Hawaii*
66. *Halpern: *A Decade of Probation*
67. Tappan: *Delinquent Girls in Court*
68. Alexander & Healy: *Roots of Crime*
69. *Healy & Bronner: *Delinquents and Criminals*
70. Cutler: *Lynch-Law*
71. Gillin: *Taming the Criminal*
72. Osborne: *Within Prison Walls*
73. Ashton: *The History of Gambling in England*
74. Whitlock: *On the Enforcement of Law in Cities*
75. Goldberg: *Child Offenders*
76. *Cressey: *The Taxi-Dance Hall*
77. Riis: *The Battle with the Slum*
78. Larson: *Lying and Its Detection*
79. Comstock: *Frauds Exposed*
80. Carpenter: *Our Convicts.* 2 vols. in one
81. †Horn: *Invisible Empire: The Story of the Ku Klux Klan, 1866–1871*
82. Faris et al.: *Intelligent Philanthropy*
83. Robinson: *History and Organization of Criminal Statistics in the U. S.*
84. Reckless: *Vice in Chicago*
85. Healy: *The Individual Delinquent*
86. *Bogen: *Jewish Philanthropy*
87. *Clinard: *The Black Market: A Study of White Collar Crime*
88. Healy: *Mental Conflicts and Misconduct*
89. Citizens' Police Committee: *Chicago Police Problems*
90. *Clay: *The Prison Chaplain*
91. *Peirce: *A Half Century with Juvenile Delinquents*
92. *Richmond: *Friendly Visiting Among the Poor*
93. Brasol: *Elements of Crime*
94. Strong: *Public Welfare Administration in Canada*
95. Beard: *Juvenile Probation*
96. Steinmetz: *The Gaming Table.* 2 vols.
97. *Crawford: *Report on the Penitentiaries of the United States*
98. *Kuhlman: *A Guide to Material on Crime and Criminal Justice*
99. Culver: *Bibliography of Crime and Criminal Justice, 1927–1931*
100. Culver: *Bibliography of Crime and Criminal Justice, 1932–1937*
101. Tompkins: *Administration of Criminal Justice, 1938–1948*
102. Tompkins: *Administration of Criminal Justice, 1949–1956*
103. Cumming: *Bibliography Dealing with Crime and Cognate Subjects*
104. *Addams et al.: *Philanthropy and Social Progress*
105. *Powell: *The American Siberia*
106. *Carpenter: *Reformatory Schools*
107. *Carpenter: *Juvenile Delinquents*
108. *Montague: *Sixty Years in Waifdom*

* new material added   † new edition, revised or enlarged

PATTERSON SMITH SERIES IN
CRIMINOLOGY, LAW ENFORCEMENT, AND SOCIAL PROBLEMS

109. *Mannheim: *Juvenile Delinquency in an English Middletown*
110. Semmes: *Crime and Punishment in Early Maryland*
111. *National Conference of Charities & Correction: *History of Child Saving in the United States*
112. †Barnes: *The Story of Punishment*
113. Phillipson: *Three Criminal Law Reformers*
114. *Drähms: *The Criminal*
115. *Terry & Pellens: *The Opium Problem*
116. *Ewing: *The Morality of Punishment*
117. †Mannheim: *Group Problems in Crime and Punishment*
118. *Michael & Adler: *Crime, Law and Social Science*
119. *Lee: *A History of Police in England*
120. †Schafer: *Compensation and Restitution to Victims of Crime*
121. †Mannheim: *Pioneers in Criminology*
122. Goebel & Naughton: *Law Enforcement in Colonial New York*
123. *Savage: *Police Records and Recollections*
124. Ives: *A History of Penal Methods*
125. *Bernard (ed.): *Americanization Studies*. 10 vols.:
    Thompson: *Schooling of the Immigrant*
    Daniels: *America via the Neighborhood*
    Thomas: *Old World Traits Transplanted*
    Speek: *A Stake in the Land*
    Davis: *Immigrant Health and the Community*
    Breckinridge: *New Homes for Old*
    Park: *The Immigrant Press and Its Control*
    Gavit: *Americans by Choice*
    Claghorn: *The Immigrant's Day in Court*
    Leiserson: *Adjusting Immigrant and Industry*
126. *Dai: *Opium Addiction in Chicago*
127. *Costello: *Our Police Protectors*
128. *Wade: *A Treatise on the Police and Crimes of the Metropolis*
129. *Robison: *Can Delinquency Be Measured?*
130. *Augustus: *John Augustus, First Probation Officer*
131. *Vollmer: *The Police and Modern Society*
132. Jessel & Horr: *Bibliographies of Works on Playing Cards and Gaming*
133. *Walling: *Recollections of a New York Chief of Police;* & Kaufmann: *Supplement on the Denver Police*
134. *Lombroso-Ferrero: *Criminal Man*
135. *Howard: *Prisons and Lazarettos*. 2 vols.:
    The State of the Prisons in England and Wales
    An Account of the Principal Lazarettos in Europe
136. *Fitzgerald: *Chronicles of Bow Street Police-Office*. 2 vols. in one
137. *Goring: *The English Convict*
138. Ribton-Turner: *A History of Vagrants and Vagrancy*
139. *Smith: *Justice and the Poor*
140. *Willard: *Tramping with Tramps*
141. *Fuld: *Police Administration*
142. *Booth: *In Darkest England and the Way Out*
143. *Darrow: *Crime, Its Cause and Treatment*
144. *Henderson (ed.): *Correction and Prevention*. 4 vols.:
    Henderson (ed.): *Prison Reform;* & Smith: *Criminal Law in the U. S.*
    Henderson (ed.): *Penal and Reformatory Institutions*
    Henderson: *Preventive Agencies and Methods*
    Hart: *Preventive Treatment of Neglected Children*
145. *Carpenter: *The Life and Work of Mary Carpenter*
146. *Proal: *Political Crime*

* new material added   † new edition, revised or enlarged

PATTERSON SMITH SERIES IN
CRIMINOLOGY, LAW ENFORCEMENT, AND SOCIAL PROBLEMS

147. *von Hentig: *Punishment*
148. *Darrow: *Resist Not Evil*
149. Grünhut: *Penal Reform*
150. *Guthrie: *Seed-Time and Harvest of Ragged Schools*
151. *Sprogle: *The Philadelphia Police*
152. †Blumer & Hauser: *Movies, Delinquency, and Crime*
153. *Calvert: *Capital Punishment in the Twentieth Century & The Death Penalty Enquiry*
154. *Pinkerton: *Thirty Years a Detective*
155. *Prison Discipline Society [Boston] Reports 1826–1854.* 6 vols.
156. *Woods (ed.): *The City Wilderness*
157. *Woods (ed.): *Americans in Process*
158. *Woods: *The Neighborhood in Nation-Building*
159. Powers & Witmer: *An Experiment in the Prevention of Delinquency*
160. *Andrews: *Bygone Punishments*
161. *Debs: *Walls and Bars*
162. *Hill: *Children of the State*
163. Stewart: *The Philanthropic Work of Josephine Shaw Lowell*
164. *Flinn: *History of the Chicago Police*
165. *Constabulary Force Commissioners: *First Report*
166. *Eldridge & Watts: *Our Rival the Rascal*
167. *Oppenheimer: *The Rationale of Punishment*
168. *Fenner: *Raising the Veil*
169. *Hill: *Suggestions for the Repression of Crime*
170. *Bleackley: *The Hangmen of England*
171. *Altgeld: *Complete Works*
172. *Watson: *The Charity Organization Movement in the United States*
173. *Woods et al.: *The Poor in Great Cities*
174. *Sampson: *Rationale of Crime*
175. *Folsom: *Our Police [Baltimore]*
176. Schmidt: *A Hangman's Diary*
177. *Osborne: *Society and Prisons*
178. *Sutton: *The New York Tombs*
179. *Morrison: *Juvenile Offenders*
180. *Parry: *The History of Torture in England*
181. Henderson: *Modern Methods of Charity*
182. Larned: *The Life and Work of William Pryor Letchworth*
183. *Coleman: *Humane Society Leaders in America*
184. *Duke: *Celebrated Criminal Cases of America*
185. *George: *The Junior Republic*
186. *Hackwood: *The Good Old Times*
187. *Fry & Cresswell: *Memoir of the Life of Elizabeth Fry.* 2 vols. in one
188. *McAdoo: *Guarding a Great City*
189. *Gray: *Prison Discipline in America*
190. *Robinson: *Should Prisoners Work?*
191. *Mayo: *Justice to All*
192. *Winter: *The New York State Reformatory in Elmira*
193. *Green: *Gambling Exposed*
194. *Woods: *Policeman and Public*
195. *Johnson: *Adventures in Social Welfare*
196. *Wines & Dwight: *Report on the Prisons and Reformatories of the United States and Canada*
197. *Salt: *The Flogging Craze*
198. *MacDonald: *Abnormal Man*
199. *Shalloo: *Private Police*
200. *Ellis: *The Criminal*

* new material added   † new edition, revised or enlarged